Cyberculture
and New Media

Cyberculture
and New Media

Edited by
Francisco J. Ricardo

Amsterdam - New York, NY 2009

©Cover image: Holger Mader, Alexander Stublić, Heike Wiermann, "But over the edges", installation, 2002

Cover design: Pier Post

The paper on which this book is printed meets the requirements of "ISO 9706:1994, Information and documentation - Paper for documents - Requirements for permanence".

ISBN: 978-90-420-2518-9
©Editions Rodopi B.V., Amsterdam - New York, NY 2009
Printed in the Netherlands

Contents

Welcome to a *Critical Issues* Project

Cyberculture and New Media appears within the Critical Issues series of publications. The aim of the series is to examine, explore and critically engage with the issues and implications created by the growing adoption of information technologies for inter-human communication and focus on the examination of the continuing impact of emergent cybermedia for human communication and culture.

Key themes in the series include:

1. **Cyberspace and Cyberculture.** Theories and Concepts of Cyberspace and Cyberculture.

2. **Cybercultures, Cybersubcultures and Online Communities.** The Rise of Web 2.0. Emerging Practices in Social Networking. The Shaping of Individual and Collective Identities. Cyber-activism and Social Mobilisation. The changing Social Identity in Cyberspace.

3. **Videogame Cultures.** The Future of Interactive Entertainment. The Aesthetic Aspects of Videogames. The Spatiology of Videogames and Virtual Worlds. Social Dimension of Online Gaming and Presence in Virtual Worlds. The History of Virtual Worlds and their Cultures.

4. **Digital and Interactive Arts** Performative and Collaborative and Use of Crossmedia. Digital Culture. Interactive Storytelling.

5. **Cybercultures and Politics** Virtual Policies in 3-D Multi-user Worlds. Cyber-Democracy and the Impact on National and Global Politics. New Media in Political Context. New Forms of Citizenship.

6. **Cybermedia and Innovation in Cyberjournalism** Histories and Theories of New Media. Cyberjournalism. Crossmedia and Digital Publishing. Digital Communications and Free Speech.

7. **Educational Use of 3-D Videogames and Virtual Worlds** Serious Games and Simulations. Virtual Communities and Collaborative Work. Cultures of Online Learning. Case Studies on Educational Use of Cybermedia and Videogames.

Dr Robert Fisher

Inter-Disciplinary.Net
http://www.inter-disciplinary.net

'Until Something Else' – A Theoretical Introduction

Francisco J. Ricardo

The present volume presents an array of essays branching from the scion of cyberculture[1]. In breadth, they address individual disciplinary problems, but read collectively, they illuminate the sweeping and defining significance of cyberculture, no longer distinct from what is implicit to culture in the framework of post-industrial society. With technology as its supramedium, "cyberculture" is the contemporary and transpicuous paraphrase of what the term, revolving around a new industrial model in the late 19th century, "culture" implied to Ferdinand Tönnies. His role in modern sociology, centering on the idea of *Gemeinschaft* and *Gesellschaft*, is of particular significance as marker for the turning point at which cyberculture diverges most dramatically from prior cultural architectures. Sensing something beyond the constrictions of positivist thinking, Tönnies felt the distance denoted between *Gemeinschaft* and *Gesellschaft* as precisely what, by 1887, the publication year of the book whose title announces these two terms, appeared to presage major adhesions for social groupings in modern society. In the pole indexed by the *Gemeinschaft*, commonly translated as *community*, lies the conceptual inventory of subjective and intrinsic motivations for collective assembly and bonding, while, opposing this specific vitality, *Gesellschaft*, *"society"*, denotes the much more instrumental type of gathering that familiarly attends to *ad hoc* aims: paid labour, civic responsibility, and motives of capital. Cyberculture's primary challenge to theory turns on the refutation of this boundary, and, consequently, the merging of community and society, dispassionately or otherwise, into a single historical event. But as these poles derive from entirely divergent impulses, they reconcile with singular experience only by the strategy of overlay that signals the contemporary structuration of desire and its expressions through the standard lens and language of existing media, which replace geographical location as the principal condition for assembly, intersubjectivity, and assent. Since this overlay of realms, of expression and media, is motorised by a continual codification of the terms of each domain through waves of technological innovation and obsolescence that permeate contemporary actions, sensibilities, and disciplines, we might look to any of these for an example of this codification through the anxiety that arises from the stylised manufacture of the archaic and the destruction of memory.

It is thus to the extent that culture's ample retinue of actions are incrementally recoded into the collimation called cyberculture—as a course through what follows the age called modernism—that we might expect to view sweeping acts of convergence reflected on any number of historical examples. These illustrate something like the regularities and patterns of the new casting aside the old in the incessant feast that is this pattern of innovation and obsolescence. We might, because of the persistence of cyberculture's incipient reconfigurations—often deployed through new technology—easily locate in any major moment within twentieth century historiography markers of the passing of one age and, simultaneously, glints of the one in advent. And so, there is, not entirely surprisingly, one inconspicuous occasion, from a time that we might call the intellectual prehistory of contemporary art, when a succinctly worded letter inscribes a moment in the dialogue between two worlds in the person of two artists, each a sovereign of his own medium:

> Dear Stieglitz__
> Even a few words I don't feel like writing.
> You know exactly what I think about photography
> I would like to see it make people despise painting
> until something else
>   will make photography unbearable__
> There we are.
>   Affectueusement,
>   Marcel Duchamp[2]

Dating from 1922, this letter, resonating in the uncharted freshness of photography's early conceptual age, is a pithy riposte to Alfred Stieglitz, who, nurturing concerns about posterity, had stirred Marcel Duchamp in previous correspondence by posing a more transcendental question, "Can a photograph have the significance of art?" It would be neither the first nor the last time that questions would hover at the interface between the historical dawn of a medium and an atemporal, universalizing category, something on the order of absolute status, or to choose Stieglitz's more personal term, significance. What makes the question permanently relevant is the premise, summarily anticipated by Stieglitz, that the standing of any medium will not merely relate to contemporary concerns and their practical necessity, but additionally occupies a manifest place in time from which scholars may construct social, scientific, and cultural retrospectives – which is to say, construct histories and world views. Equally relevant to the contemporary media arts today is that, what in 1922 is asked about photography, a medium without, at that time, a developed place or canon in art, is what is being similarly asked now about the computer game. Since, for Stieglitz, it is not the medium's continued existence that was in question—this was already assumed by his escalating level of commercial production and breadth of photographic work—the tightness of the embrace, measured via heightened social status, of technology's relationship to a society's arts need a new line of explanation.

It is in this manner, by asking about the place that the photographic medium, to choose one kind of medium, will, as a novel venue for artistic production, to choose one kind of production, occupy in the order of culture that Stieglitz presages differential legitimacies that were addressed again, almost two decades later in the galleys of an essay that itself became a defining moment in art criticism. The article is, of course, *Avant-Garde and Kitsch*, Clement Greenberg's judgment and oppositional ideology pitting the definably avant-garde, championed as guardian of a society's aesthetic standards, against the inescapably complement, in the category of *kitsch*, decried as the unconditional response to impulses of consumer haste and taste. Enumerating four expressive examples, a poem by T. S. Eliot, a Tin Pan Alley song, a painting by Georges Braque and a Saturday Evening Post cover, Greenberg assembles a cultural quartet whose individual elements are "on the order of culture, and ostensibly, parts of the same culture and products of the same society." In this broadside, etching as it does the presumable boundaries of high art, he finds that, beyond their shared contemporaneity, nothing of cultural consequence actually links them. To be sure, they are expressive tokens from entirely non-contiguous strata of *culture*, Greenberg's critical fulcrum. But in these examples there is something more specific to the question of medium and genre than the context-free expression of cultural positions as arguably high or low. That a modern poem, a parlour song, a Cubist painting, and a magazine illustration identify how distinct genres tie to distinct media is what principally puts the question, for us, in the postmodern frame, in a state of contemporary suspense, and has repositioned Greenberg as something of an archaeo-rhetorical relic, if a fiery one. For today, culture's significant expressive distinctions cut not across genres alone, but also across the specific media that encapsulate them. And operating with special relevance on the plane of the cybercultural, this synthesis is not so much framed as encoded. So while, ironically, Greenberg's criteria later came to hinge on a ready sense of medium, it is there that challenges against him proved most withering to his undignified transformation from master critic to "worm-eaten colossus"[3]. As art discovered mechanisation, Greenberg's contractile optical notions of medium, seen against its new modes of actual execution, were overpowered by new media frenetically co-fusing toward bastardisation and able to account for the ubiquitous role of appropriation and remediation in art today

It is this persevering theme's vital essence—reductive purity—that divides modernist sensibility from its subsequent condition in the postmodern encounter, and which Caroline Jones posits as Greenberg's major ideological vector[4]. Concern above all else with the narrowest exercise of the expressive strength of a medium is, for Greenberg, the vital modernist principle. The application of the sensory refinement that each medium best supports is the aim: in the case of painting, the interpretive inflection is best received and expressed by means of the flatness of the form; for sculpture, it is the rotational affordance of one's gaze in three dimensions that produces and transcends the rustle of narrative in the object. Through this interpretive specialisation, the production conditions of each medium could be used to critique the medium itself; paintings that use, evoke, or transcend the backdrop of the level plane are in conversation with the conditions of the flatness of their native medium, and thus, for Greenberg, will definably self-identify with the aesthetic traditions of modernism. The legendary proclamation, Greenberg's most oft-quoted mantra, was unequivocal: "The essence of Modernism lies, as I see it, in the use of characteristic methods of a discipline to criticize the discipline itself, not in order to subvert it but in order to entrench it more firmly in its area of competence", and reveals with the passage of time an assumption of stability and transparency of medium that is so unimaginable today that one can look to Greenberg's own examples as sites of contradiction vis-à-vis the evolving concerns of new media. On one hand, Greenberg erects high art as specifically medium-derived:

> Picasso, Braque, Mondrian, Miro, Kandinsky, Brancusi, even Klee, Matisse and Cézanne derive their chief inspiration from the medium they work in. The excitement of their art seems to lie most of all in its pure preoccupation with the invention and arrangement of spaces, surfaces, shapes, colors, etc., to the exclusion of whatever is not necessarily implicated in these factors.[5]

Immediately we might remember, however, that several expressive genres, chief among them that of collage, distort the material and aesthetic integrity of the medium as defined by Greenberg's prohibitive art panorama. We might consider collage as *not-painting*, but it is not sculpture, either; its coarse, uneven tatters, cementations of more than immediate expression, announce the commanding plan of bastard form, and thus the cacophony of a staunch anti-formalism. As neither painting nor sculpture, collage could be inaugurated as the first new art medium of 20th century sensibility. The difficulties for Greenberg in approaching this medium point to the persistence of the modernist optic in attempting to frame media that have already entered new paradigmatic space. His *Collage* essay, focusing on pasted paper, formation of shapes, and interlocking silhouettes, in short, issues of material support and the mounting of elements so physically central to collage, all but ignores the expressive force of that practice as a hard-edged support whose exploration in subsequent political uses underscores the necessary relationship of medium to message that became a cybercultural credo. That Greenberg's *Collage* essay, which remains still too under-explored, was to be read through an obliviously formal lens is evident from the resolve with which the word "flatness", mentioned twenty-four times, characterizes it.

But by 1959, the year that the essay was last revised, collage's initial play with the newspaper cutout had expanded to include photographs, print matter, and other kinds of graphic material, material whose innate textuality presented just the opportunity that many artists had been awaiting: the literal quality of words permuted visually into a new, hybridised message. So, where Joan Miró had *painted* or drawn similar suggestively textual works and otherwise merged text and image by illustrating the stanzas of Tristan Tzara, René Char and other poets, the collagists had *assembled* theirs entirely from pre-existing elements. No longer a form based on original composition, collage was the first of many *composite* practices—something gradually less framed but increasingly encoded. And when the photograph joins the textual composition, the expressive language of the collage, now as photomontage, becomes dimensionally expanded such that it becomes impossible to overlook the sensory impact favoured by John Heartfield, Raoul Hausmann, and Hannah Höch. To evaluate flatness in their own collages, whose message is transfused with stilted, often anti-propagandistic context, is to favour form against its content and to ignore the essential utility of structure as expression, a balance that defines postmodernism's production of art and meaning and returns us to the process of encoding as principle of industrial objects' translation out of culture and into cyberculture. For the composite image produced by the collage is an enunciative literalisation, a recoding in a different scope, of practice of the composite diagnostic profile which the psychoanalyst merges out of disparate observations on the patient, and of the evidence for social portraiture which the anthropologist adduces from fieldnotes on the ethnographic stay, and which the social scientist correlates from observational data. From the orderly fittings of modular architecture down to the interlaced patterns of the crossword puzzle, nothing appears created whole cloth; everything is instead assembled from prefabricated elements, programmed into a phrasal, composite whole[6].

Collage's entrance into authentic practice, just one of the theoretical inversions that recodes the previously autonomous state of art into something indistinguishably embraced with its mechanism, typifies developments predating but advancing toward the concerns of contemporary art, art in which what divides medium from content no longer matters. This is the blur maintaining that the logic of judgment informing the first half of the previous century can plausibly read in reverse today; Greenberg's ideas on kitsch, at the level of content, re-evolve as today's avant-garde at the level of technology. Here, encoded technologically, is what could pass for a cursory account of the typical simulation programmed in virtual game space:

Kitsch is mechanical and operates by formulas. Kitsch is
vicarious experience and faked sensations. Kitsch changes
according to style, but remains always the same. Kitsch is
the epitome of all that is spurious in the life of our times.[7]

Nor did this inversion erupt all at once. The intervening four
decades between Greenberg's homily on form and Baudrillard's landmark
inauguration of postmodern critique, <u>Simulation and Simulacra</u>, would seem
to trace a line directly from ideas about the purity of medium to that of
complete and vacant derivation, based on the traffic and interchange of signs,
a substitution whose performance begins as sensory artifice and culminates as
a set of codes proxying for reality itself, as we shall see.

But too easily positing Greenberg as the modernist weathervane in a
postmodern cataclysm misses the more complex problems of the art-medium,
indeed message-medium, agglomeration of cyberculture in general, outside
any disciplinary context. For however inexactly his thinking was termed
"formalist", which is to say, assuming the existence of something like pure
universals, and however we might admit of the indissoluble union of medium
and production, there is nonetheless, suggestively below the superficial, one
major distinction that *has* emerged, even as others have dissolved. It turns on
the problem of individual identity, forged in relation to time and labour as a
function of the basic product to be realised. However executed, and whether
so for art, manufacture, or information, personal effort interfaces with a long
chain of technological supports that shape the gradual output in relation to the
complexity of the *interaction*, the unit of analysis for technology's formulaic
conditions of engagement. Technology's manifestations, therefore, however
extruded, printed, or structured, conform to a perpetual level of exactitude,
similitude, and standardisation that is increasingly precise, and decreasingly
personal. The archetypal creation of cyberculture, like a collage, is explicitly
synthetic, assembled, yet increasingly *uniform*. This last adjective suggests
how post-industrial process points toward thoroughly formalist results. As
product or content are historically immediate and *of their time* whereas form,
formalism, and uniformity are abstract and timeless, which is to say,
unrealised, we locate ontological tensions underlying the production of
cyberculture. For the term *cyberculture* itself evokes the union of something
abstract and timeless – the sense of culture – with something embedded,
time-based, and historically contextualised – the cyber-stratum, the present
moment of technology's interleaving within societal function, and with a
clear preference for being encoded, the worlds of *Gemeinschaft* and
Gesellschaft encapsulated as a single word, a summary formulation. That
cybercultural thinking is in essence formal is evident in the arresting
immediacy with which pervasive encounters with technology in social,
professional, personal, and artistic acts impose logical structure, instrumental

thinking, and stimulus-response behaviour. Since such logic, thinking, and behaviour are conditioned early, at the point of interface design, they precede many possibilities for creative latitude at the individual level, imposing constraints of experience whose processing does not entirely originate within the user alone. The presence of design and interaction intrudes on expressive freedom with presupposing inferences that guide, limit, and accompany real-time reasoning with an array of predetermined tasks that the interface performs in producing whatever solution or feedback the given technology generates. As if to underscore a major formalist divide, the major thinking in fact occurs at great temporal remove prior to that which happens in real-time use, such that the design, manufacture, and functionality of an automated teller machine exceedingly dwarfs the mental commitment required to use it.

The same holds for cybercultural experiences like viewing films, chatting via mobile phones, or piloting airplanes. Time and labour have been divided, with the medium presenting much of the problem's solution already elaborated, leaving little of what executes in the present to its calculation in the here and now. It is by following its idiosyncratic impression of historical progress that technology increasingly alters this balance; to define cyberculture is to witness a further skewing of one particular asymmetry that follows the simultaneous and mutually exclusive aims of increasing complexity of construction on one end in order to augment ease of use on the other. To be sure, the human record provides no other model of collective existence in which social artefacts and affordances are divided so radically, save that which takes root in the rise of technology for organic tasks, let us say farming and transportation – technologies whose own horizons have advanced so far as to merit their own histories. But in those early deployments, the only factor subject to transformation is the labour of a task; the identity of the user remains integral to its pre-technological history; even today, the farmer is no less a farmer because he uses a mechanised tractor rather than a manual hoe. This continuation of role-person is maintained precisely because in the narrowness of the task provided, the technology does none of the actual thinking involved in the work. Thinking is at that stage still exogenous to labour, the latter being the only objective of the technological intervention. But once the horizon of technological possibility on the dimension of labour is largely conquered, the remaining challenges, now cognitive, become fertile ground for a parallel incursion.

It is in the 20th century when, confronted by military circumstances, that governments launch into major initiatives for technological performance in the cognitive rather than manual realm alone: to design anticipatory intelligence into field artillery, to decrypt enemy communications, and to calculate the procurement of materiel to large-scale operations, among other marvels of intellectual execution, these and countless other objectives are attempts at consolidating intelligence into code. For these unprecedented tasks, new varieties of professionals surface; those whose language of specialty is that of formal, uniform, formulaic, formalistic interaction: information workers, knowledge engineers, scientists, researchers. Accompanying machine-assisted cognition is humans' surrender to technology, and with it, the terms that characterize thinking: terms that can only be approached allegorically as the semblance of identity.

In the sphere of relations comprising the *cybercultural*, two strands exhibit particularly extensive levels of growth. The first appears through an insistent translation of social and communicative signs from one context onto another. Given that any cyberculture's foundations are technological, more enduring values, those connected to a personal sense of being, must derive from activities that traffic within them – art and religion provide examples for such recodification. Problematically rooted in pre-modern and early modernist references, symbols and messages of these expressive dimensions have transmuted through the rational analytic gaze of technological means and media and pressed into service in postmodern frames of expression. The allure of old world obscurities is exposed and questioned anew through the gridlike circumstances of a standard model pulsing to the pace of electronic language. Meaning once richly construed through organic, intimate, and localised connection to production–the tilling of land, the tending of livestock, securing a mode of subsistence that is not distinct from the place of existence–is now derived from the widespread and exact manipulation of tools designed to reduce time and space.

But there is another sense in which it makes sense to look at the bridge between Stieglitz, standing as the last pre-modernist of the developed image, insisting that photographs "look like photographs", and Duchamp, the first conceptual artist, for whom purity of form was anathema, as portal to the concerns of cybercultural signification, layered and multiply codifying. For to the extent that signs with variable meaning populate the cybercultural interface (now that there is no longer an unproblematic modernist *landscape*), identity, activity, and presence are all brought into focus through the measure of another benchmark crucial to these two artists, though for opposing reasons: that of the image. Here, in the emblem of the image, of imaginal construction, of imaginary virtuality, of the basis for the process of the interface, cybercultural mediation is defined, encapsulated. The image is more than an object, it is a verb, a reagent for representation, and thereby, also for reception. In this, and long before Guy Debord translates the connotational susceptibility of the *image* to its unmitigated collective commodification as *spectacle*, Stieglitz's viewfinder charts a range of imagery that relates intimately to human experience without artifice, either retrograde (informed by painterly façade) or postmodern (supporting cynical second readings)[8]. For Stieglitz, in a manner never possible for Greenberg, the image culminates as the source of reflection that Bergson pursues, while for Duchamp, as for Debord, the image serves as the target for merely probing what it is *not*. Duchamp points that absence back to art's repressive retinal obsessions, while Debord, refracting Walter Benjamin's elegy for an erstwhile aura, assumes that some iconic enzyme motors a primal code of order historically functioning through progressively autonomous art whose very independence now paradoxically threatens it[9].

The progressive degradation of ceremonial image into serviceable spectacle that Debord's *Society of the Spectacle* relates is, of course, too extensive for explication through the exclusively visual. But, however intractable within the constraints of modernism's value system of commodity exchange, only art has effectively assimilated all the contradictory tendrils that modernism's social, economic, and epistemic crises has spawned. It has accomplished this multiple adoption by the exchange of one kind of defining structure for another: the transmutation of *form* into *mode*. Old distinctions of knowledge, culture, and social stratification, wholly indispensable until the Victorian era, encounter abrupt and sustained challenges in the 20th century, which in fact undermines the stability and merits of category. Intimations of categorical collapse first take root in the intermingling problematisation of form and concept; montage, collage, bricolage, a steady profusion of appropriations, synergies and syntheses construct a model of experience that denies the separateness of observation and context. As the established impressions of form become incrementally replaced by acts of transformation centering on the interpermeation of conceptual constructs, epistemic and expressive emphasis accrues to the manner of construction, which shifts what we might call the enunciative rationale of disciplines toward new conventions of doing, that is, toward new *modes* of perception that transcend formal opacities.

In prevailing over the individuality of form, this preference for the modal, comprised within the larger overlay to which I alluded earlier, registers in several directions, of which two interest us here. These might be called transhistorical and transformal. While in disciplinary appearance, history is framed as a paradigm of continuity such that the idea of "human history" is phrased as a single object, it is in contemporary thinking that historical *moments* assume incommensurable separateness from each other, and this separateness is marked by distinctions not in time but in cultural thinking. Hence the Victorian era authenticates as historically distinct from the Edwardian, although temporally these periods are of course directly continuous, and it makes sense to assume that it is by an overlap of cultural markers such as this that we might locate that I mean by transhistorical. Restating Tönnies, Debord's anchorless Gesellschaft longs for the vital sufficiency of a bygone Gemeinschaft, an autonomy of historical moments that wants cybercultural resolution in the overlay, the simultaneity of two ages sharing signs at a temporal junction. Philosophy and art were the first to document this overlay, with Rousseau's virtuous 'noble savage' and Gauguin's entrée to primitivism, but most authoritatively later in the early Picasso, through the same modern lens that, in its own temporally continuous but seemingly disjunctive moment, also spawned Cubism. In the analytic Gesellschaft of Great War-era Europe, the intuitive spirit of preliterate art, evoking the Gemeinschaft's numinous significance, marks the first codification of a transhistorical overlay.

So it is too that an untainted, non-linguistic, perceptual probity connects Stieglitz to the projects of several of his philosophical contemporaries; inarguably to Whitehead and Wittgenstein, and not least to Henri Bergson. It was the latter's approach to intuitive process, no doubt a counter to quasi-Enlightenment precise rationalities, that, from the outset, could have supplied a *vade mecum* to Stieglitz's photography[10]. This non-rational palpability, that only a transformative escape from the logos of discourse restores essential meaning, has remained vibrant and persistent in art's transhistorical explorations, mapping a field of unanswered questions extending across a range of contemporary work. It was, for example, in 2003 that Mark Alice Durant and Jane Marsching curated *The Blur of the Otherworldly* (also co-editing the eponymous book[5]), an exhibition examining the numinous through the contemporary speculum. Surveying religious and extra-sensory imagery through postmodern, principally photographic expression, Durant and Marsching fittingly locate this overlay at the margins of perception that still stir us toward a temporal Other-time:

> Henri Bergson has described an image as something that exists halfway between a representation and the thing itself. It is not just a lifeless sign, yet it is not quite life. The image lives at the threshold, standing between us and the abstractions we use to represent ourselves. The image is a window, a doorway, a passage between the flesh of our existence and the cluttered forest of signs we have invented to communicate our inchoate selves. Before photography: words, etchings, pottery shards, carvings in stone, the artifacts left by our ancestors, the concrete pieces of a puzzle with which we attempt to reconstruct their lives.[11]

Rapt between transhistorical horns and consequentially yearning for conciliatory unison, Durant's intones an Everyman lament, a cybercultural sequel to the soul-searching of Joyce's Ulysses/Bloom:

> I desire otherworldly experiences, yet I want proof. Humans are programmed with these sometimes-contradictory impulses. By definition, having proof means

that otherworldly experiences are brought into the concrete
world of clarity and legibility. But when this happens they
are in danger of losing their mystery and power to make us
wonder. Much of human culture is a result of this ongoing
struggle between our empirical demands and the need for
an open-ended universe. We want our unshakable certainty
and yet we hunger to be haunted.[12]

The contentions bound to this antagonism are not exclusively
epistemological; they extend into ethico-cultural territory, as well. For within
a year of Durant and Marsching's show, another event broadened further still
the degree to which transhistorical anxieties operate in the present.
Concerned with the consequences that a seemingly innocuous intersection of
worlds—art and religion—provoke, Alison Edwards and Lawrence Sullivan,
then at Harvard's Center for the Study of World Religions, forced a defining
moment in empirical questions in the form of a book and conference,
Stewards of the Sacred [21]. Aiming at decisive resolution of still-remaining,
ambiguous and competing notions underlying distinctions between terms like
relic and *artwork*, Sullivan and Edwards identified a range of practices,
museological, governmental, and tribal, crucial to worlds in opposition but
co-present in the same space-time. Here, anthropologists, museum
administrators, artists, theologians, and First Nations tribal elders voiced
conflicting perspectives on the *objective* importance of unearthed and
otherwise reclaimed objects revolving on a singular transhistorical question:
which world now owns the rightful claim to the power, value, and destiny of
sacred objects? Whether as components of the archaeological record or
consecrated items in need of repatriation, all contention inculpates the
dilemmatic role, perhaps conspiratorial, played by the museum at a time
when the institution stands transhistorically across two conflicting world
views, one, belonging to contemporary institutional study, and the other,
anchored in primordial structures of birthright.

With art and culture, music, too, has echoed a transhistorical
phenomenology unique to cyberculture. Of innumerable examples, on, from
the collaborative work of Brian Eno and David Byrne has placed special
attention on the process. Presented neither as social study nor as parody, the
1981 album *My Life in the Bush of Ghosts* carved out a novel act of re-
voicing. Adopting actual recordings that depicted a range of theological
experiences—homilies, religious quarrels, songs, and exorcisms—as thematic
metonymy for a larger sonic canvas, the album mortised the playback of
these conversions, transformations, contentions, and incantations with the
minimalist pulse of postmodernity's precursor to trance. This technological
replacement of acoustic foundation is not just an incidental instance of sound
collage; in the act of substitution of an original audience present at the event

with another, pluralized across time, space, and culture, a transhistorical isthmus of worlds comes into view. It is a space otherwise unable to harmonise one culture whose embryonic spiritual roots deliver transcendence but sacrifice relativism, with another, innervated by continual flux but limited to material reality. As similar to the work of Marsching and Durant, the album, replete with transcendental, conceptual and aesthetic significance, functions within a rare ethos in which the modern work of art is pressed into service as landscape surveyor scanning through an expressive field of ancestral moments and energies.

Even so, this is not the only compound tension induced through technological postmodernity. There is, in addition to the transhistorical colligation of epochs, another tension that cyberculture's overlaying multiplicities have provoked. Rather than manifesting in the temporal dimension, its encroachment marks across the spatial axis, for which reason it is *transformal*. By this term I mean not only the substitution of form with mode, but specifically the process by which that exchange has been realized, such that form and shape now operate more as enunciative verbs than as static substances. This alteration appears most discernibly in art practices that now transcend all singularity of medium (and thus of form), yet retain the kind of pure formalism that one might have felt irrelevant to the deconstructive character of contemporary art. The theatre on which this transformal action takes place is, as I have mentioned, that of the image, but, insubstantially present only as projection, the image now assumes the dimensionality of a material support that extends beyond the two dimensions of a projection screen. Of this fusion of image and space, which may assume the name *filmic sculpture*, several examples indicate the transformal case for cybercultural encoding in spatial appearance.

Figure 1. Mader, Stublić, and Wiermann, *Façade*. Media facade, dimensions variable. Orkuveitan headquarters, Reykjavik, Iceland. ©2008, Mader, Stublić, and Wiermann. Courtesy of the artist.

The transformal might best be understood functionally, as the stipulation of one disruptive plane onto the visual structure of another. A naïve reading might assume this notion to include the realm of virtual reality, but VR follows rather the differing aim of creating non-disruptive planarity of maximal resemblance to the objectival cohesion of the physical world. Instead, the divergent stratification of space, implying among other phenomena, that of depth, which is to say *more* space, whether shallow or filled, is the rhetorical force of the transformal, which in a cybercultural context points to the function of the term I have been iterating: encoding. One exemplar of this new duality, proposed as a media façade by the German design firm of Mader, Stublić, and Wiermann on the headquarters of Orkuveita Reykjavíkur, Iceland's principal purveyor of geothermal power, melds onto the presence of an architectural body the projection of geometrical forms tightly bound to a new axis whose centre anchors to indeterminate space (figure 1). Here, emblematic of cyberculture, is the expression of transformal tension, a projective opposition between forces, one entirely physical and conveying pure convexity and; the other, purely notional and injecting into the physical a fervent concavity—with each distending toward its own direction, which is to say, its own dimension.

A similar deconstruction of planar perception is central to the work of Andrew Neumann, whose series of electronic sculptures, *Industrial Wall Panels*, expresses transformal conjugation on a variety of levels. The material choice of these sculptures accentuates one such distinction, as the organic role of the back panel, comprised of unpainted plywood, contradicts the mechanical and optical operations of the mechanism that figures over it. In opposition, too, is the stasis of the panel against the motion inherent within the metallic machinery of self-observation in continual oscillating movement like a laden pendulum or a Duchampian rotorelief whose expressive dynamism has been translated from a circular contour to a horizontal one. The layering of planes stipulated in Neumann's work is emphasised by the presence of one or various cameras trained on kinetic details of the work's own rotary motion rail system, or conversely of an abstract line painted directly onto the sculpture, a recursive act that fills the distance between conceptual forms with a new reading of the work, a reading rendered by the work onto itself. These elements orchestrate simultaneously in *Phase Cancellation with Sine Wave* (figure 2), in which each half of a double rail structure, stacked and harmonising like the staves of a piano score, sets into motion an electronic component. The bottom module, exposing its circuitry so cryptically as to render it unrecognisable, is a camera assembly whose focal interest is a horizontal sine wave painted onto the panel beneath the rail. The top element in this duo, accommodating a compact LCD monitor whose image is the signal of the sine wave captured by the camera, moves across the panel to the rotation of its own helical screw rail. Each element, camera and monitor, paces horizontally across the surface of the panel in entirely independent rhythm, so that the reality of the painted sine wave becomes relativized and deconstructed in an act of scanning that is itself explicitly decomposed into an endless continuity of states combining viewing in one direction with presenting in another. Neumann's work typifies how the transformal encoding of perception through planar differences destroys the transparency of mechanism and medium, replacing the intuitive assumptions of integration with relentless conspicuousness on implicit processes themselves.

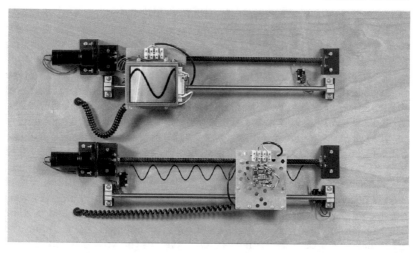

Figure 2. Andrew Neumann, *Phase Cancellation with Sine Wave*. Plywood, LCD screen, camera, motors, electronics, 32" x 18" x 7". 2002. Private collection. Courtesy of the artist.

In light of the numerous reciprocities that I have documented here, it is retrospectively arguable that the scope of possibility implied in Stieglitz's letter to Duchamp turns on the acknowledgment of mechanical process as a new aesthetic and embryonically cybercultural code rather than as embedded groundwork for something else. This shift toward process is why the same question could have been asked by Duchamp of Stieglitz. Duchamp's departure from conventional art practice, a moment seen as germinating in a diary entry containing the self-rebuking imperative to stop painting and get a job, is in many ways a permanent foray into the embrace of technical materials not only for expressive critique, but for a kind of engineering, which is to say the *capture of functionality*, that artistic practice had always ignored. The near-filmic motion that Duchamp's early painting had striven to capture through *Nude Descending a Staircase*, through the fictive documentation of gear machinery in *The Large Glass*, and through the interrogative paradox on motion of *Bicycle Wheel*, will all later amplify in his electrically powered rotorelief work, itself a mechanical kineticisation, a multi-angle take on expressive perspective, a major disavowal of painting's flatness, and collude to frame new conditions of art through an embrace of the artful media, which is to say conceptual engineering. This line of effort reveals how genuinely and repeatedly Duchamp's empirical curiosities reached into the heart of Stieglitz's own territory. For it was Stieglitz who had studied mechanical engineering in Berlin forty years earlier, and it was he again who had developed unusual expertise in photochemistry and who harvested a collection of cameras large and small with which to experimentalise the photograph. It was Stieglitz, the epitome of the artist artisan, who explored new media and confronted aesthetic and technical matter with equal skill. And, likewise, a visionary attention to multiple perspective was also valuable to Stieglitz, manifesting most momentously in vigorous and clairvoyant sponsorship of the young Picasso, for whom he organized the first solo exhibition, in 291, the legendary "Little Galleries of the Photo-Secession" which Stieglitz and Edward Steichen opened in 1911. With such foresight and foundations, one can view this perplexing question of whither photography as art as a probe to Duchamp's logic rather than as a factual quest for authenticity that Stieglitz would in any case have by then long resolved. And the probe proves fruitful, for Duchamp's answer falls neither in the class of affirmation nor of denial but, looking to the role of artistic production within the continuity of historical process, presages what has become increasingly consequential to art's encirclements around medium and materiality, namely that culture's technological and industrial affordances now provide the bulk of what defines the principal experiences, events, and objects through which both contemporary art and the culture industry articulate.

These encirclements, measurable in art's evolution through accelerating engagements with new technology and materials, are not isolated cases; they are overlooked or relegated as secondary to art's genuine modernist concerns. But as an abundance of examples of what must now be called cybercultural art, they appear in several moments and places, in the geometric symmetries in the latticed sculptured of Naum Gabo and Antoine Pevsner, Francisco Sobrino, and François Morellet, the magnetic sculpture of Len Lye and Takis, the kinetic sculpture of George Rickey, the material deconstructions of Jean Tinguely, the light dynamos of Heinz Mack, recombinant revolutions of Nicolas Schöffer's rotating objects and in the utter industrial depersonalisation of the Minimalist aesthetic. The material structure of these works expands and saturates expressive space to the point where critique folds within the fabric of work, for it is through technological proficiency that this kind of art is realized, and only through such technology that its significance would be decoded. To appraise the full extent to which such art functions as critique requires that critique itself migrate from a system built up of rational formalism and categorical abstraction toward the technological frame from which new media work is constructed and through which it codifies itself. To ask, from such a cybercultural frame, what sense it makes to view new media art through notions of flatness, to recall Greenberg's modernist norms for painting, is to prompt a backward glance all the way to photography itself, and the critical difficulties that it imposed on art's received aesthetic paradigms. For, even with its glaring representational characteristics, photography already embedded in itself a critique of culture mediated through a mechanism of production and reproduction that was no longer predominantly manual. And the perception of that distance, which locates the act of creation as something far removed from the immediate hand, was the major crisis for art and for culture, a point of simultaneous material, economic, and political transition at the turn of the last century.

Cultural production, no longer an immediate craft, becomes mechanized and industrialized into a new phenomenon that compels broad deciphering of social and technical codes. In this dual cipher, with production newly accompanied by and gradually supplanted by reproduction is the semantic etymology of *cyberculture*, the historical moment in which a conglomeration of signs produced both by humans and technology defines a turbulent sea on whose waves of innovation everything new instantly, virally, reproduced is continually rendered obsolete by further novelty, improvement, or replacement. Drawing closer to perception, this restless cultural language, manifest in the neologistic adoption, substitution, and convergence of art, system, craft, and language, is a sign of cyberculture's perpetual "until something else".

Notes

[1] The essays in the present book evolved from presentations at the 3rd Global Cybercultures Conference held from Thursday 11th August - Saturday 13th August 2005 in Prague, Czech Republic. In the interdisciplinary spirit of the conference, the essays are wide-ranging in scope; yet they trace one of two tributaries, mirrored in the two sections of the book. The empirical essays present data to build a portrait of human action through digital media, while the aesthetic essays look at new media as a field of expressive practices—visual art, film, literature, and electronic games—central to human engagement.

[2] Naumann, F., M. and Obalk, H. (eds.), *Affectt Marcel: The Selected Correspondence of Marcel Duchamp*, trans. Jill Taylor London: Thames & Hudson, 2000. The typographic configuration shown is Duchamp's.

[3] Schjeldahl, P., *The Hydrogen Jukebox: Selected Writings of Peter Schjeldahl, 1978-1990*, (Lannan Series of Contemporary Art Criticism, No 2, University of California Press, Berkeley, 1991. p. 187.

[4] See Jones, C. A., *Eyesight Alone: Clement Greenberg's Modernism and the Bureaucratization of the Senses*, University of Chicago Press, Chicago, 2005. Jones documents this reduction, and through the question, "What was it that Greenberg took to be modern, such that an artist could emerge as either premature or 'pseudo' in relation to it?" (p.150) reasons its roots to be centered in a formalism of abstraction, one in which the body does not figure (as it were) and which conversely resonates with technology. Her further

assertion that abstraction "also took from perception to purify" implicates Greenberg's characterisation of modernism in Bruno Latour's similar critique of modernity as largely manifesting through a practice of purification, of separation of "native" from "modern" sensibility, of pure from impure, whose culminating process is the scientific method, a methodological holy grail of sorts for Greenberg (See Latour, B., *We Have Never Been Modern*, trans. Catherine Porter, Harvard University Press, Cambridge, 1993.) .

[5] Greenberg, C., *Art and Culture: Critical Essays*, Beacon Press, Boston, 1965.

[6] This hybridism is for Latour, modernity's second practice, a complement to that of purification.

[7] Greenberg, *Art and Culture: Critical Essays*,

[8] It is the relevance of this organicity to modernism that Greenberg dismisses. While Picasso and Matisse had broken with nature, the work of Stieglitz, Georgia O'Keeffe, Arthur Dove, and Kandinsky, rife with "mystical overtones", was for Greenberg a "repudiation of technics and rationalism", a metaphysical "messianism" that Caroline Jones connects to multiplicity of charges: of Greenberg's view of Stieglitz as an intellectually puerile dandy; to Greenberg's view of O'Keeffe as "pseudo-modern"; and to Greenberg's inability to free the photograph from its indexicality (Cf. Jones, pp.145-175). As my later treatment of art and metaphysics reveals, these biases leave Greenberg outside the portals of cyberculture, with its propensity for assimilation through layered recoding of historical culture's many previously unconnected manifestations.

[9] "Once society has lost its myth-based community, it loses all the reference points of truly common language until such time as the divisions within the inactive community can be overcome by the inauguration of a real historical community. When art, which was the common language of social inaction, develops into independent art in the modern sense, emerging from its original religious universe and becoming individual production of separate works, it too becomes subject to the movement governing the history of all separate culture. Its declaration of independence is the beginning of its end". Debord, G., *The Society of the Spectacle*, trans. Donald Nicholson-Smith, Zone Books, Cambridge, Mass., 1967/1995.§ 186.

[10] Nor is this merely postmodern hindsight. Documenting Bergson's rejection of the conceptual method in favour of the flux-like immediacy of experience, a 1912 review of the first English translation of Time and Free Will, makes clear that the basis for just such an essentialist reading of Stieglitz was available in his own day. Bergson's "sympathetic insight" as fuel for the intuitive grasp crucial to a Stieglitz photograph is contrasted with the kind of formal/categorical reasoning that disrupts the captured phenomenon so that

"to get at reality in its living movement we must break out of the prison of concepts and immerse ourselves, as best we may, in the flux". Fawcett, E. D., 'Matter and Memory', *Mind*, 21/ 82,April 1912, 201-32.
[11] Durant, M. A., 'The Blur of the Otherworldly', *Art Journal*, 62/3,Fall 2003, 6-15.
[12] Ibid.

Bibliography

Debord, G., *The Society of the Spectacle*, trans. Donald Nicholson-Smith, Zone Books, Cambridge, Mass., 1967/1995.

Durant, M. A., 'The Blur of the Otherworldly', *Art Journal,* 62/3,Fall 2003, 6-15.

Durant, M. A. and Marsching, J. D. (eds.), *Blur of the Otherworldly: Contemporary Art, Technology, and the Paranormal* Baltimore: Center for Art and Visual Culture, UMBC, 2006.

Fawcett, E. D., 'Matter and Memory', *Mind,* 21/ 82,April 1912, 201-32.

Greenberg, C., *Art and Culture: Critical Essays*, Beacon Press, Boston, 1965.

Jones, C. A., *Eyesight Alone: Clement Greenberg's Modernism and the Bureaucratization of the Senses*, University of Chicago Press, Chicago, 2005.

Latour, B., *We Have Never Been Modern*, trans. Catherine Porter, Harvard University Press, Cambridge, 1993.

Naumann, F., M. and Obalk, H. (eds.), *Affectt Marcel: The Selected Correspondence of Marcel Duchamp*, trans. Jill Taylor London: Thames & Hudson, 2000.

Schjeldahl, P., *The Hydrogen Jukebox: Selected Writings of Peter Schjeldahl, 1978-1990*, (Lannan Series of Contemporary Art Criticism, No 2, University of California Press, Berkeley, 1991.

Sullivan, L. and Edwards, A. (eds.), *Stewards of The Sacred* Cambridge, MA: American Association of Museums with the Center for Study of World Religions, Harvard University, 2004.

Part I

The Empirical

Formalisms of Digital Text

Francisco J. Ricardo

Abstract
Critical discussions of online communication typically assume the presence of variations in language use in digital media versus traditional literature or real-time conversation. However, as there is little actual research to corroborate this claim, the question arises: what evidence exists to justify the claim that people communicate differently using digital media than in writing or in person? This is a comparative study of several measures of communicative practice across a variety of literary and speech genres, digital and embodied. It explores oral and written expression through media use as the manipulation of formal language components and affordances of a medium or genre in connection with notions of spoken or written style. A comparative analysis of sentence usage in four different communicative forms - blogs, emails, printed text, and actual speech shows that, while *mean sentence length* remained statistically equal in speech, book print, or online postings, substantial variation, as measured by lexical density, was found in the actual *richness of language* employed across these forms. While empirical in structure, this analysis is intended as a contribution to critical theory on digital media's expressive forms and uses.

Key Words: Comparative linguistics, media theory.

*****

1. Introduction

With particular relevance to the communicative affordances of new media, it could be argued that the expressive possibilities of any medium are defined by its prevalent manner of consumption, which, to posit a paraphrase to Ludwig Wittgenstein, is to say that the expressive potential of a medium is realized in its use. The present study explores oral and written expression through media use as the manipulation of formal language components and affordances of a medium or genre in connection with spoken or written style. It presents a comparative analysis of sentence usage in four different communicative forms - blogs, emails, printed text, and actual speech (which I will call genres for a unified term) - across which significant similarities, and differences, in lexical expressive practice were measured. Results show that, while mean sentence length remained unchanged in speech, book print, or online post, substantial variation was found in the richness of language employed, as defined by the lexical density metric used in computational linguistics. This density was highest for printed text, which presumably would have been extensively edited, and lowest for speech, which reflects its improvisatory nature. Blogs and emails, which share characteristics of both (given that these digital genres are written like print but improvised and unedited like speech)

2.   Primary distinctions

I open my topic with an exploratory notion: if there are detectable, structurally predetermined information variabilities across different media or genres, what are the forms of this variation? Empirical evidence demonstrating a given utterance to be more or less information-rich depending on whether it were spoken, printed on a page, or written online would prove the significance of a medium or form of presentation as a collaborator in inflecting expression. Information science already accepts that print's unique process of revision renders its content more lexically dense than that of speech. It is thus generally assumed that, in a complexity-of-language spectrum, print would lie on the pole of highest density, while speech would be positioned at its opposite, more diffuse end. The findings in the present study place show that online writing, which borrows heavily from both expressive modalities, falls provably between both.

Precedents for the notion I first broached - that where one expresses something changes how it expressed - are anchored in various fields, from the controversies of the anthropological Sapir-Whorf hypothesis of linguistic relativism, asserting as it does that thinking is structured differently in response to the unique structure and terminological emphases of the speaker's language, out to the contemporary discovery of media as an object of study, the field singularly pioneered, though unsystematically, by Marshall McLuhan. The history of language variation formerly known as historical linguistics, founded on an expansive prospect that could accommodate the word's entanglement with modern, industrialized techniques for its propagation, takes its starting point at the pummel of the first printing press and culminates in a redirection that has become entangled within the accelerating project of all media evolution, the stylisation and broadcasting of language through transmissive mechanisms. In the proliferation of such mechanisms, meaning, originally shared in a purely embodied manner, became inextricably tied to technical methods of reproduction. As the practice of language became incrementally absorbed within the affordances and conditions of the means of its production, each medium, indistinguishable from the institutions that operated it, stipulated conditions on the potential realization of the word - newspapers offered expressive possibilities to the correspondent; possibilities that were, however, circumscribed by specific journalistic stylistic standards and strict word counts. Broadcast media, too, rather than serve exclusively as passive conduit for communication at the cultural level, evolved the "encapsulated story" as its discrete object of delivery and has for its part also aggressively controlled the time and space available to expression, by limiting the coverage of stories in scope and length. In doing this, it has also demanded tacit agreement with the politics of the sponsorship model that subsidizes commercial broadcast institutions. And for their own part as well, the voice of many digital media forms, while transcending political restrictions, have also been hampered by bandwidth and detailed technical limitations. In each case, we might now ask whether the medium is the message or rather *governs* it.

From the foregoing, we might take it that the expressive potential of a medium is defined by its interface and manner of consumption, which is to say that the expressive potential of a medium is realized in its use. As an exploration in this line of inquiry, I conducted a comparative analysis of sentence usage in four different communicative forms - blogs, emails, printed text, and actual speech (which I will call genres for a unified term). The results of quantitative measures on usage data found significant similarities, and differences, in lexical expressive practice across these genres. While mean sentence length remained exactly the same regardless of whether the utterance was found in speech, printed in a book, or posted online, there was substantial variation in the richness of language employed, as defined by the lexical density metric used in computational linguistics. This density was highest for printed text, which presumably would have been extensively edited, and lowest for speech, which reflects its improvisatory nature. Blogs and emails, which share characteristics of both (given that these digital genres are written like print but improvised and unedited like speech), were statistically located at the median between oral and print forms.

This might not be an unintuitive finding; the practice of writing, always in flux, has over the last two decades been particularly impacted by the emergence of digital innovations in new text genres, chiefly, email messages, newsgroup postings, and weblogs. Many of the compositional practices of conventional (that is, print-intended) writing - the sense of a linear structure comprising a beginning, middle, and end, for example – fell into muted crisis in the new medium. In the manifest difference between physical and digital media, digital genres have evolved into environments that encourage the substitution of many established structural authorial conventions for the more convenient parameters offered by interfaces and tools embedded in the interactive genre. Length of written work, to evoke one measure, is one of the attributes in greatest deviation. The essay or chapter is practically non-existent in a medium that by nature emphasizes less the exposition of larger-scale topics than the assertion of, and reaction to, specific, closely circumscribed points. There are, to be sure, compound structures in digital writing, the canonical example being the case of discussion list threads, essentially a conversation (or various) structured around a question-and-answer or declaration-and-response built up from sequentially posted messages. There is also the genus of the blog, the online equivalent of the diary, with journal entries posted in reverse chronological order. But the pithy unit of writing that comprises these cases is distinct from the shape of expository writing: the online *post* comprising each of these forms are discrete and compacted assertions that lack the dimensional scenery-setting context of the *chapter* from the world of print. Except for the still comparatively rare case of digital literature, prevalent online forms distinguish the anatomical core of digital writing as being point-based rather than story-based. Further justifying our view of the basic semantic unit as the point are the extreme forms that promote it: media formats and software exclusively dedicated to creating and organizing and displaying points: the presentation package (e.g., Microsoft PowerPoint™), the idea processor (e.g., Inspiration), and the semantic drawing system (e.g., Microsoft Visio™). We might also note, in contrast, that no major software exists exclusively for topic-making[1]. The comparatively small thematic unit is evident at the software interface, invariably designed to manipulate diminutive units of text.

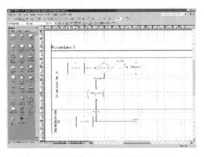

Figure 1. A Microsoft Visio™ drawing

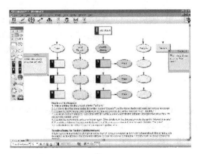

Figure 2. An Inspiration™ diagram

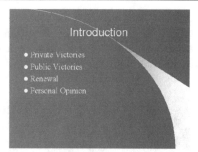

Figure 3. A Microsoft PowerPoint™ Slide

There is no hyperbole in asserting that the cultural unconsciousness of modernity harbours historically engendered motivations toward one particular kind of literacy. The form of linear thought whose logic is based on gradual development of theme or idea from context to climax begins in the educational requirement, taught for centuries and passed into the legacy of the literate scribe and scholar, that the young pupil of ancient Greece command classical logic's syllogistic structures and manoeuvre classical rhetoric's five-point techné. Modern deviations from this path, therefore, are bound to have dramatic impact. In particular, the displacement of theme-centred thinking by point-driven media introduces particular economies of language that reduce the archetypal expressive unit, the sentence, to a quasi-outmoded artefact rarely seen in these new forms. Drawings and diagrams are not new, but their prevalence as a substitute for writing mark a turning point of sorts. Point-driven writing, manifest even more emphatically in the bullet list, shifts the emphasis from style to process, seeking to communicate some kind of *how* in what is presented, and if judged only through its insistent visuality, renders the written form nearly gratuitous. Predictably, this alteration has attracted numerous lines of critique. There are some for whom the historically evolved forms of textual expression fulfil conditions of understanding that are not attainable merely with points, glyphs, or graphs, and others for whom the comparison between topical and point-driven media is not necessary, for each is its own class of communicative tool. A vexed Edward Tufte, whose background is statistical rather than literary, finds these non-manuscript forms paralysed to natural exposition or fertile idea development[2]. Narrowing on the particularly problematic category of presentation software, he associates the characteristic cascade of bullet points, garish mastheads with oversized, condescendingly obvious graphics, and distracting animations typical of its "texts" with the jarring, disconcerting experience devoid ample explanation, which is to say that Tufte traces the semantic disparity between seeing and reading. Conversely, a more exploratory construal of the problem is rendered by David Byrne, who, speaking as visual artist-critic, begins with parody by "making fun of the iconography of PowerPoint" and redirects the medium into its own kind of expressive genre unrelated to any historically determined textual function[3]. Utilizing the tools of the tool, such as its ability to render arrows, for aesthetic production in its own right, he subsumes the domain of text to that of the image.

Figure 4. *Sea of Possibilities*, David Byrne, 2003, digital image.
Courtesy Pace/MacGill Gallery

Two divergent views – one pragmatic, one aesthetic – of the same phenomenon, set the foundation for what has developed between the semi-textual and the orthodox-textual: the space of the neo-textual where oral and textual, and semi-improvised emerged, and we see a new kind of conversational writing develop in the form of blogs, emails, and other aleatory genres. History, always difficult to evade, continually integrates into communicative forms. The last stage of protracted writing, embodied in the essay or novel form, took place roughly six centuries ago. The process-based diagrammatic textuality that we identify with the algorithmic or process diagram reached completion in the twentieth century. But conversational writing has no direct ancestor, except for the personal diary, which nonetheless never assumed the sprawling and fragmentary form of common contemporary usage. In notion, however, conversational writing is not entirely new; a variety of it – "conversational literacy" – was central to the meta-analyses of oral and mediated communication of Lori Janzen-Wilde as early as 1993, just as new media communication was acquiring global prevalence. Surveying the nascent landscape of multimodal communication, she was the first to notice that lying entirely neither in print-based nor orally based genres, mediated communication synthesizes equally from both and exhibits "characteristics typically assigned to both 'oral' and 'literate' ends of the continuum"[4].

It is the features of this style that have incubated within digital media that are the foundation of many suppositions equal to those of the effects of the medium on "traditional" writing. Special "mechanics", unique this new style, are worked out through the lexical characteristics that reflect the degree of orality implicit in the medium, amenable to study in a diachronic manner. That is, displacing literariness, the orality of this mode is, over time, increasingly encoded both for visual prominence and lexical conciseness:

> The oral conventions are evident in the way people subvert or abandon traditional conventions of grammar and punctuation in electronic writing. Meaning is very often conveyed by cues recognized only by users of computer-mediated communication. Some examples are acronyms like BTW (by the way) and IMO (in my opinion), and specialized use of typography -- for example, *word* to signify italics and the use of nonverbal icons or emoticons like a smiley face :-) -- which differ from traditionally recognized textual cues.[5]

Another relation justifies the popular belief in significant differences between oral, written, and online modes of communication: the production of digital textuality in relation to what we might term a principle of commitment. To consider the conditions of speech is to accept evanescent, improvisatory modes of expression literally projected into the air. Everything more or less spontaneous in this sense is enclosed within the utterance. To produce writing, on the other hand, necessitates an engagement toward preparatory organizational work and editing prior to "committing" expression to paper, its physical support. We could see these practices as two ends of a spectrum, and see in electronic writing a middle ground with sufficient latitude to draw arbitrarily from each pole. Here, any resemblance to print text emerges from the common lexical nature of both: words uniformly arranged on a visual medium. The contrast however, is equally significant, for, as with air, the digital medium is entirely unstable, and its production is sufficiently provisional that textual operations based on structural organization, prewriting, and detailed editing run against its aleatory spirit.

And this remains the case in spite of other distinctions operating within the medium, for instance whether the genre in question is realised synchronously (e.g., in the online chat) or not (e.g., in e-mails, mailing lists, newsgroups, and discussion groups). In conventional writing, the author generally writes to make a point. But in digital conversational writing online authors may pursue another purpose, since the style of this writing appears structured so as to reflect the social network in which the authors are participating.

Moreover, a peculiar relationship, functioning as ballast, holds between physicality and orality, the absence of the former being compensated by the use of the latter. Presumably, this manifests for two reasons, because the lack of another means of communicating introduces non-verbal communication into a predominantly textual medium and because networked users, interacting in large numbers, can experience many kinds of interaction almost simultaneously. Here a nexus of language is superimposed on one of populace, a two-dimensional grid of continuous interaction: optimisations to the traditional model of expository text are essential. In defining the notion of virtual community, Howard Rheingold refers indirectly to the displacement of presence by expression, when, pondering both the breadth of collective contact and the demand for using language in the absence of material presence to assist in those relationships, he remarks that people in virtual communities continually

> exchange pleasantries and argue, engage in intellectual discourse, conduct commerce, exchange knowledge, share emotional support, make plans, brainstorm, gossip, feud, fall in love, find friends and lose them, play games, flirt, create a little high art and a lot of idle talk. People in virtual communities do just about everything people do in real life, but we leave our bodies behind.[6]

We might conclude altogether that the more one looks into conversational writing, the less it resembles traditional text either in purpose or structure. The speed and quantity of messages (again, emphasizing points rather than topics) almost compels a new definition for its medium-specific functions, and one can understand the rationale for assertions like Ferris's "computer users often treat electronic writing as an oral medium: communication is often fragmented, computer-mediated communication is used for phatic communion, and formulaic devices have arisen" or Murray's classification of such writing as comprising a "language of action".[7]

We have enough here to deepen our examination of conversational writing into specific questions posed by the foregoing comparisons. With the generous amount of speculation on the characteristics of digital conversational writing, one would expect a somewhat proportional body of observational data to support or refute theoretical claims, but this has not materialized. Considering that the operational nature and environment of digital text connects transparently to its archival, which is the task of innumerable server logs and search engine indexes, any paucity of systematic studies of data and material produced within and through the digital medium is nothing less than surprising. And it is not entirely clear what useful inferences can be drawn from much of what does exist, certainly stylistic knowledge – knowledge of what and how authors are creating online, and how the conventions adopted and evolving in their medium compare with those long established in the world of print – does not appear to be the focus of such analyses. One would, for instance, like to observe whether stylistic practices in the new medium conform to conventional modes of print-based writing: is there consensus on the length of sentences between both conventional and conversational writing? If conversational writing derives attributes from orality (i.e., Ferris's observation that "electronic writing is characterized by the use of oral conventions over traditional conventions, of argument over exposition, and of group thinking over individual thinking" is representative of this belief), how significant and present are these in any digital corpus, such as an online discussion group, or a library of similar communications documents? This invokes the idea of a spectrum of communicative modes ranging from most to least "formal" along lexical and semantic criteria, which I will explore next.

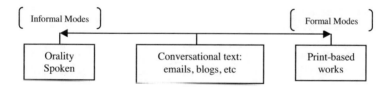

Figure 5. Spectrum of oral-literal communicative modes

Let us establish the first dimension of an analytic framework that qualitatively incorporates the different forms of writing we wish to compare. We first assume, along with the general academic consensus, that print-oriented or traditional writing stands in structural contrast with oral communication–this point has been navigated throughout an entire literature and, as mentioned earlier, Janzen-Wilde's relatively early work drew relevant conclusions for comparative media, between literacy and facilitated communication, in a meta-analysis of research, summarized in tables 1 and 2.

Table 1. Characteristics of "orality" and their relationship to facilitated communication (FC)

CHARACTERISTICS OF "ORALITY"	SOURCE	ASSOCIATED WITH FC?
Used to regulate social interactions	Westby, 1985; Hildyard & Hidi, 1985; Chafe, 1985	Yes
Topic usually here and now	Westby, 1985; Rubin, 1987	?
Familiar words; repetitive syntax and ideas	Westby, 1985; Rubin, 1987	?
Intonation and non-verbal cues important for cohesion and conveying meaning	Westby, 1985; Tannen, 1985; Hildyard & Hidi, 1985; Wallach, 1990	No
Usually has fragmented quality	Chafe, 1985; Redeker, 1984	?
Rapid rate contributes to dysfluencies	Chafe, 1985	No
Usual lack of permanence	Chafe, 1985	Depends on medium
Listeners often give immediate feedback	Redeker, 1984; Rubin, 1987	Yes

Table 2. Characteristics of "literacy" and their relationship to facilitated communication

CHARACTERISTICS OF "LITERACY"	SOURCE	ASSOCIATED WITH FC?
Slow, deliberate process because of mechanical constraints	Chafe, 1985; Rubin, 1987	Yes
No need to worry about keeping the listener's attention	Chafe, 1985	No
Often abstract or unfamiliar topics	Westby, 1985	?
Concise use of syntax and ideas	Westby	?
Cohesion based on linguistic markers	Westby, 1985; Tannen, 1985	?
Can be polished and perfected before it is read	Hildyard & Hidi, 1985; Chafe, 1985; Redeker, 1984; Rubin, 1987	Yes and no
Integrated quality	Chafe, 1985; Redeker, 1984; Westby, 1985; Rubin, 1987	?
Usually detached spatially and temporally from readers	Chafe, 1985; Redeker, 1984; Westby, 1985; Rubin, 1987	Yes and no
Visually permanent	Chafe, 1985; Redeker, 1984; Rubin, 1987	Depends on medium

From patterns evident in the communications research literature on this subject, Janzen-Wilde concludes that "characteristics of orality which are common in facilitated communication include its use in regulating social interactions and the opportunity for the listeners/ communication partners to give immediate feedback to the speaker", in this sense, conversational writing is most unlike its traditional predecessor. In the new millennium, emails and blogs are the everyday examples of conversational writing.

Content and genre present special problems for comparative media work, any conclusions deduced from textual analysis must only reflect structural features of the medium, such as specific conventions and communicative practices, rather than content features of it. The importance of structural inference can be illustrated in a simple example. Let us imagine a (flawed) comparison of print versus orality by means of examining five works of each. Our sample from print media, in other words, would comprise five novels and our oral sample, five transcripts transcribed from legal cases argued in a court of law. This assessment, after statistical analysis, would lead us to infer almost inescapably that print media are more 'romantic' and that orality, on the other hand, is more 'factual'. But this fallacy of inference would reflect the nature of the samples utilized for each medium rather any features inherent in how the medium is itself rhetorically structured. In seeking to establish objective differences of communicative practice between media, therefore, we must choose criteria that are independent of special content-level features such as "factuality" or "romance", for factuality is not intrinsic to any medium (would that it were so). We must, therefore, confine ourselves to comparing media on strictly structural features that may emerge from communicative practices within them. And the structural characteristics must be present in all the media under scrutiny. Three such structural features present themselves without content bias: sentence length, pronoun usage, and lexical density, as defined next.

If, as research cited in the *Characteristics of Literacy* table suggests, written text possesses unique structural characteristics: concise use of syntax and ideas and cohesion based on linguistic markers, then the prime measure by which we might compare communicative differences between text, orality, and conversational writing is the word length of the average sentence in each medium. If the belief is that oral media are more diffuse, "rambling", free than print-based ones, we ought to expect longer sentences from the former[8],[9],[10]. Intuitively, it is reasonable to construe the length of sentences in one medium or genre as being radically different than in another, for, why should they be the same?

Similarly, a second criterion, relative pronoun usage, is also worth exploring across media. Measuring the extent of pronoun usage across different media would indicate the degree to which speakers or writers are "close to the text" by way of direct reference, and may justify approaching the question of whether one medium is in general more impersonal than another. Again, the instinctive hypothesis might be that orality is more informal and therefore more "personal" or intimate than text, and that pronoun usage in blogs and emails lies ostensibly somewhere between both. This is intriguing, but it is worth cautioning that pronoun usage may belong more to specific kind of content than to the intrinsic structure of how communication in media takes place. Nevertheless, given this instinctive hypothesis and caveat, comparative statistics on pronoun usage are presented here without firm conclusion, should they prove helpful for future linguistic investigations in new media.

Finally, lexical density, the opposite of redundancy in language, is an indicator of the percentage of words in a text that are unique, that is, not repeated in it. The lower the lexical density, the greater the verbal redundancy and therefore the presumed ease of comprehension. The formula for calculating the lexical density D for any text is

$$D = (U/N)* 100$$

where U represents the number of unique words in a text sample, and N is its total word count. Lexical density is more than a statistical number; it confirms a principle of information theory that claims that redundancy in a message boosts its comprehension. As a cheeky example, let us imagine that you want to learn a dialectical kind of Spanish, Cuban street argot, one word at a time. Today's word is *astilla*, a noun that translates to splinter, although the slang means something completely different. With a single utterance, you might or might not guess the slang term's denotation:

Use *astilla* for dinner.

The lexical density of this utterance is 100%, in that 4 out of the 4 words are unique. In the next lesson, the key phrase becomes

Use *astilla* for dinner. use *astilla* for payment.

This utterance, with 5 out of 8 unique words has lower (63.%) lexical density, reflecting the possibility that its redundancy boosts its potential comprehension, and the student of that word may now have some feasible ideas as to the slang meaning of *astilla*. Finally the third phrase:

Use *astilla* for dinner, use *astilla* for payment, use *astilla* for purchases.

This new utterance now has only 6 unique words out of 12, or 50% lexical density, and its increased redundancy supports the possible conjecture that *astilla* translates to *money*. In this sense, comparative measures of lexical density would, with Westby's and Rubin's research corroborate or disprove the claim that orality emphasizes familiar words as well as repetitive syntax and ideas, and based on those research claims, we would expect to find lower lexical density in oral data than in print, and the density of online texts would presumably lie between both.

3.   Analysis

There is much theory on blogging, but few empirical studies, of the semantics or stylistic composition in blogs (or emails). And for extant research, methodological weaknesses pose an additional obstacle. One 2004 study, Herring et al analysed 203 blogs for linguistic measures. Its method arrived at conclusions based on the reported number of sentences detected (3260) and words collected (42930)[11]. However, this study cannot have looked at more than the first page of each blog, for in my study of 61 blogs, the scanning program written for that task requested 30 postings from each of the 61 sites, for a total of 8726 sentences and 94433 words, many more words drawn from fewer than one-third the blogs in the 2004 study. In all, the statistics in my work are based on 522 individual postings. My analysis found the average number of words per post to be 303, not similar to Herring's 210. We did, however agree on the average number of words per sentence; I found 15, Herring 16.

Herring et al count the number of paragraphs in their blog corpus, but this measure is problematic in the blog genre. A paragraph, in the realm of conventional print, is a group of one of more sentences separated by one or more blank lines. However, the definition of paragraphs is different in web genres, where, rather than being used to separate groups of ideas in the same text, paragraph breaks instead introduce whole new ideas or micro texts. Similarly, the paragraph, or a set of empty lines, to be precise, is overloaded in blog style: its serves as the default marker between blog posts; as the separator between texts and graphic elements; as a break between a text and an inserted quote; and as mere cosmetic device where inserting white space adds visual balance to existing text blocks. None of these uses is functionally related to notion of a paragraph boundary.

A more difficult problem is that of quoted phrases in blogs. Herring's count presents no definition for what constitutes a quoted phrase. Instead, they provide two separate counts, quoted sentences/fragments and quoted words per sentence, but these do not specify how quotes were counted, for, in the high intertextuality of blog style, there are at least three ways to encapsulate a quoted phrase. One is in the conventional way: by inserting the desired text within quotes. Another is by means of block text with indented margins on both sides, for which an HTML tag specifically exists. The third is not to include the text at all, but rather to link to it. This makes questionable the statistical measure presented there, the number of "quoted words per sentence", which they find to be 7.6–an almost impossible number if we accept their 13.2 "words per sentence" measure, as it would mean that over half of everything written is rendered in quotes.

Across 500 emails and 500 posts on random blogs, the pattern of sentence length for each genre appears to be very similar (see figure 6).

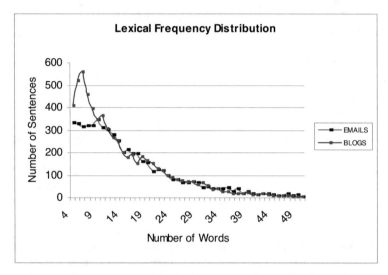

Figure 6. Frequency Distribution of sentences by word count, Emails and Blogs

If, even taking into consideration the wide disparities in style across all possible authors, significant stylistic differences are found with the distribution of sentence length in other genres, these could be attributed to the structure of the genre, and its writing practices, which for the most part lack interventions such as word count limit, editorship, and revision. All of these would influence average length of sentence measures.

Overlaying sentence length (grouped in ranges of 5 words) all communicative modes a single graphical frequency distribution, we identify the first significant difference between text and conversational writing.

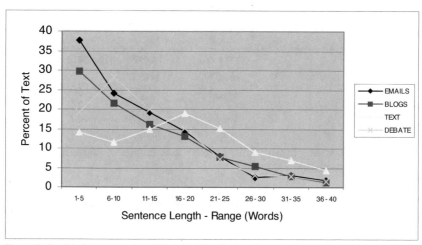

Figure 7. Graphical representation of Relative Distribution, Sentence Length Ranges, by Genre

Table 3. Relative Distribution, Sentence Length Ranges, by Genre

RANGE	EMAILS	BLOGS	TEXT	DEBATE
1-5	37.6%	29.7%	14.1%	19.2%
6-10	24.2%	21.6%	11.5%	28.2%
11-15	19.3%	16.1%	14.8%	20.1%
16 - 20	14.4%	13%	18.9%	15.1%
21 - 25	7.9%	7.7%	15.1%	7.3%
26 - 30	2.5%	5.4%	8.9%	3.2%
31 - 35	3%	2.0%	6.8%	2.8%
36 - 40	1.7%	1.4%	4.3%	1.6%

A regression analysis of emails and blogs shows a powerful (98.5%) correlation between sentence lengths across media modes (p < 0.05):

Table 4. Regression Analysis of Sentence Length Ranges – Emails and Blogs

Regression Statistics	
Multiple R	0.992762
R Square	0.985578
Adjusted R Square	0.983174
Standard Error	1.648615
Observations	8

ANOVA

	df	SS	MS	F	Significance F
Regression	1	1114.4473	1114.4473	410.03478	0.00
Residual	6	16.307602	2.7179337		
Total	7	1130.755			

Likewise, blogs and spoken text share a significant 75.4% correlation ($p < 0.05$) in length:

Table 5. Regression Analysis of Sentence Length Ranges - Blogs and Speech

Regression Statistics	
Multiple R	0.868533
R Square	0.75435
Adjusted R Square	0.713408
Standard Error	5.283954
Observations	8

ANOVA

	df	SS	MS	F	Significance F
Regression	1	514.4277	514.4277	18.42495	0.005135
Residual	6	167.521	27.92017		
Total	7	681.9488			

Similarly, the correlation relating to sentence length between email and spoken data is significantly high (70.7%, $p < 0.05$):

Table 6. Regression Analysis of Sentence Length Ranges - Email and Speech

Regression Statistics	
Multiple R	0.84133
R Square	0.707836
Adjusted R Square	0.659142
Standard Error	7.42031
Observations	8

ANOVA					
	df	SS	MS	F	Significance F
Regression	1	800.389	800.389	14.5364	0.008836
Residual	6	330.366	55.061		
Total	7	1130.755			

These analyses reveal significant similarity in sentence length across oral and conversational writing modes. Conversely, and as expected, there is a low (28.4%) correlation on sentence length between email and written text, from which we reject the null hypothesis that they are from similar populations (or lengths):

Table 7. Regression Analysis of Sentence Length Ranges - Email and Texts

Regression Statistics	
Multiple R	0.532924
R Square	0.284008
Adjusted R Square	0.164676
Standard Error	11.616156
Observations	8

ANOVA					
	df	SS	MS	F	Significance F
Regression	1	321.144	321.144	2.37998	0.173840504
Residual	6	809.610	134.935		
Total	7	1130.755			

In summary, this appears to demonstrate how much more similar, in terms of length of utterance, emails and blogs are to spoken genres than to written texts, for which reason I have in this discussion termed this class of expression, created materially as text but possessing essential qualities of speech, *conversational writing*.

One structural point about blog stylistics bears consideration: the notion of sentence must be somewhat redefined in this genre, in response to its expanded use. The blog sentence, such as it is, is deployed as a "traditional" declarative sentence as often as it is pressed into something serving the role of *caption*, that is, an utterance that is not a sentence but a verbal adjunct to reinforce an associated idea or graphic. Thus, what appear under normal grammatical conditions to be nonsensical fragments like "Rewards of some hard digging" or "gander mountain credit card" in fact emphasize the dependence of text on neighbouring non-textual elements for completeness of meaning. This fragmentary expression has become standard practice in blog writing. Typically, the fragment-caption will be a sentence missing either the verb, e.g., "Lots of diggers", "Myself with a very good find", "picture of beetle bug" or the subject, e.g., "Screening ore".

However, the results of sentence length, which show conversational writing to be of similar length as the oral utterance, does not transfer to the case of pronoun usage (see Figure 8).

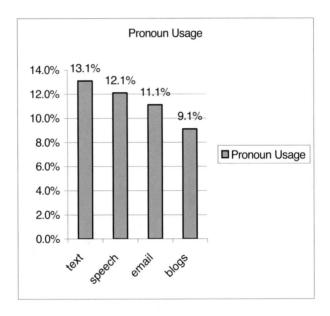

Figure 8. Relative pronoun usage in text, speech, email, and blog samples

The downward frequency slope illustrates that the literary and expository forms understood by the label "text" employ more pronouns than blogs or email samples, and approximates only speech in frequency of use. This runs counter to generally accepted arguments of orality versus literacy, with conversational writing synthesizing elements of both. However, arguments around an orality-literacy opposition so often associated first with Marshall McLuhan[12], and later with Walter Ong[13] and Jack Goody[14] did not arise in the full bloom of new media nor aim at modernity's digital textuality, and consequently they do not examine the new conventions of merging text with temporal and graphical forms in a dynamic medium. When text accompanies an image, the deixis between both is transmodal, which is to say, not merely textual. In the presence of an image a text that describes or relates it will not apply a pronoun in reference to the non-textual element; pronouns are strictly referents for linguistic content.

The general formula for determining pronoun usage is simply the percentage of words in a corpus that are pronouns. No doubt, a larger corpus is necessary to determine this more authoritatively, and we might keep in mind that some text genres are bound to use more pronouns than others. In the present case, the text corpus was comprised entirely of fiction works; if we used scientific monographs, the resulting pronoun usage would likely differ greatly. Nonetheless, as a starting point for discussion, these results induce some speculation. In particular, we might infer that blogs, addressed to a general audience, are more "impersonal" than email messages, directed at specific individuals, and both are less personal than speech, which is as we might expect, since speech is more improvisatory; and email is easier to compose than blogs. In the Enron sample, many emails were of a highly personal nature whose appropriateness in a blog format may not be evident. Further research should statistically probe the comparative degree of personal reference in blogs and emails.

The final measure of potential communicative differences, lexical density, shows the differences divided into three groups – Speech (6%); Blogs (9%) and Emails (10.7%); and Texts (17.2%). In keeping with its primary standing as a communicative structure, text possesses a higher lexical density than speech, and, in support of the hypothesis relating to the interstitial status of conversational writing, blogs and emails lie between both.

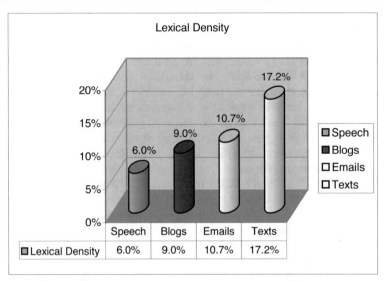

Figure 8. Relative lexical density in text, speech, email, and blog samples

4.   Conclusion

This analysis of four distinct communicative modes – speech, blogs, emails, and printed text (as fiction works) – exposes sufficiently significant differences in sentence length, pronoun usage, and lexical density between them so as to support the assertion that blogs and emails, as instances of conversational writing, conform to stylistic and structural characteristics somewhere between speech and print. This may suggest that usage of different communicative media appears to respond to fundamental differences between them, with the most marked contrast being observed in sentence length and the least, for usage of pronouns. We might say that sentence length is the most structural of our three metrics, and pronoun usage the most stylistic, with lexical density in a region lying between both. In that the observed differences were largest in the structural variables of observation, further research might similarly examine structural variables in corpus samples across these or similar communicative modalities in relation to the new expressive practices developing synthetically within digital media.

Bibliography

Byrne, D., *E.E.E.I (Envisioning Emotional Epistemological Information)*, Steidl Publishing, Göttingen, Germany, 2003.

Chafe, W. L., 'Linguistic Differences Produced by Differences between Speaking and Writing', in N. Torrance D.R. Olson, & A. Hildyard (ed.), *Literacy, Language and Learning: The Nature and Consequences of Reading and Writing*, Cambridge University Press, Cambridge, 1985.

Debord, G., *The Society of the Spectacle*, trans. Donald Nicholson-Smith, Zone Books, Cambridge, Mass., 1967/1995.

Durant, M. A., 'The Blur of the Otherworldly', *Art Journal,* 62/3,Fall 2003, 6-15.

Durant, M. A. and Marsching, J. D. (eds.), *Blur of the Otherworldly: Contemporary Art, Technology, and the Paranormal* Baltimore: Center for Art and Visual Culture, UMBC, 2006.

Fawcett, E. D., 'Matter and Memory', *Mind,* 21/ 82,April 1912, 201-32.

Ferris, S. P., 'Writing Electronically: The Effects of Computers on Traditional Writing', *Journal of Electronic Publishing,* 8 2002.

Goody, J., *The Logic of Writing and the Organization of Society*, Cambridge University Press, Cambridge, 1986.

Goody, J., *The Interface between the Written and the Oral*, Cambridge University Press, Cambridge, 1987.

Greenberg, C., *Art and Culture: Critical Essays*, Beacon Press, Boston, 1965.

Herring, S. C., Scheidt, L.A., Bonus, S., Wright, E., 'Bridging the Gap: A Genre Analysis of Weblogs', *37th Annual Hawaii International Conference on System Sciences (HICSS'04)* (2004).

Janzen-Wilde, L., 'Oral and Literate Characteristics of Facilitated Communication', *Facilitated Communication Digest,* 1993/2,1993.

Jones, C. A., *Eyesight Alone: Clement Greenberg's Modernism and the Bureaucratization of the Senses*, University of Chicago Press, Chicago, 2005.

Latour, B., *We Have Never Been Modern*, trans. Catherine Porter, Harvard University Press, Cambridge, 1993.

McLuhan, M., *The Gutenberg Galaxy: The Making of Typographic Man*, University of Toronto Press, Toronto, 1962.

Murray, D. E., 'Literacy at Work: Medium of Communication as Choice', *American Association of Applied Linguistics* (Seattle, WA, 1985).

Naumann, F., M. and Obalk, H. (eds.), *Affectt Marcel: The Selected Correspondence of Marcel Duchamp*, trans. Jill Taylor London: Thames & Hudson, 2000.

Ong, W. J., *Orality and Literacy: The Technologizing of the Word*, Methuen, New York, 1988.

Rheingold, H., *The Virtual Community: Homesteading on the Electronic Frontier*, Addison-Wesley, Reading, Mass., 1993.

Schjeldahl, P., *The Hydrogen Jukebox: Selected Writings of Peter Schjeldahl, 1978-1990*, (Lannan Series of Contemporary Art Criticism, No 2, University of California Press, Berkeley, 1991.

Sullivan, L. and Edwards, A. (eds.), *Stewards of The Sacred* Cambridge, MA: American Association of Museums with the Center for Study of World Religions, Harvard University, 2004.

Tannen, D., 'Relative Focus on Involvement in Oral and Written Discourse', in N. Torrance D.R. Olson, & A. Hildyard (ed.), *Literacy, Language and Learning: The Nature and Consequence of Reading and Writing*, Cambridge University Press, Cambridge, 1985.

Tufte, E., *The Cognitive Style of Powerpoint*, Graphics Press, Cheshire, Connecticut, 2003.

Westby, C. E., 'Learning to Talk - Talking to Learn: Oral-Literate Language Differences', in C.S. Simon (ed.), *Communication Skills and Classroom Success: Therapy Methodologies for Language-Learning Disabled Students*, College-Hill Press, San Diego, 1985.

Appendix A – Oral transcripts from radio and television broadcasts

1. *The Third Bush-Kerry Presidential Debate* (broadcast October 13, 2004, available from
   http://www.debates.org/pages/trans2004d.html)
2. *The Second Bush-Kerry Presidential Debate* (October 8, 2004,
   http://www.debates.org/pages/trans2004c.html)
3. *The First Bush-Kerry Presidential Debate* (broadcast September 30, 2004, available from http://www.debates.org/pages/trans2004a.html)
4. *The Cheney-Edwards Vice Presidential Debate* (broadcast October 5, 2004 , available from
   http://www.debates.org/pages/trans2004b.html)
5. *The Abrams Report* for July 6, 2005
   (http://www.msnbc.msn.com/id/8498010/)
6. *The Abrams Report* for July 1,2005
   (http://www.msnbc.msn.com/id/8485029/)
7. *NPR Weekend Edition on Reincarnation: Tibetan Buddhism*, radio broadcast Saturday January 10th, 1998 *Weekend Edition Saturday*; available from
   http://www.npr.org/programs/death/980110.death.html
8. Hardball with Chris Matthews July 6, 2005,
   http://www.msnbc.msn.com/id/8498025/
9. *Hardball with Chris Matthews* for June 30,2005
   (http://www.msnbc.msn.com/id/8430780/)
10. *Hardball with Chris Matthews* for June 29,2005
    (http://www.msnbc.msn.com/id/8416840/)
11. *Hardball with Chris Matthews* for July 5,2005
    (http://www.msnbc.msn.com/id/8485042/)
12. *Hardball with Chris Matthews* for July 1,2005
    (http://www.msnbc.msn.com/id/8485041/)
13. *Countdown with Keith Olbermann* for July 6, 2005
    (http://www.msnbc.msn.com/id/8498013/)

All moderator comments tags identifying the speaker, and "stubs" (pre-written introductions and transitions between commercials) were removed to preserve only the actual spoken sentences.

Appendix B – Source Texts

1. <u>Dracula</u> by Bram Stoker, electronic version courtesy of The
    University of Adelaide Library,
    http://etext.library.adelaide.edu.au/s/s87d/
2. *Evening Tide* by Neal Gordon, *Intertext*, Issue #57, December 5,
    2004, available from
    http://www.intertext.com/magazine/v13n2/eveningtide.html
3. <u>Father Christmas Must Die</u> by Patrick Whittaker *Intertext*, Issue
    #57, December 5, 2004, available from
    http://www.intertext.com/magazine/v13n2/christmas.html
4. Metamorphosis by Franz Kafka, available at
    http://www.zwyx.org/portal/kafka/kafka_metamorphosis.html
5. *Star Quality* by Melanie Miller, *Intertext*, Issue #5, January-
    February 1992, available from
    http://www.intertext.com/magazine/v2n1/star.html
6. *The Legion of Lost Gnomes* by T.G. Browning, *Intertext*, Issue #57,
    December 5, 2004, available from
    http://www.intertext.com/magazine/v13n2/gnomes.html
7. <u>War of the Worlds</u> by H.G. Wells, available from
    http://www.gutenberg.org/dirs/3/36/36.txt

All chapter and/or section numbers, headings, or titles were removed
from the texts prior to analysis.

Appendix C – The Enron Mail Corpus

In emails, inserting extraneous text (e.g., news stories from The Associated Press, Reuters) is common, and these had to be removed so that the true style of email writing could be examined. The manual distillation process the elimination of all person references as well as titles (which are not part of the body of a text). Incidentally, having controlled for spam or automatically generated titles (e.g., "Breaking News from ABCNEWS.com"), "RE:", "FWD:" and repeated entries, the average email title is 3.56 words in length. 500 random messages from the Enron email corpus were cleaned, scanned and parsed for style according to the criteria indicated below.

1. Repeated or extratextual lines were eliminated (those beginning with ">");
2. Reports included in emails were eliminated (e.g., "Energy Executive Daily");
3. Words containing "@"were eliminated as potential emails;
4. Lines containing email headers (e.g., "From:", "To:", "cc:", "Subject:", etc.) were eliminated.

The original extraction was of 99,241 words, 493,144 characters on 17,229 lines, the equivalent of 303 pages of text.

Notes

[1] One might suppose the case of outlining software as the clear exception. This class of software exhibits, after all, the swift and ready capacity for promoting, demoting and reordering items, from lines to entire paragraphs. It would thus seem the ideal topic processor were it not that what is moved is only arranged graphically, rather than semantically. The software executes no rules for identifying, relating, or maintaining coherence among the topics in the user's text.

[2] Tufte, E., *The Cognitive Style of Powerpoint*, Graphics Press, Cheshire, Connecticut, 2003.

[3] Byrne, D., *E.E.E.I (Envisioning Emotional Epistemological Information)*, Steidl Publishing, Göttingen, Germany, 2003.

[4] Janzen-Wilde, L., 'Oral and Literate Characteristics of Facilitated Communication', *Facilitated Communication Digest,* 1993/2,1993.

[5] Ferris, S. P., 'Writing Electronically: The Effects of Computers on Traditional Writing', *Journal of Electronic Publishing,* 8 2002.

[6] Rheingold, H., *The Virtual Community: Homesteading on the Electronic Frontier*, Addison-Wesley, Reading, Mass., 1993.
[7] Murray, D. E., 'Literacy at Work: Medium of Communication as Choice', *American Association of Applied Linguistics* (Seattle, WA, 1985).
[8] Chafe, W. L., 'Linguistic Differences Produced by Differences between Speaking and Writing', in N. Torrance D.R. Olson, & A. Hildyard (ed.), *Literacy, Language and Learning: The Nature and Consequences of Reading and Writing*, Cambridge University Press, Cambridge, 1985.
[9] Westby, C. E., 'Learning to Talk - Talking to Learn: Oral-Literate Language Differences', in C.S. Simon (ed.), *Communication Skills and Classroom Success: Therapy Methodologies for Language-Learning Disabled Students*, College-Hill Press, San Diego, 1985.
[10] Tannen, D., 'Relative Focus on Involvement in Oral and Written Discourse', in N. Torrance D.R. Olson, & A. Hildyard (ed.), *Literacy, Language and Learning: The Nature and Consequence of Reading and Writing*, Cambridge University Press, Cambridge, 1985.
[11] Herring, S. C., Scheidt, L.A., Bonus, S., Wright, E., 'Bridging the Gap: A Genre Analysis of Weblogs', *37th Annual Hawaii International Conference on System Sciences (HICSS'04)* (2004).
[12] See, for example, McLuhan, M., *The Gutenberg Galaxy: The Making of Typographic Man*, University of Toronto Press, Toronto, 1962.
[13] Ong, W. J., *Orality and Literacy: The Technologizing of the Word*, Methuen, New York, 1988. Ong's work emerged at the dawn of the popular computer revolution, but posited a comparative culture argument. That is, while the book has been invoked in arguments relating to the new literature of digital media, its treatment of orality is not quite focused on the speech practices of modern society. As the second chapter illustrates, Ong's argument derives its theoretical vector from the earlier work of Milman Parry and Eric Havelock on the noetic characteristics of oral cultures. Thus it is the discovery and problematisation of traditional oral cultures that is modern, not the cultures or their speech practices themselves. In that distinction, Ong's work is less apposite to contemporary models of new media communication.
[14] See Goody, J., *The Logic of Writing and the Organization of Society*, Cambridge University Press, Cambridge, 1986. Also, Goody, J., *The Interface between the Written and the Oral*, Cambridge University Press, Cambridge, 1987. As with the work of Walter Ong, Jack Goody's focus is refracted through the lens of linguistic anthropology. In his assessment of writing's impact on largely oral societies at the interface with literate modalities, in the Ancient Near East, in contemporary Africa, and in forms marginally related to the ideographic structure of technology's Western scripts (e.g., Islamic writing, cuneiform variations, Vai writing), Goody's

work is, as with Ong, critical to discussions of Western writing in general but not buttressed either by example or by empirical observation in sufficiently close comparison to new media writing to serve as a document of phenomena in digital modalities. These, I argue, have in fact drawn from existing communicative practices for the distinctive emergence their own synthetic form.

Knowledge Building and Motivations in Wikipedia: Participation as "Ba"

Sheizaf Rafaeli, Tsahi Hayat, Yaron Ariel

Abstract

The online encyclopedia Wikipedia has been one of the prominent phenomena in the emergent of online user-generated content. This study explores Wikipedians' (Wikipedia users) perceptions of Wikipedia knowledge, their sense of community and motivations for participating in Wikipedia. We suggest utilizing the constructivist approach to knowledge, as a theoretical framework for understanding the co-building of knowledge in Wikipedia. Adapting the *organizational knowledge creation model*, as proposed by Nonaka and Takeuchi, for examining Wikipedia we emphasize the importance of the context, using a concept named *Ba*. We suggest that key factors of knowledge building are the users' sense of community and processes of interactivity that are enabled by Wikipedia. A central tenet of wiki community is users' motivation to contribute. In a study exploring the success of online community, Sangwan suggested that the "Uses and Gratifications" framework be applied, and identifies three key motivators for virtual community use: Functional, Emotive and Contextual. Following these observations, we study Wikipedians' motivations, thus highlighting the users' cognitive and integrative gratifications. To survey Wikipedians on these aspects, we posted a link to an online web questionnaire in the "Community Portal" of the English and Hebrew language Wikipedias. We provide some preliminary cross-cultural survey data.

Key Words: Wikipedia, Wikipedians, knowledge building community, ba, motivations, sense of community, uses and gratifications

*****

1.   Introduction

New media go beyond traditional media modes by adapting and innovating conventions. Traditional media such as newspapers and books shift to online environments through duplication of the old genre, or by generating new genres. One interesting new medium transformation case is the on-line encyclopedia - Wikipedia. The project of Wikipedia was initiated in 2001 and currently has millions of articles in many dozens of language versions.

Thus, Wikipedia as a medium is a novel form of creating and projecting content that experiments with social structure and form. Wikipedia's success, in terms of growth, quality and popularity, hinges on the careful balance of individual effort and social control. Previous studies concerning Wikipedia investigated its functions as an on-line volunteer-contributed encyclopedia,[1] as a community,[2] the value of its content[3] and users co-authoring.[4]

This study focuses on Wikipedians - Wikipedia participants that contribute to its content and taking part (or not) in its community. After a brief description of Wikipedia features and their relevance to our study, we will turn to discuss the process of knowledge building in community and the motivations for participating in Wikipedia. We focus on two Wikipedias, the English language based and the Hebrew language based Wikipedia.

2.   What is Wikipedia?

Wikipedia is a wiki-based application. Wikis are group-editing tools that allow the creation and maintenance of online linked web pages by a group of collaborating users[5]; the term Wiki refers to the content as well as the software used to manage these pages. In a Wiki, all users are potential authors and editors. To modify a page, a user simply clicks on an "Edit page" link, changes the text in a text area, and submits the changes. The term Wiki comes from the Hawaiian language, where "Wiki Wiki" means, fast. The term itself implies the ease and the speed of use and maintenance of Web pages through Wikis. However, beginners' performance in various Wiki features, available in Wikipedia, is somewhat questionable.

Wikipedia is an on-line, user-generated, volunteer-contribution-driven encyclopedia. Each web page is an article in this online encyclopedia. Every article allows accompanying online conversation. A detailed history of changes is readily available for each article. The system allows anyone (registered or anonymous - identified only by IP number) to add, change or delete content on any of the articles. Thus, articles are authored collectively. Professional editors do not review article's content prior to publication. Instead, visitors to the online site monitor content. A few users, called bureaucrats and administrators, gain the privilege of suspending the editing of an article in case of vandalism or excessive edits. Individuals, who have interest in a specific topic, may purposefully follow recent changes and traffic. Occasional and sporadic visitors may contribute as well.

3.   Wikipedia as a knowledge building community

The process of constructing a collaboratively written encyclopedia highlights Wikipedia's communal aspects. Thus, let us first suggest a few relevant concepts relating to the process of knowledge co-building. Knowledge is a highly controversial and ambiguous concept. A large number of different (and sometimes opposing) approaches were raised to define what knowledge is.

We need to define Knowledge in relation to Data and Information, distinguish tacit and explicit knowledge, and identify its locus as either individual or collective. Any definition of knowledge must start by discriminating between "Data", "Information" and "Knowledge". Many scholars offer hierarchies of information also known as Data-Information-Knowledge and Wisdom Hierarchies.[6] A common distinction holds that:

> Data is a raw fact out of context, Information is data in context relevant to an individual, team or organization ... Knowledge evolves as new insight and experiences are brought to bear on new and existing information.[7]

An important distinction concerning knowledge should be made between Explicit Knowledge and Tacit Knowledge: Explicit Knowledge is knowledge that can be express in a tangible ways. It is only a drop in the bucket considering the entire body of knowledge.[8] Tacit knowledge, on the other hand, is personal, context - specific, and therefore difficult to communicate.[9]

Another central aspect of knowledge concerns the "locus of knowledge". We can distinguish between Individual Knowledge and Collective Knowledge. Individual Knowledge is "owned" by the individual, and is therefore transferable. Collective Knowledge is distributed and shared among members of a group; it is the "accumulated knowledge of the organization stored in its rules, procedures, routines and share norms".[10] Furthermore, collective knowledge is "Dynamic, relational, and based on human action, thus, it depends on the situation and people involved rather than absolute truth or hard facts".[11]

Let us elaborate on our suggestion to consider Wikipedia content as knowledge. Davenport and Prusak suggest a constructive definition for this purpose; they consider knowledge as "information combined with experience, context, interpretation and reflection".[12] Wikipedia obviously offers its users more than raw data. Furthermore, the process of content creation in Wikipedia facilitates the context for the combining of information (this notion will be elaborated later).

As mentioned earlier, Wikipedia contains features that enable co-authoring. The individual Wikipedian needs to externalize his knowledge, and convince other Wikipedians to combine this knowledge into Wikipedia's content. This process may foster Wikipedians' collective reflection and interpretation of Wikipedia's content. The idea that Wikipedia fosters the combination of information with context, reflection and interpretation leads us to consider Wikipedia's content not as information, but rather as knowledge. Based on the "locus of knowledge" notion, we can refer to it as a collective knowledge.

After presenting key terms concerning knowledge and offering our rationale for grasping Wikipedia's content as "collective knowledge", let us move now to explore the process building that knowledge.

Along with the Wiki literature, we claim that Wikipedia is a "knowledge building community". Note that any process of knowledge building starts with an individual who knows. The "knowledge creation metaphor of learning"[13] might be helpful for articulating individual knowledge. This metaphor regards the learning process as analogous to the process of inquiry, especially when knowledge is substantially enriched or significantly transformed. The Wikipedia environment offers its participants much stimulation for these processes. The context of Wikipedia as community is most relevant to this matter, since it enables individuals' processes means to build up collaboratively.

To examine Wikipedia as a knowledge building community let us turn to highlight the collective level. This aspect will be examined according to the "Theory of Organizational Knowledge Creation",[14] and its extension through the "ba" concept.[15] The process of knowledge creation, according to this theory, involves social interaction and the transition between tacit and explicit knowledge. Four modes of knowledge conversion proposed:
(1) Socialization: individuals share tacit knowledge through joint activities.
(2) Externalization: individuals link tacit knowledge to explicit knowledge.
(3) Combination: individuals combine different explicit ideas into more complex sets of explicit knowledge.
(4) Internalization: individuals extract knowledge from newly created tacit and explicit knowledge. A central notion of this theory is the continuation and dynamic interaction of these modes.

"Ba" is a concept proposed by the Japanese philosopher Kitaro Nishiba. "Ba" can be conceived of as a:

> Shared space for emerging relationships: physical, virtual, mental or any combination of them…According to the theory of existentialism, "ba" is a context, which harbors meaning. Thus, we consider "ba" to be shared space that serves as foundation knowledge creation.[16]

Nonaka et al. suggest four types of "ba":
(1) Originating "ba" is defined by individual and face-to-face interactions, which offer the context of socialization
(2) Dialoguing "ba" is defined by individual and face-to-face interactions, which offers the context of externalization
(3) Systemizing "ba" is defined by collective and virtual interactions, which offers the context of combination
(4) Exercising "ba" is defined by individual and virtual interactions, which offers the context of internalization.

The last three "ba": Dialoguing, Systemizing and Exercising refer to interactive processes that serve, each in its own context, as facilitators to a knowledge building community process.

In this study, Wikipedia will be discussed as a social and technical platform, which facilitates the creation of "ba". In order to understand in what ways this facilitation is expressed in Wikipedia we turn now to explore Wikipedia's communal facet.

4.   Wikipedians' sense of community

The Wikipedia project describes itself as a community. Wikipedians are invited to participate in the "Community portal" "Wikipedia wants you! Together we are building an encyclopedia and a Wiki community",[17] and community issues (from technical issues to debates) are discussed at the so-called "Village pump". Wikipedia clearly meets the basic definitions of virtual community, sharing common interests and ideas.

Paradoxically, and even though its subject matter is broad and universal, and it almost by definition does not have a unique focal point or "practice" in the sense of discipline, the Wikipedia community can be described as a community of practice. The community of practice model is based on the concept that knowledge cannot be separated from practice.[18] The model assumes that activity and mutual engagement brings members together into social entity with a shared repertoire of communal resources.[19]

Wikipedia is also a part of the growing body of open source software. Open source is the generic name to describe software whose source code can (with few restrictions) be freely modified and redistributed. Creating open source software has many similarities to Wikipedia, since both the software and the encyclopedia are created collaboratively and enable its creators the mechanisms of reputation. An open source community is able to produce software that at least matches those of commercial companies.[20]

One of the most striking features of Wikipedia are the individual Wikipedians who take the time to voluntarily contribute to its content. Those individuals are the people who establish Wikipedia's sense of community. After discussing the communal aspects of Wikipedia, an interesting question to ask will be one that concerns the individual Wikipedians' motivation for contributing to Wikipedia content.

5.   Wikipedians' motivations

Wikipedians contribute time and intellectual efforts to add and correct Wikipedia's content. The more involved Wikipedians, who are the subject of this study, also participate in many communal activities such as voting, sharing opinions about Wikipedia developments and policies, patrolling pages, communicating with new participants, and the like. Rafaeli and Ariel propose scholars should study Wikipedians' participation along five contrasting dimensions

> (1) professional versus nonprofessional participation, (2) constructive, confrontational, and vandalistic participation; (3) continuous versus one-time participation, (4) anonymous versus identifiable participation, (5) content contribution, community involvement, and (silent) participation in the form of lurking.[21]

Considering participation as a one-dimensional construct might limit our ability to seize the motivational factors driven Wikipedians. Nevertheless, we can measure the subjective Wikipedia's perceptions regarding their motivations (rather than measuring their actual performance). In order to examine Wikipedians' motivations to participate, we will use a Wikipedia survey based on the theoretical framework of a user-centered approach named "Uses and Gratifications" perspective.

Uses and Gratifications is one of the established theoretical frameworks for examining media users.[22] Media Uses and Gratifications research investigate how people use the media to gratify their needs. This theory is based on the assumption that users are active and goal oriented in their interactions with the media.

Uses and Gratifications theory established originally in the mid 20th century.[23] Katz, Blumler and Gurevitch expressed its more "formal" definitions in the mid seventies.[24] In recent years, following the rapid growth of internet users related studies; many researchers continue to utilize the Uses and Gratifications perspective. Perhaps one of the reasons for its continuing popularity is its compatibility with new media affordances, which enable more flexibility in performing interactions among users.[25]

Traditional studies of uses and gratifications tend to emphasize five generic clusters of needs the media could fulfill:

(1) Cognitive needs- represent the intrinsic desire for information acquisition for knowledge and understanding.

(2) Affective needs - are related to emotional experiences, and intrinsic desire for pleasure, entertainment and aesthetics.

(3) Integrative (personal) needs - are affiliation needs where the individual want to be part of a group, and to have a sense of belonging.

(4) Integrative (social) needs - derive from individual's desire to appear credible, be perceived as confident, and have high self-esteem.

(5) Diversion needs - relate to the need for escape and diversion from problems and routines.[26]

Most New media studies tend to follow the traditional Uses and Gratifications categories.[27] Based on the uses and gratifications perspective,

Sangwan identifies a conceptual weakness in the exploration of possible factors that motivate users to participate in virtual communities. In an attempt to understand the success of virtual communities, Sangwan studied users' motivations to become members in a fee-based knowledge community. Satisfaction or gratification, according to Sangwan, is an ex-post evaluation of member experience with the community.[28] Conceptualized gratifications as a form of subjective evaluation, implies a contextualized perspective of gratifications.

In this study, we attempt to identify the cognitive and social-integrative motivators for Wikipedians' active participation. Sangwan identifies three key motivators for virtual community use: Functional, Emotive and Contextual. These motivators represent various mixtures of needs, but essentially relate more to information acquisition than to pleasure motives.[29] Another example offered by Stafford, Stafford and Schkade who suggest cognitive gratifications' need for information acquisition as one of the principal motivators for virtual community usage.[30]

Based on the theoretical framework presented thus far we offer three research questions: (1) what are the personal motivations for participation in Wikipedia? (2) What are the aspects of community characteristics that Wikipedians demonstrate? (3) how do Wikipedians perceive the knowledge creation process in Wikipedia?

6.   Method

The data for this study were collected using an online web questionnaire, which was posted in the "Community Portal" of the English and the Hebrew Wikipedias (http://en.wikipedia.org and http://he.wikipedia.org). The target population of this questionnaire consists of highly involved Wikipedians. Using the answers received by the respondents in their questionnaires, we managed to filter the active subgroup, those members who edit Wikipedia entries at least several times a month. In order to reach this population, our questionnaire was posted on a web page dealing specifically with Wikipedia internal discussions about Wikipedia and Wikipedians. Our assumption is that people who look into the Community Portal page are Wikipedians who are actively involved in the Wikipedia project. The sample used in this study included 120 Wikipedians, 85 from The English Wikipedia and 35 from the Hebrew Wikipedia.

Our Likert-style questionnaire included a set of items regarding the respondent perceptions of Wikipedia and other Wikipedians. The questionnaire also included questions concerning the respondents' demographical background and Wikipedia uses patterns.

7.   Results

Following the main research questions, we present the Wikipedian personal motivations for participation in Wikipedia, communal attributes demonstrated by Wikipedians answers and knowledge creation process in Wikipedia according to the "ba" framework.

Wikipedians' motivations measures included eight items in which the respondents were asked to state what personally motivates them to participate in Wikipedia. Each item was a proposed motivator, which the respondent ranked using a five point scale measure, ranging from Strongly Disagree (1) to Strongly Agree (5). Data presented in figure 1 below

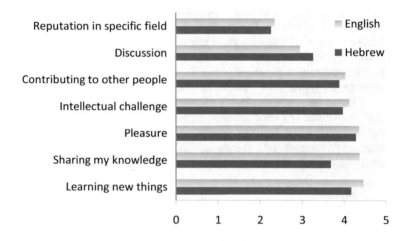

Figure 1: Wikipedians Motivations

* Standard deviation ranged between 0.7-1.3

Figure 1 shows respondents' average rankings of the relevant assertions. The data reveals that the strongest motivators are Cognitive ("Learning new things" and "Intellectual challenge") Affective ("Pleasure") and Integrative ("Sharing my knowledge" and "Contributing to other people").

Five items measured Wikipedians demonstration of communal characteristics. Respondents were asked to rank assertions regarding those aspects, between Strongly Disagree (1) and Strongly Agree (6). Table 1 displays the respondents' answers. The data from Table 1 points to some of the Wikipedians' notions of community ("I feel I belong to a group of Wikipedians", "I have contacted Wikipedians within Wikipedia"), and a sense of "team work" ("It is important to me that other Wikipedians will refer to things I'm writing", and "Writing in Wikipedia is a team work"). We can also see that there are statistically significant differences between the respondents of the English and the Hebrew version. The first difference is a higher "feeling of belonging to a group of Wikipedians" among the English version respondents. The second noticeable difference is the higher importance, accorded by the Hebrew version respondents, to other Wikipedians referring to things they are writing in Wikipedia.

Table 1: Communal aspects

		Mean (SD)
I feel I belong to a group of Wikipedians*	H	3.86 (1.16)
	E	4.78 (1.45)
I have contacted Wikipedians within Wikipedia	H	4.46 (1.56)
	E	5.00 (1.41)
I have contacted Wikipedians outside of Wikipedia	H	2.40 (1.93)
	E	3.51 (5.34)
Writing in Wikipedia is a "Team work"	H	2.54 (1.50)
	E	5.14 (1.20)
It is important to me that other Wikipedians will refer to the things I'm writing in Wikipedia*	H	4.66 (1.26)
	E	3.65 (1.40)

* Statistically significant differences

The knowledge building process was measured by four groups of assertions that were built according to the four modes of knowledge conversion adapted from the theory of organizational knowledge creation. Each group contains the answers to relevant assertions in four categories: Socialization, Externalization, Combination and Internalization. Respondents ranked the assertion ranging from Strongly Disagree (1) to Strongly Agree (6). Table 2 displays the respondents' answers in the category of socialization mode

Table 2: Knowledge building - Socialization mode

		Mean (SD)
Participating in Wikipedia should be open to everyone	H	5.11 (1.2)
	E	5.25 (1.1)
The significant contributors to Wikipedia are those that identify themselves and are not anonymous *	H	5.03 (1.3)
	E	3.92 (1.4)
Wikipedia is an egalitarian space for its participants.	H	4.14 (1.2)
	E	4.55 (1.2)
Participation in Wikipedia should be monitored to some degree*	H	2.54 (1.5)
	E	3.45 (1.5)

* Statistically significant differences between English and Hebrew versions
** E=English; Heb=Hebrew

Respondents' answers in the Socialization mode revealed that the Wikipedians are compatible with the Wikipedia notion of open participation and egalitarian space. Nevertheless, some Wikipedians call for monitoring of both Wikipedia's content and of the Wikipedians.

Another finding is a statistically significant difference between the respondents of the English and the Hebrew version regarding two assertions. In the Hebrew sub-sample, identified users were valued more than the anonymous ones. The second difference is that English Wikipedians are more in favor of monitoring the participation in Wikipedia.

An example of externalization (see Table 3) could be seen in the process of joint creation of concepts, through collective reflection. The fact that Wikipedians find it important that other Wikipedians will refer to what they are writing, implies exactly such a process. The process of "combining" knowledge in Wikipedia is done collectively.

The Combination mode is based on combining new knowledge into existing sets of knowledge. This process is inherent to the knowledge co-building-taking place in Wikipedia. We have already seen that the Wikipedians consider this to be "team work". Therefore, we can really look at the Wikipedia content building as a group task or accomplishment, rather than individual personal effort. Furthermore, the findings regarding this mode indicate that the Wikipedians do take a position regarding to Wikipedia's content. This point of view is expressed in their negative attitude toward copying information from other sources into Wikipedia, and toward inaccurate writing that can be found in Wikipedia. These judgments expressed by the Wikipedians, might derive from their desire to preserve the quality of the knowledge that is being created. Misshaping this knowledge can harm any Wikipedian's efforts to imprint their own knowledge into Wikipedia.

The mode of Internalization, deals with the opportunity to share explicit knowledge among individuals. The data presented here are meant to assess how likely Wikipedians are to internalize Wikipedia's knowledge. Table 2 reveals that Wikipedians believe that Wikipedia is a good source for knowledge regarding other sources on the Internet. They also think that Wikipedia contributes to the knowledge of its active users. Those points of view may facilitate the Internalization mode.

Table 3: Knowledge building-Externalization, Combination & Internalization

Externalization mode		Mean (SD)
It is important to me that other Wikipedians will refer to things I'm Writing in Wikipedia	H	4.66 (1.30)
	E	3.70 (1.40)
Writing in Wikipedia is "team work"	H	5.00 (1.16)
	E	5.14 (1.20)

Combination mode		
When people copy from other sources into Wikipedia, it makes me angry	E	4.80 (1.40)
	H	5.10 (1.20)
When people write inaccuracies in Wikipedia, it makes me angry	E	4.10 (1.15)
	H	4.30 (1.60)

Internalization mode		
Wikipedia is better in comparison to other information sources on the Internet	H	3.80 (1.1)
	E	4.19 (1.5)
Wikipedia contributes to the knowledge of its active users	H	5.47 (1.1)
	E	5.35 (.70)

* Statistically significant differences between English and Hebrew versions
** E=English; Heb=Hebrew

8.   Discussion

The survey results reported here was conducted during the Spring and Summer of 2005, prior to the public furor around Seigenthaler's false Wikipedia biography[31], and prior to the publication of the editorial and "Quality test" conducted by the editors of the Nature journal.[32] Our findings regarding the knowledge building process indicate that Wikipedia can be considered as a knowledge building community. Furthermore, Wikipedia platform combined with Wikipedians' knowledge building norms provides what was previously referred to elsewhere as "ba". Exploring Wikipedias as a "ba" facilitator, we propose that Wikipedia provides a unique context for the process of knowledge building. This context is based on Wikipedians perception of Wikipedia as a platform for an egalitarian teamwork. Evidently, we should also account for the fact that within this Wikipedais' "ba", there are Wikipedians who call for broader supervision over Wikipedia's content, and over other Wikipedians.

Based on the examination of communal aspects, deriving from Wikipedais' "ba", we propose that Wikipedia should be observed as a community. Recall that Wikipedia is a community that has semi "defined" boundaries (the Wikipedia platform). Most Wikipedians do not contact each other outside of Wikipedia. This community is based on interaction that revolves around the process of knowledge building. The process and these boundaries can be viewed as the forces that facilitate the evolvement of Wikipedians into a "Community of Practice". Wikipedians fit into the description of CP by forming a social collective of individuals, which deals with similar problems that matter to them. This Community of Practice, as well as the sense of community that Wikipedians share, serve together as key factors in fostering the process of knowledge building taking place in Wikipedia.

The assessment of Wikipedians' motivation was based on the "Uses and Gratifications" perspective. The results indicate that Wikipedians motivations are mainly cognitive, affective and integrative. Nevertheless, at least two motivators ("sharing my knowledge" and "contributing to others") have a selfless flavor. These were both ranked high in comparison to other ranked motivation descriptors. We should consider the idea that Wikipedians really do contribute to Wikipedia (at least partially) based on altruistic reasons, or at least sharing and collaborating for non-selfish reasons. Quoting Benkler's portrayals of Wikipedia (and Wikipedians) mechanisms:

> Perhaps the most interesting characteristic about Wikipedia is the self-conscious-social-norms-based dedication to objective writing... It depends on self-conscious use of open discourse, usually aimed at consensus... The project relies instead on social norms to secure the dedication of project participants to objective writing. So, while not entirely anarchic, the project is nonetheless substantially more social, human, and intensively discourse- and trust-based than the other major projects described here.[33]

The findings explored in this study are from two different Wikipedia communities. The first is the English Wikipedia, which is the oldest Wikipedia (over five years old at the time of this study) and the largest one, both in content and in the number of its active users. The Hebrew Wikipedia was three years old. At the time of writing, this Wikipedia could be considered medium sized with respect to the number of articles, and the number of its active users.

The different characteristics of the two Wikipedias might explain the differences in some of the findings. One more important aspect, that might explain those differences, is the fact that the Wikipedians of the Hebrew Wikipedia were largely concentrated in a small geographic area, and had a much better opportunity to meet "face to face", a fact that must be further explored to see how it affects the communal aspects of Wikipedia.

Given the availability of multiple Wikipedias rooted in different cultural and linguistic groups, the ongoing comparative study of Wikipedia, following the example provided here, is clearly indicated.

Notes

[1] W Emigh and S. Herring, 'Collaborative Authoring on the Web: A Genre Analysis of Online Encyclopedias'. Proceedings of the *39th Hawaii International Conference on System Sciences*, Hawaii, 2004.
[2] A Ciffolilli, 'Phantom authority, self–selective recruitment and retention of members in virtual communities: The case of Wikipedia'. *First Monday,* vol. 8, no. 12, September 2003, viewed on 15 May 2008, <http://firstmonday.org/issues/issue8_12/ciffolilli/index.html>.
[3] A Lih, 'Wikipedia as Participatory Journalism: Reliable Sources? Metrics for evaluating collaborative media as a news resource'. Proceedings of the *International Symposium on Online Journalism*, Texas, 2004.
[4] F Viegas, M Wattenberg and D Kushal, 'Studying Cooperation and Conflict between Authors with history flow Visualizations'. *CHI*, Vienna, 2004.
[5] B Leuf and W Cunningham, *The Wiki way: quick collaboration on the Web*, Addison-Wesley Longman Publishing, Boston, 2001, p.5.
[6] V Barabba, and G Zaltman, *Hearing the Voice of the Market*, Harvard Business School Press, Boston, 1999, p. 24.
[7] D Coleman and D Furey, 'Collaborative Infrastructures for Knowledge Management'. *Collaborative Strategies LLC*, March 1996, viewed on 15 May 2008, <http://www.collaborate.com/mem/hot_tip/tip1096.php3>.
[8] I Nonaka, 'A Dynamic Theory of Organizational Knowledge Creation'. *Organization Science*, vol. 5, no. 1, 1994, pp. 14-37.
[9] Nonaka and Takeuchi, op. cit., p.89.
[10] A Lam, 'Alternative societal models of learning and innovation in the knowledge economy'. *International Social Science Journal*, vol. 171, no. 1, 2002, pp. 67-82
[11] G Von Krogh, I Kazou and I Nonaka, *Enabling knowledge creation: How to unlock the mystery of tacit knowledge and release the power of innovation*, Oxford University Press, New York, 2000, p. 52.
[12] T Davenport and L Prusak, *Working Knowledge: How organizations manage what they know*, Harvard Business School Press, Boston, 1998, p.38.
[13] S Paavola, L Lipponen and K Hakkarainen, 'Epistemological Foundations for CSCL: A Comparison of Three Models of Innovative Knowledge Communities'. In: Proceedings of the *Computer-Supported Collaborative Learning (CSCL)*, Colorado, 2002.

[14] I Nonaka and H Takeuchi, *The Knowledge-Creating Company*, Oxford University Press, New York, 1995, p.17.

[15] I Nonaka and N Konno, 'The Concept of 'Ba': Building a Foundation for Knowledge Creation'. *California Management Review*, vol. 40, no. 3, 1998, pp. 40–54.

[16] ibid., p.41.

[17] Wikipedia, *Wikipedia: The Free Encyclopedia*, July 2005, viewed on 1 October 2005, <http://en.wikipedia.org/wiki/Wikipedia>.

[18] Nonaka and Takeuchi, op. cit., p. 55.

[19] E Wagner, 'Communities of practice: the structure of knowledge stewarding', in *The present and the promise of knowledge management*, C Despres and D Chauvel (eds), Butterworth-Heinemann, Boston, 2000, pp. 78-92.

[20] N Nilendu and T R Madanmohan, *Competing on Open Source: Strategies and Practice*, April 2002, viewed on 1 October 2005, <http://opensource.mit.edu/papers/madanmohan.pdf>.

[21] S Rafaeli and Y Ariel, 'Online motivational factors: Incentives for Participation and Contribution in Wikipedia', in *Psychological Aspects of Cyberspace: Theory, Research, Applications*, A Barak (ed), Cambridge University Press, Cambridge, 2008, pp.247-267

[22] T Liebes, 'Herzog's "On Borrowed Experience": Its Place in the Debate over the Active Audience', in *Canonic Texts in Media Research: Are there any? Should there be? How about these?*, E Katz, D J Peters, T Liebes and A Orloff (eds), Polity Press & Blackwell Publishing, Cambridge, 2003, p. 156-190.

[23] H Herzog, 'On Borrowed Experience'. *Studies in Philosophy and Social Science*, vol. 11, no. 1, 1944, pp. 65-95.

[24] E Katz, J Blumler and M Gurevitch, 'Uses and Gratifications Research'. *Public Opinion Quarterly*, vol. 37, no. 4, 1973, pp. 509-523.

[25] S Sangwan, 'Virtual Community Success: A Users and Gratifications Perspective'. Proceedings of the *38th HICSS Conference*, Hawaii, 2005.

[26] Katz, Blumler and Gurevitch, op. cit, p. 515.

[27] E Ruggiero, 'Uses and gratification theory in the 21st century'. *Mass Communication & Society*, vol. 3, no. 1, 2000, pp. 3-37.

[28] Sangwan, op. cit., p. 6.

[29] ibid., p. 4.

[30] ibid., p. 3.

[31] J Seigenthaler, 'A false Wikipedia 'biography''. *USA TODAY*, 29 November 2005, viewed on 16 December 2006, <http://www.usatoday.com/news/opinion/editorials/2005-11-29-wikipedia-edit_x.htm>.

[32] J Giles, 'Internet encyclopedias go head to head', *Nature*, 14 December 2005, viewed on 16 December 2006, <http://www.nature.com/news/2005/051212/full/438900a.html>.
[33] Y Benkler, *The Wealth of Networks: How Social Production Transforms Markets and Freedom*, Yale University Press, New Haven, 2006, p. 7.

Bibliography

Barabba, V. and G. Zaltman, *Hearing the Voice of the Market*. Harvard Business School Press, Boston, 1999.

Benkler, Y., *The Wealth of Networks: How Social Production Transforms Markets and Freedom*. Yale University Press, New Haven, 2006.

Coleman, D. and D. Furey, 'Collaborative Infrastructures for Knowledge Management'. *Collaborative Strategies LLC*, March 1996, viewed on 15 May 2008, <http://www.collaborate.com/mem/hot_tip/tip1096.php3>.

Ciffolilli, A., 'Phantom authority, self–selective recruitment and retention of members in virtual communities: The case of Wikipedia'. *First Monday,* vol. 8, no. 12, September 2003, viewed on 15 May 2008, <http://firstmonday.org/issues/issue8_12/ciffolilli/index.html>.

Davenport, T. and L. Prusak, *Working Knowledge: How organizations manage what they know*. Harvard Business School Press, Boston, 1998.

Emigh, W. and S. Herring, 'Collaborative Authoring on the Web: A Genre Analysis of Online Encyclopedias'. *Proceedings of the 39th Huwuii International Conference on System Sciences*, Hawaii, 2004.

Giles, J., 'Internet encyclopedias go head to head'. *Nature*, 14 December 2005, viewed on 16 December 2006, <http://www.nature.com/news/2005/051212/full/438900a.html>.

Herzog, H., 'On Borrowed Experience'. *Studies in Philosophy and Social Science*, vol. 11, no. 1, 1944, pp. 65-95.

Katz, E., J. Blumler and M. Gurevitch, 'Uses and Gratifications Research'. *Public Opinion Quarterly*, vol. 37, no. 4, 1973, pp. 509-523.

Lam, A., 'Alternative societal models of learning and innovation in the knowledge economy'. *International Social Science Journal*, vol. 171, no. 1, 2002, pp. 67-82.

Leuf, B. and W. Cunningham, *The Wiki way: quick collaboration on the Web*. Addison-Wesley Longman Publishing, Boston, 2001.

Lih, A., 'Wikipedia as Participatory Journalism: Reliable Sources? Metrics for evaluating collaborative media as a news resource'. Proceedings of the *International Symposium on Online Journalism*, Texas, 2004.

Nilendu, N. and T. R. Madanmohan, *Competing on Open Source: Strategies and Practice*, April 2002, viewed on 1 October 2005, <http://opensource.mit.edu/papers/madanmohan.pdf>.

Nonaka, I., 'A Dynamic Theory of Organizational Knowledge Creation'. *Organization Science*, vol. 5, no. 1, 1994, pp. 14-37.

Nonaka, I. and H. Takeuchi, *The Knowledge-Creating Company*. Oxford University Press, New York, 1995, p.17.

Nonaka, I. and N. Konno, 'The Concept of 'Ba': Building a Foundation for Knowledge Creation'. *California Management Review*, vol. 40, no. 3, 1998, pp. 40–54.

Paavola, S., L. Lipponen and K. Hakkarainen, 'Epistemological Foundations for CSCL: A Comparison of Three Models of Innovative Knowledge Communities'. In: Proceedings of the *Computer-Supported Collaborative Learning (CSCL)*, Colorado, 2002.

Sangwan, S., 'Virtual Community Success: A Users and Gratifications Perspective', Proceedings of the *38th HICSS Conference*, Hawaii, 2005.

Stafford, T., M. Stafford and L. Schkade, 'Determining Uses and Gratifications for the Internet'. *Decision Sciences Atlanta*, vol. 35, no. 2, 2004, pp. 259-288.

Liebes, T., 'Herzog's "On Borrowed Experience": Its Place in the Debate over the Active Audience', in *Canonic Texts in Media Research: Are there any? Should there be? How about these?* E. Katz, D. J. Peters, T. Liebes and

A. Orloff (eds), Polity Press & Blackwell Publishing Cambridge, 2003, p. 156-190.

Viegas, F., M. Wattenberg and D. Kushal, 'Studying Cooperation and Conflict between Authors with history flow Visualizations'. *CHI*, Vienna, 2004.

Von Krogh, D., I. Kazou, and I. Nonaka, *Enabling knowledge creation: How to unlock the mystery of tacit knowledge and release the power of innovation.* Oxford University Press, New York, 2000.

Wagner, E., 'Communities of practice: the structure of knowledge stewarding', in *The present and the promise of knowledge management.* C. Despres and D. Chauvel (eds), Butterworth-Heinemann, Boston, 2000.

Rafaeli, S. and Y. Ariel, 'Online motivational factors: Incentives for Participation and Contribution in Wikipedia' in *Psychological Aspects of Cyberspace: Theory, Research, Applications.* A. Barak (ed), Cambridge University Press, Cambridge, 2008, p.247- 267.

Ruggiero, E., 'Uses and gratification theory in the 21st century'. *Mass Communication & Society*, vol. 3, no. 1, 2000, pp. 3-37.

Seigenthaler, J. 'A false Wikipedia 'biography''. *USA TODAY*, 29 November 2005, viewed on 16 December 2006, <http://www.usatoday.com/news/opinion/editorials/2005-11-29-wikipedia-edit_x.htm>.

Wikipedia, *Wikipedia: The Free Encyclopedia*, July 2005, viewed on 1 October 2005, <http://en.wikipedia.org/wiki/Wikipedia>.

Acknowledgments
Research for this article was supported by a grant from The Hubert Burda Center for Innovative Communications at Ben Gurion University of the Negev

On the Way to the Cyber-Arab-Culture:
International Communication, Telecommunications Policies, and Democracy

Mahmoud Eid

Abstract
        Cyberspace is the most significant technological development of the late twentieth century. Yet it is inseparable from its cultural context. Hence the creation and continued evolution of cyberculture, developed through social interaction in the electronic environment of cyberspace. This chapter describes Cyber-Arab-Culture as one example of a newly emerging cyberculture, produced through the interactive processes of *globalization, democratization, privatization, digitization,* and *Arabization.* Globalization of media markets, digitization, and new media have led to an unprecedented democratization of international communication. Democratization is a gradual, ongoing process in Arab countries, with various requirements still to be achieved. Telecommunications policies have accomplished significant economic development in the region, most notably the privatization of administration, manufacturing, and service delivery. New media have influenced the region, and particularly its culture, through increasing access by the Arab public to international media content. Arabization of new media content has been a major goal in the region. Cyber-Arab-Culture is expected to facilitate the spread of Arab cultural values on the Internet; however, there have been anti-Cyber-Arab-Culture practices that impede the evolution of this new cyberculture. Arabs are encouraged to continue to develop and enhance Cyber-Arab-Culture, relying on their own widespread cultural patterns: primarily their basic cultural values, language, and verbal communication patterns.

        Key Words: Cyberculture, Cyber-Arab-Culture, Arab World, International Communication, Globalization, Democratization, Telecommunications Policies, Privatization, Digitization, Arabization.

*****

1.   Introduction: Cyberspace and Cyberculture
        There have been several waves of change in information and communication technology that have influenced the lives of post-industrial societies. These include the spread of the personal computer, the fax, multimedia, the laptop, the personal digital assistant (PDA), cellular communication, satellite communications, fiber optics, the Internet, artificial

intelligence, mobile connectivity to the Internet, the continuous exponential growth in the capacity of computers, smart agents and virtual reality.[1] "Cyberspace" is the term that encompasses most of these technologies. It is one of the most significant technological developments of the late twentieth century.

In his 1984 science fiction novel *Neuromancer*, William Gibson describes cyberspace in the following often-cited passage:

> A consensual hallucination experienced daily by billions of legitimate operators, in every nation, by children being taught mathematical concepts. . . . A graphic representation of data abstracted from the banks of every computer in the human system. Unthinkable complexity. Lines of light ranged in the nonspace of the mind, clusters and constellations of data. Like city lights, receding.[2]

Since Gibson published *Neuromancer* the word cyberspace has become common parlance. The term is used synonymously with other phrases such as cyberia, virtual space, virtual worlds, dataspace, the digital domain, the electronic realm, the information sphere, virtual reality, computer networking, and the Internet. In *Neuromancer*, cyberspace is a "dataspace," a vast "world in the wires" known as "the matrix," where transnational companies trade in information in a visual, Cartesian and electronic space. Here data reside in colourful architectural forms in a space where the imagination enters and interacts. *Neuromancer* paints a dystopian picture of the near future, where the urban fabric is in decay, technology and information are power, and humans and machines merge to become one. Since Gibson's novel, the word cyberspace has generally been used to describe emerging computer-mediated communications and virtual reality technologies. Both these cyberspatial technologies allow people to interact with other people or with computer-simulated worlds. These technologies fit with Gibson's description of a consensual hallucination because there are well known consensual protocols or rules, and because the medium of interaction loosely simulates real-world interaction. However, the emerging technologies do more than just electronically simulate traditional forms of communication; they also provide new means of interaction.[3]

> New technologies alter the structure of our interests: the things we think about. They alter the character of our symbols: the things we think with. And they alter the nature of community: the arena in which thoughts develop.[4]

Cyberspace is a global network of computers, linked through communications infrastructure that facilitates interaction between remote actors. Cyberspace is hardware and software, and it is images and ideas; these are inseparable. Cyberspace can be divided generally into three domains: the Internet, intranets and virtual reality. The Internet is a vast collection of computers linked to networks within larger networks spanning the globe. It is a huge, anarchic, self-organizing and relatively un-policed system, which allows unlimited access to other connected people, and the information stored on public databases and computer sites. The Internet consists of several separate but interconnected networked spaces, each consisting of thousands of individual networks. These spaces are all linked through common communication protocols (i.e., ways of exchanging information). Intranets have the same general architectural form as the Internet, allowing the transfer of multimedia data, but are private, corporate networks linking the offices, production sites, and distribution sites of a particular company or group of linked institutions around the world. These are closed networks; using specific lines leased from telecommunications providers, with no, or very limited, public access to files. Virtual reality technologies partially or totally immerse users in an interactive, visual, artificial, computer-generated environment. Instead of being spectators watching a static screen, users participate in an environment that responds. Virtual reality has three essential components: it is inclusive; it is interactive; and the interaction is in real time.[5]

Through social interaction in the electronic environment of cyberspace, a new kind of culture has developed, referred to as "cyberculture." The concept of cyberculture refers to the unique culture associated with computer-mediated communication (CMC) and online interaction. This includes the emergence of special forms of language and symbols, and the development of rituals, conventions, norms, and rules of conduct for CMC. Cyberspace technologies not only constitute a site for new cultural formations, but also affect pre-existing elements of culture, situated in other kinds of spaces; more and more, we are likely to find mainstream culture mimicking cyberculture in a variety of ways.[6]

Given that cyberspace provides new kinds of human interactions that do not always fit with non-cyber interactions and that require a new, broader perspective on what constitutes reality, the very existence of cyberspace necessitates a re-definition of human values and assumptions about people's moral perspectives.[7] Human values and assumptions are part of the cultural context we live in. Therefore, Bell argues that "setting up a distinction between cyberspace and cyberculture is a false dichotomy" because "cyberspace is always cyberculture, in that we cannot separate cyberspace from its cultural contexts."[8]

> Gibson's original use of the word *space* in cyberspace
> relates to electronic spaces created by computer-based
> media. Today, it has been adapted by an emerging
> *cyberculture* as a general term for digital media space.
> Cyberculture represents the merging of the present and the
> future and the total encroachment of technology into human
> lives.[9]

In this chapter, I describe cyberspace in one particular cultural context – namely, the Arab world. Cyberspace and new technologies in the Arab world have created a new cyberculture that I refer to here as "Cyber-Arab-Culture." This newly emerging cyberculture is described here as a product of the notions and processes of *globalization, democratization, privatization, digitization* and *Arabization*.

2.   Globalization: International Communication and the Flow of Information

International communication can be understood as communication that occurs across international borders. International communication in the contemporary world "encompasses political, economic, social, cultural and military concerns."[10] The focus of scholars studying international communication in the early decades was on the flows of information between and among nations.[11] Another understanding of international communication focused on propaganda. Harold Lasswell's analysis of propaganda in World War I assumed that no government could control the minds of people without using propaganda, and therefore the mass media could move societies for good or ill. U.S. President Woodrow Wilson and scholars of that period, such as Walter Lippmann, advocated using the mass media for the betterment of all people. The idealism of international communication scholars in that early era, particularly concerning the media's potential for improving the world, continues to some extent today.

Linked to the research undertaken in international communication, as McDowell explains, are the unbalanced flows of news and entertainment between countries, and the rise of the large digital delivery corporations in telecommunications, software, online media, and other communications spheres. The implications of these developments, and the factors underlying them, are important elements of such research. But more significantly, McDowell considers the role of the state in shaping national media, and the roles of intergovernmental organizations in shaping world media industries, flows and uses.[12] McDowell shows that "effects of the dominance of media corporations on individuals, cultures, and politics across national boundaries have been debated at different times, whether called cultural imperialism or transnational media."[13] In fact, "one-way media content flow from one country to the other affects the culture and cultural industries in the recipient country."[14]

International communication expanded markedly during the first half of the 20th century through wireless communication and broadcasting technologies. A new paradigm began to emerge in the 1960s, when a series of innovations in the field of telecommunications provoked a second explosive expansion of international communication. Most noteworthy was the invention of fiber optic cables and geo-stationary communication satellites, which were increasingly developed into global networks under the auspices of international organizations such as Intelsat and the International Telecommunications Union. At the start of the 21st century, a borderless media system has developed whose backbone is a global communication network comprising fiber optic pipes and TV broadcast satellites. Its expansion is driven by the internationalization – or to use the popular term, globalization – of media markets following deregulation and a worldwide integration of the media industry. Global communication adds to the flow of information, networks of communication and systems of exchange. As such, a new international communication paradigm is emerging. The information technology revolution has further deepened the integration between computing, telecommunications, and electronic media. Outcomes of this process include the digitization of broadcasting systems and the emergence of new digital media. A transnational media order is coming into being that is re-mapping media spaces and involving new media practices, flows, and products. The new media are opening up public access to international communication. The World Wide Web gives instant access to international content, and e-mails facilitate interpersonal communication across borders. These tools are more individual-centred and are less government-controlled than old pathways to international communication. Digitization and the new media have led to a democratization of international communication.[15]

3.   Democratization: Major Obstacles in the Arab World

In the era of globalization, with increasing reliance on the information society and new media, healthier environments for democracy have become a necessity. Democracy cannot survive without the achievement, and maintenance, of a set of preconditions. For any political system to be democratic, there has to be a considerable understanding amongst the populace of the process of democratization. Democracy presupposes that citizens have achieved self-discipline and political tolerance, without which it cannot survive. Popular participation is an indispensable part of a democratic system. Public deliberation is essential to democracy, to ensure that the public's policy preferences – upon which democratic decisions are based – are informed, enlightened, and authentic. Democracy requires the construction of a vibrant, vigorous, and pluralistic civil society.

Without such a civil society, democracy cannot be developed and secured. A democratic revolution is the cumulative achievement of citizens who become actively involved in civic movements and independent media. Democracy involves wide access by citizens to government information, and the freedom to debate political issues at both interpersonal and societal levels, the latter often through independent media. In sum, the democratization process aims at bringing decision-making closer to the people affected by those decisions and diffusing power in society. Furthermore, it includes notions of access and accessibility, equal opportunity, fairness, and equity in social relations. Put simply, democracy is not just a form of government. It is a pattern of thought and a way of life.[16]

> The globalization of national economies has also implied the institutionalization of more liberal and democratic schemes of governance around the world, including the Arab region.[17]

In the Arab world, the term "democratization" does not necessarily imply the same thing it does in the Western world. Ideas like the people's right to elect leaders at specified intervals, according to a carefully agreed-upon procedure; the occasional exchange of leadership roles between government and opposition; and the concept of loyal opposition, have not yet taken root anywhere in the Arab world. Freedoms generally associated with human rights are still in the painful process of asserting themselves. However, throughout the Arab region the democratization process is ongoing, with some regimes more liberal than others.[18] Although many Arab countries have experienced a degree of political liberalism at some point in their contemporary history – most notably Egypt, Iraq, Jordan, Kuwait, Lebanon, Morocco, and Syria – none of these experiences has given rise to fully fledged democratic systems.[19] "Democratisation is not only about allowing multi-party elections or enabling the independence of the judiciary, but also about reconfiguring relations of power in order to open spaces for pluralism, diversity and inclusiveness."[20] The failure of political regimes in the Arab world to deliver on democracy is coupled with other failures, such as the slow pace of development and lack of responsiveness to rapid social change. In fact, a system could not be described as democratic "if a democratic principle could be used to usurp the individual rights of expression and association on which the whole system was dependant."[21]

In many areas of the world, democracy does not seem able to find suitable environments in which to flourish. In the Arab world, the appropriateness of democracy is widely debated, which in turn appears to have an impact on the use of new media. The achievement of a democratic environment in the Arab world will require a more pluralistic civil society, widening access to government information, more freedom of expression and debate on political issues, the spread of social equity, and a multi-voice, independent media. Arab political institutions will need to remove measures restricting the media's ability to do their job, such as government pressure, censorship, abuse of media personnel, regulations against privatization, and limits on freedom of expression. The smooth, free flow of information should be encouraged in the direction of democratization. Government fears regarding the spread of sensitive political and religious discussions through new media, along with its desire to protect cultural identities, should not be used to justify control over, or ban access to, information. Instead, these fears and desires should be properly discussed and openly communicated between Arab governments and their publics. Internet usage should be open to those seeking information in all fields in Arab societies and not limited to specific purposes such as university or corporate use.[22]

Censorship continues to be a major problem that renders the Arab media ideologically dependent. The Arab region is confronted with local rather than global problems in the development of networking, for example, restrictive media policies by their own governments and lack of acceptance of new media by state authorities. Governments in the Arab world have adopted various means to restrict the flow of information online. There is a tradition of Arab ministries of information wishing to control – or at best, influence – the information their citizens receive, often through government ownership of electronic media. Kuwait ensures that no pornography or politically subversive commentary is available. Abu Dhabi's Internet clubs ban sexual, religious, and political materials on the Internet to respect local laws. Bahrain, which went online in December 1995 through the government-run phone company, Batelco, installed an expensive system to block access to certain Internet sites. Jordan's authorities asked GlobeNet, a U.S. firm that won a contract to provide Internet service in 1995, to install a special screening facility to control sexually explicit material. Saudi Arabia confines Internet access to universities and hospitals, and inspects all local accounts through the Ministry of Interior, claiming to be protecting people from pornographic and other harmful effects of the Internet. Morocco procures Internet service and governs all aspects of the Internet's operations. Internet service is targeted at the banking and insurance sectors, universities, and multinational corporations. Most Arab governments justify their restrictions on Internet access as necessary to protect cultural identity.[23]

As a new medium in the Arab world, the Internet is facing obstacles similar to those from which the traditional Arab media still suffer. Most notably, censorship is targeting new media in the same way as traditional media.[24] In spite of the fact that residents of the Middle East are going online in increasing numbers, many governments in that region are hoping to control access to sensitive political and religious discussion, as well as sex-related material.[25] In the Arab world, freedom of speech and information is severely limited, even on the Internet, with the single common denominator a perceived need by the region's governments to protect cultural identity. Arab countries feel that they are being threatened from the outside. Some of them see this threat as an attempt by the United States to spread its perceived neglect of ethics into Arab households. Others fear misinformation strategies by the Israelis, who are perceived as masters at manipulating information for their own ends.[26]

4.   Privatization: Arab   Telecommunications   Policies   and Development
    The globalization of media has had a strong influence on the development, policy, and regulation of communication systems all over the world. Information technology and the telecommunications industry have been profoundly influenced by globalization. The convergence of computers, telecommunications, and information technology is expected to bring new telecommunication products and services, over time, within reach of ever larger proportions of the global population. This trend has led to new demands by customers, suppliers, and operators, and is exerting tremendous pressure for changes in the traditional policy and regulatory framework of the telecommunication sector in most countries of the world.[27]

> In today's world of instant communication and global
> media sources, the censorial culture has ceased to have any
> reason for existence. Authoritarian regimes are coming
> under increasing pressure to allow privatization and
> democratization, to respect human rights, and to guarantee
> freedom of expression.[28]

    As a result of an increasing vision of telecommunications as a key factor for Arab economic development, the first International Telecommunications Union Arab Regional Telecommunication Development Conference, held in Cairo in October 1992, adopted a resolution on the restructuring of the telecommunications sector in the Arab states. This resolution urged countries to study and propose appropriate national policies for information and telecommunications that will cover the regulation and operation of the sector.[29] In Algeria, for example, "with enormous under-development in the telecommunications sector and a government committed to economic expansion coupled with higher than average government revenues in 2000, the sector looks set for a significant overhaul in the immediate future."[30] In Lebanon, the size of the telecommunications market is estimated at around US$4 billion. Contracts have been signed with Alcatel-

CIT, Siemens and Ericsson for supply and installation of digital exchanges. Lebanon has over one million new telephone lines, compared with less than 300,000 lines at the end of the civil war in 1991.[31] In Saudi Arabia, "following 40 years of slow growth, the telecommunications industry expanded with remarkable speed, from a rudimentary network of 188,000 working lines in 1978 to about 858,000 lines only five years later – an increase of 455%."[32] Jordan has taken several steps toward improving its telecommunications sector; however, "these initial steps will have to be accelerated if the country is to achieve its vision as a centre of international trade and finance."[33] Bahrain has shown "an extraordinary capability for acquiring and using advanced telecommunications. Consequently, the island nation has become a vital regional telecommunications centre in the Middle East."[34]

The ongoing developments in telecommunications have paved the road for Arab countries to go online and join the global information superhighway. Their level of development cannot be assumed to be homogeneous, as individual countries differ greatly in educational standards, financial strength, and willingness to innovate. The development of telecommunications has differed greatly from one country to another in the Arab world. Although the twenty-two Arab countries are similar in religion, customs and values, history, and language, they differ in many other aspects, including wealth, population, area, geographical location, political direction, and foreign relations.[35] Differences among these countries have been clearly reflected in such things as telecommunications infrastructure, information and media productions, communication policies, and cultural industries.[36] Examples of highly qualified Arab countries in the telecommunications sector are Egypt and the United Arab Emirates. In Egypt, telecommunications are controlled by Telecom Egypt, "a joint-stock company in which the Egyptian government owns the majority [of] shares With over 9 million subscribers, Telecom Egypt is the biggest telecommunications operation in the Arab world."[37] The United Arab Emirates subscribes to the Arab Satellite Communications Organization (Arabsat) and has upgraded its entire telecommunications service with digital technology. Emirates Telecommunications (Etisalat), the United Arab Emirates' federal telecommunications authority, launched its Emirate Internet and Multimedia unit after a major organizational overhaul. Other e-services into which Etisalat is moving include Warraq, an online encyclopedia of Arabic literature, and a bilingual search engine enhancing Arabic-language Internet browsing.[38]

The privatization of administration, manufacturing, and service delivery has been one of the more obvious features of Arab economies in recent years. For a variety of reasons, Arab governments have sought to change arrangements created in earlier phases of public ownership and control. In its continuing attempts to attract more foreign investment, the Lebanese government is considering privatizing some public services. The Lebanese political establishment has generally been against wide-scale privatization, but economic pressure could breach that political obstacle and lead to an increasing role for the private sector in the economy. The Algerian officials dealing with privatization issues increasingly target foreign investors, who for a long period were prevented from entering the country's private-sector market. Despite continued fears over job losses, the privatization of a number of companies in Jordan has been carried out since 2000; 40% of the Jordan Telecommunications Company was sold for over US$500 million.[39]

There are numerous Internet service providers (ISP) in operation in Arab countries providing several services such as dial-up, ISDN, leased, ADSL, Web hosting, and e-mail services.[40] Egypt has the largest number of Internet service providers, while a notable number of Arab countries have only one Internet service provider in operation. Monopolies in the Internet market raise the cost of an Internet connection in most Arab countries, and to some extent contribute to a deterioration of the service. For political reasons, most Arab governments try to create a monopoly in the ISP market by preventing new firms from entering the market (e.g. by controlling licenses). Another reason Internet costs are high and connection speeds low in Arab countries is that Internet service providers are not allowed to provide their own international gateways. In most Arab countries, the total cost of Internet access is way beyond the purchasing power of average citizens, especially when adding the high cost of making local calls to the cost of an ISP connection. For example, in Saudi Arabia, local calls cost three times as much as the cost of an ISP connection. Only individuals living in Kuwait and the United Arab Emirates can obtain access to the Internet for less than US$20 per month.[41]

Recently, there has been a "rapid growth in Internet subscriptions in the majority of Arab countries as the cost of connections came down and the number of Arabic-language websites increased. But overall Internet penetration remained very limited."[42] There is a huge digital divide between the Arab world and the world as a whole, in terms of Internet usage in proportion to population. The entire Arab-world percentage of world Internet usage is only 1.9%. That is, among the more than 316 million Arab peoples (4.9% of the world population) in twenty-two countries, only 19 million have access to the Internet, with a penetration rate (6.1%) much less than the world average penetration rate (15.7%). Arab countries with the highest rates of Internet access are Egypt (0.489%), Morocco (0.342%), and Saudi Arabia (0.248%), while those with the lowest rates are Comoros (0.001%), Djibouti (0.001%), and Mauritania (0.001%). However, the Arab countries with the highest percentages of Internet access do not have the highest penetration rates (i.e., the percentage of those who use the Internet in proportion to the total population in these countries). Arab countries that have the highest penetration rates are the United Arab Emirates (35.8%), Kuwait (22.8%), Bahrain (21.1%), and Qatar (20.7%). In sum, there is no one country in the Arab world that has a high percentage of Internet access and, at the same time, high penetration rates, albeit Morocco (0.342%; 11.6%) and Saudi Arabia (0.248%; 10.8%) are doing well on both levels of global usage and penetration, respectively. In sum, people in the Arab region do not, in general, have sufficient access to media and information technologies compared to global rates, other countries in the region, or in proportion to the population of the Arab world. Statistics show that access to the Internet in the Arab world is restricted to the elite, who have the skills and financial power necessary to take advantage of this medium. The current picture of the Arab telecommunications sector, media and information production, and cultural industries demonstrates that, while the Arab world may appear to have the technological qualifications, there are still many deficiencies that stop it from playing any significant role in the era of globalization.[43]

5.   Digitization: New Media and the Arab Publics

Digitally based communication technologies have catapulted modern Arab societies into globalization, placing further pressures on them to cope with the imperatives of the new information age. The digital communications revolution sweeping through the Arab world has stimulated intellectual and political debates, spawning numerous views on the social, economic, and cultural implications of new media.[44] The Internet makes possible certain forms of communication that go beyond the unidirectional pattern characteristic of the traditional media. E-mail, for example, offers direct communication similar to letter writing plus a medium for discussion via mailing lists. The discussion forums (newsgroups) offered by the Usenet, similar to mailing lists, provide for joint and simultaneous discussion between numerous participants.[45]

Much has been said recently about the possibility of the Internet enhancing democracy. Many claims have been based upon actual online practices. As well, there has been rapid growth in online political projects and Internet democracy experiments being carried out by governments, corporate interests, and citizen groups. Within these rhetorics and practices, three dominant "camps" have emerged – *communitarian, liberal individualist,* and *deliberative*. The communitarian camp stresses the possibility of the Internet enhancing community spirit and values. The liberal individualist camp sees the Internet as assisting the expression of individual interests. The deliberative camp promotes the Internet as the means for an expansion of the public sphere of rational-critical citizen discourse that is autonomous from state and corporate power and through which public opinion may be formed that can hold official decision-makers accountable. The deliberative camp is less prominent than the other two within Internet rhetoric and practice, yet the decentralized communications enabled through Web publishing, electronic bulletin boards, e-mail lists, and chat rooms does seem to provide public spaces for rational-critical discourse. The deliberative position also offers a more powerful democratic model. Both communitarian and liberal individualist models posit a unitary subject, whether it be the undifferentiated community or the isolated ego. As such, both fail to take seriously the multiple differences between subjects within pluralist societies. Moreover, both assume a pre-discursive political subject that requires little in the way of public discourse. In contrast, dialogue and difference are central to the deliberative model. The latter model assumes that difference always exists between subjects, difference which necessitates a process of rational-critical discourse in order for privately-oriented individuals to become publicly-oriented citizens and for public opinion to develop that can rationally guide democratic decision-making. Despite the fact that cyberspace has never been a space free of offline administrative power; that the Internet is largely developed, monitored, and regulated by government and controlled by corporate interests; and that online commerce dominates the Web, an enormous amount of discourse takes place online in a manner relatively autonomous from state and economic affairs.[46]

New media, particularly the Internet and satellite television, have flourished, occupying many of the channels through which the exchange of ideas and information can take place, even across borders, eroding barriers that formerly impeded the flow of information. The introduction of these technologies has had tremendous ramifications in the Arab world, particularly concerning culture and identity, and one can look to the changing nature of the region's popular music industry as an example. The Arab audience's taste is increasingly becoming more sophisticated and diverse, given the introduction of satellite television that gives access to the Arab public not only to local and regional programming, but also to international programming. Arab satellite channels are not only competing with their regional counterparts, but with their international ones as well. The consequence then is an empowerment of the audience and an improvement in their satisfaction. This phenomenon is affecting the Arab popular music industry in several ways. It has given greater importance to the visual aspects of popular music because of the mushrooming Arab satellite music television stations, modelled after their foreign competitors such as MTV. Viewers can now vote for their favourite videos by sending e-mails or text messages from their cellular phones to the channels, resulting in a more defined measure of singers' popularity. Not only does the Arab audience take the artist's voice and lyrics into consideration, they now also consider the artist's image to be of equal importance. Furthermore, they no longer have the attention span for

singers to perform two-hour songs, as Umm Kulthoum did while standing
still on stage. Instead, they expect the experience to be participatory,
stimulating all of their senses. New media have therefore increased
competition between Arab singers by rendering conformity and uniformity
obsolete. Many Arab singers, such as Amr Diab and Elissa, had to learn the
technique of hybridizing Arabic pop music by incorporating foreign
elements, such as techno and Spanish flamenco music, into their songs and
performances. Critics have also contested the trend among producers to
reintroduce classic songs such as those of Abdel-Halim Hafez by remixing
them with techno music. Despite their objections, these songs continue to
gain popularity and attention, both in the region and abroad. Arab pop music,
mainly through music videos, is witnessing an explosion of overt female
sexuality as a result of the quest to innovate. Nancy Ajram and Haifa Wehbe
are forcibly pushing the boundaries and paving the way for other female
singers to capitalize on their femininity in order to secure a bigger
following.[47]

New media have helped bring Arab music into the international pop
music scene. New media as a facilitating agent for globalization, thereby
affecting culture and identity, is not exclusive to the Arab region. What
makes the situation in the Arab world unique is that before the introduction of
the Internet and satellite television, governments heavily controlled the media
environment and censorship was the custom. New media offer the Arab
public an alternative, more open media environment. As a result of the
symbiotic relationship that exists between technology and communication,
the Arab world will continue to witness an evolving popular music industry
with the introduction of every new medium and technological advance. With
the onset of each evolution, Arab artists will attempt to adapt and reinvent
themselves. Those who do so successfully will emerge in the limelight both
at home and abroad, ensuring that Arab pop music continues to garner
international attention. The new media phenomenon in the Arab world has
found recent expression in the show *Superstar*, the Arab world's version of
the U.S. program *American Idol*. Arab *Superstar* is a joint venture between
TV 19 (the UK-based creator of the *Pop Idol* concept), Warner Music
International and its Middle Eastern licensee, Music Master International.
The program was broadcast regionally by the Lebanese satellite channel
Future TV. The 10,000 entrants from across the Arab world who originally
applied to appear on the show were narrowed down to 12 finalists from seven
different countries. Over 21 weeks, viewers got to vote by fax, Internet, or
cell phone for their favourite singers, who covered a variety of musical styles
from Arabic pop to traditional dance and classical music—there was no
Western pop. Viewer response to the program surpassed all expectations.
Jordan, Lebanon, and Syria witnessed lavish campaigns including large

television screens, posters, and e-mail messages urging fans to vote for each national representative.[48]

Dynamics of hegemony and resistance generally operate not in crude dichotomies, but in complex social fields replete with contradictions, ambiguities, and paradoxes. It is particularly interesting when music that is considered "rebellious" ultimately legitimizes Arab regimes. Shaaban Abdel-Rahim's music is one such example. This Egyptian *shaabi* (popular) singer took the musical and political worlds by storm with his unusual lyrics, which, in an earthy colloquial language, discusses matters such as cigarettes, the news, fictional television characters, the state of Arabic music and, most importantly, politics. After spending 20 years as a laundry man and part-time singer at Egyptian weddings, the illiterate villager became a phenomenon in 2001 with his infamous song, "I Hate Israel." Abdel-Rahim appears to have earned street credibility by singing things that no one else dares express. Looking at the politics behind the production of this song, however, complicates this image. When the song was first released two years before, the lyrics said, "I Hate Israel and Love Amr Mussa" (the leader of the Arab League). Soon after, the song was altered to include, "I love Hosni Mubarak" (the President of Egypt). Thus, while his song is a reflection of the role of Arabic pop as an arena for dissent and protest against Israeli and U.S. policy, it also serves as a legitimating force for the Egyptian regime.[49]

6.   Arabization: Technology and the Arabic Language

It has been evident throughout the last decade that the Arabization of computer software and hardware has contributed to the digitalization of Arab communications.[50] Arabic is the official language of the twenty-two Arab countries. Each of these nations has a pressing need to adapt Arabic to the demands of modern science and technology. Although language planning in the Arab world purportedly enjoys support from government, education, and business, this professed support is often no more substantial than the ephemeral political unions of various Arab countries. Language planning is an issue of contemporary concern around the globe. Every sovereign nation wishes to preserve its national tongue and maintain its status as a preferred medium of communication. However, the phenomenon of globalization, coupled with the increasing hegemony of English, has motivated many nations to revisit their language planning policies with a view to ensuring and strengthening the preeminence of their own languages. The Arabic-speaking countries, while recalling with pride their historical dominance in the medieval scientific arena, are now struggling to protect their language from an inundation of foreign, modern terminology. The main goals of the official agencies of language planning in the Arab world have always been the regeneration of Arabic as an effective communication medium for modern science and technology, as well as the preservation of the purity of the language. All proposals for change are carefully scrutinized to ensure compatibility with the phonological, syntactic, and morphological structure of Arabic. The majority of Arabic planners show considerable reluctance to tamper with the fundamental linguistic and grammatical principles of the language. Although the Arab countries have strong practical and economic reasons to collaborate on scientific and technological issues, including terminology and standardization, the lack of inter-Arab cooperation has stunted this potential route for development. Arab researchers have designed a computerized model for which Arabic is the governing language rather than English. This model can be readily adapted to work with English. This potentially powerful tool for modernizing the functions of language use from the Arabic perspective should motivate Arab institutions and governments to sponsor more innovative language solutions of this nature.[51]

Egypt has been the best example of provoking the awareness and usage of the Arabic Internet as well as Arabizing its content. The Internet was introduced to Egypt in October 1993 by the Cabinet Information and Decision Support Center. In January 2002, the Egyptian government started a plan to increase Internet connectivity. Access to the network became free for all, through any of the sixty-eight Internet service providers then serving the Egyptian market. Users only had to pay the small price of a telephone call while connected to the Internet. Egypt's online government portal is a well-developed site that has recently started to offer several e-government services. These include automobile license renewals, traffic ticket payments, phone bill payments, electric bill payments, filing for taxes, and university applications. E-commerce has started to emerge in Egyptian society, albeit at a slow pace. Efforts in this regard include establishing Web sites for major Egyptian financial institutions, including the Central Bank of Egypt and the National Bank of Egypt. Banks have started aggressive marketing campaigns to spread the adoption and use of credit cards in the cash-oriented Egyptian society. Other Egyptian sites have also tried to find creative ways to answer customer demands and overcome e-commerce obstacles. For example, Otlob.com allows users to place online orders for a variety of foods, pharmaceuticals, flowers, and video rentals, which they would receive in thirty minutes to an hour. The site offers access to over three hundred restaurants and had over four thousand registered users, averaging 25,000 hits per day. Egypt's biggest portal, Masrawy (http://www.masrawy.com), offers a database of contact information to more than 12,000 businesses in Egypt. The site also offers real-time information on the Egyptian and international stock markets. Other portals, such as Yallabina (http://www.yallabina.com), offer information from an Egyptian cultural perspective. The Internet has also allowed for media convergence, the medium itself being used as a news provider (online newspapers and magazines) as well as an online radio and television broadcaster. Throughout the years, Egypt has led the Arab world in introducing such media Web sites and Arabizing their content. These efforts started in 1996 when Egypt's Information Highway Project was launched, putting the first Arabic Web pages on the Internet. The Egyptian newspaper *Al Gomhuria* was the first Arab publication to launch an electronic version in 1996. The *Al Ahram* newspaper, which has been Egypt's most widely distributed daily newspaper since 1876, followed with its own electronic version in 1998. Today, most Arabic- and English-language Egyptian newspapers and magazines have electronic versions on the Web. One Web site, Sahafa Online (http://www.sahafa.com), listed at least 250 online publications within the Arab world.[52]

The features of the Arabic language are reflected in the design, layout, format, structure, and commercial activities in the major Arabic e-mail, chat, and news Web sites. Language requirements; various Arabic language accents; preferences of pictures, fonts, and colours; an Arabic style of goods consumption; and so on are examples of factors that formulate or determine the nature of such Arabic Web sites.[53] A Web site is a multimedia image. "Egyptianness," for example, must be represented through graphic symbols. For the most part, Egyptian web producers did not attempt to create site designs from scratch. Rather, they drew on existing non-Egyptian models (particularly yahoo.com) and sought to offer Egyptian inflections that would make the sites more accessible to the typical Egyptian. Web producers used three key modes of representing the "typically Egyptian": naming, creating logos, and limiting content to that deemed consistent with Egyptian "traditions." For Web producers, names are a vital advertisement whose connotations signify information about the site. Naming is a semiotic process through which a hypermedia producer constructs a single verbal sign that indexes the site, both figuratively and literally. Ideally, the name will have connotations that signify, to the desired audience, some of the functions and meanings of the site. Constructing a domain name can be in part a process of exclusion; to create an Egyptian site is to create a site that is not American, French, Japanese, etc. If one's goal is to create an Egyptian web portal for Egyptian customers, the name should be instantly recognizable as Egyptian to Egyptian users, but obscure to others. The most common strategy for accomplishing this is the use of Egyptian colloquial Arabic, rather than English or Modern Standard Arabic. Logos are graphic images designed to generate site coherence and offer a visual supplement to the verbal sign that is the domain name. As coherent units, their significance is largely dependent on arbitrary cultural codes. Examples of basic patterns in the construction of logos for Egyptian websites are: using a topical icon and giving it an Egyptian, or at least Arabic, inflection; playing with the tensions involved in particular markers of Egyptian or Arabic tradition; and the appropriation and transformation of ancient Egyptian signifiers. Appeals to tradition are used by web producers in Egypt as a gloss for what are sometimes called "silential" relations or the "unsaid" – meanings generated by what is not said in comparison to what is, or what could be, said. In the case of Egyptian web producers, the effort is to ensure that sites do not contain content that would contradict Egypt's "traditional" outlook, as interpreted by the producers. Web producers are particularly cautious about sexually explicit materials that might conflict with local notions of *'ayb* (shame). Rather than maximizing the total number of hits, sites offering "Egyptian" search engines seek to ensure that the content of the hits is in line with what they understand to be local traditional values.[54]

7.   Conclusion: The "Cyber-Arab-Culture"

The Arab world and the Islamic world are inseparable on the issue of being defensive of their traditions and values, and are justifiably proud of the great cultural legacy preserved through the use of the Arabic language, Middle Eastern customs, and media. Some Arab countries are also fearful of the political/religious repercussions of an online influx of alien values. An anti-Western, Islamic fundamentalist reaction to the sudden easy availability of pop-culture products has been taking place for some time, and the predominant fear of the government is the destabilization of some Arab nations. Arab media have responded to the cyber era by applying rules of censorship that are imposed by different nations. In the West, freedom of expression is considered a basic right of every citizen, that should be protected at all costs. Within the Arab world, this type of censorship is easily tolerated, and even expected as a form of civic responsibility.[55]

> Arab media may be unique in that they convey sociocultural values on two levels, namely to the large pan-Arab audience and to the smaller nation-state one. A great deal that is of cultural value to an individual Arab is commonly shared with other Arabs throughout the area. Arab media convey such cultural messages. On the other hand, other cultural aspects are strictly local and are shared only with others who live within the borders of a country or region. Arab media also convey effectively these local Arab values.[56]

The newly produced Cyber-Arab-Culture can also facilitate the spread of such cultural values in cyberspace. However, there are on-line practices – which will here be called anti-Cyber-Arab-Culture practices – which diminish the rise of such cyberculture. For example, there has been a failure by Arab policy decision-makers to enhance the Arabic Internet, as a result of their unsuccessful educational programs to help users understand the real benefits of the Internet and direct them toward constructive ways of using it. Cybercafés in Egypt, for example, play a limited role in developing computer and Internet literacy among Egyptians. Situations in other Arab countries are not at all different. Therefore, various strategies are needed to educate Arabs about better ways of using the Internet and direct their enthusiasm toward useful developmental projects.[57]

Another practice illustrates how Arabization occurs at the level of the chat room. Some Arabic speakers use English format in their Arabic chat Web sites, due to the pervasiveness of the English language or global Internet-speak. In their text communications – through e-mails, chat rooms, or cellular messages – Arab chatters are influenced by the existing, English-dominated nature of the Internet. But they assert their own cultural heritage by using English in Arabic ways. For example, in chat rooms, when Arab participants use speech-like patterns in their online English textual communication, they follow an informal, socially agreed-upon system, or style, of characters. These characters are written in English but some have either Arabic-meaning readability (e.g., *salam* is the Arabic word for "peace"), similarities with some Arabic letters (e.g., the number 7 looks like the Arabic letter *ha'a*), or are newly innovated abbreviations to speed up communication (e.g., ASAWRAWB, which is an abbreviation of the main greeting among Arab Muslims: *Al-Salamo Alykom Wa Rahmato Allah Wa Barakatoh*).[58]

Moreover, Egyptian Web producers are deeply influenced by national and international discourses that frame information technologies as a national mission for socioeconomic development. In the absence of clear definitions of the Web audience, Web producers imagined a "typical" Egyptian that contradicted their own experiences as users of the Web. Producers largely borrowed preexisting models, using design elements to "inflect" their sites with Egyptian motifs. Building on nationalist discourses of development, Web producers were able to offer investors a compelling vision of a culturally "Egyptian" Web site that would bring Egyptian consumers to the Internet. Web producers attempted to mobilize this audience by designing sites that mixed English and Arabic, employed Egyptian colloquial Arabic, and used traditional and ancient symbols to generate an Egyptian "feel" to the sites. However, the conceptual models of access and related design strategies created by Egyptian Web producers were out of touch with Egyptian social realities, as there was a significant disconnect between the potential audience imagined by Web producers and those Egyptians who actually had access to the Internet.[59]

Arabs should thus enhance Cyber-Arab-Culture by relying on their own cultural communication patterns. Across the Arabic world, there are widespread cultural communication patterns that can be grouped under various themes. Of most relevance here are *basic cultural values* and *language and verbal communication patterns*. There is an array of values considered prevalent in Arab societies: endurance and rectitude; loyalty and dignity; generosity, courage, and self-respect; and pride, rivalry, and revenge. The most common basic cultural values include: a) collectivism; b) hospitality; and c) honour. *Collectivism* is reflected in social life in the Arab region, which is characterized by "situation-centeredness," in which loyalty to one's extended family and larger "in-group" takes precedence over individual needs and goals. Impressed on children very early, *hospitality* reflects a desired personal quality and symbolizes status. Hospitality predates the *zakat* (the Muslim duty of giving 2.5% of one's wealth to the poor, which serves to counterbalance disparity between rich and poor). Certain occasions require elaborate displays of hospitality; these include marriage, burial, circumcision, the completion of house building, and during the holy month of Ramadan, village wide visiting and sharing of meals. *Honour,* or *'ird*, is a controlling value, legitimating the family structure and the "modesty code" required of both men and women. Honour is manifested in sexual conduct and behaviours which exhibit or regulate manliness, such as the number of sons a man fathers and the extent of hospitality one bestows. One's honour determines one's image. The key to saving face is the assiduous avoidance of shame. As primary possessors of *'ird*, men – including fathers, brothers, father's brothers, and paternal cousins – strictly enforce norms related to honour by ensuring that the women of their family conduct themselves properly and, thus, maintain a chaste reputation.[60]

In research on language and verbal communication patterns, studies related to the Arabic language have focused primarily on: a) the multiple forms of Arabic; b) code-switching; and c) communicative style. As one of the six official languages of the United Nations, Arabic is spoken by approximately 200 million people, excluding non-Arab Muslims. While the classical Arabic of the *Qur'an*, (Islam's Holy Book) is considered the highest and unequalled language, other forms of Arabic also exist. Modern Standard Arabic, or *Fusha*, is the language of governments, media, and public and religious speakers. Colloquial Arabic dialects have developed within countries, and are the languages of everyday interaction. Because of the variability of local dialects, it is inaccurate to assume that Tunisians and Iraqis, for example, readily understand one another in intercultural interaction. Egyptian Arabic, however, is more readily understood in the region than the multitude of other local dialects, mainly due to Egypt's far-reaching and popular film industry. Arabic speakers not only code-switch between the different forms of Arabic, many also code-switch between Arabic, French and/or English, the latter languages borrowed during colonial occupation. As a rhetorical device, code-switching allows bilinguals to select contextually appropriate speech which carries certain connotations, emphasizes certain points, and regulates the flow of discourse. Whether communicating in Arabic or other languages, research indicates that native

Arabic speakers share common features of communicative style, which may conflict with styles of other language speakers. Reported features include: 1) repetition; 2) indirectness; 3) elaborateness; and 4) affectiveness. Repetition is a major feature at the very heart of the Arabic language and discourse. Indirectness refers to a speaker's concealment of desired wants, needs, or goals during discourse. Elaborateness refers to rich and expressive language use. Native Arabic speakers may use substantially more words to communicate verbally than do speakers of some other languages. Two rhetorical patterns contribute to the perception of elaborate Arab communicative style: exaggeration (*mubalagha*) and assertion (*tawkid*). These patterns serve a crucial function of regulating credibility during interaction. When Arabs are communicating with each other, they are forced to exaggerate and over-assert in order not to be misunderstood. Affectiveness, or "intuitive-affective style of emotional appeal," relates to organizational patterns and the presentation of ideas and arguments. Arabs predominantly use the "presentation" form of persuasion, in which people and not ideas are most responsible for influencing others.[61]

The preceding explanation of Arab cultural communication patterns indicates the uniqueness of Arab culture which, like any other culture, requires careful adoption of new cultural forms in media and cyberspace to ensure the preservation of cultural values. A Cyber-Arab-Culture has been created already in cyberspace, through the notions and processes of globalization, democratization, privatization, digitization, and Arabization. However, its current status does not offer a promising future, given the previously demonstrated examples of anti-Cyber-Arab-Culture practices. These pose a danger: the potential to absorb the defects and disadvantages of the above processes rather than benefiting from their advantages. This could lead to the dissolution of this newly produced cyberculture, as a result of its inability to resist global practices that conflict with Arab cultural values. To avoid this danger, usage of new media technologies must be open to reflecting and encouraging Arab cultural communication patterns, rather than diminishing them and imitating western patterns incompatible with Arab culture. If Cyber-Arab-Culture is not permitted to flourish, there is a dangerous potential for the distortion of Arab culture in cyberspace, and the creation of contradictory practices that might work against the development and betterment of Arab societies.

Notes

[1] A Aviram, 'From "Computers in the Classroom" to Mindful Radical Adaptation by Education Systems to the Emerging Cyber Culture'. *Journal of Educational Change*, vol. 1, 2000, pp. 331-332.

[2] W Gibson, *Neuromancer*. Ace Books, New York, 1984, p. 67.

[3] S Barnes, 'Cyberspace: Creating Paradoxes for the Ecology of Self', in *Communication and Cyberspace: Social Interaction in an Electronic Environment*. L Strate, R L Jacobson and S B Gibson (eds), Hampton Press, Cresskill, New Jersey, 2003, p. 230; R Kitchin, *Cyberspace: The World in the Wires*. John Wiley & Sons Ltd., Chichester, 1998, p. 2.

[4] Kitchin, op. cit., p. 74.

[5] D Bell, *An Introduction to Cybercultures*. Routledge, London, 2001, p. 7; Kitchin, op. cit., pp. 2-8.

[6] L Strate, R L Jacobson and S B Gibson, 'Surveying the Electronic Landscape: An Introduction to Communication and Cyberspace', in *Communication and Cyberspace: Social Interaction in an Electronic Environment*. L Strate, R L Jacobson and S B Gibson (eds), Hampton Press, Cresskill, New Jersey, 2003, pp. 12-15.

[7] A Miah, 'Virtually Nothing: Re-evaluating the Significance of Cyberspace'. *Leisure Studies*, vol. 19-3, 2000, p. 222.

[8] Bell, op. cit., p. 8.

[9] Barnes, op. cit., p. 231.

[10] D Thussu, *International Communication: Continuity and Change*. Arnold, London, 2000, p. 2.

[11] E M Rogers and W B Hart, 'The Histories of Intercultural, International, and Development Communication', in *Handbook of International and Intercultural Communication*. W B Gudykunst and D Mody (eds), Sage Publications, Thousand Oaks, California, 2002, pp. 6-9.

[12] S D McDowell, 'Theory and Research in International Communication: A Historical and Institutional Account', in *Handbook of International and Intercultural Communication*. W B Gudykunst and B Mody (eds), Sage Publications, Thousand Oaks, California, 2002, pp. 295-308.

[13] Ibid, p. 295.

[14] A J Bhuiyan, *Mass Media, Communication, and Culture in Bangladesh in the Shadow of a Big Neighbor*. Unpublished Master's Thesis, Carleton University, Ottawa, 2002, p. iii.

[15] J K Chalaby, 'From Internationalization to Transnationalization'. *Global Media and Communication*, vol. 1-1, 2005, pp. 29-31.

[16] P A Bruck, 'Communication and the Democratization of Culture: Strategies for Social Theory, Strategies for Dialogue', in *Democratization and the Media: An East-West Dialogue*. S Splichal, J Hochheimer and K Jakubowicz (eds), Communication and Culture Colloquia, Yugoslavia, 1990, pp. 56-72; L Diamond, 'Civil Society and the Struggle for Democracy', in *The Democratic Revolution: Struggles for Freedom and Pluralism in the Developing World*. L Diamond (ed), Freedom House, New York, 1992, pp. 1-27; M Eid, 'Engendering the Arabic Internet: Modern Challenges in the Information Society', in *New Media and Public Relations*. S C Duhé (ed), Peter Lang Publishing, New York, 2007, pp. 247-268; S Langdon, *Global Poverty, Democracy and North-South Change*. Garamond Press, Toronto, 1999; B A Ojo, 'The Military and the Democratization Process in Africa', in *Contemporary African Politics: A Comparative Study of Political Transition to Democratic Legitimacy*. B A Ojo (ed), University Press of America, Lauham, Maryland, 1999, pp. 51-63; B Page, *Who Deliberates? Mass Media in Modern Democracy*. The University of Chicago Press, London, 1996; M Raboy, 'Policy-Making and Democratization: The Case of Canadian Broadcasting', in *Democratization and the Media: An East-West Dialogue*. S Splichal, J Hochheimer and K Jakubowicz (eds), Communication and Culture Colloquia, Yugoslavia, 1990, pp. 108-120; K Raffer and M A M Salih, 'Rich Arabs and Poor Arabs: An Introduction to Intra-Arab Issues', in *The Least Developed and the Oil-Rich Arab Countries: Dependence, Interdependence or Patronage?* K Raffer and M A M Salih (eds), St. Martin's Press, New York, 1992, pp. 1-12.

[17] M Ayish, 'The Changing Face of Arab Communications: Media Survival in the Information Age', in *Mass Media, Politics, and Society in the Middle East*, K Hafez (ed), Hampton Press, Cresskill, New Jersey, 2001, p. 123.

[18] K S A Jaber, 'The Democratic Process in Syria, Lebanon, and Jordan', in *Democratization in the Middle East: Experiences, Struggles, Challenges*. A Saikal and A Schnabel (eds), United Nations University Press, Tokyo, 2003, p. 127.

[19] R Aliboni and L Guazzone, 'Democracy in the Arab Countries and the West'. *Mediterranean Politics*, vol. 9-1, 2004, p. 82.

[20] N Pratt, 'Identity, Culture and Democratization: The Case of Egypt'. *New Political Science*, vol. 27-1, 2005, p. 86.

[21] G S Adam, 'Truth, the State, and Democracy: The Scope of the Legal Right of Free Expression'. *Canadian Journal of Communication*, vol. 17-3, 1992, p. 13.

[22] Eid, op. cit., pp. 248, 262.

[23] D A Boyd, 'Saudi Arabia's International Media Strategy: Influence Through Multinational Ownership', in *Mass Media, Politics, and Society in the Middle East*. K Hafez (ed), Hampton Press, Cresskill, New Jersey, 2001, p. 56; Eid, op. cit.; H Kirchner, 'Internet in the Arab World: A Step Towards "Information Society"', in *Mass Media, Politics, and Society in the Middle East*. K Hafez (ed), Hampton Press, Cresskill, New Jersey, 2001, p. 137; The Internet in the Mideast and North Africa: Free Expression and Censorship, *Human Rights Watch*, 1999, viewed on 28 March 2008, <http://www.hrw.org/hrw/advocacy/internet/mena/download.htm>.

[24] Eid, op. cit., p. 250.

[25] K Sorensen, 'Silencing the Net: The Threat to Freedom of Expression On-line'. *Human Rights Watch,* vol. 8-2, 1996, pp. 18-19.

[26] Kirchner, op. cit., pp. 151-152.

[27] Eid, op. cit., pp. 250-251.

[28] H Amin, 'Freedom as a Value in Arab Media: Perceptions and Attitudes Among Journalists'. *Political Communication*, vol. 19-2, 2002, p. 132.

[29] Telecommunication Policies for the Arab Region – the Arab Book, *Regional Telecommunication Development Conference for the Arab States -- Lebanon*, 11-15 November, 1996, ITU, Telecommunication Development Bureau, Beirut, Lebanon, viewed on 1 April 2008, <http://www.itu.int/itudoc/itu-d/rtdc96/010v2e_ww2.doc>.

[30] Algeria, *World of Information Business Intelligence Reports*, vol. 1, 2001, Walden Publishing, Essex, UK, p. 35.

[31] Lebanon, *World of Information Business Intelligence Reports*, vol. 1, 2001, Walden Publishing, Essex, UK, p. 26.

[32] A D Kayal, 'Telecommunications in Saudi Arabia: A Paradigm of Rapid Progress', in *Telecommunications in Western Asia and the Middle East*. E M Noam (ed), Oxford University Press, New York, 1997, p. 163.

[33] P V Vivekanand and J E Kollar, 'Telecommunications in Jordan', in E M Noam (ed), *Telecommunications in Western Asia and the Middle East*. Oxford University Press, New York, 1997, p. 157.

[34] D Winterford and R E Looney, 'Advanced Telecommunications and the Economic Diversification of Bahrain', in *Telecommunications in Western Asia and the Middle East*. E M Noam (ed), Oxford University Press, New York, 1997, p. 223.

[35] Arab countries fall into four categories with regard to their economic structure: 1) low-income countries that are poor in natural resources, manpower skills, and financial capacities; 2) non-oil-exporting, middle-income countries that, in general, have large populations and skills but limited natural resources and small financial capacities; 3) oil-exporting

countries without large financial surpluses, using all their income plus additional borrowing to finance development; and 4) oil-rich exporting countries with relatively small populations, which are the main sources of aid and financing for many development projects in other Arab countries. Raffer and Salih, op. cit., p. 1.

[36] Eid, op. cit., p. 252.

[37] R A Abdulla, 'An Overview of Media Developments in Egypt: Does the Internet Make a Difference?' *Global Media Journal: Mediterranean Edition*, vol. 1-1, 2006, p. 94.

[38] United Arab Emirates, *World of Information Business Intelligence Reports*, vol. 1, 2001, Walden Publishing, Essex, UK, p. 34.

[39] Algeria, op. cit., p. 40; Jordan, *World of Information Business Intelligence Reports*, vol. 1, 2001, Walden Publishing, Essex, UK, p. 21; Lebanon, op. cit., p. 30; T Younis, 'Privatization: A Review of Policy and Implementation in Selected Arab Countries'. *International Journal of Public Sector Management*, vol. 9-3, 1996, p. 18.

[40] There are three categories of Internet providers in the Arab world: 1) countries with a single provider, most often a government post, telegraph, and telephone provider, such as Jordan, the United Arab Emirates, Bahrain, Qatar, Kuwait, and Oman; 2) countries with multiple providers, such as Lebanon, Egypt, and Morocco; and 3) countries where Internet services are confined to research centres and universities or are not available at all, such as Iraq, Syria, Sudan, and Libya. Ayish, op. cit., p. 121.

[41] A M Aladwani, 'Key Internet Characteristics and E-Commerce Issues in Arab Countries'. *Information Technology & People*, vol. 16-1, 2003, pp. 13-14.

[42] N Sakr, 'Freedom of Expression, Accountability and Development in the Arab Region'. *Journal of Human Development*, vol. 4-1, 2003, p. 42.

[43] Eid, op. cit., pp. 252-255.

[44] Ayish, op. cit., pp. 111-112.

[45] Kirchner, op. cit., p. 138.

[46] L Dahlberg, 'The Internet and Democratic Discourse: Exploring the Prospects of Online Deliberative Forums Extending the Public Sphere'. *Information, Communication & Society*, vol. 4-4, 2001, pp. 615-617.

[47] S Abdel-Nabi, J Agha, J Choucair and M Mikdashi, 'Pop Goes the Arab World: Popular Music, Gender, Politics, and Transnationalism in the Arab World'. *Hawwa*, vol. 2-2, 2004, pp. 232-235.

[48] Ibid, pp. 236-237.

[49] Ibid, pp. 240-241.

[50] Ayish, op. cit., p. 128.

[51] H M Elkhafaifi, 'Arabic Language Planning in the Age of Globalization'. *Language Problems & Language Planning*, vol. 26-3, 2002, pp. 253-256, 262.

[52] Abdulla, op. cit., pp. 94-97.

[53] Eid, op. cit., p. 260.

[54] M A Peterson and I Panovic, 'Accessing Egypt: Making Myths and Producing Web Sites in Cyber-Cairo'. *New Review of Hypermedia and Multimedia*, vol. 10-2, 2004, pp. 207-213.

[55] H Amin, 'Mass Media in the Arab States Between Diversification and Stagnation: An Overview', in *Mass Media, Politics, and Society in the Middle East*. K. Hafez (ed), Hampton Press, Cresskill, New Jersey, 2001, p. 39.

[56] W Rugh, *Arab Mass Media: Newspapers, Radio, and Television in Arab Politics*. Praeger, Westport, Connecticut, 2004, pp. 19-20.

[57] A M El-Gody, 'The Role of Cyber Cafés in Developing Internet Literacy in Egypt', in *Civic Discourse and Digital Age Communications in the Middle East*. L A Gher and H Amin (eds), Ablex Publishing Corporation, Stamford, Connecticut, 2000, pp. 272-273.

[58] Eid, op. cit., p. 260.

[59] Peterson and Panovic, op. cit., pp. 199-200.

[60] E Feghali, 'Arab Cultural Communication Patterns'. *International Journal of Intercultural Relations*, vol. 21-3, 1997, pp. 351-355.

[61] Ibid, pp. 356-361.

Bibliography

Abdel-Nabi, S., J. Agha, J. Choucair and M. Mikdashi, 'Pop Goes the Arab World: Popular Music, Gender, Politics, and Transnationalism in the Arab World'. *Hawwa*, vol. 2-2, 2004, pp. 231-254.

Abdulla, R. A., 'An Overview of Media Developments in Egypt: Does the Internet Make a Difference?' *Global Media Journal: Mediterranean Edition*, vol. 1-1, 2006, pp. 88-97.

Adam, G. S., 'Truth, the State, and Democracy: The Scope of the Legal Right of Free Expression'. *Canadian Journal of Communication*, vol. 17-3, 1992, pp. 1-17.

Aladwani, A. M., 'Key Internet Characteristics and E-Commerce Issues in Arab Countries'. *Information Technology & People*, vol. 16-1, 2003, pp. 9-20.

Algeria, *World of Information Business Intelligence Reports*, vol. 1, 2001, Walden Publishing, Essex, UK, pp. 1-54.

Aliboni, R. and L. Guazzone, 'Democracy in the Arab Countries and the West'. *Mediterranean Politics*, vol. 9-1, 2004, pp. 82-93.

Amin, H., 'Mass Media in the Arab States Between Diversification and Stagnation: An Overview', in *Mass Media, Politics, and Society in the Middle East*. K. Hafez (ed), Hampton Press, Cresskill, New Jersey, 2001, pp. 23-41.

——, H., 'Freedom as a Value in Arab Media: Perceptions and Attitudes Among Journalists'. *Political Communication*, vol. 19-2, 2002, pp. 125-135.

Aviram, A., 'From "Computers in the Classroom" to Mindful Radical Adaptation by Education Systems to the Emerging Cyber Culture'. *Journal of Educational Change*, vol. 1, 2000, pp. 331-352.

Ayish, M., 'The Changing Face of Arab Communications: Media Survival in the Information Age', in *Mass Media, Politics, and Society in the Middle East*, K. Hafez (ed), Hampton Press, Cresskill, New Jersey, 2001, pp. 111-136.

Barnes, S., 'Cyberspace: Creating Paradoxes for the Ecology of Self', in *Communication and Cyberspace: Social Interaction in an Electronic Environment*. L. Strate, R. L. Jacobson and S. B. Gibson (eds), Hampton Press, Cresskill, New Jersey, 2003, pp. 229-253.

Bell, D., *An Introduction to Cybercultures*. Routledge, London, 2001.

Bhuiyan, A. J., *Mass Media, Communication, and Culture in Bangladesh in the Shadow of a Big Neighbor*. Unpublished Master's Thesis, Carleton University, Ottawa, 2002.

Boyd, D. A., 'Saudi Arabia's International Media Strategy: Influence Through Multinational Ownership', in *Mass Media, Politics, and Society in the Middle East*. K. Hafez (ed), Hampton Press, Cresskill, New Jersey, 2001, pp. 43-60.

Bruck, P. A., 'Communication and the Democratization of Culture: Strategies for Social Theory, Strategies for Dialogue', in *Democratization and the Media: An East-West Dialogue*. S. Splichal, J. Hochheimer and K. Jakubowicz (eds), Communication and Culture Colloquia, Yugoslavia, 1990, pp. 56-72.

Chalaby, J. K., 'From Internationalization to Transnationalization'. *Global Media and Communication*, vol. 1-1, 2005, pp. 28-33.

Dahlberg, L., 'The Internet and Democratic Discourse: Exploring the Prospects of Online Deliberative Forums Extending the Public Sphere'. *Information, Communication & Society*, vol. 4-4, 2001, pp. 615-633.

Diamond, L., 'Civil Society and the Struggle for Democracy', in *The Democratic Revolution: Struggles for Freedom and Pluralism in the Developing World*. L. Diamond (ed), Freedom House, New York, 1992, pp. 1-27.

Eid, M., 'Engendering the Arabic Internet: Modern Challenges in the Information Society', in *New Media and Public Relations*. S. C. Duhé (ed), Peter Lang Publishing, New York, 2007, pp. 247-268.

El-Gody, A. M., 'The Role of Cyber Cafés in Developing Internet Literacy in Egypt', in *Civic Discourse and Digital Age Communications in the Middle East*. L. A. Gher and H. Amin (eds), Ablex Publishing Corporation, Stamford, Connecticut, 2000, pp. 271-273.

Elkhafaifi, H. M., 'Arabic Language Planning in the Age of Globalization'. *Language Problems & Language Planning*, vol. 26-3, 2002, pp. 253-269.

Feghali, E., 'Arab Cultural Communication Patterns'. *International Journal of Intercultural Relations*, vol. 21-3, 1997, pp. 345-378.

Gibson, W., *Neuromancer*. Ace Books, New York, 1984.

Jaber, K. S. A. 'The Democratic Process in Syria, Lebanon, and Jordan', in *Democratization in the Middle East: Experiences, Struggles, Challenges*. A. Saikal and A. Schnabel (eds), United Nations University Press, Tokyo, 2003, pp. 127-141.

Jordan, *World of Information Business Intelligence Reports*, vol. 1, 2001, Walden Publishing, Essex, UK, pp. 1-40.

Kayal, A. D., 'Telecommunications in Saudi Arabia: A Paradigm of Rapid Progress', in *Telecommunications in Western Asia and the Middle East*. E. M. Noam (ed), Oxford University Press, New York, 1997, pp. 163-171.

Kirchner, H., 'Internet in the Arab World: A Step Towards "Information Society"', in *Mass Media, Politics, and Society in the Middle East*. K. Hafez (ed), Hampton Press, Cresskill, New Jersey, 2001, pp. 137-158.

Kitchin, R., *Cyberspace: The World in the Wires*. John Wiley & Sons Ltd., Chichester, 1998.

Langdon, S., *Global Poverty, Democracy and North-South Change*. Garamond Press, Toronto, 1999.

Lebanon, *World of Information Business Intelligence Reports*, vol. 1, 2001, Walden Publishing, Essex, UK, pp. 1-42.

McDowell, S. D., 'Theory and Research in International Communication: A Historical and Institutional Account', in *Handbook of International and Intercultural Communication*. W. B. Gudykunst and B. Mody (eds), Sage Publications, Thousand Oaks, California, 2002, pp. 295-308.

Miah, A., 'Virtually Nothing: Re-evaluating the Significance of Cyberspace'. *Leisure Studies*, vol. 19-3, 2000, pp. 211-225.

Ojo, B. A., 'The Military and the Democratization Process in Africa', in *Contemporary African Politics: A Comparative Study of Political Transition to Democratic Legitimacy*. B. A. Ojo (ed), University Press of America, Lauham, Maryland, 1999, pp. 51-63.

Page, B., *Who Deliberates? Mass Media in Modern Democracy*. The University of Chicago Press, London, 1996.

Peterson, M. A. and I. Panovic, 'Accessing Egypt: Making Myths and Producing Web Sites in Cyber-Cairo'. *New Review of Hypermedia and Multimedia*, vol. 10-2, 2004, pp. 199-219.

Pratt, N., 'Identity, Culture and Democratization: The Case of Egypt'. *New Political Science*, vol. 27-1, 2005, pp. 69-86.

Raboy, M., 'Policy-Making and Democratization: The Case of Canadian Broadcasting', in *Democratization and the Media: An East-West Dialogue*. S. Splichal, J. Hochheimer and K. Jakubowicz (eds), Communication and Culture Colloquia, Yugoslavia, 1990, pp. 108-120.

Raffer, K. and M. A. M. Salih, 'Rich Arabs and Poor Arabs: An Introduction to Intra-Arab Issues', in *The Least Developed and the Oil-Rich Arab Countries: Dependence, Interdependence or Patronage?* K. Raffer and M. A. M. Salih (eds), St. Martin's Press, New York, 1992, pp. 1-12.

Rogers, E. M. and W. B. Hart, 'The Histories of Intercultural, International, and Development Communication', in *Handbook of International and Intercultural Communication*. W. B. Gudykunst and B. Mody (eds), Sage Publications, Thousand Oaks, California, 2002, pp. 1-18.

Rugh, W., *Arab Mass Media: Newspapers, Radio, and Television in Arab Politics*. Praeger, Westport, Connecticut, 2004.

Sakr, N., 'Freedom of Expression, Accountability and Development in the Arab Region'. *Journal of Human Development*, vol. 4-1, 2003, pp. 29-46.

Sorensen, K., 'Silencing the Net: The Threat to Freedom of Expression On-line'. *Human Rights Watch,* vol. 8-2, 1996, pp. 1-24.

Strate, L., R. L. Jacobson and S. B. Gibson, 'Surveying the Electronic Landscape: An Introduction to Communication and Cyberspace', in *Communication and Cyberspace: Social Interaction in an Electronic Environment*. L. Strate, R. L. Jacobson and S. B. Gibson (eds), Hampton Press, Cresskill, New Jersey, 2003, pp. 1-26.

Telecommunication Policies for the Arab Region – the Arab Book, *Regional Telecommunication Development Conference for the Arab States -- Lebanon*, 11-15 November, 1996, ITU, Telecommunication Development Bureau, Beirut, Lebanon, viewed on 1 April 2008, <http://www.itu.int/itudoc/itu-d/rtdc96/010v2e_ww2.doc>.

The Internet in the Mideast and North Africa: Free Expression and Censorship, *Human Rights Watch*, 1999, viewed on 28 March 2008, <http://www.hrw.org/hrw/advocacy/internet/mena/download.htm>.

Thussu, D., *International Communication: Continuity and Change*. Arnold, London, 2000.

United Arab Emirates, *World of Information Business Intelligence Reports*, vol. 1, 2001, Walden Publishing, Essex, UK, pp. 1-58.

Vivekanand, P. V. and J. E. Kollar, 'Telecommunications in Jordan', in E. M. Noam (ed), *Telecommunications in Western Asia and the Middle East*. Oxford University Press, New York, 1997, pp. 157-162.

Winterford, D. and R. E. Looney, 'Advanced Telecommunications and the Economic Diversification of Bahrain', in *Telecommunications in Western Asia and the Middle East*. E. M. Noam (ed), Oxford University Press, New York, 1997, pp. 223-235.

Younis, T. 'Privatization: A Review of Policy and Implementation in Selected Arab Countries'. *International Journal of Public Sector Management*, vol. 9-3, 1996, pp. 18-25.

The Challenge of Intercultural Electronic Learning: English as Lingua Franca

Rita Zaltsman

Abstract
        This is a study of the use of English as a language of intercultural communication (as a *lingua franca*) in virtual global educational settings.[1] The work is based on the discourse analysis of the cross-cultural online seminar *IKARUS: Teaching and Learning in Virtual Learning Environments,* supported by the European Commission, as part of its project on distance education. The linguistic problems of English as a lingua franca of virtual educational settings are related to cross-cultural communication between contextually different cultures (juxtaposition high/low, cultural dichotomy of West-East). The linguacultural aspects of intercultural online learning are examined and the issues of "electronic English" are discussed. The paper concludes with the most relevant findings of the study.

        Key Words: Cross-cultural communication, e-learning, discourse analysis, cyberculture, English, lingua franca.

*****

1.   Introduction

        English as a lingua franca (ELF) is a medium of communication between people of different native languages for whom English is a second language.[2]
        English has become the language most commonly used for international communication, mainly due to historical reasons: the quantity of English speakers in the world (according to David Crystal,[3] 1.7 billion people, only 340 million of whom are English native speakers) considerably exceeds the quantity of French or Spanish speakers. It is expected that within the next few years the number of people speaking English as a second language will exceed the number of native English speakers: the global English language learning market is one of the fastest growing educational markets in the world and it continues to increase exponentially.
        World languages have been affected by English (e.g. French: *le Web, les hackers, le chat*), although for some languages the acquisition of English borrowings was not an absolute necessity: in Dutch, for example, its number is limited. Results from large scale interviews also show that most native speakers of Dutch do not experience the strong position of English as a threat to their native language.[4]

The globalisation of online learning has resulted in an increasing number of cross-cultural distance learning projects in which English has a dominant position as a communication lingua franca. The latter is a matter of great concern for the future of virtual learning in the world: together with the expansion of Western technologies and the distribution of ELF in global distance learning, there appears a kind of cultural imperialism of the West as nearly 60 % of all virtual education in the world today is being conducted in English.

Nevertheless, the problem of ELF in global e-learning has been insufficiently studied, whereas there is a lot of serious research on ELF in non-virtual settings.[5]

2.   Background

According to Samovar, Porter, and Stefani,[6] language is a reflection of how we perceive the world surrounding us.

> Any transformation of the language influences our basic
> values and assumptions, that is, our culture, defined as the
> collective programming of the mind which distinguishes the
> members of one group or category of people from another.[7]

Therefore, any attempt to influence culture inevitably affects language, which means that language is deeply rooted in culture and the latter has a profound impact on language. To underline such a close interrelationship between them both, in 1994, Michael Agar introduced a concept of *linguaculture*.

The present paper is based on the following cross-cultural oppositions:

a) *dichotomy of West/East:* G.Hofstede stated that some essential patterns of thinking, feeling, acting and communication significantly differ in various cultures. Eastern cultures (e.g. China, Japan, Thailand) are collectivist, with a strong sense of community, traditionally focused on roles, status and relationships: the interests of others have a priority; communication is primarily concerned with maintaining group harmony (a "loss of face" phenomenon). Whereas the Western are individuum-centred, logical, rational, independent, direct and success-oriented. Their ethics are based on professionalism and personal achievements (e.g. USA, Germany, England).

b) *high versus low context theory:* E.Hall's theory is based on the juxtaposition of cultural context (West versus East), which is directly related to their contrasting conversational practices: Western cultures are "speaking" communities: in the West, language is a means to find and convey information, which is why Westerners initiate discussions more often than

Easterners. In Eastern cultures, communication partners first listen to and establish the other's position, then react to it and formulate their own. For that reason, they are often indicated as *silent* cultures. In general, Easterners perceive communication with Westerners as an unpleasant experience ("foreigner complex") and tend to avoid it.

> What do non-Japanese teachers find challenging about teaching Japanese learners? Long pauses before answering a teacher's question; lack of eye contact; long silences; not initiating; very quiet voicing that is hard to hear; consulting with classmates before answering; and insistence on accuracy. These features can be extremely frustrating for teachers.[8]

Identifying/being aware of cultural contrasts (*differences in building and maintaining relationships; differences in communication: direct versus indirect; verbal versus nonverbal; the time challenge: past-, present-, or future-oriented; etc.*) are often crucial for successful communication and learning. When ignored, these factors can make effective communication and learning collaboration in online communities extremely complicated. This issue acquires much more significance when the communities are intercultural and the communication is conducted in a non-native language.

3.   Methodology

The present paper focuses on linguacultural peculiarities of learning in global virtual settings. Through lexical, graphical, and semantic observations of a particular communication process, we have made an attempt to identify online students' attitude toward linguacultural barriers in virtual environments and indicate the role of ELF in cross-cultural e-learning.

The present study is based on the discourse analysis of a cross-cultural online seminar *IKARUS: Teaching and Learning in Virtual Learning Environments*. According to Stubbs, 1983, discourse analysis "is concerned with language use beyond the boundaries of a sentence/utterance".

IKARUS (an acronym of a German term: "**I**nternet-basiertes **K**ollaboratives **AR**beiten in **U**niversitären Lehr- und Lern-**S**zenarien" - "Internet based collaborative work in university teaching and learning environments") was conducted by the University of Saarland, Germany, together with e-learning European competency centres from Sweden, Spain and Greece and funded by the European Commission.

The main goals of the online seminar were: a) to promote intercultural understanding and co-operation among people from different countries and encourage the development of international perspectives in organisational communication; b) to provide opportunities for students, faculty, and institutions to participate in transatlantic dialogue and collaboration.

The concept was based on the *learning by doing* approach: the students collaborated in groups and reflected the pros and cons of cross-cultural collaborative online learning - thus, the content was identical with the method.

Initially, 175 students from 28 countries were registered in the course: Westerners were very well represented by Germany (34%), Sweden (15%), Austria (12%), the Netherlands (2%), the USA (4%) and Canada (4%); Easterners by: Greece (12%), Malaysia (4%), Egypt (1.5%), Taiwan, Columbia (each - 0.8%), etc.

Thus, 71% of the participants represented Western, 29% - Eastern cultures.

Average age: 32 years; males - 42%, females - 58%.

Students represented 48% of the participants, university lecturers and scientific workers - 34%, postgraduate students - 6%, Ph.D. candidates - 12%, people interested in distance learning - 6%.

The level of English language proficiency: 12% - native speakers, 32% - advanced/good level, 56% - standard level (enough to be enrolled).

The study reported here has been centred around the correlation between some dimensions of culture and ELF:

1. cross-cultural dimension of online learning
2. cultural context, East/West dichotomy
3. limitations of virtual learning: the ways to compensate missing visual, auditory and kinesthetic signals
4. the quality of communication in its relation to ELF issues

Note that for the purpose of this research, the terms *e-learning, online learning, distance learning, distance education and virtual learning,* denoting the process of learning at a distance on the Internet setting without face-to-face communication between learning participants, have been used interchangeably.

4.   Key Findings

In the following, we provide the analysis of the online asynchronous discussion (forum inputs) with particular attention paid to the cultural aspects of transnational global e-learning as correlated with ELF.

First, the discussion focuses on the issues of cultural barriers in virtual settings, in particular, on the differences in time orientation in cultures of various contexts (all citations below are reproduced with original spelling and punctuation - R.Z.):

> Some of us (including me as I found out to my
> astonishment) seem to like to go ahead from the beginning,
> discuss their point of view [...], simply they want to start
> working. Others are used to seeing the whole thing a little
> more relaxed: The deadline is then-and-then - why
> bothering weeks ahead?

It turns out, however, that due to time zone differences Easterners
can acquire some extra time which they need to actually start learning.

This "delayed reaction time" phenomenon seems to significantly
influence online communication: e.g. a 12-hour time zone difference between
the USA and China, which normally hinders communication, has also
another (positive) aspect – the Chinese are given additional time to think their
answers through and formulate arguments. Thus, the Internet turns into an
ideal communication setting for these two contextually different cultures.

This means that a) virtual communities are not culture-free settings
as the Internet effects the quality of online communication; b) a cyber
environment can play not only a destructive role in online learning (due to
preferences for written communication, a contrasting values paradigm in
different cultures, etc.), but also a constructive role making online
communication across cultures less complicated.

Thus, virtual settings can bring cultures of different contexts closer
together through bridging a "cultural divide."

The further dispute centres on communication, active participation,
and collaboration in the seminar that the participants consider crucial for e-
learning. Although it takes a great amount of time to learn online ("It took me
the whole day until 23.30 CET in the evening to get the final paper finished
and uploaded."), they indicate their satisfaction with this kind of learning
primarily due to their successful integration into virtual groups:

> This sense of flow is something I experienced within
> IKARUS! It was the final chatting session of the groupwork
> and we had to finish our paper. There was a lot to do, but
> everybody contributed. In the end I worked simultaneously
> on a part of the paper and chatted, did some formatting etc.
> Three hours of real flow. It was a great experience...

The emphasis is put on the factors that affect this process, in
particular, a social/cultural dimension within online classes:

> ... it was fun [...] to see a team of four completely different
> people actually working together and 'creating' something
> out of nowhere.

Thus, the general perception remains that a sense of belonging to the team is essential for the quality of online learning.

On the other hand, as indicated, learning in online settings is often accompanied with dissatisfaction:

> My first experience in a virtual learning context was that my own language (English, not mother tongue but usually quite easily spoken) changed. I felt very clumsy and staggering around. Then I realized that it wasn't the language but the setting making me somehow insecure. I thought that it was about the division between written and spoken language. When I write in online situations I feel that I need to be fast and sharp. If I write 'on my own' my metaphors, my sentences my 'style' is different. Being and writing online my language is 'strange', it differs from other situations.

Further, the limitations of online learning are highlighted: some students favour its convenience ("anytime-anywhere-24/7 possibilities"), others feel dissatisfied ("time consuming", "too much work", "the tempo is very high"), frustrated ("I feel lost"), or lonely ("online learning is a lonely business"):

> ... this is definitively not working for me. I simply don't know what I'm doing or what I'm supposed to do. I need face to face interaction, I need total physical immersion in the learning environment, I need more focused discussions, etc. I'm glad I went through this experience before enrolling in an online grad program. I would go totally crazy.

This has a direct impact on learning results: less than a half of the participants were certified at the end of the course - course start date: March, 1st (175 participants); course finish date: June, 1st (70 participants). A high dropout rate (59%) indicates that the seminar has not met the needs of the majority of the students. It should be taken into account, however, that the course has been offered at no cost and, as one of the learners has noted, "to drop out was much easier as compared to a commercial course."

The next question that logically follows, is: what else denotes the quality of virtual communication/learning?

> For many people, even though they are conversant in English, not hearing the voice of the person talking to you

is a 'language barrier'. It takes some time to understand an individual's personality through the written word and some people can come off as curt or uncaring or downright rude without meaning to.

This argument turns out to be debatable: some participants consider such characteristics as speech tempo, dialect, humour perception across cultures, or non-verbal signals to be more relevant for efficient communication. In their view, it is predominantly false pronunciation and an accent that considerably determine its quality.

Gradually, the community proceeds to discussing the pitfalls in intercultural communication caused by latent meanings within the same language. The major issue is whether the initial message coincides with the decoded information or not:

> ... once at school we were playing Chinese whispers and half of us were Arab and the other half Europeans... the meanings got totally distorted across the cultures!!! in this case, we were teenagers and the Europeans would say some daring word and the Arabs would hear it as something very neutral!

Some participants suppose that they would have experienced greater psychological comfort if the seminar had been conducted in their native language:

> ... I say in all sincerity that I would like to write and participate more in this seminar if I write either in Swedish or Spanish. Sometimes I don't find the right expressions to explain in English and it's a bit frustrated. But I hope that such a seminars on internet like this one can be given in our mother tongues in the very near future.

In general, however, the students appreciate the choice of English as a communication lingua franca:

> I think it's easier if the groupmembers have the same language, because you don't have to work with the language at all and you understand everything, it's easy then.

On the whole, the level of language proficiency of non-native English speakers (representatives of Eastern cultures) has been compatible with that of their Western communication partners. The discourse observation clearly shows that ELF was playing the role of a powerful bridge-builder, which resulted in a qualitative collaboration between opposite cultural contexts:

> It would be difficult to experience flow if I had to interrupt my thinking/working process with the search for words or if I checked my grammar all the time (this might result in a lot of mistakes, but what the hack ... ;-).

Notable is that some Easterners have unexpectedly demonstrated more competency in English than their Western co-students. Easterners attribute this to the language environment they were brought up in:

> I'm Egyptian but my Arabic and English are almost the same level... This is because I always went to a British school with British/Australian teachers, then American University, then worked in an American multinational.

A Chinese student living in the Netherlands regrets not being able to communicate in pure British/American English (which nobody expects her to) as she has been brought up under the conditions of linguistic diversity:

> I was born in Malaysia with Chinese parentage. Left Malaysia since 19. Since then lived in UK, NL [Netherlands], US. I have just moved back to NL June 2001. Have worked in Korea, China, Australia, South American regions etc.

The growth of the level of English language proficiency may also be attributed to the shift to conversational learning in the East. To understand this, have a look at the previous English learning situation in China:

> Owing to the powerful influence of the traditional language teaching methods, both teachers and students typically adopt the grammar-translation method. This method focuses on grammar and vocabulary, on linguistic phenomena rather than on reading. Little or no attention is paid to speaking or listening.[9]

In the new millennium, the methods of English learning in the East have been revolutionised: it is no longer limited to learning grammar and practising translation as it used to be. This resulted in the increasing level of

English language proficiency, not only in China, but in the Eastern world on the whole. English has become the preferred choice of communication in the second language situations for Easterners - consequently, they (here: a Chinese Malaysian) feel "quite at home with it":

> I considered myself to be quite good with computer and the Internet. But [...] I am quite 'blind' to computer software instructions in Chinese. Therefore, I prefer *to have everything in English at least I can understand a bit better*.

It is notable that Easterners (here: several cultural convergents - a Chinese Malaysian and an Egyptian, both using distance learning for their Ph.D. in England) displayed a high level of language competency, success-oriented thinking and greatly contributed to collaborative work. They demonstrated fluent English, were working hard to earn more credits, were creative, helpful and competitive as well as often initiated group discussions. Online tutors were not absolute authorities for them - they challenged them, presented their views, even if the latter differed from that of the instructors'.

This indicates that cultural differences in virtual settings along West/East paradigm are no longer contrasting: Easterners from academic circles who are taking part in cross-cultural online projects seem to little differ in their classroom conduct or language fluency from their Western co-students.

Interestingly, a Swedish student states that successful online communication and learning cannot be secured only through fluent English and provides reasons for that:

> ... I now know that this way of learning is not mine. I [...] miss the personal contact which inspires me, I *need to see reactions on faces in order to feel safe in conversing*.
>
> [...] there is a huge part of communication going on when we are talking that is not language. And a large amount (if not all) is lost when we communicate in writing, even worse: electronic writing.

The present discourse is rich in such *electronic writing* which is represented mostly graphically - with emoticons and smileys which are universally accepted methods of linguistic compression widely used in computer-mediated communication. Both emoticons and smileys add meaning and emotional charge to written texts. Some students view them as "the jargon that can be understood without too many words", or as a part of another language ("I view this as Italian or Spanish words"). In general, emoticons and smileys are used to avoid many misunderstandings. Having admitted that he personally hated emoticons, a German student receives the following response:

> ... when I read your post and you write that you HATE emoticons, I do not know if you are saying this with a twinkle in your eye, or if you are 100% serious about this. An emoticon [...] could have made this clear.
>
> I can tell other people what I feel/think about a situation with just one 'smiley' and that makes it quite easy...

This quote suggests that online learners view computer graphics as a method for punctuating messages. Though some find it "quite amusing when educated adults communicate via 'a very happy smiley or shouting smiley'."

Alongside emoticons and smileys, some other variants of "electronic English" are extensively used in the given discourse, in particular:

- *exclamations (reflect the emotional state of a "speaker"):*
  Wouldn't you rather curl up at home with a nice glass of wine and your warm friendly laptop?!!!!!!
- *capitalisation (enables transference of the height of the tone - a large font, as is known, in the Internet culture is equivalent to shouting):*
  We are undertaking an educational activity so the PRODUCT is LEARNING.
- *letter addition:*
  Well, we European will just let you stewed...... for a bit...loooooooooooonger...
  OOOOOOOOOOOUCH!!!!!! Sorry for the mistake guys. I plead to your mercy.
- *shortenings:*
  U ("you"), tho ("though"), rite ("right"), CU ("see you"), f2f ("face-to-face")
- *acronyms:*
  BTW - By the Way
  LOL - Laughing 0ut Loud
  IMHO - In my Humble Opinion
- *computer slang:*
  My two pennies worth (a contribution to conversation or debate)
- *occasionalisms:*
  Xcuse me - excuse me
  www - world wide waiting
- *dots (adequate to a pause in oral speech - shows the speech tempo):*

> As to the groupwork I found it very hard to bring together all group members and in the end I spend the entire sunday to 'organise' the final paper ..... There once again I spent more time than expected .....

- *paraverbal methods (a descriptive presentation of an emotional reaction in written discourse): <hehe>, <smile>, <grin>:*
  ... are there any left??? hehe.

All of these types of e-writing are commonly used in online communication to save time and space. They serve as substitute emotions (or their textual description) because of visual, auditory, and kinesthetic deficits of online communication and learning. It is significant that both cultural groups have made an extensive use of non-animated/animated smileys or emoticons expressing positive/negative emotions: energy/sadness, optimism/depression, etc. In general, participants have no problems with decoding computer graphics. Text compression, in their view, is even obligatory as "the writing is taking up so much more time and care." Notable is the correlation between the number of language substitutes and the level of emotional distance between communicants: *the higher emotional contact between participants, the greater the number of language substitutions.*

The same is true in relation to the use of "multilanguages" - Genglish, Spanglish, Chinglish, Swenglish or other "Englishes":

> Funnily, it is easiest for me to communicate with someone who speaks both languages because we (my friends and colleagues) usually speak a combination of the languages (2 words in Arabic and 2 in English per sentence)! even on MSN or email!

Why do online students feel comfortable when speaking both English and their native language? The given discourse contains the answer to this question: the students seem to greatly enjoy an exciting experience of belonging to the community of co-thinkers. For them, interacting online means talking, they communicate as if it were speaking face to face: ("I'm writing what I would say... Looking forward to 'talking' to you soon again! ..."). Hence, some misspelled words, wrong punctuation or the use of hybrid forms - e.g.: "feber" (Genglish: German - "der Fieber", English - "a fever"). The latter shows that while writing in English, students might be thinking in their native languages, which does not seem to have destructed communication. The response: "I hope your fever is better already!" (a respond to the posting where "feber" has been used) shows that the message was unerroneously delivered. For them, it is evidently more important to convey an idea or to deliver a message than to think about correct grammatical constructions or the choice of lexical units.

To secure a qualitative online communication in ELF both Easterners and Westerners:

- make use of intercultural English (avoiding local "Englishes")
- do not use idiomatic or slang expressions or substitute them with a suitable equivalent
- search for synonyms to make messages "digestable"
- apply for help: clarify, ask for additional information
- use supportive lexical units
- employ humour and laughter and their graphical equivalents - smileys or emoticons
- ask for/give feedback: retrieve information about lexical difficulties from their communication partners; ask their partners if they are comfortable with their English
- are sensitive to the peculiarities of linguacultural communication in different cultures
- are especially tolerant and empathic when communicating with cultures of opposite context

This clearly testifies *the shift of roles* in online cross-cultural communities as compared to monocultural communities: the communication partners not only "consume" the delivered information but actively cooperate with each other in reconstructing the meaning and creating understanding.

Seminar participants are competent and fluent English speakers. Neither high nor low context cultures dominate the conversation with the both groups taking turns in initiating discussions and promoting a dialogue. The feedback is constructive, they enjoy being listened to, encouraging each other to respond, and sharing their thoughts and knowledge. They feel safe to express themselves, and as a result, experience some kind of a *'we - feeling'*.

The English in the seminar is academic: both parties practise a Western (direct, without status-priorities open) way of discourse. There is no language deficit, the spelling system presents mixed American/British forms (tending more to English spelling) and uses international grammar. The participants are capable of discussing complex didactical, psycholinguistical or philosophical topics in English: their lexicon is rich and phraseological competency is relatively high. In general, their language proficiency is good enough for a qualitative online communication with a learning objective.

The following data reflects the communication patterns being viewed cross-culturally (words/per message):

Westerners: n (max) = 467; n (min) = 27
Easterners: n (max) = 136; n (min) = 17

Although the data above shows evident discrepancies in the length of the contributions, there is no Western dominance observed in their quality. The examined discourse demonstrates no misconceptions and misjudgments between representatives of opposite cultural context caused by the use of erroneous English lexical or phraseological units.

5.   Conclusions and Future Research Directions

In this seminar, the English language has played the role of a powerful bridge-builder able to connect people of diverse backgrounds in online learning communities.

The obtained findings can lead to the following conclusions:

- there's no "language divide" between Eastern and Western cultures as far as language competency is concerned
- cyberculture, as a common educational environment, can help bridge cultures and languages
- different "Englishes" are/will be turning into a universal lingua franca for online communication across cultures
- cultures of different context tend to converge in online educational settings, which influences English as a language of international communication

Additional research is necessary in tracking the cross-cultural communication pitfalls caused by semantic differences between the same notions/concepts in various cultures. The same lexical units may not have equivalent meanings which can result in misinterpretation and miscommunication: when using a lexical unit in English, we involuntarily attribute to it the meanings it has in our native language, even though the same unit in other linguacultures may have a completely different scope of meanings. E.g., the word "president" in the American electoral discourse denotes a person, who is democratically elected and has a limited power, whereas in Russian it means "a person elected by establishment" - an equivalent of the word "tsar" (in the Russian culture it is a person with unlimited authority, "God's chosen representative on earth").

Thus, the meanings are culturally dependent and are not semantically equivalent in different cultures. Hence, further research will be concentrated on linguacultural varieties of English and their relevance for valid cross-cultural communication in educational online settings.

Notes

[1] This paper has benefited from comments made by Ann Snowden. I remain responsible for any errors and welcome corrections or comments to <rzaltzma@yahoo.de>

---

[2] Gnutzmann, C., 'Englisch als Globale Lingua Franca: Funktion und Entwicklung - Fragen des Lehrens und Lernens - Lernziel *Mehrsprachigkeit*' (in German), in *Fremdsprachen Lehren und Lernen* 29, 2000, pp. 23-36.

[3] Crystal, D., *English as a Global Language*. Cambridge University Press, Cambridge, 1997.

[4] Booij, G., *English as the Lingua Franca of Europe; a Dutch Perspective*. Lingua e Stile 36, 2001, pp. 351-361.

[5] See, for example, Gramkow-Andersen, 1993; Firth, 1996, J. House, 1982, 2001, 2004, - In: Meierkord, C., 'Interpreting Successful Lingua Franca Interaction. An Analysis of Non-Native-/Non-Native Small Talk Conversations in English', in *Linguistik Online*, 5/1, 2000, viewed on 16 April 2008.
<http://www.linguistik-online.de/1_00/MEIERKOR.HTM>

[6] Samovar, L., and Porter, R. (eds.). *Intercultural Communication: a Reader*. Belmont, CA, Wadsworth, 1997.

[7] Hofstede, G., *Cultures and Organizations: Software of the Mind*. McGraw-Hill, London UK, 1991.

[8] Gray, P. and Leather, S., *Safety and Challenge for Japanese Learners of English*. Delta Publishing, United Kingdom, 1999.

[9] Huang, Y. and Xu, H., 'Trends in English Language Education in China', *in English as Second Language Magazine*. N11-12, 1999.

Bibliography

Agar, M., *Language Shock: Understanding the Culture of Conversation*. William Morrow and Co., New York, 1994.

Boutonnet, J., 'Irony: stylistic aspects,' in *The Encyclopedia of Language and Linguistics*, K.Brown (ed.), Elsevier, Amsterdam, 2005.

Chase, M., et al. *Intercultural Challenges in Networked Learning: Hard Technologies Meet Soft Skills*, in *First Monday* (Online Journal), vol. 7 and 8., 2002, viewed on 20 April 2008.
<http://firstmonday.org/issues/issue7_8/chase/index.html>

Dahl, S., *Communications and Culture Transformation: Cultural Diversity, Globalization and Cultural Convergence*. ECE, London, 2000, viewed on 19 April 2008.
<http://www.stephweb.com/capstone/capstone.shtml>

Edmundson, A., 'The Cross-Cultural Dimensions of E-Learning', in *Turkish Online Journal of Distance Education-TOJDE*, Vol. 4 N.3, 2003.

Guttfreund, D., 'Effects of Language Usage on the Emotional Experience of Spanish-English and English-Spanish Bilinguals', in *Journal of Consulting and Clinical Psychology*, 58 (5), 1990.

Hall, E., *The Hidden Dimension*. Doubleday and Company, New York, 1966.

Kauffmann, I. and Scheuermann, F., *Studieren im globalen Dorf: Juristische Online-Ausbildung in Saarbrücken*. JurPC Web-Dok. 154/1998, Abs. 1 – 24, viewed on 20 April 2008.
<http://www.jurpc.de/aufsatz/19980154.htm#fn0">

Piller, I., 'Language Choice in Bilingual, Cross-Cultural Interpersonal Communication', in *Linguistik Online*, 5/1, 2000, viewed on 16 April 2008.
<http://www.linguistik-online.de/1_00/PILLER.HTM>

Stubbs, M., *Discourse Analysis*. Blaekwell, Oxford, 1996.

Ting-Toomey, S., *Communicating Across Cultures*. The Guilford Press, New York, 1999, pp. 194-230.

Wierzbicka, A., *Jewish Cultural Scripts and the Interpretation of the Bible*. Journal of Pragmatics, Vol. 36, Issue 3, 2004, p. 575-599.

Zaltsman, R., 'Communication Barriers and Conflict in Cross-Cultural e-Learning', in *Globalized E-Learning Cultural Challenges*. Edmundson, A. (ed.), Information Science Publishing, Hershey, PA, 2007, pp. 291-307.

Part II

The Aesthetic

The Implicit Body

Nicole Ridgway and Nathaniel Stern

Abstract
This essay follows scholars who have revisited the crisis narrative of disembodiment in relation to technology to argue instead that electronic digitality, far from eviscerating the real and occluding the body, invests in bodily affectivity. As such, we argue, it has the capacity to engender a non-representational experience that mixes affection, memory and perception in the emergence of bodiliness. It is our contention that those interactive works that fall within the broad rubric of "body art," albeit with a new twist, perform a doubled gesture: they both force us to rethink the extant relationship *in* the in-between of body and technology, and invite us to experiment with the *of* of the relation of body and technology.

If "explicit body" performance explicated bodies in social relation to unfold layers of signification, then "implicit body" art allows us to experience the enfolding field out of which bodies come to sense, but as something unaccomplished, as the limit and expression of meaning.

Here interaction encompasses a taking place that inaugurates rather than enacts an *a priori* script. While new media has displayed a tendency to take interaction literally as "doing" something, this approach argues that interaction is incipient action, in which an implicit body emerges alongside an unfinished art work; and being bodily materializes in the in-between of interaction.

Key Words: embodiment, disembodiment, digital/interactive art, affect, perception, vision, touch, emergence

*****

Lev Manovich contends, while contesting the validity of the nomenclature, that "interactive art" is a "laboratory" in which the compelling questions of our age are being examined.[1] Despite the problematic overtones of empiricism here, his implied assertion that it is in the place of new media art that new media (broadly understood) are being investigated is an interesting one. So too is the turn by a number of recent philosophers (Dag Petersson, Mark BN Hansen, and Brian Massumi, amongst others) to discussions of digital interactive art to interrogate our cherished, critical categories of understanding the world in general, and the body, in particular. Following and developing this turn, it is our contention that those interactive works that fall within the broad rubric of "body art," albeit with a new twist, perform a doubled gesture: they both force us to rethink the extant relationship *in* the in- between of body and technology, and invite us to experiment with the *of* of the relation of body and technology.

In her essay "Will the Real Body Stand Up?" Allucquere Roseanne Stone argues, via the work of Frances Barker, that the retreat of the body in the West into text, and/or brute physicality, is both being continued and refigured through the mediation of computing technology. This history of "disembodiment" in Western thinking can be traced from, amongst others, Plato "who argued that the world of the senses is a mere copy of an abstract reality" via Descartes who asserted "that certain knowledge can only begin when we remove ourselves as far as possible from the senses."[2] Like many other critics, artists and scholars in the field of new media, Stone contends that, "The discourse of visionary virtual world builders is rife with images of imaginal bodies, freed from the constraints that flesh imposes ... Forgetting about the body is an old Cartesian trick ..."[3] Imaginal bodies abound, for example, in the dreams of disembodied brains in the artificial intelligence movement (especially in the pioneering work of Hans Moravec), in the downloaded selves of the cyberpunk imaginary, and is given new life with the creation of the world wide web and so-called "cyberspace."[4] Here the "myth of disembodiment" - "the [drive] to escape the limitations of the flesh"[5]- finds its apotheosis in John Perry Barlow's assertion: "cyberspace is not where bodies live."[6] With both Barlow and Moravec, the metaphoric and literal retreat from the flesh goes hand in hand with the literal and conceptual ascension of transparency - light, abstraction and vision.

New media philosopher Mark BN Hansen has extensively critiqued studies of technology rooted in writing (what he calls "the systemic-semiotic perspective" linked to "discursive-representationalist reason"). He contends that the "intertwined themes of occularcentrism and disembodiment have been central to critical studies of new media ... [and that] metaphors of vision and light have always been coupled with notions of ... immateriality, but in an era saturated with computer-generated imaging modalities, the theme of disembodiment has taken on radical new dimensions."[7]

William Mitchell asserts, for example, that, "A worldwide network of digital imaging systems is swiftly, silently constituting itself as the decentered [sic] subject's reconfigured eye."[8] Vivian Sobchack speaks of electronic space as "a phenomenological structure of sensual and psychological experience that seems to belong to no-body."[9] Friedlich Kittler goes so far as to contend that with digital convergence human perception is becoming obsolete.[10]

In his examination of the digital image in "postphotography," Hansen suggests that Deleuze's analysis of cinema-based "machinic vision'"(as well as the digital arts theories that follow its trajectory) eliminates the contribution of the body so that the resulting image is seen as "the function of a purely formal technical agency;" namely, the camera or computer.[11] Here the disembodied, but still human, eye of the Renaissance is replaced with that of a lens or digital sensor. This "radical disembodiment of perception" imagines an eye and brain that act only as "conception qua subtraction" in the selection and reflection of images and information.[12]

Along with scholars such as Jonathan Crary, Hansen calls, therefore, for a "reconstruction of the technical history of vision,"[13] one which puts the body, as whole, back into sight: a "shift from an optical to a haptic mode of perception."[14] He advocates a Bergsonist reconfiguration of seeing which "is always mixed with affection and memory, [and the] bodily faculties that mark the positive contribution of the body to the process of perception."[15] In this reconfiguration the "viewer is always already in the image, necessarily and inevitably positioned within a field of interacting images,"[16] and "perception... [is] itself a part of matter as a whole."[17]

In the posthuman perceptual regime brought about by technology, Hansen goes on to argue, "the selection of information is no longer performed exclusively or even primarily by the human component (the body-brain as the center of indetermination)," however, he contends, "machinic vision must be differentiated from the automation of vision... [and] the human must be resituated in the space of this very difference ..."[18] Whereas "automation seeks to replace human vision tout court, machinic vision simply expands the range of perception well beyond the organic-physiological constraints of human embodiment."[19] Like Virilio's "vision machines," Hansen contends that new media art, far from retracting from the body, actually invests in "alternative ... bodily underpinnings of human vision."[20]

While it is certainly true that "compared to the analogical arts - which are always instantiated in a fixed, Euclidean space - the digital arts seem abstract, ephemeral, without substance," this sense of "becoming immaterial" is contingent on two misrecognitions, David Rodowick asserts.[21] Firstly, a misrecognition of the "question of materiality [and embodiment] in relation to technology"[22] and, secondly, a misrecognition in which the unravelling of "spatial coherence" is read as a "desubstantialization" (one in which the openness to time is also erased - because these works are not, as Mitchell argues, "finished").[23]

Interactive body art can, and may, make us think again about these misrecognitions, and challenges us to explore anew the relation of body and technology without returning to the crisis narrative of disembodiment.[24] This paper follows those new media scholars who have, in recent years, revisited the ideas of occularcentrism and disembodiment in relation to technology to argue its inverse. That is, to argue that, "electronic digitality, far from eviscerating the real and occluding the body, invests in bodily affectivity. As such, it has the capacity to go beyond the aesthetic perception of the object" and engender a "non-representational experience."[25] Technologies affect what it means to be an embodied agent and, as such, we need an approach to digitality that acknowledges affect, perception, bodiliness and cognition.

Ursula Frohne and Christian Katti, in their discussion of the politics of the body and language in new media, contend that the "'body' and 'language' gained new significance with the emergence of action, performance, and conceptual art," and retrospectively, "they may be considered preliminary impulses for the introduction of 'new media'."[26] This historical trajectory foregrounds, they argue, the need "to develop a critical concept of media that neither presupposes nor excludes the categories of body and language ... to address the political implications for changing notions of the body and language under the impact of electronic space and communication."[27]

Much of the work in action, performance and concept art that prefigures "new media" art draws attention to the dominant structures of representation and meaning-making, and works to reveal the body as a site of inscription, surveillance and power. While these works may not invest in bodily affectivity of the participant, they do ask the spectator to grapple with "the body's" explication in discourse and in art practices (for example, in primitivism), and attempt to make visible the relations of seeing - who sees and who is seen - embedded in these discourses and practices. Because these works also disrupt inherited structures of representation (and question the hegemonic relationship between the so-called "real" and the "copy," the "subject" and the "object") we start here in taking up the challenge to develop a critical vocabulary that does not exclude or presuppose the body.

The "explicit body," a term coined by Rebecca Schneider to describe feminist performance art, speaks to a "mass of orifices and appendages, details and tactile surfaces ... [that] in representation is foremost a site of social markings, physical parts and gestural signatures of gender, race, class, age, sexuality - all of which bear ghosts of historical meaning, markings delineating social hierarchies of privilege and deprivilege."[28] The explicit body in performance "explicate[s] bodies in social relation" and "renders the symbolic [as] literal" in order to "pose a threat ... [to] implicit structures of comprehensibility."[29] It is a body which is scarred by a history larger than the bodies' wearer - we are peeling away to reveal what is already there, but unbeknownst to us.[30]

Through an "explosive literality," and with an eye towards the Latin root *explicare* (or, *to unfold*), the explicit body is performed to "peel back layers of signification," to "expose not an originary, true, or redemptive body, but the sedimented layers of signification themselves."[31] Explicit body performance deploys the material body to collide the literal against the symbolic order of meaning in order to implode the binary logics of capitalism and patriarchy and reveal, to paraphrase Judith Butler, which bodies come to matter and why.

In the work of performance and visual artist Karen Finely, for example, the explicit body is wielded to intervene in the spectacle of engenderment. According to Jill Dolan, in her performances Finely does not offer herself as an object of desire but rather desecrates herself as an object of male desire, as commodity to be consumed.[32] Confounding the expectations of conventional theatrical spectatorship, Finley de-idealises and de-sacralises the body and draws attention to female bodies as site of prohibitions.[33] By taking the signifier for the body, the performances reveal the markings of embodiment and draw us to the place where meaning collapses.[34] Here the explicit body literalizes the legislative frontier, that aspect of power, which both authorises and invalidates representations, and gestures to that which is un-representable.

Within the framework of the performance art, body art and Happenings movements that Schneider writes about, this notion of the explicit body is extremely productive. It "unfolds" and reveals to us our stories, preconceptions and, perhaps most importantly to Schneider, social relations.

Under the conditions of digitality, there's potential for another shift in subject / object and performer / audience hierarchies, and thus a shift in how we might read such explicit inscriptions and/or come to perceive our embodiment. We propose that the "flesh" can perhaps be thought of as more of a palimpsest, where we inscribe and scratch away, and enfold, alongside our continuous unfolding, in order to not uncover or discover our bodies, but to emerge as bodies (both legible and illegible), as not-yet-bodies, as bodies in process - implied bodies, in relation and drawn out. Like a moebius strip, where the root of explicit is *to unfold*, to imply is *to enfold*. And, like a moebius strip again, the relationship between them is neither dichotomous nor dialectical. We ponder this continuum not as a binary between emergence and positioning, between regulatory operations and becomings, or between implicit and explicit. It is rather a both/and, a co-telling - in, of and by the flesh.[35]

Interactive body art allows us to live through that out of which the explicit experience of embodiment emerges. In allowing us to touch/be touched by what Hansen calls the "nonlived" (the affective excess out of which perception comes)[36] and Massumi calls the "virtual" (the reserve of differentiation or qualitative transformation in every event),[37] the implicit body, like passage, precedes construction. As Massumi avers, "process always has ontological priority" in that "it constitutes the field of emergence."[38]

Interactive art, with its potential to be process rather than construction, may allow, as Margaret Morse argues, the visitor to perform the piece: she "*is* the piece as its experiential subject, not by identification, but in body."[39] Interactive work is, at its best, "unfinished"[40] work that requires a "co-joining"[41] of work and participant. The participant, in other words, is central to the final "materialisation of the work" (and the work, we will argue, is central to the materialisation of the participant).[42] While all art is to a lesser or greater extent "interactive," interactive work requires more than the work of the imagination because it is, as Pierre Levy states, created by the body[43] and, in part, experienced as a kind of learning "with the body itself."[44]

While new media has, for the most part, "displayed a tendency to take interaction literally as 'doing' something," interaction may also, with its combination "of attention and distraction, intention and passivity - woven through with the reciprocities of sensation, affectivity and conscious reflection," be an incipient locus of action.[45] As such, it may be a space in which an implicit body emerges alongside an unfinished art work; a space in which embodiment is performed but not necessarily as the result of conscious (or explicit) actions.

> Paul Ricoeur reminds us that inter-action is not only a doing and a making, but also a receiving and enduring. It speaks to not only the ability to effect, but the ability to be affected. As a site of emergence - like Adorno's configurations - inter-action may 'unfold the space between subjects and objects' such that subjects and objects are implicated in the space of unfolding. Here interaction encompasses a taking place that inaugurates rather than enacts an *a priori* script.[46]

David Rokeby is a Canadian-based artist whose installations use custom-made "artificial perception systems"[47] that directly engage with the body, by provoking unusual performances in their participants. His *Very Nervous System* (1986-1990) was perhaps one of the first and most important artworks to place emphasis on the performed and decentralized space of an interactive work. The piece's current incarnation - it's gone through several generations - uses "video cameras, image processors, computers, synthesizers and a sound system to create a space in which the movements of one's body create sound and/or music."[48] In his artist statement, Rokeby describes his thinking behind the creation of the work:

> I created the work for many reasons, but perhaps the most pervasive … was a simple impulse towards contrariness … Because the computer is purely logical, the language of interaction should strive to be intuitive. Because the computer removes you from your body, the body should be strongly engaged. Because the computer's activity takes place on the tiny playing fields of integrated circuits, the

encounter with the computer should take place in human-scaled physical space. Because the computer is objective and disinterested, the experience should be intimate.[49]

The work is amongst the first "interactive body" works where work and participants co-create each other's materiality. Participants look like they are dancing to a strange sonic composition, but are actually creating it in a real-time, response-driven environment, which uses a feedback loop in order to guarantee a non-repeatable experience. Rokeby turns the body into an improvisational jazz instrument that births both an experience of a non-lived and/or virtual embodiment as well as unique aural creations. It is through their interaction that "the 'spectator' is more than a participant, [in that they become] both participant in and creator of the simulation."[50]

Near the birth-time of video installation, Margaret Morse argued for kinaesthetic insights with regard to such work, and looked at how it is tied to the action (or inaction) of the viewer; she argued for the space between, the element of surprise, and thought as to how these works mediate a mediated culture: as interweaving the corporeal and conceptual. Morse argued that such work "allows the visitor rather than the artist to perform the piece," a participant "is the piece as its experiential subject, not by identification, but in body."[51] Morse pushed a "vocabulary for kinesthetic 'insights' for learning at the level of the body ego and its orientation in space."[52]

More recently, digital artist and scholar Ken Feingold has argued for the importance of touch, vision, and an affective body moving through space as integral to participation in, and "materialisation of the work."[53] These interactive works are then emergent, rather than extant pieces of art. "This is methexis in operation and not representation … meaning is produced as an embodied, situated, event."[54] The work takes on its own momentum, its own rhythm and intensity"[55] and through its "radical material performativity"[56] it produces techné as poeisis in Heidegger's sense of starting something on its way.[57]

Both Hansen and Massumi would juxtapose this observation with conceptual art to say, further, that this work does not involve the visualisation of an abstract idea, but the experiential and embodied enactment of a work. Here they would warn us to be weary of the logic of representational claims made on behalf of the image, and call for a new vocabulary of forms, rather than the transfer of old visual habits into a new mode.

Rokeby's work stretches the perceptions of the "natural" body. Playing with synaesthesia the work reworks both image and vision. It enables our experience of new forms of embodied human perception through our coupling with the computer. Here the computer is not a technical extension beyond body-brain, it is an augmentation for vision *and* a catalyst for bodily affection that allows the participant to touch the non-lived and the virtual. As such, it forces us to rethink the materiality of the work and the body, of the image and perception.

In our experience of digital immersion vision and body themselves becomes emergent. Digital imaging re-members that perception "takes place in a rich and evolving field to which bodily modalities of tactility, proprioception, memory, and duration ... make an irreducible and constitutive contribution,"[58] and inaugurates "a fundamental shift in the 'economy' of perception from vision to bodily affectivity."[59] In the words of Henri Bergson:

> [We] have to take into account the fact that our body is not
> a mathematical point in space, that its virtual actions are
> complicated by, and impregnated with, real actions, or, in
> other words, that there is no perception without affection.
> Affection is, then, that part or aspect of the inside of our
> body which we mix with the image of external bodies ...[60]

The body, in short, "has become the crucial mediator between information and form (image): the supplemental sensorimotor intervention it operates coincides with the process through which the image ... is created."[61] New media artworks, says Hansen, "literally compel us to "see" with our bodies."[62] On the one hand, is the affective and proprioceptive body, on the other, is an embodied (computer) prosthesis as catalyst. In the "digital middle," haptic vision emerges through a cooperative effort. Body and image mediate one another, and the locus of perception is between and of the two.

Media convergence under digitality, thus, increases rather than decreases the centrality of the body. Its processual features make interaction affective; and this affectivity is the condition for the emergence of, rather than result of, perception because affectivity is not a mode of perception - perception appeals to structures already constituted – but a relation, an interval and an incipience.

In his analysis of digital art Hansen correlates affectivity with a shift from visual space to haptic space, from the body as a locus of perception to the body as an affective source for haptic space. Here, drawing on, but radically rethinking, the understanding of the haptic in aesthetic discourse, he asserts that digital art makes primary the "affective and introceptive sensory processes that generate a 'haptic spatiality,' an internally grounded image of the body prior to and independent of external geometrical space."[63] This work solicits a haptic mode that requires that we "transform the haptic from a modality of vision (perception) into a modality of bodily sense (affection)."[64] Because these are computer-generated forms that we can only experience via 'analogy' as something felt in our bodies, they situate the viewer-participant between "the machinic space of the image and the normal geometric space of visual perception."[65] This work, therefore, opens a non-representational and non-visual space that fosters the affective and proprioceptive experience of the body and, as such, compromises a new form of 'affection-image'[66] - "a digital affection-image that unfolds in and as the viewer-participants's bodily intuition of the sheer alienness of these forms."[67]

Hansen turns to the work of new biologists such as Hans Jonas to show how the force-experience of touch and proprioception are "reality-generating" elements:

> Of particular interest will be the resonance between this deployment and philosophical and scientific work that has shown how vision is grounded upon touch. This resonance will serve to underwrite a neo-Bergsonist claim that virtual reality realizes an aesthetic function insofar as it couples new perceptual domains with the 'reality-conferring' experience of touch (or what Bergson calls 'affection').[68]

Jonas' work on vision and touch approximates, says Hansen, Bergson's on perception and affection in that vision, like perception, is defined by a certain detachment from its objects. "Likewise, as '*real* action,' affection approximates touch, since in both cases what is at stake is some kind of 'force-experience.'"[69] What Jonas then adds, according to Hansen, to the Bergsonist understanding is "a clarification of how touch-affection functions as the 'understructure' of vision-perception." And, as an understructure, allows us to account for the way in which it's potential "for generating 'reality' can be 'lent' to the most schematic artificial environments,"[70] thus constituting the post-visual topography of new media art. In order to develop Bergson's insights he again turns to the world of science (to argue with Dorion Sagan that recent psychoanalytic and phenomenological critiques of mind fail to disturb the "monolithic notion of 'the' body"[71]) and to the early phenomenology of Merleau-Ponty to explore the concept of "body schema" outside of the projective understanding - that is, of body image - derived from theorists such as Jacques Lacan, Judith Butler, and Elizabeth Grosz (which, he argues, is, in turn, derived from a Freudian source).

For Hansen, body-schema, "Far from being a mediator between the subject and the environment that would condition bodily activity," (and far from being an image as it is for Lacan, Butler and Grosz), "is cosubstantial with the activity of the body," and, as such, "is dynamically constitutive of the spatiality of the world."[72] Merleau-Ponty, argues Hansen, accords to spatiality a constitutive role in bodily experience. It is not simply an effect of representations, even bodily representations, as it is generative of space as well as the body.

> We might say that the body schema, like touch in the
> higher office accorded it by Jonas, forms an *infraempirical*
> form: one that is immanent to bodily life without being
> reducible to its empirical contents; moreover, like Jonas's
> conception, the body schema involves vision and touch
> (along with the other senses) in an irreducible co-
> functioning that, in and of itself, indicts the more abstract,
> visual conception of the body-image.[73]

This conception of the body-schema, says Hansen, resonates with the potential for thinking psychasthenia beyond the optical and projective. As with his mediation on the haptic, Hansen here advocates for the importance of the body as a filter and for the framing function of the embodied viewer participant, thereby drawing attention to the role of bodily affectivity in "producing and maintaining ... experience."[74]

Thinking alongside Hansen's work forms an important foundation for the thinking of the implicit body in interactive body art. However, while this work takes us outside of the crisis narratives of disembodiment and the recursive hegemony of visuality, it tends to embody a preformist understanding of enfleshment. As we will explore in the last part of this paper, assuming a body prior to interaction and/or subsuming touch into the haptic may run the risk of reiterating an implied reference to an *a priori* materiality. The implicit body, we are arguing, is not found in the co-mediation of body and image - in what Hansen calls the "digital middle" of body and prosthesis[75] - it is rather in the *of* of the relation of co-emergence; it is incipience of a not-yet extant flesh doubled with a not-yet finished artwork. Here, digitality engenders a horizon in spatial-temporal location (an interval) in which the advent of the subject is simultaneously the advent of the object: the implicit body.

It is also important to bear in mind Dag Petersson's caveat, a caution against regarding computers as prostheses. This, he says, would place computing under the dominance of reflection. Speaking of the work of the artist Marcaccio, he argues that

> knowledge does not form materiality; knowledge is formed
> by materiality... the body of movement [in interactive art]
> has a capacity for conceptualization that is not opposed to
> the materiality of the conceptualized. Instead of the
> traditional hierarchical order that arises from such a
> metaphysical opposition, materiality is a constellation of
> curves that conditions knowledge. But this knowledge has a
> particular capacity to understand and conceptualize the

materiality that conditions it. It is not expressible as reflection, but as composition.[76]

In a recent paper on interaction as relation, Nicole Ridgway, following Deleuze, argues that this meeting of materiality and concept in interactive art happens as a modality of performance rather than preformism: "not the realization of a preformed order, it is rather constant emergences; a dynamic and processual becoming; the interval of relation: unique, improvisational, reciprocal, participative, and affective."[77]

Rafael Lozano-Hemmer is a Canadian Mexican artist who develops 'Relational Architectures': large-scale, public, interactive installations that attempt to "transform urban spaces and create connective environments."[78] *Body Movies* (Lozano-Hemmer, 2000) casts an archive of thousands of images taken on the streets of cities all over the world, onto large buildings, using robotically controlled projectors located around a square. Huge floodlights wash out these photographs so they can only be seen when passers-by block out the whiteness with their shadows and reveal the projections underneath. Said shadows range in size from 2 to 22 meters, depending on a visitor's distance from the light.[79] When pedestrians have aligned their shadows with all the persona-images in the portrait, a new photograph is triggered, and the inter-play begins again. (See Figure 1)

In addition to Lozano-Hemmer's deployment of the haptic, his works effectively accomplishes Deleuze's time-image: severing the connections between situations and actions so that we experience "direct images of time."[80] What Deleuze finds in the time-image is a shift from "the Kantian subject to the decentred subject of postmodernity."[81] The time-image severs time from movement and space from location; it enables a viewer to draw out that part of an event that cannot be reduced to the limited image we see on screen. Lozano-Hemmer's work gives "discourse to the body ... the body is no longer the obstacle that separates thought from itself ... it is on the contrary that which it plunges into or must plunge into, in order to reach the unthought ... it forces us to think, and forces us to think what is concealed from thought."[82]

Figure 1. *Body Movies* (2000). Rafael Lozano-Hemmer. Interactive
installation and relational architecture, dimensions variable. Image
courtesy of the artist.

Body Movies enables a subject to experience the "present as a
thickness comprised of protentions and retentions," and a past not lived by
themselves.[83] Here, time is always a reserve, shot through with unanticipated
lines of action, potentialities. This time is always outside the image, in the
interval, and we "must ... allow the now of perception to be contaminated
with affection; we must identify that threshold with which perception of the
flux of an object affects itself and thus generates a supplementary perception,
a perception of the flux itself, time consciousness."[84]

Lozano-Hemmer encourages an engagement with the "alien
memories" present in his work, a "focus on the new temporal relationships
that emerge from the artificial situation ... [of] 'relationship-specific' art."[85]
It "ensures our openness to the preindividual, the preperceptual, the new, and
with it, the very future-directedness of the constitutively incomplete
present."[86] Like Leibniz's incompossible worlds, there "are innumerable
variations of the future virtually present in the moment we now inhabit."[87]

This is not memory content (politics of memory), but rather a
mediation of the between of perception and content: it both exceeds and
forms the preconditions of perception. Massumi says that in a space such as
Lozano-Hemmer's "energetic impulses... take place in every level of the
body... [through] proprioceptive receptors in our muscles and our joints."[88]
Action is performed and felt "in the flesh," and we have the "conversion of

the materiality of the body into an event, it is a relay between its corporeal and incorporeal dimensions. This is not yet a subject."[89]

In her *External Measures Series*, interactive artist Camille Utterback's goal is to "create an aesthetic system which responds fluidly and intriguingly to physical movement in the exhibit space."[90] *Untitled 5* uses body tracking and custom software, in order to turn the body into a painterly tool for an ever-changing visual feedback system. (See Figure 2)

> The existence, positions, and behaviors [sic] of various parts of the projected image depend entirely on people's presence and movement in the exhibit area.... Out of a working 'palette' of these animated marks, she composes an overall composition... Integral to the piece are the animated mark's cumulative interaction with each other over time... Engaging with this work creates a visceral sense of unfolding... is the experience of embodied existence itself.[91]

Figure 2. *Untitled 5* (2004). Interactive installation by Camille Utterback.
Interactive installation and software, dimensions variable. Image courtesy of
the artist

In his chapter, "The Affective Topology of New Media Art,"
Hansen builds on Deleuze's time-image, and correlative any-space-whatever,
and introduces what he calls the digital image, and the digital any-space-
whatever (DASW). The DASW is a space felt in the body rather than
experienced as visually extended apprehensible space.

The DASW is a process of "modulation that is operated by the
affective body itself."[92] By experiencing 'in our flesh' a projected digital
image of something that does not exist 'in the flesh,' the work provokes a
virtualization of the body. The DASW "lacks an 'originary' contact with a
space of human activity"[93] and instead becomes tactile when it "*takes place*

in the body of the spectator."[94] Hansen says that it is literally "the production of place within the body."[95]

Similar to Hansen's reading of *Skulls*,[96] *Untitled 5* "invests [in] proprioception as a fundamentally embodied and nonvisual modality of experience" that yields a bodily intuition of affective space that itself forms a "sensually produced resemblance" to "the forces of our digital technosphere."[97]

In its utilization of the DASW, *Untitled 5* also mobilizes the time-image. The organically animated inscriptions that others create, and leave behind, effect, and are affected by, new participants in the space. In other words, each new participants' feedback loop of space, flesh, time and embodiment co-emerges alongside past and future productions of the DASW.

step inside, a work by Nathaniel Stern (one of the authors of this chapter), is an immersive space that, like Utterback's *Untitled 5,* requires the interactions of its participants to emerge.[98] (See Figure 3) The piece "provokes us to re-think our selves," both in and as bodies, "as 'collage[s] in motion,' and... implies multiplicity and movement as intrinsic to our being; it asks viewers to explore the noise and stillness attendant on the performance of self." Stern describes the work on his web site as follows:

> When 'stepping inside' the 3 x 3 x 3 meter interaction space, viewer-participants are immediately confronted with an amplified and echoed trail of noise. This, they'll soon discover, is the sound of each footstep they take, of all the footwork in the room.
>
> A video camera, opposite them and connected to the step inside software, reads their bodies, and separates them out from the background. However, instead of a video mirror, they see only a profile, and are disallowed a frontal reflection. This left-hand 'projection' fills their 2-D forms with white noise. The amplitude of the echoed footsteps controls the video's opacity. The 'result' becomes a variable wave of embodied noise.

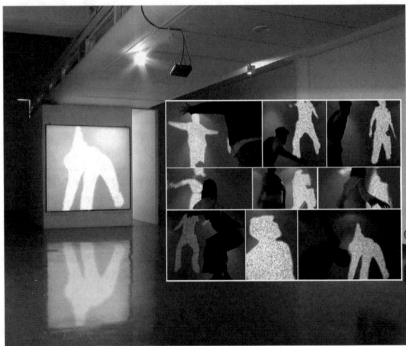

Figure 3. *step inside* (2004), 3x3x3 meters (inside, outside variable),
Nathaniel Stern. Installation view and performance documentation.

A wall panel text invites "participants to perform, direct, react to,
and interact with, the images and sounds they create. It asks them to try
walking, crawling, gesturing, with their bodies; play between silence and
tapping, scratching, audio-theatrics on the floor." Over time, Stern observes,
"I've watched astute experimenters adapt their bodies to direct their images
and sounds - a purposeful performative act."

The projection wall is actually a two-sided screen, so there are both
interactive participants, and more passive viewers engaging with the *step
inside* installation.

> External, non-participant viewers will also see the
> performer's projected image, but not their bodies or actions
> inside the space. They can only guess the intent of step
> inside's participant, who can likewise only attempt to
> promote a well-read representation of self. There's a literal
> wall between what we project with our performance, and
> how this might be perceived.

By cutting a performer off from his or her mirror image, as well as the external reactions of the audience, the work tempts us to leave behind reflection and self-consciousness and, rather, occupy a place of play and intimacy.[99]

A major difference between *step inside* and the aforementioned works is its literalized performance space. Participants "step inside," and attempt to perform body and space, while external viewers see only their projected images. There's a literal wall placed between performance (active participant) and perception (passive viewer). Hansen's DASW becomes a doubled gesture of affect and experience that is equally shared, but not equally produced, between the two.

Affect, says Massumi, is irreducibly bodily and autonimic, but it is not pre-social, pre-reflexive or unconscious: It is "asocial ... it includes social elements but mixes them with elements belonging to other levels of functioning and combines them according to a different logic [because] the trace of past actions, including a trace of their contexts, are conserved in the brain and the flesh, but out of mind and body."[100] *step inside* catalyzes a dissolution of those boundaries characteristic of the body as bearer of the looking agent, creating for the participant an experience of the temporary suspension of the differentiation between bodily interiority and spatial exteriority. As the visual (representational) boundaries between body and world dissolve in favour of an affective contact, what is brought to the fore is an energetic connection of the body with, and in, the world. At stake, are "the body and art as cooperative sites of potential resistance, counterinvestments in the automation of meaning, begging us to 'look again'."[101]

Here, elements from the social and the affective body are accented together, to make explicit the implicit, and versa vice. The "body" is an incipience and a tendency with regards to expression and action: it is not yet accomplished. Interactive art becomes an interface between explicit and implicit orders.[102]

The implicit bundles "potential functions, [it is] an infolding or contraction of potential interactions (intension). The playing out of those potentials requires an unfolding in three-dimensional space and linear time - extension as actualization; actualization as expression ... Implicit form ... is ... relationality autonomized as a dimension of the real."[103]

While this rethinking of embodiment (in particular in relation to vision and touch) and technology certainly moves us far beyond the old "Cartesian trick" of which Stone speaks, it tends to leave intact one of the most intractable aspects of the bodiliness of humanism; namely, an essential materiality that comes before (whether it be culture or language or ideology). In other words, the "body" of new media as explored by Hansen (and others) does not go far enough towards thinking a thinking body that Massumi says is both an *infolding* of potential interactions and an *unfolding* as actualization.

A body that is a "dimension of the real"[104] not a mirror of an *a priori* body that precedes construction and discourse; a body that is a figure of thought outside dominant Western conceptions and that can begin to speak of the relationality of materiality and the materiality of the body as event not thing.[105]

As anthropologist Marilyn Strathern points out, it would be a mistake to think we know what a body *is* when we see one.[106] For example, with regards to certain "feminist quests" to critique and alter dominant Western modes of embodiment she comments: "Sometimes, though, the discourse on the embodiment of vision seems to share with rather than obviate an earlier representationalist obsession with uncovering facts about the world. Embodiment is brought from under the text - a hidden influence is made explicit, and analysis invites us to see what we did not see before."[107] There may be, she argues, that in the visual play of embodiment there is nothing to be "uncovered" about embodiment "since the body is the medium - and deliberately incomplete."[108]

For Massumi what we have to do is think the body neither as naïve realism nor subjectivism, neither as concrete materialism nor linguistic text, but rather as "in motion ... in an immediate, unfolding relation to its own nonpresent potential."[109] From Deleuze, he asserts that this relation is real but abstract: "never present in position, only ever in passing ... a body in its indeterminacy (its openness to an elsewhere and otherwise than it is, in only here and now."[110] In a completely different context, cultural theorist Tom Cohen thinks through the work of Walter Benjamin to think materiality again - not as immediacy, immanence, closed ontology, or an ideality of a before - as an "as if" that precedes phenomenalization and mimesis. In other words, as a virtuality or site of emergence that is non-representational. [111]

What is common to all of these attempts is the thinking of thinking bodies and materiality that requires that we think anteriority and inscription again; that we think them not as anthropomorphised figures in which interiority is privileged. From de Man, Cohen argues that to achieve this thinking again we need to explore a radical exteriority (an "ex-scription") that does not deny the material nature of language and representation, but instead works with that which precedes the production of referents. This is not, he is at pains to show, the pre-discursive or extra-discursive (that is removed from power and mediations).[112] Here materiality is neither referential, nor subjective, nor mimetic, nor present as positivity. It is rather present as the non-figural, as trace, as movement, and as force.[113]

This thinking of the body - as we are arguing, this thinking of the body as implicit - means accepting the paradox that there is an incorporeal dimension to the body (a dimension that Hansen in his turn to biology, for example, occludes somewhat). For Massumi, it is with regards to this "real incorporeality of the concrete" that contemporary theory struggles,[114] and it is precisely here that interactive body art experiments in Manovich's sense.

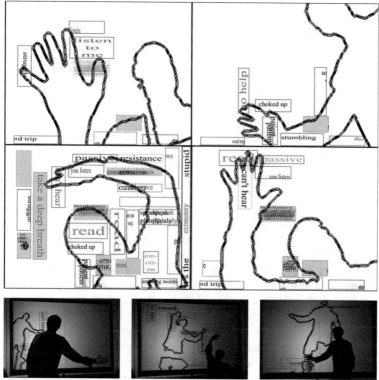

Figure 4. *stuttering* (2003), one channel interactive video installation, dimensions variable, Nathaniel Stern. Four screenshots and three documentation stills.

Nathaniel Stern's *stuttering* (2003) simultaneously involves viewers in the laborious, embodied experience of communication, and problematizes the abstraction of the body into language. Participants cross a threshold into the installation space, and walk across printed transparencies "containing quotes and passages about stutterers, situations in which stuttering, in its broadest sense, is common, and suggestions of when and where we should 'make stutters,' in order to break 'seamless' communication."[115] They are confronted with a projection that "is broken into a Mondrian-like mirror, where each sub-section, initialized by body-tracking software, animates one of the floor-found quotes; every animation is accompanied by an audio recitation of its text." (See Figure 4)

> *stuttering* thus creates a tense environment through its
> inescapable barrage of stuttering sound and visual
> stuttering: noise. Only by lessening their participation will
> the information explosion slow into an understandable text
> for the viewer.... Their minimal movements, and the
> phrases they trigger, literally create new meaning.

> The spaces between speaking and listening, between
> language and the body, add to the complex experience of
> communication. *stuttering* is not displaying data, but rather,
> pushing us to explore these practices of speaking and
> listening...

... and to do so in, and as, and with, our bodies. *stuttering* "suggests
that communication comes to and from us, in ways that even we do not fully
comprehend."

Most *stuttering* performances begin with a barrage of noise and
motion, but its participants inevitably slow, so as to hear the work's voice.
"The piece asks them not to interact," and often results in Bhuto-like
gestures, a heightened body-awareness, a flesh informed by and influential in
language, but that cannot be captured or experienced in full. *stuttering*
performs what Massumi says theory struggles with - the "real incorporeality
of the concrete" - and frames us as of the between and in relation.[116]

French philosopher Jean-Luc Nancy is one of the central thinkers to
take up this struggle, and thus, helps us understand the embodiment of
interactive art as implicit. For Nancy, our language and discourse are
remarkably inadequate with regards to the question of embodiment.[117] In *On
Touching - Jean Luc Nancy*, Derrida's moving tribute to Nancy, Derrida
asserts that the corpus of Nancy is an "implacable deconstruction of modern
philosophies of the body proper and the 'flesh'."[118]

> And all of the ways of thinking the 'body proper,' the
> laborious efforts to reappropriate what was believed to be
> unfortunately 'objectified' or 'reified;' all of the ways of
> thinking about the body proper are contortions of
> comparable scope: they end up with nothing but the
> expulsion of what one wished for.[119]

While Nancy does not reject ontology he does reject the traditional
questions of ontology - What is Being? What is Meaning? - instantiating
instead a questioning of the mode of questioning, and asking (with
Heidegger) "how it is that the world and we ourselves as part of the world are
accessible and available to meaning."[120] Nancy's unequivocal answer is:

"There is no meaning if meaning is not shared (*partagé*)."[121] And so too, as we will explore in more detail, there is no unified, integrated *a priori* "body" only bodiliness as shared, as being-with, and as exscribed.

In "Corpus," "Exscription" and "Being Singular Plural" especially, Nancy sets out to develop the relationship of embodiment to meaning and ethical obligation. In order to think the body not as an object of knowledge (acknowledging the irony and difficulty of this task), Nancy re-conceives of embodiment in terms of "tact," "touch," "spacing," and "being-with." However, even in the face of his own endeavours, Nancy reminds us that we are always faced with a double failure: "a failure to produce a discourse on the body, also the failure not to produce discourse on it."[122]

Despite the series of changing metaphors and figures by which the body has been explored (for example: plague, machine, flesh) the Western "philosophico-theological corpus of bodies" is still supported by "the spine of mimesis, of representation, and of the sign."[123] The body as sign (as thing) is grasped as an instrument or mechanism or expression of meaning, as something that attaches itself to sense rather than as sense. Because, Heidegger asserts, "...we do not 'have' a body; rather, we 'are' bodily."[124]

According to Nancy, "body" can, and has been, represented/signified in discourse but it has never been written as "neither substance, nor phenomenon, nor flesh, nor signification."[125] Nancy's "corpus" is one attempt to catalogue different modes of bodiliness and being in the world and with others in such a way that the body "implicitly emerges."[126] This "body" is "affected in and through the other, responds to the call of the other, is exposed to the other, as something (no-thing) unfinished and unaccomplished."[127] An implicit body, perhaps? A body not *of* essence or substance but *as* series? A series or multiplicity of contiguous states that is neither fullness nor nothingness, outside nor inside, part nor whole, function nor totality, but is rather "folded, refolded, unfolded, multiplied ... "[128]

Touch is principal to Nancy's thinking/writing of the ways in which bodies *are* meaning - the ways in which they are the limit and expression of meaning. Derrida tells us that for Nancy, "touch" is multivalent, incorporating both of the senses of the "sense of touch" and the sense of "to touch someone" - to come into contact with, to move, or affect. And, as we shall discuss in more detail below, touch here incorporates a paradoxical intangibility at the very heart of tactility.

For Derrida, the "corpus" of Jean-Luc Nancy both explicitly and implicitly, revisits and challenges the "haptocentric tradition"[129] within Western philosophy. This tradition, which has attempted to retain touch within sight and (as so many commentators have pointed out) asserts the supremacy of the visible - the incorporeal gaze and the disembodied knower - "obeys the eye only to the extent that a haptic intuitionism comes to accomplish it, fulfil it, and satisfy the intentional movement of a desire as the desire for presence."[130] The history of haptics reveals a similarity across shifts in approaches; namely, the exposure of visible form to the incorporeal look fulfilled by the promise of the immediacy of haptical intuitionism.[131] Even the great "idealist tradition" (from Plato to Berkeley, from Kant to Husserl) relies on figures of touch as the assurance of access to immediate presence. Pace Hansen, Nancy reads Western philosophy from Aristotle to Merleau-Ponty to show how it has characterized and/or understood touch as giving access to immediacy, as central to the provision of continuity and synchrony. This tradition accords to touch "*immediate* external perception" and sets it up as "co-extensive with the *living body*."[132] Touch is then what founds the two more objective senses; that is, sight and hearing.

In contradistinction to this tradition, Nancy, in his meditations on touch as "syncope" emphasizes touch as deferral, as a technical supplement (in the Derridean sense) in relation to bodiliness. In the haptocentric tradition the assurance of touch is on the side of the act or the actual, and this assurance institutes a resistance to the virtualization of touch. Nancy's work, on the other hand, explicitly intimates a thinking of the virtualization of touch.[133] "There is no 'the' body; there is no 'the' sense of touch; there is no 'the' *res extensa*."[134] Syncope allows instead the thinking of touch as virtual, as partaking of an originary separation or spacing, or what Nancy elsewhere calls *partagé* (a sharing out at the heart of all self-relation).[135]

Touch is, for Nancy, unparadoxically always a sharing *and* a separation, it is an instance of both contact *and* difference. It is touch with tact. We touch the limit of the other but the other is not immediately given to our touch. Our touching does not fix and confer meaning - bring to presence - the other as same, but is touching "in both a tangible and intangible sense, to gain access to her specificity, to be exposed to it, to be affected by it and to respond to it, not to subsume or annihilate it."[136]

This is an aesthetic model of contact that rules out the "fantasy of immediacy."[137] Here neither the artist is inscribed within the work, nor is the viewer-participant inscribed via the work - they are not touched/moved by the work in the sense that they have accessed the heart of the work, or felt it in all its fullness/presence.

Touch is syncopated - interrupted - or exscribed.[138] So too then, Nancy writes the body as "being-exscribed" [*l'être-excrit*], not only inscribed. The body comes to sense; it is not only an effect of signification. For Nancy, writing (or in our case, interactive body art) "exscribes meaning" and materiality every bit as much as it "inscribes significations." It exscribes meaning; that is, it shows that what matters "is outside the text, takes place outside writing ... to write [to interact] ... is to be exposed, to expose oneself, to this not-having."[139] What is exscribed, this outside, is neither a referent nor a material datum, nor is it the immanence of a thing-in-itself or the un-representable; it is instead a recognition that what is present in writing is there in its absence. As deconstruction shows us, the designation of identities or the representation of things as things (for example, bodies as objects of knowledge) can only be accomplished by "forgetting" that every representation is haunted by what Derrida calls the "impossible" - "that which exceeds and at the same time is at the heart of representational logic."[140] "By inscribing significations, we exscribe the presence of what withdraws from all significations, being itself (life, passion, matter ...).[141]

We could say then, paraphrasing Nancy, that bodies are not un-representable; they are rather presented as "exscribed." As such, bodies *take place* neither *in* discourse nor *in* matter ... they take place *at* the limit, *as the limit*."[142]

In touching and being touched (in interacting) we encounter the limit, or what Baross describes as the "in-between par excellence."[143] Since "to touch" is always "shared in-between," "touch is always already reciprocal ..."[144] "If we accept the claims made by Derrida and Baross that the 'self' comes into being only in and through the sensuous relation with the other, in and through exposure to the limit, to that which is not self (but is nevertheless internal to it), then we can see how touch,"[145] and by extension the body, is not simply an object of the self's perceiving consciousness (or an expression of its affective interiority), but is also a body in and through exscription.[146]

This figuration of touch moves us outside of the humanism of the tradition (of, for example, Merleau-Ponty where touch always privileges the human hand and in fact is central to the definition of humanness), and allows us to explore the non-human aspect of touch.[147] What sets Nancy's thinking apart in this regard "is the way it locates the technical supplement, the expropriation of the proper by the prosthetic, right at the phenomenological threshold of the lived or proper body."[148] "[I]t is the thinking of a technè of bodies as thinking of the prosthetic supplement [not addition] that will mark the greatest difference, it seems to me, between Nancy's discourse and other more or less contemporary discourses about the "body proper" or 'flesh'.[149] At the heart of touching is the intrusion of technics - the syncope [150] introduced by "body ecotechnics."[151] (This is a world of bodies "neither transcendental nor immanent.")[152]

In order for something to appear as a determinate something "there must exist a limit or border by which both the identity and difference of the thing are constituted."[153] Coming into touch with something - coming into contact with the limit that enables something to take place - produces a body. A body that is multiple in its circulation of touches and separations as it divides and relates to itself and others multiply.[154]

Being bodily (being bodily as implicit rather than explicit) implicates an exteriority "in 'me'"[155] but "everything is outside another outside."[156] Derrida elaborates: "the being outside an other outside forms the fold of a becoming inside of the first outside, and so forth."[157] "Hence, by reason of this folding, here are the *interiority-effects* of a structure made up of nothing but surfaces and outsides without insides."[158]

Being bodily here materializes in the in-between of interaction, but in a way that does not imply the immediate presence of a body. As Haraway argues, objects, be they bodies, affects, memories, or discourses, are boundary projects productive of, not just produced by, meanings, subjects, places, temporalities - the implicit body is a body that is emergent; a locus of exchange, force and semiosis.[159]

Notes

[1] L Manovich, 'The Poetics of Augmented Space' in A Everett and J Caldwell (eds), *New Media: Theories and Practices of Digitextuality*, Routledge, New York and London, 2002 <http://www.manovich.net/DOCS/augmented_space.doc> (viewed 5 July, 2005).

[2] DJ Bolter and D Gromala, *Windows and Mirrors: Interaction Design, Digital Art, and the Myth of Transparency*, MIT Press, Cambridge and London, 2003, p. 118.

[3] RA Stone, 'Will the Real Body Please Stand Up?' in M Benedikt (ed), *Cyberspace: First Steps*, MIT Press, Cambridge, 1991, np. <http://www.molodiez.org/net/real_body2.html> (viewed 5 July, 2005). Pre-eminent amongst these other scholars is Katherine Hayles, in for example, *How We Became Posthuman: Virtual Bodies in Cybernetics, Literature, and Informatics*, University of Chicago Press, Chicago, 1999.

[4] Bolter and Gromala, p. 119.

[5] Ibid.

[6] Ibid, p. 120.

[7] T Lenoir, 'Foreword' in *New Philosophy for New Media*, by MBN Hansen, MIT Press, Cambridge, MA, 2004, p. XIII.

[8] W Mitchell, *The Reconfigured Eye: Visual Truth in the Post-Photographic Age*, MIT Press, Cambridge, MA, 1992, p. 57, quoted in Lenoir, *New Philosophy for New Media*, p. XIV.

[9] V Sobchack, *Screening Space: The American Science Fiction Film*, Ungar Press, New York, 1987, in Stone, np.

[10] Lenoir in Hansen, pp. XVII-XVIII. Here, Lenoir uses a quote from Friedlich Kittler's *Gramophone, Film Typewriter* (Stanford University Press, Stanford, 1999), and poses Hansen and Kittler as polar opposites. While the

latter argues that convergence will lead to a disappearance of flesh and objects, the former finds embodiment accented.

[11] MBN Hansen, 'Seeing with the Body: The Digital Image in Postphotography,' *Diacritics,* Volume 31, No 4, 2001, p. 57.

[12] Ibid.

[13] Ibid.

[14] Ibid, p. 63.

[15] Ibid, p. 57.

[16] Ibid, p. 58. The turn from the optical to the haptical can be seen in a number of recent works that address in particular film and video, for example, in Jean Arnaud's analysis of filmmaker Michael Snow's work ('Touching to See,' *October*, Issue 114, Fall 2005, pp. 5-16) and Laura Marks' *Touch: Sensuous Theory and Multisensory Media* (University of Minnesota Press, Minneapolis, 2006). Marks explores the affective and embodied experience of new media objects as well as film and video. Like Hansen, she uses the work of Deleuze (and, thus, Bergson) to rethink the perceptual event. Interestingly, she extends the haptic-optical synaesthetic strategy to the sense of smell and to the erotic (in her meditation on the screen as skin). For Marks too, the notion of digital culture as immaterial and transcendent requires critique, and she extends many of her explorations of the haptic and material into the realm of code. She argues that alongside its embodiment vis-à-vis the viewer-participant, digital media embody a materiality at the level of code, as well as on social and global levels.

[17] Ibid, p. 57.

[18] Ibid, p. 58.

[19] Ibid.

[20] Ibid, p. 59.

[21] DN Rodowick, *Reading the Figural, Or, Philosophy after the New Media,* Duke University Press, Durham and London, 2001, p. 212.

[22] Ibid, p. 213.

[23] Ibid, p. 212.

[24] Bearing in mind of course the caveat that even theorists such as Derrida, Bourdieu, and Baudrillard, are all engaged, asserts Hansen in *New Philosophy for New Media*, in a common pattern of reduction - what he calls technesis, "in which a stated interest in embracing technological materiality is compromised in order to safeguard the integrity and autonomy of thought and representation" (p. XIX).

[25] N Ridgway, 'In Excess of the Already Constituted: Interaction as Performance' in D Riha (ed), *New Media and Technological Cultures,* Rodopi Press, Oxford, Forthcoming 2008.

[26] U Frohne and C Katti, 'Crossing Boundaries in Cyberspace? The Politics of 'Body' and 'Language' after the Emergence of New Media,' *Art Journal*, Volume 59 No 4, Winter 2000, p. 9.
[27] Ibid.
[28] R Schneider, *The Explicit Body in Performance*, Routledge, London, 1997, p. 2.
[29] Ibid.
[30] Ibid, pp. 1-3.
[31] Ibid.
[32] J Dolan, 'Bending Gender to Fit the Canon: The Politics of Production' in L Hart (ed), *Making a Spectacle: Feminist Essays on Contemporary Women's Theatre*, University of Michigan Press, Ann Arbor, MI, 1989.
[33] See E Fuchs, 'Staging the Obscene Body,' *TDR*, Volume 33 Number 1, 1989.
[34] See E Diamond, 'Mimesis, Mimicry, and the True Real,' *Modern Drama*, Volume 32 Number 1, 1989 and 'The Shudder of Catharsis' in A Parker and EK Sedgwick (eds), *Performance and Performativity*, Routledge, London, 1995.
[35] The Australian performance and new media artist Stelarc provides an interesting bridge between the performance of the explicit body in performance and digital art. From his earliest works with suspensions to his latest with prostheses, Stelarc has "with the use of harsh procedures [re-examined] the body itself and its representation." In "contact with new technologies" (B Kunst, 'Orifices and Fluids,' *Frakcija*, Numbers 6/7, January, 1998, <http://www2.arnes.si/~ljintima2/kunst/t-oaf.html> (viewed January 10, 2006), Stelarc blurs the distinction "between what an organism is and what a mechanism is" (M J Jones, 'Stelarc,' *Cyberstage*, Issue 1.2, Spring, 1995 <http://www.cyberstage.org/archive/cstage12/stelrc.htm> (viewed January 10, 2001).
[36] Hansen, *New Philosophy for New Media*, p. 614
[37] B Massumi, *Parables for the Virtual: Movement, Affect, Sensation*, Duke University Press, Durham, NC, 2002, p. 8.
[38] Ibid.
[39] M Morse, 'Video Installation Art: The Body, the Image, and the Space-in-Between' in D Hall & SJ Fifer (eds), *Illuminating Video*, Aperture, New York, 1991, p. 155. With regards to the contemporary use of the term "interactive" it is interesting to note, with Ann-Sargent Wooster, that "It was less than thirty years ago when the term *interactive* was first used in reference to computers, and it was used to describe the then breathtaking but now humble function of being able to interrupt a computer run" ('Reach out and Touch Someone: The Romance of Interactivity' in Ibid, p. 288). "Computers

have gone from the most basic form of interactivity, *interruption* to *selection* ... to the highest form of interactivity, *responsiveness* ..." (Ibid, p. 290; her emphasis).

[40] Brian Eno in K Kelly, 'Gossip is Philosophy: An Interview with Brian Eno,' *Wired,* Volume 3 Number 5, May, 1995 <http://www.wired.com/wired/3.05/eno.html?pg=4&topic=   > (viewed January, 2002).

[41] M Morse, *Virtualities: Television, Media Art, and Cyberculture*, Indiana University Press, Bloomington, Indianapolis, 1998, p. 16.

[42] K Feingold, 'The Interactive Art Gambit' in M Rieser and A Zapp (eds), *The New Screen Media: Cinema/Art/Narrative,* BFI Publishing, London, 2002), p. 127.

[43] P Levy, 'The Art of Cyberspace' in T Drucker (ed), *Electronic Culture: Technology and Visual Representation*, Aperture Press, London, 1996, p. 366.

[44] Morse, *Virtualities*, p. 34. It is important to remember that interactive computing more broadly has many downsides, as Lev Manovich clearly articulates in a recent chapter entitled "The Myth of Interactivity" (*The Language of New Media*, MIT Press, Boston, 2001). Here, interactivity (on, for example, the World Wide Web), at worst becomes a glorified delivery system for commodities, or at best allows us to be swept away by someone else's vision. Alongside these downsides, Manovich warns that too much facile interactivity inculcates a mistaken sense in the user that the world is fragmented, conditional and subject to their control. Jean Baudrillard too rings bells of warning with regards to the increase use of interactivity: "... we are threatened on all sides by interactivity ... distance is everywhere abolished" and so-called "tactile interactivity" ('Violence of the Virtual and Integral Reality,' *International Journal of Baudrillard Studies*, 2005 <http://www.ubishops.ca/baudrillardstudies/vol2_2/baudrillard.htm> (viewed January 27, 2006), p. 7) in which we "become actors" provides a closed feedback loop that destroys agency and "strangerness" (Ibid, p. 15).

[45] Ridgway, forthcoming 2008.

[46] Ibid, from her footnote: See for example, S Helmling, 'Constellation and Critique: Adorno's Constellation, Benjamin's Dialectical Image,' *Postmodern Culture*, Volume 14 Number 1, 2003 <http://www.aith.virginia/edu/pmc> (viewed February 4, 2004) and L Lawlor, *Imagination and Chance: The Difference Between the Thought of Ricoeur and Derrida*, State University of New York Press, New York, 1992.

[47] D Rokeby, 'David Rokeby - Media Installation Artist,' 2002 <http://homepage.mac.com/davidrokeby/home.html> (viewed January 16, 2006).

[48] D Rokeby, 'Very Nervous System,' 1990
<http://homepage.mac.com/davidrokeby/home.html> (viewed July 12, 2005).
[49] Ibid.
[50] Stone, p. 112.
[51] Morse, 'Video Installation Art,' p. 155.
[52] Ibid, p. 153.
[53] Feingold, p. 127.
[54] P Carter, *The Lie of the Land*, Faber & Faber, London, 1996, p. 84 cited in B Bolt, *Art Beyond Representation: The Performative Power of the Image*, I.B. Tauris, London and New York, 2004, p. 142.
[55] Bolt, p. 1.
[56] Ibid, p. 10.
[57] See, ibid, p. 61.
[58] Ibid, p. 59.
[59] Ibid, p. 71.
[60] H Bergson, *Matter and Memory*, NM Paul and WS Palmer (trans), Dover Philosophical Classics, 2004, p. 58 quoted in Ibid, p. 58.
[61] Hansen, 'Seeing with the Body,' p. 79.
[62] Ibid, p. 63.
[63] Lenoir in Ibid, p. XXIII.
[64] Hansen, *New Philosophy for New Media*, p. 229.
[65] Ibid, p. 203.
[66] Hansen's use of Deleuze's affection-image is discussed in more detail later in this chapter.
[67] Hansen, *New Philosophy for New Media*, p. 204.
[68] MBN Hansen, 'Embodying Virtual Reality: Touch and Self-Movement in the Work of Char Davies,' *Critical Matrix: The Princeton Journal of Women, Gender and Culture*, Volume 12 Numbers 1-2, 2001
<   http://www.immersence.com/publications/2001/2001-MHansen.html> (viewed 11 January, 2005).
[69] Ibid.
[70] Ibid.
[71] Hansen, 'Seeing with the Body,' p. 16.
[72] Hansen, 'Embodying Virtual Reality.'
[73] Ibid.
[74] Ibid.
[75] Ibid.
[76] D Petersson, 'On the Aesthetics of Digitization,' *NMEDIAC*, Volume 2 Number 1, Summer 2003
<http://www.ibiblio.org/nmediac/summer2003/digitization_files/index.html> (viewed July 11, 2005).

[77] Ridgway, forthcoming.

[78] R Lozano-Hemmer, 'Relational Architectures: Rafael Lozano-Hemmer,' 2003   <http://www.absolutearts.com/artsnews/2003/05/28/31074.html> (viewed July 8, 2005).

[79] R Lozano-Hemmer, 'Body Movies: Relational Architecture 6,' 2001 <http://www.absolutearts.com/artsnews/2001/08/31/29058.html>   (viewed July 8, 2005).

[80] D Toole, 'Of Lingering Eyes and Talking Things, Adorno and Deleuze on Philosophy since Auschwitz,' *Philosophy Today*, Volume 37 Numbers 3-4, Fall 1993, p. 232.

[81] Ibid.

[82] G Deleuze, *Cinema 2: The Time-Image*, H Tomlinson and R Galeta (trans), University of Minnesota Press, Minnesota, 1989, p. 173.

[83] Hansen, *New Philosophy for New Media*, p. 597. Note that here, Hansen is speaking of his "digital image," which, he contends, accomplishes a bit more than Deleuze's time-image. The digital image correlates affectivity with a shift from the body as a locus of perception to the body as affective source.

[84] Ibid, p. 602.

[85] Rafael Lozano-Hemmer quoted in J Sullivan, 'Body Movies - Experimental: An Interview with Rafael Lozano-Hemmer,' 2002 <http://www.idonline.com/imdr02/body.asp> (viewed July 8, 2005).

[86] Hansen, *New Philosophy for New Media*, p. 268.

[87] Rodowick, p. 228.

[88] Brian Massumi quoted in 'Brian Massumi: Entrevistado por Maria Teresa Cruz,' by MT Cruz, 2003
<http://www.interact.com.pt/interact8/entrev/entrev1.html> (viewed February 2, 2005).

[89] Massumi, *Parables for the Virtual*, p. 14.

[90] C Utterback, 'Untitled 5,' 2004
 <http://camilleutterback.com/untitled5.html> (viewed July 12, 2005).

[91] Ibid.

[92] Hansen, *New Philosophy for New Media*, p. 220.

[93] Ibid, p. 205.

[94] Ibid, p. 211.

[95] Ibid.

[96] Ibid. In Chapter Six, Hansen argues that *Skulls* (Robert Lazzarini, 2000), a digital sculpture that updates and dialogues with *The Ambassadors* (Hans Holbein, 1533) assists in production of the digital any-space-whatever.

[97] Ibid, p. 206.

[98] N Stern, 'step inside,' 2004,

<http://nathanielstern.com/works/interactive/step-inside.html> (viewed July 5, 2005). Until again noted, the following quotations are all my own text from this site.

[99] Paraphrased from N Ridgway, 'Between Text and Flesh,' *New York Arts Magazine*, September-October, 2006.

[100] Massumi, *Parables for The Virtual*, p. 30.

[101] Nathaniel Stern quoted in R Borland, 'Nathaniel Stern,' *Artthrob Artbio*, 2006 <http://www.artthrob.co.za/06feb/artbio.html> (viewed April 10, 2006). Originally sent in an email from Stern to Borland when the latter was writing this article, Stern is speaking to/with Hansen, who initially said, "the body becomes the site of a potential resistance to-or more exactly, a potential counterinvestment alongside of-the automation of vision" (Hansen, *New Philosophy for New Media*, pp. 6-7).

[102] Massumi, *Parables for the Virtual,* p. 37.

[103] Ibid, pp. 34-5.

[104] Ibid.

[105] Ibid, p. 14.

[106] In her examination of Hagen cosmology - in which persons are understood to be entities with relations integral to them - what is seen as a "body" is what is brought forth as an outcome of relations. Here, persons are "fractally realized" rather than essentially determined (M Strathern, 'The Limits of Auto-anthropology,' in A Jackson (ed), *Anthropology at Home*, Tavistock, London, 1995, p. 250.

[107] Ibid, p. 243.

[108] Ibid.

[109] Massumi, *Parables for the Virtual*, p. 4.

[110] Ibid, p. 5. Rosi Braidotti reads Deleuze and Nietzsche from a feminist perspective to explore embodiment as emergent, rhizomatic, inter-related, as an interface of forces. Here affectivity is pre-discursive - not as a "before" but as an unthought/non-thought within thought (See *Nomadic Subjects: Embodiment and Sexual Difference in Contemporary Feminist Theory*, Columbia University Press, New York, 1994). In thinking through the *a priori* and Nietzsche, Judith Butler asks which bodies come to matter and why. She reminds us of the importance of power (regulatory norms and matrices of intelligibility) and that materialization *takes place*: it is a series of practices that produces, over time, the effects of insides and outsides (boundaries, surfaces and depths). In her analyses, she provides a very cogent and provocative critique of constructionism and its instantiation of an *a priori* body: the tabula rasa body biological material that is inscribed by the social, cultural, political etc. (See *Gender Trouble: Feminism and the Subversion of Identity*, Routledge, New York, 1989).

[111] See T Cohen, *Ideology and Inscription: Cultural Studies after Benjamin, de Man and Bakhtin*, Cambridge University Press, Cambridge, 1998, p. 8 and p. 41.

[112] Ibid, p. 46.

[113] Ibid, p. 83 and p. 112.

[114] Massumi, *Parables of the Virtual*, p. 5.

[115] N Stern, 'stuttering,' 2003, <http://nathanielstern.com/works/interactive/stuttering.html> (viewed January 5, 2006). Until again noted, the following quotations are all my own text from this site.

[116] Massumi, *Parables for the Virtual*, p. 5. For an extended exploration of this discussion of the between (as interval and relation) see, N Ridgway, "Of the Between - Thinking the (Im)Mediate," in D Mayer-Dinkgräfe (ed), *Consciousness, Theatre, Literature and the Arts*, Cambridge Scholars Press, Cambridge, 2008.

[117] For example, Elizabeth Grosz in *Volatile Bodies: Towards a Corporeal Feminism* (Indiana University Press, Indiana, 1994) argues that we need to develop feminist concepts and understandings of embodied subjectivity that move beyond hierarchical binaries to better adequate language to embodiment. She argues that we use the concept of a field in rethinking the practices/technè of corporeality. Due to the scope of this essay, there is insufficient space to address the all-important question of gender, but will be taken up in a longer study.

[118] J Derrida, *On Touching – Jean-Luc Nancy*, C Irizarry (trans), Stanford University Press, Stanford, 2005, p. 63.

[119] JL Nancy, *Corpus*, Métailié, Paris, 1992, p. 9 quoted in Ibid, p. 63.

[120] D Perpich, 'Corpus Meum: Disintegrating Bodies and the Ideal of Integrity,' *Hypatia,* Volume 20 Number 3, Summer 2005, p. 76.

[121] Nancy in Ibid, p. 76.

[122] JL Nancy, *The Experience of Freedom*, Stanford University Press, Stanford, 1993, p. 190. Nancy acknowledges the tension inherent in recreating "the body" in discourse, but wants to eschew both the tendency to arrest the affect, plurality and difference of the body, and the tendency to reinstate the body as something un-representable. In the Western tradition he questions, Nancy reiterates what other scholars have discussed at length; namely, that the body has been set up as opposed to speech and language, and to thought and rationality. It has all too often been figured as ineffable, passive, material, un-representable, as, in other words, outside of or beneath language and sense. Those selfsame opponents to this figuration of the body have all too often reiterated this modality of thinking, he argues.

[123] Nancy, *Corpus*, p. 192.

[124] S Sorial, 'Heidegger, Jean-Luc Nancy, and the Question of Dasein's Embodiment: An Ethics of Touch and Spacing,' *Philosophy Today*, Volume 48 Number 2, Summer 2004, p. 218.

[125] Perpich, p. 78.

[126] Sorial, p. 221.

[127] JF Lyotard, *The Differend: Phrases in Dispute*, G Van Den Abbeele (trans), University of Minnesota Press, Minneapolis, 1988, p. 112 quoted in N Sullivan, 'Being-Exposed: 'The Poetics of Sex' and Other Matters of Tact,' *Transformations*, Issue 8, July 2004, <http://transformation.cqu.edu.au/journal/issue_08/article_04.shtml> (viewed 2, December 2005). What is at stake for Nancy in this is far-ranging and paramount: "The body, as an expression of meaning by virtue of its singularity or alterity, is the site where both ethics and community take place." (Sorial, p. 4) "We" is, for Nancy, the expression of a plurality. It expresses "'our' being divided and entangled: 'one' is not 'with' in some general sort of way ... a 'we', even one that is not articulated, is the condition for the possibility of each 'I'" (Nancy in Sorial, p. 3). While the subject is always singular, she is not isolated in her difference, but is rather exposed to, affected and touched by, the other. The central point here is that "we" are always in relation; we are always "I" as something shared with others, not as a fused collective or a collection of autonomous individuals. This is an ethical mode of being that seeks out and affirms otherness. It is a tactful, rather than tactical response, "the testimony of a fracture, of the opening onto the other," rather than "an experience conducted by an I in the quest for self-knowledge" (Lyotard in Sullivan, p. 6). Touch then, for Nancy, opens up spaces strangeness. An ethics that is tactful recognizes the need to maintain the space between self and other, and to make contact.

[128] Nancy, *Corpus,* np. quoted in Perpich, p. 82.

[129] Derrida, p. 41.

[130] Ibid, p. 39.

[131] Ibid, pp. 121-123. See also pp. 124-125 for a brief discussion of Deleuze and Guattari's attempt to open up a non-optical haptic.

[132] Ibid, p. 53.

[133] See Ibid, pp. 300-303 for Derrida's discussion of the virtualization of touch and the examples he gives from contemporary digital technologies.

[134] Nancy, *Corpus*, p. 104 quoted in Ibid, p. 288.

[135] M Naas, 'In and Out of Touch: Derrida's *Le Toucher*,' *Research in Phenomenology*, Volume 31, 2001, <http://proquest.umi.com.innopac.wits.ac.za:80/pqdweb?did=785059751&si d=2&Fmt=3&clinetid=57035&ROT=309&VName=PQD> (viewed 3 August 2005), p. 258. *Partagé* refers to both that which is shared in common and that

which is divided out or shared between. Here meanings (and/or bodies) are never monolithic; they are not *a priori* or intermediate. Rather meaning is *of* the relation between singular beings as a modality of "contiguity not continuity" (JL Nancy, *Being Singular Plural*, RD Richardson and A O'Byrne (trans), University of Stanford Press, Stanford, 2000, quoted in Perpich, p. 76.) Before "touching" or *partagé* there is no ordered whole (and touching is not the expression of a rational, intentional, self-reflexive consciousness). "All of being is in touch with all of being, but the law of touching is separation; moreover, it is the heterogeneity of surfaces that touch each other ... If 'to come into contact' is to begin to make sense of one another, then this 'coming' penetrates nothing; there is no intermediate and mediating milieu. Meaning is not a milieu in which we are immersed" (Ibid).
[136] Sorial, p. 78.
[137] M Crowley, 'Bataille's Tacky Touch,' *MLN*, Volume 119 Number 4, September 2004, p. 777.
[138] Ibid, p. 778.
[139] JL Nancy, 'Exscription,' in Brian Holmes et al (trans), *The Birth to Presence*, Stanford University Press, Stanford, 1993, p. 338.
[140] Sullivan, p. 1.
[141] Nancy, 'Exscription,' pp. 338-9.
[142] Our emphasis. Nancy, *Corpus*, quoted in Perpich, p. 79. Perception, for Nancy, not only opens onto the embodied (affectivity in Hansen's sense) but also to the reciprocal "of" of relation (in other words, an affect that traverses the inside - outside binary, and one that is not only located within an extant/*a priori* body).
[143] Z Baross, 'The (False) Gifts of Writing,' *New Literary History*, Volume 31 Number 3, 2000, p. 437 quoted in Sullivan, p. 7.
[144] Ibid.
[145] Ibid.
[146] While inscription and exscription are mutually constitutive they are also incommensurable: Bodies are first "to be touched. Bodies are first masses, masses offered without anything to articulate, without anything to discourse about ... discharges of writing rather than surfaces to be covered in writings. Discharges, abandonments, retreats. No 'written bodies,' no writing on the body, nor any of this graphosomatology into which the mystery of the Incarnation and of the body as pure sign of itself is sometimes converted 'modern style'. For indeed, the body is not a locus of writing ... it is always what writing exscribes. In all writing a body is traced, is the tracing and the trace - is the letter, yet never the letter ... a body is what cannot be read in writing ... it is by touching the Other that a body is a body ..." (Nancy, *Corpus*, p. 204).

[147] In "Tangent Three," Derrida critiques Merleau-Ponty for figuring touch as direct contact with the other's body and, thereby, the appropriation of the other's alterity. In the classic haptocentric move, Merleau-Ponty also conflates sight and touch occasionally, while subordinating touch to sight for the most part. (Although there are later Merleau-Ponty's who deliver this critique to earlier Merleau-Ponty's, the latter work still, for Derrida, stumbles on the "anthropology of touch" (Naas, p. 560). In Tangents Four and Five, Derrida looks at the work of Chrétien and Franck who are credited with radicalizing our understanding of touch and "showing the way the non-proper (what is other or from the other) always interrupts the proper of 'my flesh' [thereby rupturing] the auto-affection of a phenomenology" but ultimately end up affirming the privilege of man's hand by not taking into account "the role of the techno-prosthesis located as the 'heart' of the so-called 'lived' or 'body proper'" (Ibid).

[148] Naas, p. 559.

[149] Derrida, pp. 96-7.

[150] Ibid, p. 113 and p. 273.

[151] Ibid, p. 127. Derrida most often, although not always, uses Nancy's terms - the 'techne of the body' or 'ecotechnics' - instead of those more commonly used - 'the technical,' of techne, and 'technology' or even 'the question of technics' - "in order to follow him and warn against the general-singular ('the' technical) and against the modern doxa always prone to misusing this conceptual bent or alibi." Nancy in "A Finite Thinking" calls for vigilance with regards 'technology' as a 'fetish-word': "There is no 'the' … here … there is not 'the' technical, merely a multiplicity of technologies." Earlier he has marked his analysis with these two other propositions: "'The' technical is nothing other than the 'technique' of compensating for the nonimmanence of existence in the given"; or: "'The' technical - understood this time as the 'essential' technicity that is also the irreducible multiplicity of technologies - compensates for the absence of nothing; it fills in for and supplements nothing'" (Ibid, pp. 286-7).

[152] Ibid, p. 129.

[153] Perpich, p. 6.

[154] Is this problematic for bodies that have had the privilege of being seen as self-identical and whole? Nancy, as so many, pays scant attention to gender, for example. But, argues Perpich, his account address "those bodies considered borderline without having to position them at the outer limits (or, for that matter, at the center)" (p. 7). His work also augments the work of feminist philosophers such as Judith Butler in its movement beyond the a priori instantiation of social constructionism - the sexed body that is prior to the social inscription of gender.

155 Nancy, *Being Singular Plural*, quoted in Perpich, p. 76.
156 Nancy, unaccredited paraphrase in Derrida, p. 14.
157 Derrida, p. 14.
158 Ibid.
159 DJ Haraway, 'Situated Knowledges: The Science Question in Feminism and the Privilege of Partial Perspective' in *Simians, Cyborgs, and Women: the Reinvention of Nature*, Routledge, New York, 1991, p. 190.

Bibliography

Baross, Z., 'The (False) Gifts of Writing,' *New Literary History*, Volume 31 Number 3, 2000, pp. 435-458.

Bergson, H., *Matter and Memory*. NM Paul and WS Palmer (trans), Dover Philosophical Classics, 2004.

Bolt, B., *Art Beyond Representation: The Performative Power of the Image*. I.B. Tauris, London and New York, 2004.
Bolter, DJ and Gromala, D., *Windows and Mirrors: Interaction Design, Digital Art, and the Myth of Transparency*. MIT Press, Cambridge and London, 2003.

Borland, R., 'Nathaniel Stern,' *Artthrob Artbio*, 2006
<http://www.artthrob.co.za/06feb/artbio.html> (viewed April 10, 2006).

Carter, P., *The Lie of the Land*. Faber & Faber, London, 1996.

Cohen, T., *Ideology and Inscription: Cultural Studies after Benjamin, de Man and Bakhtin*. Cambridge University Press, Cambridge, 1998.

Crowley, M., 'Bataille's Tacky Touch,' *MLN*, Volume 119 Number 4, September 2004, pp. 766-780.

Cruz, MT., 'Brian Massumi: Entrevistado por Maria Teresa Cruz,' 2003
<http://www.interact.com.pt/interact8/entrev/entrev1.html> (viewed February 2, 2005).

Deleuze, G., *Cinema 2: The Time-Image*. H Tomlinson and R Galeta (trans), University of Minnesota Press, Minnesota, 1989.

Derrida, J., *On Touching – Jean-Luc Nancy*. C Irizarry (trans), Stanford University Press, Stanford, 2005.

Diamond, E., 'Mimesis, Mimicry, and the True Real,' *Modern Drama*, Volume 32 Number 1, 1989, pp. 58-72.

_____, 'The Shudder of Catharsis' in A Parker and EK Sedgwick (eds), *Performance and Performativity*. Routledge, London, 1995, pp. 152-171.

Dolan, J., 'Bending Gender to Fit the Canon: The Politics of Production' in L Hart (ed), *Making a Spectacle: Feminist Essays on Contemporary Women's Theatre*. University of Michigan Press, Ann Arbor, MI, 1989, pp. 318-344.

Feingold, K., 'The Interactive Art Gambit' in M Rieser and A Zapp (eds), *The New Screen Media: Cinema/Art/Narrative*. BFI Publishing, London, 2002).

Frohne U. and Katti, C., 'Crossing Boundaries in Cyberspace? The Politics of 'Body' and 'Language' after the Emergence of New Media,' *Art Journal*, Volume 59 No 4, Winter 2000, pp. 9-13.

Fuchs, E., 'Staging the Obscene Body,' *TDR*, Volume 33 Number 1, 1989, pp. 33-58.

Hansen, MBN., *Embodying Technesis: Technology Beyond Writing*. The University of Michigan Press, Ann Arbor, 2000.

_____, 'Seeing with the Body: The Digital Image in Postphotography,' *Diacritics*, Volume 31, No 4, 2001, pp. 54-84.

_____, 'Embodying Virtual Reality: Touch and Self-Movement in the Work of Char Davies,' *Critical Matrix: The Princeton Journal of Women, Gender and Culture*, Volume 12 Numbers 1-2, 2001, pp. 112-147.
<   http://www.immersence.com/publications/2001/2001-MHansen.html> (viewed 11 January, 2005).

_____, *New Philosophy for New Media*. Foreword by T Lenoir, MIT Press, Cambridge, MA, 2004.

Haraway, DJ., 'Situated Knowledges: The Science Question in Feminism and the Privilege of Partial Perspective' in *Simians, Cyborgs, and Women: the Reinvention of Nature*. Routledge, New York, 1991, pp. 183-201.

Kelly, K., 'Gossip is Philosophy: An Interview with Brian Eno,' *Wired*, Volume 3 Number 5, May, 1995 http://www.wired.com/wired/3.05/eno.html?pg=4&topic=   (viewed January, 2002).

Kittler, F., *Gramophone, Film Typewriter*. Stanford University Press, Stanford, 1999.

Levy, P., 'The Art of Cyberspace' in T Drucker (ed), *Electronic Culture: Technology and Visual Representation*. Aperture Press, London, 1996.

Lozano-Hemmer, R., 'Body Movies: Relational Architecture 6,' 2001 <http://www.absolutearts.com/artsnews/2001/08/31/29058.html>   (viewed July 8, 2005).

_____, 'Relational Architectures: Rafael Lozano-Hemmer,' 2003 <http://www.absolutearts.com/artsnews/2003/05/28/31074.html> (viewed July 8, 2005).

Lyotard, JF., *The Differend: Phrases in Dispute*. G Van Den Abbeele (trans), University of Minnesota Press, Minneapolis, 1988.

Manovich, L., 'The Poetics of Augmented Space' in A Everett and J Caldwell (eds), *New Media: Theories and Practices of Digitextuality*. Routledge, New York and London, 2002, pp. 75-91. <http://www.manovich.net/DOCS/augmented_space.doc> (viewed 5 July, 2005), pp. 75-91.

Massumi, B., *Parables for the Virtual: Movement, Affect, Sensation*. Duke University Press, Durham, NC, 2002.

Mitchell, W., *The Reconfigured Eye: Visual Truth in the Post-Photographic Age*. MIT Press, Cambridge, MA, 1992.

Morse, M., 'Video Installation Art: The Body, the Image, and the Space-in-Between' in D Hall & SJ Fifer (eds), *Illuminating Video*. Aperture, New York, 1991, pp. 153- 167.

_____, *Virtualities: Television, Media Art, and Cyberculture*. Indiana University Press, Bloomington, Indianapolis, 1998.

Naas, M., 'In and Out of Touch: Derrida's *Le Toucher*,' *Research in Phenomenology*, Volume 31, 2001, pp. 258-60 <http://proquest.umi.com.innopac.wits.ac.za:80/pqdweb?did=785059751&sid=2&Fmt=3&clinetid=57035&ROT=309&VName=PQD> (viewed 3 August 2005).

Nancy, JL., *Corpus*. Métailié, Paris, 1992.

_____, 'Exscription,' in Brian Holmes et al (trans), *The Birth to Presence*. Stanford University Press, Stanford, 1993.

_____, *The Experience of Freedom*. Stanford University Press, Stanford, 1993.

Perpich, D., 'Corpus Meum: Disintegrating Bodies and the Ideal of Integrity,' *Hypatia,* Volume 20 Number 3, Summer 2005, pp. 75-91.

Petersson, D., 'On the Aesthetics of Digitization,' *NMEDIAC,* Volume 2 Number 1, Summer 2003 <http://www.ibiblio.org/nmediac/summer2003/digitization_files/index.html> (viewed July 11, 2005).

Ridgway, N., 'In Excess of the Already Constituted: Interaction as Performance' in D Riha (ed), *New Media and Technological Cultures*. Rodopi Press, Oxford, Forthcoming 2008.

_____, 'Between Text and Flesh,' *New York Arts Magazine*, September-October, 2006.

Rodowick, DN., *Reading the Figural, Or, Philosophy after the New Media*. Duke University Press, Durham and London, 2001.

Rokeby, D., 'Very Nervous System,' 1990 <http://homepage.mac.com/davidrokeby/home.html> (viewed July 12, 2005).

_____, 'David Rokeby - Media Installation Artist,' 2002 <http://homepage.mac.com/davidrokeby/home.html> (viewed January 16, 2006).

Sobchack, V., *Screening Space: The American Science Fiction Film.* Ungar Press, New York, 1987.

Sorial, S., 'Heidegger, Jean-Luc Nancy, and the Question of Dasein's Embodiment: An Ethics of Touch and Spacing,' *Philosophy Today*, Volume 48 Number 2, Summer 2004, pp. 216-230.

Stern, N., 'stuttering,' 2003,
http://nathanielstern.com/works/interactive/stuttering.html (viewed January 5, 2006).

_____, 'step inside,' 2004, <http://nathanielstern.com/works/interactive/step-inside.html> (viewed July 5, 2005).

Stone, RA., 'Will the Real Body Please Stand Up?' in M Benedikt (ed), *Cyberspace: First Steps.* MIT Press, Cambridge, 1991, pp. 81-118. <http://www.molodiez.org/net/real_body2.html> (viewed 5 July, 2005).

Strathern, M., 'The Limits of Auto-anthropology,' in A Jackson (ed), *Anthropology at Home.* Tavistock, London, 1995, p. 59-67.

Sullivan, J., 'Body Movies - Experimental: An Interview with Rafael Lozano-Hemmer,' 2002   <http://www.idonline.com/imdr02/body.asp> (viewed July 8, 2005).

Sullivan, N., 'Being-Exposed: 'The Poetics of Sex' and Other Matters of Tact,' *Transformations*, Issue 8, July 2004,
<http://transformation.cqu.edu.au/journal/issue_08/article_04.shtml> (viewed 2, December 2005).

Toole, D., 'Of Lingering Eyes and Talking Things, Adorno and Deleuze on Philosophy since Auschwitz,' *Philosophy Today*, Volume 37 Numbers 3-4, Fall 1993, pp. 227-246.

Utterback, C., 'Untitled 5,' 2004
<http://camilleutterback.com/untitled5.html> (viewed July 12, 2005).

Cyborg Goddesses: The Mainframe Revisited

Leman Giresunlu

Abstract
   In current popular film media, human technology interface representations are often characterised through the female gender in the role of both creator and terminator, lending an omnipotent attribute to this gender. The use of godly female images in the service of human-to-machine technology interfaces is also reminiscent of both major technological innovations and well-known vessels in history and literature, all of which took names with feminine qualities. Thus, the mythological goddess cult's manifestations evident in Anatolia and neighboring regions inspired echoes in classical American literature as well as in current popular films. This affords a comparative cultural perspective evolving towards futuristic openings.
   Current science fiction movies employ the omnipotent female image with a dual capacity of realizing good and evil combined into one, as evinced in several well-established works, *Lara Croft: Tomb Raider*, *Lara Croft: the Cradle of Life*, *Resident Evil*, *Resident Evil: Apocalypse*, *Resident Evil: Extinction*, *Minority Report*, *I Robot* and *Ghost in the Shell*. These movies incite critical questioning of faith, science, technology, self and identity formation in race, class and gender from a feminist perspective and as an alternative to conventional codifications of power.

Key Words: American Literature, Archaeology, Mythology, Popular Culture, Science Fiction, Cyborg, Goddess, Donna Haraway, Hollywood.

*****

1.   Introduction

   I will analyze gender articulations along race and class lines in human machine interfaces seen in recent movies such as, *Lara Croft: Tomb Raider, Lara Croft: The Cradle of Life, Resident Evil, Resident Evil: Apocalypse, Minority Report, I Robot, Ghost in the Shell, Ghost in the Shell 2: Innocence*. In these examples, human-machine interfaces manifest through the female gender as a creator, and terminator, lending a godly attribute to the gender. The choice of an omnipotent female image to negotiate the human machine interface is reminiscent of significant technological inventions or well-known vessels in history and literature, christened with names projecting feminine aspects. Almost any quick glance at classic and recent works provides a rather long list of such examples: the vessels Rachel and Pequod in Herman Melville's *Moby Dick*; the mainframe computer Red Queen in the movie *Resident Evil*, where, additionally, Queen's holographic representation emerges in the shape of a little girl called Alice; the mainframe computer V.I.K.I sporting a female look, and voice in the movie *I Robot*; in *Minority Report* the Pre-Crime system's inventor, the female botanist; and, in the same film, the pre-cog Agatha, another key female figure. In this context the movies *Ghost in the Shell* and *Ghost in the Shell* 2: *Innocence* relate questions of self and identity formation played out in the character of a cyborg woman. Even in titles, the gender allusion carries; the Latin definition of "Matrix" is the "female animal used for breeding, parent plant, from matr-, mater" or "something within or from which something else originates, develops, or takes form."[1] With the presence of so many female figures as major carriers and symbols of technology in science fiction films, we might probe their conceptualization as embodiments of good and evil combined into one.

2.   The *Cyborg Goddess* versus Donna Haraway's *Cyborg: A Manifesto* in Question

The science fiction story context, generally presenting a clean and cold medium, might be said to complement for the inadequacies of the human body's watery environment, and recent science fiction movie media further supplements female presence with superior human qualities. To this end, I probe how female images in recent science fiction films seem to appear laden with capacities for good and evil, amalgamated into one. In this duality, such female representations often function to pose questions of faith, of science and of technology from a feminist perspective and pose an alternative to conventional androcentric codifications of power. Technologically enhanced bodies, cyborgs, which appear in both genders, tend to possess superlative qualia from both worlds, human and machine. The cyborg as a concept thus constitutes a potential basis for speculative dialogue between the sciences and the arts, promising to offer up hope within artistic imagination as well as holding up a sign of impending scientific advancement. In short, we might take cyborg imagery as the humanities' and sciences' meeting point, a site where art's play with ambiguities, paradoxes, and irony meet with science's need for precision.

Dani Cavallaro analyzes the cyborg as a principally masculine body and points out both *pure* and *impure* qualities of the cyborg. Indicating how powerful female characters appear to be held in check as "an ideal to aspired to by women who are still subjected to injustice"[2], Cavallaro identifies the cyborg body as a male body and views the cyborg embodying *two opposite fantasies*:

> that of the pure body and that of the impure body. On one level, the cyborg presents a sealed, clean, hard, tight and uncontaminated body. It offers the ideal of a body that does

not eat, drink, cry, sweat, urinate, defecate, menstruate, ejaculate: a body that does not suffer any illnesses and does not die. This Puritanical body without secretions and indiscretions incarnates a fantasy of omnipotence. The mechanical parts that replace ordinary anatomical parts are supposed to enhance the body's power potential and repudiate its association with *leaky* materiality.[3]

In addition to the variants of masculine appearance, cyborgs have also assumed the ideal form of the full-fledged, voluptuous female persona. To radical feminists who object to objectifications of the female body, such one-dimensional characterization may be problematic. Against this hyperbole, Donna Haraway's genderless cyborg body, possessed of an oppositional voice, strives for recognition in the manifold realms of technology, science and politics. As it is, Haraway's cyborg is both highly topical and timeless, being both a response to the Star Wars space project of the1980s in the United States, as well as a specific statement on the attitudes of the new right towards women in the same era, and in general:

> Cyborg imagery can suggest a way out of the maze of dualisms in which we have explained our bodies and our tools to ourselves. This is a dream not of a common language, but of a powerful infidel heteroglossia. It is an imagination of a feminist speaking in tongues to strike fear into the circuits of the supersavers of the new right. It means both building and destroying machines, identities, categories, relationships, space stories. Though both are bound in the spiral dance, I would rather be a cyborg than a goddess.[4]

Differently than Haraway's oppositional cyborg, I insist upon the *cyborg goddess* imagery, one more amenable to a playful stance. The *cyborg goddess* image in the contemporary science fiction film appears as a being capable of inflicting pain and pleasure simultaneously, echoing historical roots of the Judeo-Christian tradition of the creator god, a being equally capable of loving and destroying. Gradually all through history of technology, such belief system produced a human understanding striving to become a godly creator willing to attain redemption while reaching perfection:

> ...the religious roots of modern technological enchantment extend a thousand years further back in the formation of Western consciousness, to the time when the useful arts

first became implicated in the Christian project of redemption. The worldly means of survival were henceforth turned toward the other-worldly end of salvation, and over the next millennium, the heretofore most material and humble activities became increasingly invested with spiritual significance and a transcendent meaning—the recovery of mankind's lost divinity.[5]

As David F. Noble illustrates in his work, the *Religion of Technology* the "legacy of the religion of technology is still with us." He further remarks:

> Like the technologists themselves, we routinely expect far more from our artificial contrivances than mere convenience, comfort, or even survival. We demand deliverance. This is apparent in our virtual obsession with technological development, in our extravagant anticipations of every new technical advance—however much each fails to deliver on its promise—and most important, in our utter inability to think and act rationally about this presumably most rational of human endeavors. [...] (the religion of technology) is offered in the hope that we might learn to disabuse ourselves of the other-worldly dreams that lie at the heart of our technological enterprise, in order to begin to redirect our astonishing capabilities toward more worldly and humane ends."[6]

As David F. Noble illustrates, the religious rhetoric that gave impetus to technologic developments in the western mind, secularizes through time especially in the positivistic understanding of the socialists (Owenites). However, the religious rhetoric is still visible in many parts of space related, atomic and genetic research in the United States. Noble in the final chapter of his book also illustrates his awareness of the predominant masculine influence within technological research intertwined with the religious rhetoric.[7] In this respect Noble quotes from Carol Cohn's study "Nuclear Language" (1987) where she "described the vivid vocabulary of male competition and sexual domination that routinely came into play in discussion of nuclear warfare, and the overt phallic imagery of missiles."[8] Brian Easlea argues that the field of the nuclear is a rather womanless environment which "appropriates" "female powers of procreation" in order to express "the development and detonation of atomic and hydrogen bombs from the beginning" with "recurring pseudo-maternal metaphors."[9]

In this respect, the current *cyborg goddess* imagery that I propose in this study may appear to embody the replica of a male-centric understanding of science and technology as progress: an understanding which appropriates into its womanless world feminine metaphors as the *goddess.* However the *cyborg goddesses,* as represented in the films and literature work, which I analyze in this study is a display of the changing perceptions in regard of female representations in film media through time. Especially in current film media a transformative aspect is more and more visible. Differently than a cyborg only understanding as suggested by Dana Haraway for matters of offering a way out from the duality, the *cyborg goddess* imagery instead purports to achieve the very transformative aspect, by means of compensating for the spiritual side deemed to be missing within the high-tech environment. In this respect R. L. Rutsky in his work *High Techne: Art and Technology from the Machine Aesthetic to the Posthuman* points out to recent conditions regarding the relationship between the high-tech and the spiritual:

> In an age of high tech, however, this return of the magical or the spiritual in representations of technological life no longer seems to be seen as simply monstrous or threatening. Thus, for example, movements and discourses as various as techno-paganism, "new-edge" science, cyber-shamanism, and rave culture have drawn on magical, spiritual, and metaphysical discourses to figure their own relation to a technology, to a techno-cultural space or world, that often seems to have taken on a life of its own. Techno-pagans, for example, see the techno-cultural world as magical, as inhabited by unseen forces, spirits, gods. They therefore interact with technology not simply as an instrument or tool, but as something with its own autonomy or agency, which is not simply under their control. Yet, they do not then see this technology simply as dangerous, "out of control," or monstrous. Their relation to it is more a matter of interaction, cooperation, respect—of allowing that technological agency to go on in its own terms and even to be guided by it. [10]

However earlier Haraway's ironic dream divided the spiral dance of the cyborg, and the goddess from each other in saying: "though both are bound in the spiral dance, I would rather be a cyborg than a goddess."[11] Haraway's stance was for purposes of political positioning especially contingent with an evolving understanding of multiculturalism in the United States in the 1980s which was needy of reconciliation within a technological rhetoric as a corrective for the deficiencies of a self and other dialectic. In this respect Haraway's relativistic and hybrid cyborg is a genderless, non-totalizing entity that is wary of all boundaries as well as their "deconstruction." However otherwise than Haraway's argument, with the goddess pertaining to the mythological, and the cyborg to the technological as separate, they both appear recombined in one catering to current fantasies awaiting "entertainment" in current film media. Therefore it appears that a spiral dance of entertainment and fun combined along with information and knowledge is inseparable from each other. Such inseparable dance partners as well as the *cyborg* and the *goddess* intertwined is a reminder of a DNA spiral with multiple combinations. This visual, literal as well as metaphoric imagery laden with a potential for cultural exchange obviously differs from what a singular oppositional cyborg may propose as a political entity. One hopes that the *cyborg goddess* may carry on the promise of multiple sets of performative exchanges to the future. However to argue for the potentialities of the self and the other from the perspective of mere dynamics of oppression in the current technological era does not appear as a viable cue anymore. At this point Haraway seems to discard diversified exchanges among different individuals as a root for a multiplicity of performances in the sciences and culture. Instead, her wary yet deconstructive stance which places and removes the individual at different positions of self-hood renders this opening altogether obsolete by proposing it as a mere illusion only:

> The self is the One who is not dominated, who knows that by the service of the other, the other is the one who holds the future, who knows that by the experience of domination, which gives the lie to the autonomy of the self. To be One is to be autonomous, to be powerful, to be God; but to be One is to be an illusion, and so to be involved in a dialectic of apocalypse with the other. Yet to be other is to be multiple, without clear boundary, frayed, insubstantial. One is too few, but two are too many. High-tech culture challenges these dualisms in intriguing ways. It is not clear who makes and who is made in the relation between human and machine. It is not clear what is mind and what body in machines that resolve into coding practices. In so far as we know ourselves in both formal discourse (for example, biology) and in daily practice (for example, the homework economy in the integrated circuit), we find ourselves to be a cyborg, hybrids, mosaics, chimeras. Biological organisms have become biotic systems, communications devices like others. There is no fundamental, ontological separation in our formal knowledge of machine and organism, of

technical and organic. [...] One consequence is that our
sense of connection to our tools is heightened.[12]

Haraway appears to object the illusory aspect of the oneness of the
autonomous self and seems to evade the dialectic of apocalypse for the
benefit of the other. Apocalypse already inhere the religious connotation,
which appears as the impetus in the forward move of the history of the
sciences in western thinking. At this point Haraway appears to intertwine her
denial of the sciences' historical condition and its underlying mindset along
with a postmodernist sensitivity supportive of the other. In this respect she
seems to position the other in regard of a self which should be wary of the
sciences' historical evolution but at the same time cognizant of its new others
who are in need to reconcile with the high–tech center. Therefore Haraway's
position appears to be part of integrating the disenfranchised into the
scientific center. Although quite inspiring and wrought with a certain critical
potential, this vision pertaining to the interactions between the self and the
other projects a cynical impasse. With the denial of the illusory aspect of the
One, the fiction, Haraway generates the separation between the cyborg and
the goddess. Therefore, in total opposition to Haraway what will be even
more exciting to explore in this study is the potential of that *too many* aspects
of the *two*. In this respect Haraway regards high-tech culture as a challenge to
the dualisms of the machine and the organic body. Yet this is just another
indication to her preference for the material only. However such challenge if
is to be integrated along multiplicities in gender perceptions in the film media
then the material gains furthermore a touch of interpretation.

In the current science-fiction film, gender roles acquire attributes
different than their traditional ones with the female gender that is usually
regarded to be chaotic, irrational, and weak. On the other hand, traditionally
the masculine gender characteristics imply a rational order, strength and
superiority. In recent science fiction films, female figures as well acquire a
strong role. Thus, they start to look and act superhuman and godly. Although
the term *goddess* bears a certain religious connotation, in this study it is not
religiosity in the conventional sense. These current goddesses do not have
shrines of their own, just as their ancient counterparts did. The current
goddesses do not invite potential believers to worship them either, unless
they acquire their own fan groups and admirers. These new figures transform
into *goddesses* when they become *popular culture media icons*. With the
actress Angelina Jolie, in the role of Lara Croft, and Mila Jovovich as Alice,
the superwoman protagonists etch into public viewers' minds with their
strength and heroic deeds as enacted in the films they take part. The
corresponding films generate around the protagonists an aura allowing for
their popularity to thrive as exemplary superhuman female figures. At this
point they acquire a *goddess-like* quality. Therefore popular media as part of

the celebrity cult highlights these superwomen protagonists as almost akin to their ancient counterparts. Since these superwomen protagonists manifest in multiple versions, such as Lara and Alice, they reminisce ancient times when deities prevailed in diversity. Therefore through films analyzed in this study it becomes obvious that within historic, mythological and futuristic contexts the female gender is made to manifest at multiple dimensions in time. Therefore the *cyborg-goddesses'* popularity encompass all times of the universe. Capable to extend their presence within a physical conception of time, therefore they seem ingrained into the scientific universe. Furthermore, the protagonists' mythological and archeological references allow for fact and fiction to intertwine in order to highlight the ambiguous and the humane. As will be mentioned in this study later, within *cyborg-goddesses'* scope of interest lies universal concerns dealt as part of ancient, esoteric as well as utopic, futuristic contexts. Therefore at all modes of presence the *cyborg-goddesses* edge with the universal. In this respect as a gender category they are females and they have a grasp of superhuman qualifications. As such they come near to traditional male heroic representations in films. For some, these female protagonists' approximation to male heroic qualifications may appear as a challenge to them. Albeit, such approximation's potential challenges gets to be reduced to a minimum with the *cyborg godesses'* closeness to the universals.

Furthermore, one is even inclined to think that the *cyborg goddess* figure maybe a bisexual's fantasy in disguise: as both male and female. As such the *cyborg goddess* becomes a multiple media to cope with the deficiencies of each, yet to maximize the benefits of both genders. Since bisexuality may appear inherently subversive of established gender borders, and mainstream convictions, what could be better off than giving to this superhuman character a beautiful female shape to disguise the intent, and to let conquer all hearts. In many respects this fantasy is quite well synchronized with all mainstream modes of being which is rooted in the teachings of the enlightenment thriving for progress, especially visible in issues such as human cloning as in the movie *Resident Evil: Extinction* (2007).

In this respect, *cyborg goddesses* perform their mainstream role, as popular culture media icons in current science fiction films. As such, they are fully feminine and sexy beings, capable of good and evil simultaneously. They also haul the more difficult task of the consciousness raiser in helping to transform all embedded prejudices and stereotypes in the conventional western sense in local and global human cultures. Thus, the *cyborg goddess* as a shape shifting and therefore a most ironic being is capable of making use of pleasure and pain, joy and sorrow and stay ever alive in any condition, no matter the forcefulness of the circumstances. In this sense, the *cyborg goddess* stands for the animus principle, an impetus, a momentum, which gives a jump-start to newness in the movie, as well as the video game screen.

Differently from Haraway's lonesome cyborg, the *cyborg goddess* also as a creature of complete fiction functions as a fusion of multiple values, deliberately making use of the factual, mythical, scientific, fictional as well as her sexy body image as tools of material reality and utopia in achieving the social, cultural, and political tasks Haraway designated earlier in her *Cyborg Manifesto*.

However Haraway's preference, which appears to be on the side of the cyborg rather than the goddess, and therefore dividing them from one another, is a position she takes to the detriment of subscribing to the very problematic divisiveness the western binary mindset ever dictated. This stance is highly consistent with Haraway's materialist political position. With Sadie Plant in *The Future Looms: Weaving Women and Cybernetics* [13], it is also possible to understand Haraway's binary divisive approach as a legitimization tool, a mask, or a veil she puts over the real innovative and challenging and material intent her article promises. Although her stance appears innovative, she simultaneously appears to undo it by concealing with her divisiveness. This concealment bears the very mechanism Sadie Plant refers to in her article *The Future Looms*: weaving as a feminine practice projected by men onto women for purposes of masking a blatant nature. In this respect Haraway's concealment of the materiality of her cyborg becomes possible through acquiring a divisive attitude and therefore siding with the binary. Therefore Haraway resides within and without the material. In Plant's view this concealment mechanism is inherent in women's centuries-old act of weaving. Theoretically she highlights this point with Freud and Luce Irigaray. In her article Plant mentions of computer's history along Babbage's the Difference Engine and later the Analytical Engine that Ada Lovelace brought into fruition as an idea after Jacquard's weaving method which paved the way to the modern day computers' underlying technique. According to Plant weaving as an inspiration bears Freud's imprint who argues for the following:

> weaving imitates the concealment of the womb: the Greek hystera; the Latin matrix. Weaving is woman's compensation for the absence of the penis, the void, the woman of whom, as he famously insists, there is 'nothing to be seen.' [14]

Plant further mentions Luce Irigaray who argues that "Woman can, it seems (only) imitate nature. Duplicate what nature offers and produces. In a kind of technical assistance and substitution" [15]. In this respect, Sadie Plant reminds that:

This is a concealment on which man insists: this is the denial of matter that has made his culture—and his technologies possible. For Irigaray, this flight from the material is also an escape from the mother. Looking back on his origins, man sees only the flaw, the incompletion, the wound, a void. This is the site of life, of reproduction, of materiality, but it is also horrible and empty, the great embarrassment, the unforgivable slash across an otherwise perfect canvas. And so it must be covered, and woman put on display as the veils that conceal her: she becomes the cover girl, star of the screen. Like every good commodity, she is packaged and wrapped to facilitate easy exchange and consumption. But as her own veils she is already hyperreal: her screens conceal only the flaw, the void, the unnatural element already secreted within and as nature. She has to be covered, not simply because she is too natural, but because she would otherwise reveal the terrifying virtuality of the natural. Covered up, she is always already the epitome of artifice. Implicit in Irigaray's work is the suggestion that the matter denied by human culture is a virtual system, which subtends its extension in the form of nature. The virtual is the abstract machine from which the actual emerges; nature is already the camouflage of matter, the veils that conceal its operations. There is indeed nothing there, underneath or behind this disguise, or at least nothing actual, nothing formed. Perhaps this is nature as the machinic phylum, the virtual synthesizer; matter as a simulation machine, and nature as its actualization. What man sees is nature as extension and form, but this sense of nature is simply the camouflage, the veil again, which conceals its virtuality.[16]

In addition, Plant recognizes and glorifies the feminine within the scientific community, while being wary of her overall interactions with this masculine culture. However, as the next quotation indicates, Plant recognizes the "complexity" of the feminine, which distinguishes her from the masculine:

Cybernetic systems are fatal to his culture; they invade as a return of the repressed, but what returns is no longer the same: cybernetics transforms woman and nature, but they do not return from man's past, as his origins. Instead, they come around to face him, wheeling round from his future, the virtual system to which he has always been heading. The machines and the women mimic their humanity, but they never simply become it. They may aspire to be the same as man, but in every effort they become more complex than he has ever been.... Woman cannot exist *like man*; neither can the machine. As soon as her mimicry earns equality, she is already something, and somewhere, other than him. A computer that passes the Turing test is always more than a human intelligence; simulation always takes the mimic over the brink.

'There is nothing like unto women' writes Irigaray: 'They go beyond all simulation' (Irigaray, 1991:39). Perhaps it was always the crack, the slit, which marked her out, but what she has missed is not the identity of the masculine. Her missing piece, what was never allowed to appear, was her own connection to the virtual, the repressed dynamic of matter.[17]

Sadie Plant recognizes the female dynamics within the sciences as a full display of complexity capable of *taking over the brink of simulation*. Whereas Haraway's obvious use of the concealment effect in making use of her token divisiveness in separating the cyborg from the goddess does not much prevent her from falling into the false consciousness of her own other: the masculine's binary world. Thus, Haraway's strategic token disguise left unexplained by her and overused unknowingly for long, risks permanence to the detriment of any positive future gains in the name of complexity and creativity. Therefore, Haraway's time bound *manifesto* would stay ever as a *token* and therefore clearly legitimized within the system.

Regardless the intent, Haraway's historic preference of the cyborg to the goddess contradicts in many respects with current socio-political and economic developments of the 2000s. These times define a moment of pragmatic, and effective paramount mergers, between all sorts of technologically well-developed large-scale multinational companies, therefore inviting the conceptual configurations of traditional nation-states for adjustments to new social and cultural conditions. The cohabitation of entirely different cultures, enforce more and more recognition for tolerance. The inevitable coexistence of diverse belief systems regenerate the global economic production for having it run at the right track; and therefore generating a feedback system in all walks of economic and cultural production for a more humane life style of quality in an increasingly individualistic and competitive world. Therefore, each new era brings its own complexities geared obviously to *take the mimic over the brink of simulation*. That is, simulation furthers its intent in a transformative aspect of women and nature that brings it to fruition.

3.   *The Cyborg Goddess*: in between Medias

In an era of swift social and cultural changes the journey of the *cyborg goddess* differently from the cyborg and the goddess, entails an oscillation between the video game as well as the movie screen. Therefore, this status of the *cyborg goddess* adds just another dimension to her shape shifting status as a typical representation of antique goddesses in current times. The multiple presences of the *cyborg goddess* manifest in individualized, personalized and in a one on one partnership with immersed video gamers as well as expanding her area of influence and fame into the movie screen: from a local to global scale and vice versa.

In this in-between journey of media spaces, the *cyborg goddess* may appear as a pawn of its originators and creators, as well as an alien bound up with a story of origin enfolding in time towards recognition. However, the journey of the *cyborg goddess* in between media also gives the impression for a goddess pilgrimage[18] occurring in reverse order with the use of cyber media as a tool. Kathryn Rountree in her article *Goddess pilgrims as tourists: inscribing the body through sacred travel* claims that the major intention of goddess pilgrimages to ancient sites is to have "a contemporary political consciousness which desires to continue transforming their patriarchal societies."[19] Therefore, although goddess pilgrimages may sound nostalgic they are *not backward-looking*. According to Rountree during the spiritual experiences in goddess pilgrimages the following happens:

> authority is taken to lie within rather than without (hence the absence of supplication by Goddess pilgrims), the divine is immanent, and healing and transformation occur through individuals working with ritual and meditation.[20]

In addition, those pagan pilgrims seek for *healing and transformation* rather than looking for "material or spiritual favors, where devotion is exchanged for the removal of sin" as "any healing or transformation sought by a Goddess pilgrim is not thought of as being part of a deal with a divinity, and there is no supplication on the pilgrim's part."[21]

The *cyborg goddess* as *a popular media icon* gains similar devotees as her ancient counterparts have. These *cyborg goddesses* as emphasized earlier proliferate in parallel with the capitalist economic culture. Similar to the temporal sensitivities of goddess pilgrimages where "the gap between the past and the present collapses"[22] the *cyborg goddess* appears in a setting where the notion of time collapses in the same manner, as if to generate a complete sense of immersion and oneness with the story line as a total experience of nostalgia as well as transformation.

However, in its current formats, and differently from its ancient counterparts the *cyborg goddess* awaits no more the visits of the pilgrims travelling towards her shrine in search of spiritual fulfillment. The *cyborg goddess* as a recent phenomenon reaches out to the postmodern day fan groups in their personal computers in gaming and or in movie format. Therefore, she does not only allow for an interactive experience, but also enables for divers gender experiences, and performative indulgences of all sorts. As an example Angelina Jolie's real life shape exists as a model for an avatar in *Second Life*, the multi-user online game.[23] In this respect, current media offers *choice* with online game formatting, while the films continue to generate a one-size fits-all voyage of the movie screen spectacle. Thus, both *Lara Croft* and *Resident Evil* movies with their video game/movie screen fan entourage proliferate a new generation of *cyborg goddess* sympathizers cognizant of a complex attitude within the context of science, technology and politics as inclusive of the female medium for a negotiation of all former and current conflict points. In this respect, a closer look at the video game versions of the *Lara Croft* and *Resident Evil* series may clarify the contextual implications of both media comparatively. However, this study will leave the analysis of the video games to a future task.

4.   The *Cyborg Goddess*: A Story of Origin

Ancient mythological times undeniably constitute of a source of inspiration for movies and video games such as *Lara Croft* and *Resident Evil*. Ancient mythology as regenerated in the literatures and cultures of the western world constitute also of a source to the symbolic order of such movies. However, certain feminists such as Kate Millett in their analysis of canonical literature works in terms of context and imagery of women employed, observed the traces of classical mythology bearing the fruits of a pacifying and oppressive misogynist intellect. Kate Millett in this regard argues for the following:

> Primitive society practices its misogyny in terms of taboo
> and mana, which evolve into explanatory myth. In
> historical cultures, this is transformed into ethical, then
> literary, and in the modern period, scientific rationalisations
> for the sexual politic. Myth is, of course, a felicitous
> advance in the level of propaganda, since it so often bases
> its arguments on ethics or theories of origins. The two
> leading myths of Western culture are the classical tale of
> Pandora's box and the Biblical story of the Fall. In both
> cases earlier mana concepts of feminine evil have passed
> through a final literary phase to become highly influential
> ethical justifications of things as they are.

Patriarchy has God on its side. One of its most effective agents of control is the powerfully expeditious character of its doctrines as to the nature and origin of the female and the attribution to her alone of the dangers and evils it imputes to sexuality. The Greek example is interesting here: when it wishes to exalt sexuality it celebrates fertility through the phallus; when it wishes to denigrate sexuality, it cites Pandora. Patriarchal religion and ethics tend to lump the female and sex together as if the whole burden of the onus and stigma it attaches to sex were the fault of the female alone. Thereby sex, which is known to be unclean, sinful, and debilitating, pertains to the female, and the male identity is preserved as a human, rather than a sexual one.

The Pandora myth is one of two important Western archetypes that condemn the female through her sexuality and explain her position as her well-deserved punishment for the primal sin under whose unfortunate consequences the race yet labours. Ethics have entered the scene, replacing the simplicities of ritual, taboo, and mana. The more sophisticated vehicle of myth also provides official explanations of sexual history. In Hesiod's tale, Zeus, a rancorous and arbitrary father figure, in sending Epimetheus evil in the form of female genitalia, is actually chastising him for adult heterosexual knowledge and activity. In opening the vessel she brings (the vulva or hymen, Pandora's "Box") the male satisfies his curiosity but sustains the discovery only by punishing himself at the hands of the father god with death and the assorted calamities of postlapsarian life. The patriarchal trait of male rivalry across age or status line, particularly those of powerful father and rival son, is present as well as the ubiquitous maligning of the female.

Pandora appears a discredited version of a Mediterranean fertility goddess, for in Hesiod's Theogony she wears a wreath of flowers and a sculptured diadem in which are caned all the creatures of land and sea. Hesiod ascribes to her the introduction of sexuality which puts an end to the golden age when "the races of men had been living on earth free from all evils, free from laborious work, and free from all wearing sickness." Pandora was the origin of "the damnable race of women - a plague which men must live with." The introduction of what are seen to be the evils of the male human condition came through the introduction of the female and what is said to be her unique product, sexuality. In *Works And Days* Hesiod elaborates on Pandora and what she represents - a perilous temptation with "the mind of a bitch and a thievish nature," full of "the cruelty of desire and longings that wear out the body," 'lies and cunning words and a deceitful soul," a snare sent by Zeus to be "the ruin of men." [24]

However, even a cursory look at ancient mythology's record on the significance of the term "goddess", especially around the cult of Cybele B.C. 6500-7000, points to a noteworthy connection.[25] Cybele, whose cult birthplace is considered to be Anatolia, was recognized as a major goddess throughout diverse locations, there and the broader Middle East, including the Trojans, Ephesians, Hittites, Sumerians, Phrygians, in Lydia, in Crete, in Egypt, and around Lake Nemi in Italy. She was also regarded as a goddess of the Amazons by the Black Sea region. The various names the cult of Cybele acquired ranged from Kubaba (in Kültepe tabletes), Artemis (in Ephesus), Mã (in Tokat Gümenek), Marienna (in Sumerians), Arinna (among the Hittite), Isis (in Egypt), Lat (in Syria), Rhea (in Crete), to Venus (around the region by Lake Nemi in Italy), and with the Greek word "meter" or the Roman word "mater" added to various place names she became the goddess of these particular regions.[26] Amidst the competitive and warring civilizations of the time, the Cybele cult survived, and was recognized as a belief system in the region. The female goddess' role in her times concerned of the regeneration of nature and the maintenance of its fertility to the detriment of the male principle as depicted in sacrificial stories in mythology. Therefore, the goddess cult was maintained in cycles of death, and regeneration through sacrificial ceremonies. The Cybele cult's fame and fashion spread until Rome, to become one of the reasons, which attracted Romans to Anatolia.

Kathryn Rountree's study on goddess pilgrimages refers to the goddess figures in the Mediterranean region, and refers especially to the goddess pilgrimages made toward Turkey, Crete and Malta.[27] The nature of these goddess pilgrimages was unification with the empowering aspects the memory of these goddess cults generated. Thus, they were helping to heal against the "wounds of patriarchy"[28]: almost an observation reminiscent of the potential the female gender has to offer in terms of an ability to surpass mimicry just as Sadie Plant refers to within the context of women and cybernetics. [29]

While the origin of the goddess cult provides for such historical and archaeological knowledge, one also needs to make sure of the reasons concerning the regeneration of the goddess cult and other mythological creatures and phenomena in recent times and especially in science fiction movies. My guess is that since the prevalent "god" concept possesses a rather masculine quality there obviously happens to be a need to regenerate its omnipotent female counterpart as a symbol of power. Therefore, alternatives to the male worship figure develop. Within the current capitalist context, this division brings along diversity and a freedom to choose. A selection of alternatives alongside the main providers of belief although may appear to provide diversity, may as well cater similarity, eventually all serving the same purpose: a generous contribution to the shrine of the generic mainframe program of the market economy.

While reconsidering the term goddess along Donna Haraway's definitions of the cyborg in *The Cyborg Manifesto,*[30] one realizes that a cyborg as a utopic entity is beyond genders, conventional binaries, and is devoid of any story of origin. In contemporary science fiction movies, female types have enhanced, altered and shape shifting qualities. They look like a female but they possess superhuman strength. In this respect, they show resemblance to ancient goddesses in constant negotiation with life and death. The presence of an alternative figure with the looks of a female and a strength surpassing the male may appear as a challenge to the mainstream masculine figure and "god." However, the presence of an alternative also means an opportunity for further choice, therefore an invitation to democratization. In this respect, an alternative is equally valuable as the main provider of belief. Furthermore, the image of a cyborg today has developed as an *illegitimate militaristic offspring*[31] as Dana Haraway puts it. Yet the cyborg's *goddess* imagery is an acquisition from its ancient origins, presumably all the way from the Cybele cult.

However, to recognize Cybele as a source of origin for the *cyborg goddess* phenomenon is obviously a challenge to Haraway's cyborg with no origin. Specifically, the cyborg with *no origin story* is bound to undo itself. In this respect, it appears as if it is less constrained than its counter-part. However, the denial of an origin renders the idea of a linear sense of history, and evolution look obsolete in time. If the cyborg is to be considered as an entity, which has originated overnight, then the entire succession of philosophical and technologic developments in time, giving way to the idea of the cyborg is factually nullified. This can happen in a utopic condition only. Therefore, Dana Haraway's *Cyborg Manifesto* maybe read only as a utopic philosophical construction: a further science fiction fantasy, which will allow the reading of other texts. That is, the *Cyborg Manifesto* as a fictive key of the science fiction world will help open the fictive side of the locks and amplify the meaning process. However, Haraway's proposition is an inspiration in an unconventional, yet seemingly liberating way to the world of fiction and meaning making. By this means, Haraway frees herself from the probable ontological accusations of the scientific world as well as the realm of history, which bases its ontology on the idea of historical progress. Haraway with her denial of a story of origin to the cyborg she also denies a chance to all other first origins and their line of gradual succession, development or progress therefore she sounds almost deconstructive within herself. Therefore, she is legitimating the excessiveness of her cutting-edge aspect.

5.   Cyborg Goddesses: Diversity with Style, Beatrice, Lara Croft, and Alice

In the Cybele cult a sacrificial twist is visible in antiquity. It manifests to the detriment of the male figure. In American literature, the sacrificial twist reappears in Nathaniel Hawthorne's *Rappacinni's Daughter*[32], this time to the detriment of the feminine protagonist. However, in current science fiction movies, the sacrificial potential manifests for both genders simultaneously, to the regeneration of either ones interchangeably via death. The sacrificial, rather apocalyptic aspect always induces an equivocal regeneration of technology and culture through time. In Nathaniel Hawthorne's *Rappacinni's Daughter* this role was Beatrice's.

Infused with Dr. Rappaccini's garden's poison, Beatrice self-destructs in the presence of male scientists and her lover: in the meanwhile killing them emotionally. In the story Beatrice is a young woman who was brought-up by her botanist father within their luscious garden full of poisonous plants. Rappaccini had brought up her daughter infused with poison so that she would be immune to all sorts of manipulation during her life. The poison Beatrice regularly inhales from the plants in their garden transforms her breath into pure poison itself, which is soon to affect her relationship with her young male suitor and conclude in Beatrice's subsequent death. Giovanni, Beatrice's suitor becomes upset to realize that his love for Beatrice is doomed to be a poisonous union to the detriment of tearing both of them apart from the rest of the world. Thus, he revolts and finds the solution in accepting Professor Baglioni's potion in cure for Beatrice. This cure happens to be stored in a well-wrought vial, the design of Benvenuto Cellini, which also has to say a lot about the arts and its composure in relation to the human condition. Thus with Baglioni's antidote Giovanni is to do away with Rappaccini's poison for good. Beatrice's encounter with Giovanni renders Rappaccini's victory with the poisonous garden to become Beatrice's misery. Giovanni and Beatrice become mirror reflections for each other. Eventually Beatrice selects Giovanni as her future mate. However, she keeps a grain of skepticism in regard of Giovanni's temperamental nature. Still, Beatrice does away with her father's protectiveness by drinking Baglioni's antidote. The following final conversations between Beatrice and Rappaccini highlight their condition:

"My daughter," said Rappaccini, "thou art no longer lonely in the world. Pluck one of those precious gems from thy sister shrub and bid thy bridegroom wear it in his bosom. It will not harm him now. My science and the sympathy between thee and him have so wrought within his system that he now stands apart from common men, as thou dost, daughter of my pride and triumph, from ordinary women. Pass on, then, through the world, most dear to one another, and dreadful to all besides!"

"My father," said Beatrice, feebly,—and still as she spoke she kept her hand upon her heart,—"wherefore didst thou inflict this miserable doom upon thy child?"

"Miserable!" exclaimed Rappaccini. "What mean you, foolish girl? Dost thou deem it misery to be endowed with marvellous gifts against which no power nor strength could avail an enemy—misery, to be able to quell the mightiest with a breath—misery, to be as terrible as thou art beautiful? Wouldst thou, then, have preferred the condition of a weak woman, exposed to all evil and capable of none?"

"I would fain have been loved, not feared," murmured Beatrice, sinking down upon the ground. "But now it matters not. I am going, father, where the evil which thou hast striven to mingle with my being will pass away like a dream—like the fragrance of these poisonous flowers, which will no longer taint my breath among the flowers of Eden. Farewell, Giovanni! Thy words of hatred are like lead within my heart; but they, too, will fall away as I ascend. Oh, was there not, from the first, more poison in thy nature than in mine?"

To Beatrice,—so radically had her earthly part been wrought upon by Rappaccini's skill,—as poison had been life, so the powerful antidote was death; and thus the poor victim of man's ingenuity and of thwarted nature, and of the fatality that attends all such efforts of perverted wisdom, perished there, at the feet of her father and Giovanni. Just at that moment Professor Pietro Baglioni looked forth from the window, and called loudly, in a tone of triumph mixed with horror, to the thunder stricken man of science,—

"Rappaccini! Rappaccini! and is this the upshot of your experiment!" [33]

Beatrice's ultimate preference was for being loved, and not feared. Giovanni receives Beatrice's cure from another scientist: Professor Pietro Baglioni. However, the antidote instead of curing kills her. The subtlety and ambiguity over the limits of science and technology, this time also infuses into the context of romantic relationships. Therefore in the sacrifice of the female element, poison, antidote, science, technology, art, and patriarchy (the vial keeping the antidote) strives. Therefore, by means of the female element as a vessel meaning is established.

Current *cyborg goddesses* appear to be more stoic and, omnipotent, as opposed to Rappaccini's Beatrice whose, choice for "being loved but not feared" lead directly to her death. The current *cyborg goddesses* are capable of good and evil, beauty and gore simultaneously, more or less consciously they earn a godly attribute, and they manage to survive physically. They even become more or less victorious over evil, yet at the same time, they do not resist much to become evil, or at least they appear so. Current *cyborg goddesses* have become the very being Rappaccini wanted her daughter to become, which Beatrice had chosen to reject in Hawthorne's story. Thus, current *cyborg goddesses* become active shapers of the system itself. They have all become Beatrices with a poisonous breath. Once resistant to the system and willing to trade it with an alternative, they seem to realize that "resistance is futile" and that there is no way out other than playing by the rules of the system. With the powerful poison taking over their system, they have become the system. It is also possible to say that they have appropriated the system. Thus, they seem to delay their physical death. They are not total losers any more, but they become themselves staunch manipulators. They have a godly attribute on the one hand and we call them goddesses: since they appear as an alternative to the male-order. However, at the same time they look like the male-order and doing away with it whenever the occasion occurs.

It appears, as if from Hawthorne onwards women's representation have changed. However, in this respect, ambiguities persist in the ideological plane in regard of individual freedom's compliance with a pre-programmed decision making mainframe. In this context therefore, Hawthorne's story is also a critical note over the dilemma of choosing one's loyalties. That is, just as a cure may turn out to be poisonous and vice versa: thus, are loyalties. In current movies, as noted in this paper, the *cyborg goddesses* occupy major roles as carriers of good and evil, beauty and gore all at once. Dr. Hinemann in the *Minority Report* is a female counterpart to Hawthorne's botanist Dr. Rappaccini. She is an exemplar for coercive inquisitiveness into the depths of human consciousness. Times are long past since intrusive and manipulative scientists were all males as in the style of Hawthorne's Dr. Chillingworth[34] or Dr. Rappaccini as the sole inquisitors of the scientific world in American literature.

In Herman Melville's *Moby Dick,* the sinking of Pequod, the ship is an ironic implication over the potential destructiveness of the gains culture makes in spite of the destruction of nature through time. The name Pequod is also a reference to the Native Indian tribe, an obvious allusion to matriarchal rule. Similarly, Rachel, the ship, sets sail in search of its orphans amidst the rubble of the sinking whaling ship Pequod. On the other hand, Philip K. Dick's science fiction work *Minority Report,* in film depicts a crime prevention project developed in the United States in a future time. Gifted pre-cogs detect and warn about crimes expected to take place in the future, which eventually leads in the incarceration of potential criminals. The most gifted of the pre-cogs is a woman called Agatha. However the crime prevention project later proves non-operative, and gets terminated due to innocent individuals' detention. The originator of the pre crime system happens to be another woman scientist. However, her equivocal success as an innovator is a reminder of that delicate balance the American Civil War contributed to history. A historical gun presented as a gift to Civil War generals, used as a prop, at the final scenes of the film, allows contemplation over this theme. The pre crime system's boss covers up a crime he commits. In the meanwhile the protagonist hero (Tom Cruise), his major detective, struggles to clear himself from being detained as a potential criminal and eliminated from the scene. Tom Cruise's discovery of his boss' crimes leads to the conclusion. A night of celebration in honor of the pre crime system's success turns out to be a public discovery of its failure. The historic gun presented as a gift to the boss results in its firing and his accidental death. The symbolic use of the gun is a demonstration for the punishment of abusive uses of science, therefore, bringing in a closure. The sacrificial twist leaning towards both ends in the current gender spectrum also reveals on the loss of innocence with the incorporation of science into nature.

Although Donna Haraway's *Cyborg Manifesto* indicates a withering of innocence within the cyborg context, it is possible to detect the opposite. As a further example of its kind, the movie *Ghost in the Shell* both challenges and is supportive of the issue of innocence in the person of major Kusanagi (Motoko) who is blended within the project 2501, the Puppet Master emerging as neither of them but a new born into the net which is "vast and infinite."[35] Innocence's meaning therefore transfers through shifting genders as mere shells into the ever-expanding net as a ghostly presence.

The shell likeness of genders as feminine and masculine, as vessels of technology once were carried through the shell-like aspect of the cult of Cybele, along her multiple facets in Anatolia and the neighboring regions as a major belief system allowing for the expansion and prosperity of civilizations. Once sacrificial of the masculine persona, the belief has evolved. After travelling continents, it has transformed and blended through time into a global context and slanted to the other side for searches of the feminine persona as an object of sacrifice. Today these shell-like genders are interchangeably sacrificing and regenerating one another's images as new names, vessels and shells of invention. In addition, these shell-like genders are cognizant yet also are flexible about their origins and they playfully celebrate the vastness of the net expanding into infinity.

6.   Lara Croft

In the *Lara Croft* series, the protagonist Lara Croft is an aristocratic lady and quite an aloof person. In access to cyber world she proves to be quite dexterous, and does so by means of her helper technicians. Unlike Alice, science's intrusive hand appears to have left Lara Croft's body intact. Lara is to use these devices as mere tools only.

Lara Croft as the bearer and user of technology is also to keep the true values of humanity intact: she is to prevent the world from the contamination of evil: greed, and violence. Although stricken by curiosity herself, she is the keeper of historical archeological treasures of aesthetic value. Despite geared for higher good, her involvement into action can nevertheless become harmful to historical sites. She is a Victorian goddess of virtue in a world juggling for illegal profits, including the production of biological weapons. In this respect, *Lara Croft: the Cradle of Life* also points to ethical aspects of scientific research. In the movie a Nobel Prize-winning scientist involves in the production of illegal biological weapons to acquire more power. In the same movie, the mythical Pandora's Box contains evil, which would be better off if unrevealed to the scientist especially. Lara's role in this context is to prevent history from repeating itself, and resulting in self-destruction.

Therefore, Lara represents timely interference into moments of crisis, which otherwise would be detrimental to humanity. Similarly in the *Tomb Raider* Lara is to interfere into a cosmic, planetary line up to prevent into the world's destruction. Just like in the *Cradle of Life*, in the *Tomb Raider* as well Lara is to visit many archaeological sites of spiritual and cosmic value in the four corners of the world. Oftentimes the cultural and historical context inviting for Lara's interference appears infused with use of high-powered technological devices. In the *Lara Croft* movies Lara with her interest in archaeology and her godly presence and interference into time, reveals her divine presence. She transcends the limits of time to bring together the past and the present for a higher good in order to resolve universal dilemmas.

Croft in her endeavor against destructive aspects of science and technology, takes her cue from the humanities. That is, historical legends, myths and her father's personal letters and his compassion comprise of her source of information and strength to fight against the greedy individuals in the sciences. Historical institutions such as British Royalty and a secret organization approve her quest against evil, in the *Cradle of Life* and the *Tomb Raider*.

Lara Croft can selflessly indulge into physical challenges to achieve her goals, and quite successfully manages to stay alive. Accordingly, *Lara Croft* movies turn out to be a display of extreme sports of all kinds. From horseback riding, biking, jet piloting, parachuting, air gliding, hiking, martial arts, scuba diving to Safari Lara Croft proves her aptitude in diverse areas of extreme sporting. Despite such strenuous pursuits, Lara's poise in social and cultural matters repeats itself in emotional concerns. She rejects emotional involvements, as if to reiterate the familiar code of honor of the quest epic hero who chastely avoids temptations of all sorts. Lara's distrust of men is justified at each stage whenever another one betrays her. They each appear to be more interested in material gains rather than in Lara's higher ideals or her love for the humanity. Terry Sheridan, a character in both the *Tomb Raider* and the *Cradle of Life* is a temptation on Lara's way to victory. Although he is quite an able partner, and an attractive lover to fall for, he is a traitor of the highest kind. Eventually in the *Cradle of Life*, during the chase for the Pandora's Box, Terry Sheridan perishes. Thus, Lara Croft stands out as a quite stoic *cyborg goddess* who combines in one beauty, and toughness.

Lara Croft may appear free but she is a subject of her queen, who in her turn is yet another symbolic carrier or vessel of the *ideological state apparatus* with a cultural, technological twist of her own. In the theoretical plane, this powerful and gender-laden weight of conceptual symbolism and performance politics is actually part of all contexts from cyber environments to queer terminology. Thus, it marks a decision in terms of individual freedoms and loyalties in all dimensions.

7.   Alice

As far as loyalty to duty goes, in the *Resident Evil* movies Alice is similar to Lara Croft. However, Alice is a clumsy person. She is not prudent enough. This fallacy eventually causes her secret negotiation with an Umbrella Corporation's Laboratory employee to bring the corporation down. Alice's husband Spence secretly tapes the conversation from distance and traps her. Spence manipulates this secret information for his individual profit. In this respect, Spence is the traitor just as Terry Sheridan is for Lara Croft. Spence is not interested in protecting humanity against an equally manipulative corporate giant. Therefore, Alice gets trapped, in between her husband, and the corporation. Spence claims he does not believe in change. He is more into exploiting the giant Corporation to the detriment of others' well being. He says:

> You...really believe that ... people like him (indicating
> Matt, the other idealist, and ironically the future victim of

the Nemesis program- who passed for a cop in order to enter the laboratories of the Umbrella Corporation and who is willing to put the Umbrella Corporation down) will ever change anything? No ... nothing ... ever ... changes.[36]

In sum, *Resident Evil* movies display a group of idealist rescuers' struggles against technology gone bad. However, the movie is also critical of idealism's power and the struggle for change. Alice in the *Resident Evil* movies is an epitome of idealism. Yet during the first two movies, her clumsiness results in the struggle against the ills of technology to look as clumsy and inadequate in contrast to the corporate system's evil yet initial impeccable precision. In this respect, the film is critical but at the same time cautious of its position during its visit to the mainframe by means of the beautiful and powerful *cyborg goddess*, Alice. Thus, idealism gains a beautiful yet clumsy attribute with an equivocally evolving but powerful female gender.

On the other hand, materialism and the egoistic attempt are both to win and lose while stabilizing a male gender attribute for itself in the *Resident Evil* films. The traitor Spence's manipulative male image loses its power to the deadly bites of the zombie woman scientist, and the monstrous lab creature. The male image in Spence's person also loses in not willing to listen to Alice's female voice. Especially in regard of what she has to say about the latest horrific happenings in the Hive. Spence insists in opening the infected laboratory. Therefore, the treacherous male image causes the devastation of the entire Raccoon city inhabitants twice: first, by the viral infestation of the Hive underground, and then with a nuclear blast from above ground launched to wipe out the contamination.

Nevertheless, despite the high price to pay, the materialist and manipulative mentality is a winner especially in regard of research over the accelerated evolution of the human species in the Hive. Foremost, the male scientist develops the T-virus in order to strengthen his daughter Angela's weak body. In addition, the creation of the super strong mutant humanoid creature in the Hive is another example to such experiments. Later in *Resident Evil: Apocalypse* Matt's regeneration as Project Nemesis follows. Eventually Alice marks the following stage of evolution enabled via bio-chemical enhancement as the second movie *Resident Evil: Apocalypse* concludes. The final instance is Alice's multiplication by cloning in *Resident Evil: Extinction*. The ultimate point reached in the experimentation for a superior human being in *Resident Evil* films thus epitomizes in Alice. Therefore, the post-human creature achieved to the detriment of the inhabitants of an entire city happens to be of a feminine allure in the *Resident Evil* films. It is also to notice that, compared to the earlier big-clawed mutant humanoid creature in the Hive, as well as Matt's monstrous transformation in the Nemesis Project, the bio-genetically manipulated Alice does not deteriorate in her eugenics. In the world of science, beauty survives the beast.

Therefore, during the *Resident Evil* films' sequels, the vessel or the latest biogenetic creations carrier happen to be all female figures. That is, the T-virus' production happens to be for the bodily enhancement of a weak little girl called Angela.[37] Subsequently, the mainframe computer the *Red Queen*'s[38] holographic representation speaking in British accent happens to be a girl's image. The Red Queen safe-keeps and controls the Hive. Rain is another dedicated and selfless female rescue officer. In this line of female figures, Alice the protagonist is the accidental instigator of evil in Raccoon City, but also Angela's rescuer. Thus, different shades of the female image occur as part of a technological invention. This image combines in one various qualifications: such as good, evil, innocence, clumsiness, beauty, ugliness, dedication, destruction, love, sex, altruism, determinism, will, kindness, strength, and endurance. These qualifications of the female vessel appear in the context of race, class, gender as well as generations. In the movie Alice and Rain, one blond, and the other a dark skinned woman, symbolize racial diversity. The Queen obviously stands for the class issue, while the little girl obviously introduces a generational perspective within the female context as part of the carrier of new technology into the future.

In the *Resident Evil* films, the female image appears as part of the technological, viral evolutionary and genetic experiments. However, the female image also appears along the idea of massive extinction such as the Holocaust. In this respect, the *Resident Evil* movies call forth for the reconsideration of the meaning of life, death and being one more time. Specific clues regarding the Holocaust in the *Resident Evil* films are as follows: Alice's dramatic clothing; her high black leather boots and red dress half covering her body, and Spence's black leather jacket in the first film. They are a reminder of a military outlook. A major hint regarding the Holocaust is the infection of the Hive workers by the virus spreading through the air conditioning system. Later the computerized system puts the employees into temporary sleep by pouring gas all over them. Similarly, the poison puts Alice to sleep as well while she was taking a shower in the mansion. All seem to connect as a reminder of the historic Holocaust representations in the media. The train scene is reminiscent of the media images regarding the trains, which carried Nazi victims to concentration camps during the Second World War. In the movie, the underground train connecting the Hive to the upper ground level; and the terror scenes generated by the mutant humanoid biological weapon creature's attacks haunting for flesh, add further into the idea. Thus from a critical perspective the Hive, and the quiet suburban neighborhood with both ends connected by the train, happen to be symbolic for those double concentration camps of corporate employees in work and in leisure. The movie in the opening remarks already indicates the people's entrapment in between. Therefore, it also caters to the paranoia lore prevalent in American society in regard of high technology:

> 9 out of 10 homes contain (Umbrella Corporation's) products. It's political and financial influence is felt everywhere. In public it's the world's leading supplier of: computer technology, medical products, (and) health care. Unknown even to its employees, its massive profits are generated by military technology, genetic experimentation (and) viral weaponry.[39]

In this respect, the movie creates a cross-cultural critical approach against all kinds of oppression, evil and terror in the past and the present, at home and abroad. Similarly, the pre and post contamination zombie-like Hive employees are a criticism of the mindless, soulless and memory defective ignorant masses striving only to appease their primal drives for food. These masses since have no memory, cannot recall the mentality and dynamics of the Nazi terror in the past, and in a different geographical context, neither can they recognize similar manipulative mindsets endemic of giant corporations for which they are willingly enslaving themselves. In this respect, the movie is also a critique of potential oppression and abuse giant and impersonalized corporations may generate. As in the case of the Umbrella Corporation, marriages between men and women require the corporation's approval. This constitutes an example for corporate intrusion into domesticity, in the film.

However, in reference to the first and second movies, *Resident Evil* and *Resident Evil: Apocalypse* it is worth the mention that the choice of the name *Raccoon* for a city in this movie is a reference to the animal Raccoon which generally lives in pairs. That is, they come in twos. Therefore, the city's name as *Raccoon* enforces furthermore the binary mindset. Basically, the use of the binary implies the possibility that in addition to the actual incident occurring in Raccoon city, other similar incidents maybe currently happening somewhere else in the present, might have happened already in the past, or may as well happen in the future. Thus, the doubling format through the name of the animal *Raccoon* for the city in *Resident Evil* movies enables a sense of continuity, and sameness in place and in time. On another note, the name *Raccoon* chosen for a city is also symbolic in regard of the pastoral element, amidst the bustle for technology. However, Raccoon city and its residents disappear in the nuclear blast implemented in order to contain the virus from spreading any further. Therefore, the natural element symbolized in the raccoons, terminates.

In this respect, the idea of massive extinction resulting from misuses of technology is also the subject matter of the third and final film in the trilogy: *Resident Evil: Extinction*. The T-virus contamination, wiping out all living beings and leaving the rest zombie-like, enacts major scenes on the Nevada desert. Therefore, desert scenes intertwine with high-technology science laboratories. In this sequel to the film, entry to the high technology lab is through a shabby hut in the middle of the desert, as opposed to the mansion in the first two films: reinforcing strong suggestions of extinction in the desert. Alice in her sand color sexy attire operates with high-powered in built and external weapons to rescue the survivors together with other officers she meets. Superimposed over this background is Alice's cloning. The scientist this time ventures into multiplying Alice innumerably to obtain the antidote through her blood. Alice's multiplication however is a hopeful remark of survival to the benefit of those who still exists in the north. Therefore, the female figure is yet again future's hope after the techno deluge.

Thus, as opposed to the emphasized technological dimension, the pastoral element loses ground. The friendly raccoon of the former two films, in *Resident Evil: Extinction* leaves its place to the crows. Alice destroys all contaminated and mutated ferocious crows feeding over contaminated humans. Quite a gothic literary symbol the crows, get wiped-out in Alice's concentrated superhuman power. Therefore, in the *Resident Evil* films a technologically enhanced human nature wins over both bland nature and evil. Alice's artificially multiplied body is another example to this condition. In the American myth and symbol context, Leo Marx's *The Machine in the Garden,* (1964) emphasizes the train as a well-known symbol for technology, just as the bridge is, in Alan Trachtenberg's the *Brooklyn Bridge: Myth and Symbol for a Nation,* (1979). These are former examples bringing together the technologic and the natural as part of an understanding of a usable past bringing together fact and fiction. The contemporary technologic era evolves exponentially in an accelerated pace. All the way from the Corliss engine, the steamboat, the train, the cars, the rockets, and computers towards an age of genetics an update in reconciliation of new means of technologic expression along with classical understandings of myth and symbol seems to indicate a necessity. In this respect, scientific developments along with literary and cultural reference points need reevaluation at each stage in relation to their cultural contexts.

Within the context of the *cyborg goddess,* the feminine as technology's vessel adds further into the myth and symbol construction. Different from Donna Haraway's cyborg with no origin story but a mere oppositional utopic construction at the critical edge, the *cyborg goddess,* combines in one the past, present and the future. All the way from the Cybele cult onwards as a builder of civilizations, an understanding of regeneration by means of violence oscillated from gender to gender through history. First, to the detriment of the male gender, then the feminine and now in the present times, of both sides interchangeably. Yet the current *cyborg goddess*' stance, as enhanced with technology and diversified culturally performs as a savior against the ills humanity faces in the presence of greed. Yet, the *cyborg goddess* differently from previous examples, she is equipped with the system's tools, and knows how to transform them in her own ways for a more humane future. An innumerably cloned Alice running north to rescue survivors constitutes an example. The *cyborg goddess* mentioned in this section is a being launched within popular culture. Movies and computer games constitute of her realm of action. The *cyborg goddess*, as a clean and cold medium, is a product of computer technology, if one that bears within it the feminine as the carrier of a transformative future.

Notes

[1] "Matrix," *Merriam-Webster Online Dictionary*, viewed on 20 April 2008. <http://www.m-w.com>.

[2] Dani Cavallaro, *Cyberpunk and Cyberculture: Science Fiction and the Work of William Gibson*, the Athlone Press, London, 2000, p. 47-48.

[3] Dani Cavallaro, p. 47.

[4] Donna Haraway, "A Cyborg Manifesto: Science, technology and socialist-feminism in the late twentieth century" in *The Cybercultures Reader,* David Bell and Barbara M. Kennedy (eds). Routledge, New York, 2001, p. 316.

[5] David. F. Noble, *The Religion of Technology: the Divinity of Man and the Spirit of Invention*. Penguin Books, New York, 1999, p. 6

[6] David F. Noble, ibid.

[7] David F. Noble, pp. 209-228.

[8] David F. Noble, p. 224.

[9] David F. Noble, ibid.

[10] R. L. Rutsky in his work *High Techne: Art and Technology from the Machine Aesthetic to the Posthuman,* University of Minnesota Press, Minneapolis, 1999. p.18.

[11] Donna Haraway, "A Cyborg Manifesto: Science, technology and socialist-feminism in the late twentieth century" in *The Cybercultures Reader,* David Bell and Barbara M. Kennedy (eds). Routledge, New York, 2001, p. 316.

[12] Donna Haraway, p. 313.

[13] Sadie Plant, "The Future Looms: Weaving Women and Cybernetics" in *Cyberspace/Cyberbodies/Cyberpunk: Cultures of Technological Embodiment*, Mike Featherstone and Roger Burrows (eds). Sage Publications, London, 1996, pp. 45-64.

[14] Ibid. p. 46. As quoted from Sigmund Freud, *New Introductory Lectures on Psychoanalysis, Pelican, London*, 1973.

[15] Ibid. pp. 60-61. As quoted from Luce Irigaray, *Speculum of the Other Woman, Cornell University Press, New York,* 1985, p. 115.

[16] Ibid. p. 60.

[17] Sadie Plant, p. 63. As quoted from Luce Irigaray, *Marine Lover of Friedrich Nietzsche*, Columbia University Press, New York, 1991.

[18] Kathryn Rountree, *Goddess pilgrims as tourists: inscribing the body through sacred travel,* Sociology of Religion, Winter, 2002. Viewed on 20 April 2008. <http://www.findarticles.com/p/articles/mi_m0SOR/is_4_63/ai_96254892>.

[19] Ibid. p.14

[20] Ibid. p.13.

[21] Ibid.

[22] Ibid. p.7.

[23] L Giresunlu, *Interview with Sofia Corleone in Second Life*, personal communication, 5 May 2008.

[24] Kate Millett, "Theory of Sexual Politics". *Sexual Politics* The Second Chapter (1969) Granada Publishing. Viewed on 20 April 2008. <http://www.marxists.org/subject/women/authors/millett-kate/theory.htm >.

[25] "Kybele," Azra Erhat, *Mitoloji Sözlüğü*, Remzi Kitabevi, Istanbul, 1978. pp. 199-203.

[26] Ibid.

[27] Kathryn Rountree, Ibid.

[28] Ibid. p. 7. Rountree cites Carol Christ, "Carol Christ: Words About the Goddess and Greece and her Life." Viewed on 14 May, 2008. <http://www.goddessariadne.org/carolwords.htm>.

[29] Sadie Plant, Ibid. p. 63.

[30] Donna Haraway, "A Cyborg Manifesto: Science, technology and socialist-feminism in the late twentieth century," in *The Cybercultures Reader,* David Bell and Barbara M. Kennedy (eds). Routledge, New York, 2001. pp. 291-324.

[31] Ibid., p. 293.

[32] Nathaniel, Hawthorne. *The Scarlet Letter and Rappaccini's Daughter.* [book on line] P.F. Collier & Son, New York, 1917, viewed on 20 April, 2008. available from Bartleby.com, 2000. <www.bartleby.com/310/1/>.

[33] Ibid.

[34] Nathaniel Hawthorne, *The Scarlet Letter,* (1850) Random House, New York, 2000.

[35] Mamoru Oshii, *Ghost in the Shell*, (1995) (Masamune Shirow/Kodansha LTD/Bandai Visual Co., LTD/ Elizabeth Stroll 2004, video recording. [Title 01. Chapter 14. M. 17. S. 20].

[36] Paul W. S. Anderson, *Resident Evil*, New Films, 2003, video recording. [Title 01. Ch.15. 1:11:37] Italicized emphasis within parenthesis is mine.

[37] However, the virus manifests in a variety of ways in different biologic environments. The T-virus empowers the weak body of the scientist's daughter Angela. The same virus when inhaled mutates healthy men and women into zombies who in turn infect others with their bites. The anti-virus does not save the already bitten person from mutating into a zombie.

[38] At this point it is also necessary to indicate the way in which the rescue officers treat the "state of the art computer" called the Red Queen, whenever they realize that the computer is sealing off the Hive in order to prevent the virus from spreading above ground level. The language used while speaking to, and about the Red Queen is sexist. The female characters as well use this sexist language. Here are some examples: Alice: "I am turning her back on", Rain: "That homicidal bitch killed my team", Alice: "That homicidal bitch maybe our only way out of here." One of the male officers: "The way she is treated, I'm sure she's gonna be real happy to help us out!" [*Resident Evil* (2003) Title: 01 Ch: 12 0:55.18] Rain: "Give me that fucking switch, I am gonna fry her ass" [*Resident Evil* (2003) Title: 01 Ch. 12 0:55:55] Regardless the child hologram and voice the Red Queen is speaking through, the female officers treat her in the most sexist and aggressive possible language generally known to be used in different contexts by macho male types. The switching of gender language styles from males and their use by females in this movie is quite significant in this respect. On another note it is also significant to hear the holographic girl's voice speak of herself as the following: "I have been a bad bad girl" [*Resident Evil* (2003) Title: 01. Ch: 16 01:13:38] to indicate that she has sent the mutant creature, the biological weapon, in order to have Spence killed. However within the sexist context it is obvious that grown ups' gender positions and identifications are also imposed over child images. Among other critical positions to be taken over this issue in future research however in practical terms the Red Queen appears to react in every possible way in order to keep infection from spreading further outside the Hive. However, unlike the Queen bee of a beehive whose sole job is to lay eggs, the Hive laboratory's Red Queen destroys human life in protection of the research lab. That is, the Queen bee's queen-likeness is kept, however its image is transformed to its opposite. In addition, it is transposed onto an artificial technological creation: the mainframe computer, which appears aggressive and can destroy human lives. This irony further carries onto the speech patterns of the female characters, as

well as into their actions. They as well kill in order to survive. Rain however selflessly accepts death as Red Queen's order, to enable the uninfected ones to leave the Hive. Yet Alice instead of killing Rain, she disobeys the computer, and smashes the screen through which the Red Queen speaks to them. This very moment the system shuts down. Eventually to realize that it was a male rescue officer, Kaplan who had finally managed to disable the computer. [*Resident Evil* (2003) Title: 01 Ch: 17 01:17:36] However, Rain's death, although delayed, would soon arrive with Alice's bullet, since Rain would inevitably become a zombie caused by infection.

[39] *Resident Evil,* 2003 The audience receives this information in the opening scene. Emphasis within parenthesis is mine.

Bibliography

Anderson, Paul W. S., *Resident Evil*. New Films, 2003. Video recording.

_____ , *Resident Evil: Apocalypse*. Screen Gems,/Davis Films/ Impact (Canada) Inc. Constantin Film (Un)limited. 2004. Video recording.

_____ , *Resident Evil: Extinction*. Constantin Film, 2007. Video recording.

Cavallaro Dani, *Cyberpunk and Cyberculture: Science Fiction and the Work of William Gibson*. the Athlone Press, London, 2000.

DeBont, Jan. *Lara Croft: The Cradle of Life*. Paramount Pictures, 2003. Video recording.

Erhat, Azra. *Mitoloji Sözlüğü*. Remzi Kitabevi, Istanbul, 1978.

Giresunlu, L *Interview with Sofia Corleone in Second Life*, personal communication, 5 May 2008.

Gordon, Lawrence. *Lara Croft: Tomb Raider*. Paramount Pictures, 2002. Video recording.

Haraway, Donna. "A Cyborg Manifesto: Science, technology and socialist-feminism in the late twentieth century." in *The Cybercultures Reader,* David

Bell and Barbara M. Kennedy (eds). Routledge, New York, 2001, pp.290-324.

Hawthorne, Nathaniel. The Scarlet Letter and Rappaccini's Daughter. [book on line]. P.F. Collier & Son, New York, 1917, viewed on 20 April, 2008; available from Bartleby.com, 2000 <www.bartleby.com/310/1/>.

Hawthorne, Nathaniel. *The Scarlet Letter*. Random House, New York, 2000.

Marx, Leo. *The Machine in the Garden: Technology and the Pastoral Ideal in America*. Oxford University Press, New York, 1964.

Melville, Herman. *Moby Dick*. Penguin Books, New York, 1994.

Millett, Kate. "Theory of Sexual Politics". *Sexual Politics*
The Second Chapter (1969) Granada Publishing. Viewed on 20 April, 2008.
<http://www.marxists.org/subject/women/authors/millett-kate/theory.htm >.

Noble, David F. *The Religion of Technology: the Divinity of Man and the Spirit of Invention*. Penguin Books, New York, 1999.

Oshii, Mamoru. *Ghost in the Shell*. (1995). Masamune Shirow/Kodansha LTD/Bandai Visual Co., LTD/ Elizabeth Stroll, 2004. Video recording.

Plant, Sadie. "The Future Looms: Weaving Women and Cybernetics" in *Cyberspace/Cyberbodies/Cyberpunk: Cultures of Technological Embodiment*, Mike Featherstone and Roger Burrows (eds), Sage Publications, London, 1996.

Proyas, Alex. *I Robot*. Twentieth Century Fox, 2005. Video recording.

Rountree, Kathryn. *Goddess pilgrims as tourists: inscribing the body through sacred travel,* Sociology of Religion, Winter, 2002. Viewed on 20 April, 2008.<http://www.findarticles.com/p/articles/mi_m0SOR/is_4_63/ai_962548 92>.

Spielberg, Steven. *Minority Report*. Twentieth Century Fox and Dreamworks, 2002. Video recording.

Trachtenberg, Alan. *Brooklyn Bridge: Myth and Symbol for a Nation*. University of Chicago Press, Chicago, 1979.

De-Colonizing Cyberspace:
Post-Colonial Strategies in Cyberfiction

Maria Bäcke

Abstract

Increasingly important information and communication technologies (ICT) play a significant role – sometimes as an image, sometimes as a tool – for authors like Ellen Ullman, Melissa Scott, Jeanette Winterson and Pat Cadigan. In their novels they explore patterns of power, hierarchy and colonization through the destabilization of space and transgress boundaries in the space they create. By making connections between post-colonial/post-structural/post-modern theory and technology, I explore the authors' reasons for making these transgressions. Édouard Glissant explains how computers, and computer-mediated text, can generate a "space within the indeterminacy of axioms" and how this opens up possibilities to create a space where imaginative and ideological liberation is possible. Glissant's idea of indeterminacy grows out of Gilles Deleuze and Felix Guattari's discussion about space and how it is structured. The virtual, seemingly topographical, space of the Internet has been described, on the one hand, as an information highway (*striated* space) and, on the other, as a web, where it is possible to surf (*smooth* space). I connect these concepts to the novels and explore to what extent the authors use these strategies to de-colonize the fictional, digital space their characters inhabit.

Key Words: Literature, ICT, novels, hierarchy, power, Deleuze, Guattari, Castells, Glissant

*****

Cyberspace is sometimes used as a synonym for the Internet, but the two concepts are not entirely identical. The Internet is more limited and often related to the real world, whereas Cyberspace is a broader term, a metaphor for the thought-space created by information and communication technologies – a space often explored in movies, games or literature. Cyberspace is an idea of a new land full of opportunities, a territory ready to be explored. But there is irony here, since, although Cyberspace is visualized as free space, the vast majority of the people, who are doing the visualizing, are white, middle class males in their late twenties or early thirties, living in the suburbs of large cities in industrialized countries. I would argue that this gender-, class-, age-, and ethnicity-based digital divide has had a great influence on people's view of Cyberspace, and reinforces the myth of the

"Cyberspace Cowboy". Space generated by ICT equals male space, a space colonized by men. Happily, this is of course not always the case. In the following I will be discussing the gender boundaries in Cyberspace, and how female cyberfiction authors claim their own space, choose their own issues and ways of writing. Simply by choosing to write cyberfiction they attempt to decolonize a genre already colonized by male authors.

I have examined five contemporary books written by female authors: *Close to the Machine* by computer programmer Ellen Ullman, *The Jazz* by sci-fi author Melissa Scott, *The PowerBook* by fiction author Jeanette Winterson, and the novels *Avatar* and *Dervish is Digital* by "the queen of Cyberpunk," Pat Cadigan. By using ICT, sometimes as an image, sometimes as a tool, these authors explore patterns of power, hierarchy and colonization in Cyberspace. I will, by linking post-colonial/post-structural/post-modern theory and technology, explore the way they transgress boundaries in the space they create.

Although I will use Manuel Castells' four-layered theory on Internet cultures as a structure, the underlying theory of this paper has its origin in Gilles Deleuze and Félix Guattari's ideas. The rhizome – a fluctuating "web" or a "root-and-branch-system" without centre or definition, always on the verge of becoming something else – is linked to postcolonial theory by Édouard Glissant who highlights the benefits of its multiplicity: "Rhisomatic thought is ... extended through a relationship with the Other" which challenges the intolerance of the single root of the colonizer, the norm against which the colonized struggle.[1] Glissant stresses the limitation of the dichotomy between self and other, since this means that the colonized is always-and only-defined and measured against the colonizer. Decolonization, however, has the possibility to destabilize this dichotomy and create a space – a rhizome – that takes a multitude of viewpoints into account.[2]

What Glissant labels decolonization can be related to Deleuze and Guattari's idea of smooth and striated space.[3] Smooth space is open, nomadic, flowing and flexible, whereas the striated spaces are described as grid-like in structure, relying on clear definitions, and always trying to bring the smooth spaces under their control. The creation of smooth space – ultimately an act of decolonization – is addressed by the cyberfeminist Donna J. Haraway in "A Cyborg Manifesto." The "post-gender" cyborg[4], an ambiguous hybrid of machine and organism, has the power to effectively destabilize all boundaries, and cyborg writing, "the technology of cyborgs", creates something that comes close to smooth space:

> Cyborg writing is about the power to survive ... seizing the
> tools to mark the world that marked them as other. The
> tools are often stories.... In retelling origin stories, cyborg
> authors subvert the central myths of origin of Western

culture.... Feminist cyborg stories have the task of recoding communication ... to subvert command and control.[5]

The primary aim of feminist cyborg writing is thus to decolonize pre-existing control, which can be easily transferred to the works of female cyberfiction authors.

But what pre-existing control is there to decolonize? Cyberspace is usually considered a smooth space where anything is possible, but by now it can be argued that both the Internet and Cyberspace already have been colonized. We know how it "works". In his book *The Internet Galaxy*, Manuel Castells discusses the cultures he sees on the Internet today and divides them into four layers: the techno-meritocratic, the hacker, the virtual communitarian and the entrepreneurial culture.[6]

The techno-elites focus on the technical solutions. They build the systems and networks, and formulate rules, protocols, that govern how information is sent and packaged. With its root in academia and science, this culture promotes openness, and technological discovery is usually subject to peer review. "This is a culture of belief in the inherent good of scientific and technological development as a key component in the progress of humankind".[7] It is also a fairly hierarchic culture, where a few authority figures assign projects and control the resources.[8] One of the novels, Ellen Ullman's *Close to the Machine*, highlights a computer programmer view on Internet and its impacts. The narrator, a middle-aged female programmer, works with her younger male colleagues on different projects. All of them are focussed on the code, the beauty and elegance of the syntax, and regardless of employer, their aim is to deliver software as free of bugs as possible. They hardly ever think of the end-user, and if they do, it is in abstract terms. They are completely focussed on a technology that seems to develop at the speed of light. The Internet is new and not even the narrator understands it fully. Her colleague Brian does, though:

> And his vision of the Internet had the same quality of bizarre hyperreality – all the hallucinatory detail of a dream.... For as 'technical' as I might appear to my clients, as close to the machine as I was from their point of view, that's as far away as I was from Brian. He exploded the Net for me.... a complicated sea of intelligent devices, where the distinction between hardware and software began to blur and few people knew how to navigate. Brian knew how to navigate. And because he knew, he would control the routes. He was quite straightforward about this: he wanted influence, and he wanted influence because he knew more than most people and because he was right.[9]

This quotation clearly illustrates how competent programmers are able to gain power through their expert knowledge, but this is also what the narrator reacts strongly against. Human emotions seem to have no place and she asks Brian if he has morals, a question he prefers to ignore.[10] She has seen computers as neutral tools, but she discovers that "there is something in the system itself, in the formal logic of programs and data, that recreates the world in its own image".[11] She notices that the very language people use to describe the machine – by calling the microprocessor a 'brain' or saying that the machine has 'memory' – shows that computers are given human attributes, but, as she continues, "[i]t is a projection of a very slim part of ourselves: that portion devoted to logic, order, rule, and clarity. It is as if we took the game of chess and declared it the highest order of human existence".[12] She realizes that what she has thought of as "sexy bouts of software writing" has an enormous and not always positive impact on real world social life.[13] In her realizations she shows a rebellious wish to destabilize the techno-meritocratic world view, and she stresses the benefits of the rhizomatic innovative and unconventional thinking of a good programmer when she argues: "'I mean, you don't want them to stop being cats,' I kept on bravely. 'You don't want obedient dogs. You want all that weird strangeness that makes a good programmer'".[14]

The second culture defined by Castells is that of the hackers, a culture just as techno-oriented as the techno-meritocratic one, but at the same time often more imaginative and innovative. The hackers often bridge the gap between the techno-meritocratic culture and the entrepreneurs.[15] A keyword in this type of culture is 'freedom': "Freedom to create, freedom to appropriate ... and freedom to redistribute this knowledge" in any way possible.[16] Castells points out that any software development made by a hacker usually is posted on the Internet as a 'gift' for other developers to work on.[17] This is exactly what happens in Melissa Scott's *The Jazz*. In a society controlled by large corporations, the main character Tin Lizzy, works as a "back-tech provider" for Testify, a lose-knit virtual community that hosts and spreads "jazz" – unauthorized computer programs developed outside the studios of the large corporations. In order to avoid the striations of this extremely regulated society, and to be able to work, she has become used to creating smooth space. Being a "back-tech," Tin Lizzy checks and adjusts code submitted by programmers before their work is to be released on Testify, and this is where she meets Keyz, a sixteen-year-old programmer who has stumbled upon a help program, a 'spellchecker' for code. Keyz has used this program when writing his own "jazz" and the result is remarkable and attracts enormous attention.[18] The problem is that this 'spellchecker' program belongs to America's largest computer corporation, known for their relentless pursuit of anyone using what they consider their property. Copyright lawsuits can be expensive and Testify's policy is to avoid any connection to illegal hacking. Testify therefore closes the door on the sixteen-year-old, while the CEO of the computer company puts his private police on the case.[19] Tin Lizzy does not feel comfortable abandoning a boy and she decides to help Keyz, a decision that puts her in great jeopardy. In order to do that, Tin Lizzy uses her imagination and innovative thinking – and her programming skills. In the eyes of the society/corporation she is the "other"; she is unpredictable and deviates from their norm – and therefore they attempt to stop her. Paradoxically Tin Lizzy stands up for a human viewpoint against both Testify and the computer company by using her computer skills. An interesting contrast to the experiences of the narrator in *Close to the Machine* is that Tin Lizzy's choices in the *The Jazz* are not primarily directed against her own hacker culture, most likely because it is not a striated culture to begin with. Instead her fight highlights the tension between hackers and entrepreneurs, between freedom and money, and problems that arise in a society controlled by large corporations. With her actions she attempts to decolonize the space colonized by the computer company.

The virtual communitarians, the third layer of culture Castells defines, has shaped the "social forms, processes, and uses" on the Internet.[20] Virtual communities, exemplified by MUDs, are described as places where mostly teenagers and college students can experiment with role-playing and fake identities.[21] But not all users are teenagers and role-playing might not be the only reason for joining various forms of online communities. As Castells puts it: "The social world of the Internet is as diverse, and contradictory, as society is".[22] Two features stand out, though: 'free communication' and 'shared interests'.[23] Pat Cadigan's two novels, *Avatar* and *Dervish is Digital*, both deal with the communal aspect of Cyberspace, and both are set in societies where the (predominantly male) decision-makers are reluctant to use innovations, whereas the female characters are portrayed as less afraid to embrace new technology.

Avatar is a children's book and focuses on Max and his friend Sarah Jane, who are brought up in a low-tech society where most people have never driven a car and where the Internet is viewed with suspicion. Max has been paralyzed in a diving accident, which physically ties him to his hospital bed, and he sees few choices for the future. Despite their distrust, the Council of Elders grants Max the use of high-tech prosthetics, involving the use of the Internet. Sarah Jane becomes Max's body in the sense that she, by bringing a camera and a rig that is connected to him in his bed at the hospital, enables him to go to school with her and to take part in her life. Their virtual connection in the real world continues in Cyberspace after a while, where none of them can be said to have a body. The main issue is identity and how it is perceived and authenticated in a virtual environment. According to Max's prejudices anything that happens in a virtual environment is not real, but when Sarah Jane's body is hi-jacked by an alien-something she is not

entirely unhappy with-and she exists in Cyberspace only, Max is forced to
reconsider: "No doubt about it, this was the real Sarah Jane-and boy, how
weird was that? The real one being the cartoon in the Web and the fake being
the flesh-and-blood avatar in the real world".[24] Their meeting confirms that
the relationship between Max and Sarah Jane is real regardless of
environment. Max's emotional reaction in the novel becomes the only proof
he needs, but also the only one he will ever get. In this children's book
Cadigan thus attempts to destabilize both the reader's view on virtual and
real, traditional gender roles, the question of identity, and the preconception
that emotions have no place in technology.

   Similar questions are posed in *Dervish is Digital*, where the female
police officer at techno-crime, Doré Konstantin, is busy investigating crimes
taking place in a virtual world. The novel is written for an adult audience and
its tone is darker. The novel explores privacy, safety, and law enforcement in
the virtual environment and the main concern is control. To what degree can
someone control someone else in Cyberspace and to what extent could it in
that case influence the real world existence? The book discusses the problem
of retaining individual integrity in Cyberspace when any data collected can
be stored and used for manipulation and control. In the novel an individual is
not 'safe' even if he or she takes on another identity, since the characters'
personality shines through and is possible to trace.[25] This means that what has
been considered one of Cyberspace's main advantages – the freedom to
invent personas to hide the real-world self – is not available anymore in this
novel. Konstantin's real-world self almost dies because of what happens to
her in Cyberspace. Freedom – or smooth space – has given way for striation
and control.

   The fourth and last of Manuel Castells' cultures, the entrepreneurial
one, was the primary shaping force behind the Internet's expansion.[26] The
entrepreneurs actually make money out of ideas, out of creating the future.
Castells argues that the entrepreneurs with technological capacity have
managed to make the Internet the backbone of our lives.[27] Cyberspace thus
has its firm base in the new economy developed hand in hand with ICT. In
Jeanette Winterson's *The PowerBook* the narrator is an e-writer called Ali or
Alix – the narrator's gender is never entirely clear – who makes a living by
selling stories, "Freedom for just one night," on the Internet.[28] Customers are
free to invent a persona; the real world name, age, gender, or occupation is
irrelevant. Only the personality remains; free from real world expectations
and obligations. Ali, or Alix, is selling the ultimate consumer dream, and
might therefore seem like a shrewd entrepreneur when defying the rules of
the physical world and offering the customer a virtual one.[29] The narrator
makes the most of Cyberspace's possibilities to destabilize time and space
and believes that the virtual world has little impact on the real one, but
ultimately the narrator falls in his or her own trap when s/he falls in love with

the client. As Haraway puts it: "the boundary between science fiction and social reality is an optical illusion."[30] Winterson thus knits Cyberspace closely to the real world, and once again emotions are used to destabilize and decolonize the idea of Cyberspace as an unreal, antiseptic, and purely technical world.

Above all the novels question the view of women as hopelessly incompetent users of technology, since the female characters interact on an equal level with male characters. Sometimes they even challenge the validity of the male norm. At other times the women actually take over and re-define the technology and its uses. Cadigan and Winterson focus on the individual, the human being that happens to communicate with other human beings via a new medium. All four authors decolonize the image of the male Cyberspace by stressing that emotions, values and ethics are just as important in Cyberspace as they are in the real world. By showing Cyberspace from a female point of view, the authors attempt to reverse othering and question the single root of a Cyberspace colonized by men. While breaking the Cyberspace Cowboy traditions, these authors thus present ICT as a neutral tool that gives women opportunities to mould and decolonize Cyberspace.

Notes

[1]Édouard Glissant, *Poetics of Relation*. University of Michigan Press, Ann Arbor, 1997, p. 11, 14.

[2] Édouard. Glissant, p. 17.

[3] Gilles Deleuze and Felix Guattari, *Nomadology: The War Machine*. Transl. B Massumi. Semiotext(e), New York, 1986, p. 34-36.

[4] Donna J. Haraway, *Simians, Cyborgs and Women: The Reinvention of Nature*. Routledge, New York, 1991, p. 176.

[5] Donna Haraway, p. 175.

[6] Manuel Castells, *The Internet Galaxy: Reflections on the Internet, Business, and Society*. Oxford University Press, Oxford, 2001, p. 37.

[7] Ibid., p. 39.

[8] Ibid., p. 39.

[9] Ibid., p. 41.

[10] Ibid., p. 51.

[11] Ibid., p. 89.

[12] Ibid., p. 89.

[13] Ibid., p. 59.

[14] Ibid., p. 20.

[15] Ibid., p. 20.

[16] Ibid., p. 46-47.
[17] Ibid., p. 47.
[18] Melissa Scott, *The Jazz*. Tom Doherty, New York, 2000, p. 35.
[19] Scott, p. 43.
[20] Manuel Castells, op. cit., p. 53.
[21] Ibid., p. 54.
[22] Ibid., p. 54.
[23] Ibid., p. 54-55.
[24] Pat Cadigan, *The Web: Avatar*. Dolphin, London, 1999, p. 62.
[25] Pat Cadigan, *Dervish is Digital*. Tom Doherty, New York, 2002, p. 114.
[26] Manuel Castells, op. cit., p. 55.
[27] Ibid., p. 57.
[28] Jeanette Winterson, *The PowerBook*. Vintage, London, 2000, p. 3.
[29] Jeanette Winterson, p. 53.
[30] Donna J Haraway, p. 149.

Bibliography

Cadigan, P., *The Web: Avatar*. Dolphin, London, 1999.

—, *Dervish is Digital*. Tom Doherty, New York, 2002.

Castells, M., *The Internet Galaxy: Reflections on the Internet, Business, and Society*. Oxford University Press, Oxford, 2001.

Deleuze, G. and F. Guattari, *Nomadology: The War Machine*. Transl. Brian Massumi. Semiotext(e), New York, 1986.

Glissant, É., *Poetics of Relation*. University of Michigan Press, Ann Arbor, 1997.

Haraway, D. J., *Simians, Cyborgs and Women: The Reinvention of Nature*. Routledge, New York, 1991.

Scott, M., *The Jazz*. Tom Doherty, New York, 2000.

Winterson, J., *The PowerBook*. Vintage, London, 2000.

The Différance Engine:
Videogames as Deconstructive Spacetime

Tony Richards

Abstract
The purpose here is to intervene within some dominant strands of videogame scholarship and propose a more *problematic relation* to our object. The two dominant tendencies taken-up here represent what has come to be self-styled as a media studies *2.0* model, over and against a supposedly previously dominant (and retroactivated as outmoded) *1.0.*[1] Proposed in opposition to these somewhat sweeping positions will be a *deconstructive* model which, while disagreeing with these theoretical 'algorithms', would not believe itself to be leading a charge toward any notionally more thoroughgoingly circumnavigating *3.0* account. Specifically, while the 2.0 account proposes a *"new"* active first-person *Performative* framework versus an *"old"* third-person indicative *Constative*, we would recommend a reworked *iterative-Performative* as propounded in the works of Derrida and Butler.

Keywords: différance, undecidable, narrative, first-person, third-person, performative, constative, interpellation, suture, reflexivity.

*****

1.   Introduction

To briefly recount the saga: the outmoded 1.0 account[2] tended to grant supremacy to the machine, supply, or server side of the communicative equation leaving for the *audience* only an intractable, non inter*actable* blank space to be crowded-out by an insuperable-power: the subject(-*objective*) is overwhelmed by the text's all too powerful mode-of-address. Within this previously dominant model of domination then each 'text' would form (from its *secured* vantage point) a linear-perspectival control-engine that would either hypodermically *inject* (older-outmoded theory) or *interpellate* (more modern-outmoded theory) their object-individual as *their* subject. This denial of any space either to play or to poke *polysemical* holes into the socialising fabric of the oncoming text constituted the figure then of an indivisible *program(me)* acting as some locally firewalled representative of a much larger media-industrial eco-system. While some theorists felt that this did a disservice to the multifarious positionality of the receiving audiences (that there was always a residual *meaning allowance* or a polysemic-*playspace*[3] within the static and weaved net of a particular text's 'material' signifiers), there was still nonetheless a strong server-sided control of what *composed* the message (to borrow de Certeau's language: there is still an organised supermarket from which we *must* shop, even if we get to *play* a little within its space[4]).

Let us timeshift. The tectonic plates of the media were noticeably shifting around the early 1990's. A crossing of the divisive *stage-boundary* began (hypercards for example[5]) with the birth of '*the wreader*', a sort of Barthesian writerly but this time adding signifier, paradigm and pathway choices (what Aarseth would later call 'variable expression'[6]) to the aforementioned *semantic latitude* of those signifieds. The recent birth of these inter*actors* began to make such ageing theories, even of semantic/subcultural play[7], seem untenable. The tectonics of the object itself began to drift from under these theorists' weary feet.

This move then from texts with relatively determining meta-narrators[8] to texts that stepped outside of such trajectorial-boundaries demanded a somewhat different outlook if a media theorist's reflections were to keep pace with media *practsumption* (consumption-practice*)* and to offer something fit for a changing media infrastructure. As example of this *reality-pull*, in the UK a lively email debate amongst scholars[9] ensued within which a number of *new-broom* media educators pointed out the changing shape of their student's more ludic[10] media experiences (algorithmically: how can we carry on teaching film and media theory 1.0 when students have moved on to the internet, mobile phones and games and whose media experiences are thus far from continuous and playless?). In place of the ideologically determined subject exemplified by Althusser et al, these scholars suggested *Media Studies 2.0* where a *reflexive subject*, prepared for variously by Caillois, Butler and Giddens, might provide a more fitting analytic. Before however looking at 2.0's more proper and up-to-date approach let us look in a little more detail at this 1.0 model's attempted expansion into new media territory.

2.   Theory 1.0: Third-Personed Spectatorial-Constatives

As an exemplar for the problematic extension of so-called media theory 1.0 into the alien realm of games let us present a brief case study. Rehak[11] re-issues (into games) interpellation or the '*hey you!*' function of the text, from its original setting within film theory[12] and puts it to work in its new surroundings by finding equivalents or *replacements* within the videogame. This occurs in much the same way as when for film theory MacCabe[13] famously replaced literature's omniscient written third-person commentary (operating everywhere that is outside character quotations) with the film camera and edit's positioning of what he termed dominant specularity. Rehak's replacement (or *supplementation*) of the film camera function in the game actually makes the immersion or 'loss' to *the space* more powerful than ever:

[F]irst, the use of subjective POV to create a newly participatory role for the spectator; and second, the concept of interpellation and its function, within discourse, in constructing apparently unified subject positions [...] the subject position created through shot-reverse-shot is replaced in the FPS [*first-person shooter*] by a camera simulated through software rendering of these three-dimensional spaces [...] literalises the conceit of an embedded *diegetic participant* [my emphasis] that cinema, because of its material technologies, can only imply.[14]

While in many ways an impressively argued paper, the above excerpt betokens an overly optimistic reorienting of apparatus theory imported inappropriately into the game's quite undecidable 'spacetime'. For here to speak of a "*diegetic* participant" is to take the concept of '*diegesis*' (storyworld) and to concomitantly equate the player as an insider-*character* (or here paradoxically flipped *outsider*-captured) embedded within a 'space' which is in fact neither *quite* text nor non-text (*non-text* would be something anarchically without overarching arché-textual structure like the internet): being neither decidedly *diegetic* nor *extra-diegetic*[15]. This undecidable *difficulty* will later form an important component within our own investigation of the *gamic spacetime*.

Further, according to Rehak the *suturing function* of the cinematic shot-reverse-shot (presumed to subject the spectator within the *difference* of framing positions[16]) finds a direct equivalence in the game's free-roaming simulated camera that would here make the player forget their difference and distance from the presumed diegesis. A sort of *umbilical-alliance* here comports the *game-control* as of a prosthetic extension (for that control would extend the screen outward) and in so *prosthetising-the-player* would swallow the player into the 'diegetic' matrix and make of them a mere *third-person-subject of the space*[17].

As third-person *subject* of the space the gamer would seem to *misrecognise* their pre-textual identity for that of a character *already embedded* within the game's "diegesis". To unpack this problematic idea of a diegetic *already*-embeddedness it will be worth looking in a little more detail at this borrowed model of the cinematic subjection and misrecognition before returning to Rehak's own gamic application. According to Doane[18] identification within the cinematic apparatus works on three distinct levels. After Metz[19] she points out that these three modes of identification are with the *character*, of *objects* (and issues) and finally with the *projection/screen* as an act of 'the gaze' or looking in itself. This latter identification acts as a mode of *primary identification* which subsumes and forms the condition of the possibility of the other two (which are *contentual* and thus downstream or secondary in form).

By the mere *act of looking* the cinematic spectator *forgets* their own distinction and is thus enveloped by and made *subject of the apparatus*. Doane points out that '[T]he pleasure of misrecognition ultimately lies in the confirmation of the subject's mastery over the signifier'[20]. This "*mastery*" is however the very *misrecognition* that is their actual *non-mastery* (for this gaze or look does not master, bring-forth or *change* the signifier). This act of *looking* within an apparatus which *envelopes* causes the spectator to misrecognise *their* look for a look which has the power to *bring-forth*. On this model, this *misrecognised power* to bring-forth, to master or 'write' the space in-front in fact writes or inscribes the passive spectator themselves: the mistaken feeling of *performing* (of *being* the hero) within the film constitutes the spectator's very passivity or actual non-mastery. For the primary-projection of the screen itself and the secondary-look of the protagonist within that screen *hollows-out* both the spectator's subjection as well as the film's own fixed narratological futurity. This voyeuristic misrecognition of having *potency* over the cinematic signifier would seem then to write, inscribe or *suture* them securely into the screen-space; writing them '*in*' as though they were the themselves third-person constative character already hardwired and pre-written within the film's screenplay or cinematic ecriture. Such a *self-less* cinematic subjection leaves no room for any play or indeterminacy over the signifier. *How can this be for the videogame?*

By expanding this model into the game any screen/*play* is thus turned into a more powerfully functioning and diegetically immersed linearising *screened*play. To return again to Rehack. Another strategic re-encounter with cinematic suture makes the point of a cinematic sort of subjection all the more strongly:

> The film spectator's role as an implied observer of narrative events -an "absent one" flickering ghostlike through the diegesis, positioned anew from shot to shot- is concretised in the video game imaginary through the figure of the avatar, a "present one" standing in for the player, who chooses the path of the camera-body with apparent freedom. The disavowal necessary to gameplay is like the "Yes, that's what I see" of successful cinematic suture, but goes further: it is "Yes, that's what I *do*"[21]

This "*Yes*" is of course an inauthentic and very small 'yes' which would remediate the succumbing-slumber of a massed cinematic '*they-self*[22]' which then '*[b]ecomes an extreme form of subject positioning, a scenario of continuous suture*'[23]. Without the 'breaks' that film's shot-reverse-shot lends to the viewer, the *"continuous suture"* of the game actually makes for a more powerfully immersive apparatus or mechanism; one, as it were, *without* breaks[24]. This all begins to sound so much like slavery. For the game *program's* the gamer, just as the programmer would first have *presumably* programmed 'the program'[25]..

While on the 1.0 side we have the remediated[26] locked *conveyer-belt* of the filmic world so theorised, on the other (new side) we have a theory which would supplant such subjections. For these media 'performances' really cannot be seen as 'programs' and call for a much freer inter*actor* to marry-up with the much freer *post-programming* of this modern world. Enter 2.0.

3.   Theory 2.0: First-Person Performatives

Here we can see coming into view a first-person experience in the sense of someone who comes *'before'* something in all their phenomenological purity. Keeping this in mind it is important to explore here two key components in 2.0's armoury: *'reflexivity'* and *'performativity'*. To take the first. Key Media 2.0 theorist Gauntlett argues that sociologist Giddens' notion of reflexive identity provides a key lever in coming to a clearer theoretical understanding of the contours of the present media landscape:

> Giddens is fascinated by the growing amounts of reflexivity
> in all aspects of society, from formal government at one
> end of the scale to intimate sexual relationships at the other
> [...]. Doing things just because people did them in the past
> is – is the opposite of modern reflexivity.[27]

Thus we seem to have moved on from a traditional society with its unreflective *doing-as-is-done*; a machinic society of robotically pre-conscious *'they-selfs'* where audiences were locked into the linearity of the media's handiwork. For here at least 2.0 *agrees* with 1.0, but argues however that now the world has moved along from such multitudinal *'they-selfs'* to more singularly present *'my-self'* narrations and more singular life-times. To outline the contours of these flexible identities Gauntlett utilises Judith Butler's notion of the 'Performative' but must first provide a little more *flexibility* for it in order to purchase a little more *freedom* for his own performative:

> Furthermore we do not need to worry too much about this
> [that the perfomative is not radically free of the materiality
> of the body]: every thinker puts forward tools which we can
> choose to use, or modify, or reject. I feel that the tools in

> '*Gender Trouble*' are more useful, relevant and exciting
> than some of the more cautious ideas in Butler's later
> works[28]

This above statement of 'intent' in itself *performs* a radical misunderstanding of a quotation it so recently (on the same page) utilised. Gauntlett finds some of Butler's later positions too "depressing" and "cautious"' and would prefer to take ideas from an earlier more *vital* time in her writings. But is not Butler pointing out within the quotation that in the previous book she had *already said* what she was so "depressingly" saying in the later one? She does this because she says that she is (having to) anchor and restate her position *for those who skipped too lightly over what she had originally stated*: thus in a strong sense she is here *arguing* for this later book contribution to be placed, as an *interpretative buttress*, within the space of those earlier passages to fend off such misinterpretations. Like the one Gauntlett is here making. For she says:

> One of the interpretations that has been made of Gender
> Trouble is that there is no sex, there is only gender, and
> gender is performative. People then go on to think that if
> gender is performative it must be radically free. And it has
> seemed to many that the materiality of body is vacated or
> ignored or neglected here – disavowed, even [...] I think
> that I overrode the category of sex too quickly in Gender
> Trouble. I try to reconsider it in Bodies that Matter, and to
> emphasise the place of constraint in the very production of
> sex.[29]

Thus a double (*portfolio*) choice is being made here by Gauntlett as to what one *takes* from an informing theorist but without uniformly sticking to their word: one on the surface, the other buried out in the open. Whilst our point here may seem just a little too '*pedantic*' there seems to be operating within Gauntlett a radical free-wheeling form of 'choice' radically independent of the materials being foraged upon. Taken within this rather flexible context there can never be any such thing as a (wilful) *misreading* and one can never then be accused of being *selective* or *deceptive* in cutting-up and wearing the parchments of one's sources: a very anarchic database or *portfolio*[30].

These notions of 'reflexivity' and the individualised 'performative' along with related notions of what have been termed 'portfolio identities'[31] aim towards a free-floating subjectivity cut free from the shackles of the traditional *pre-reflexive*, 'tied' or localised identities. A reflexive performativity such as this however appears to be a rather crude notion, tautologically pointing toward the *figure* of somebody standing on the *ground* of their own two feet. There is here within this '*reflexive-performativity*' a sort of giddy *auto-erotic* freedom (a much simplified Nietzschean self-making) which would see itself as existing a level-above and beyond the old *traditional* or *grounded* identities. Sherry Turkle along the similar lines talks of new media as spaces that allow us to explore and expand our *individual* identities[32]. On this model networking sites (also 'Second-Life' and videogames) would allow us to create ourselves *again* and show ourselves as new faces *each time* anew to the world (a morphous or protean *being-outside-the-world*).

An interestingly befuddled argument on the morphous and playful performativeness by Filiciak[33] would merit further symptomatic investigation for the problem of identity which would seem to be both free (in that like Gauntlett he celebrates the protean nature of "postmodern" identity opportunities within games) yet sees the player as soon to be swallowed up into some cyberspatial self-forgetting (which presumably would land us back into a form of slavery?). He argues thus:

> We are creating our "self" not as a linear process of construction and striving towards some original target – each identity we create is a temporary formation. Erosion of our individual "self" in macro scale is reflected in the fall of collected identities, like a nation [...] we cannot talk anymore about a single identity that produces temporary identities subordinate to itself. Thus in the era of electronic media we should rather talk about hyperidentity, which is related to identity as hypertext to a text.[34]

However four pages earlier we find that such playful opportunities for morphing our identities is based yet again on a model where the player finds themselves con-fused with the textual universe within which they find themselves wrapped up. The power of Cinematic identification again finds itself rehoused:

> The process of secondary identification taking place in cinema theatres depends paradoxically on distance while in the case of games we encounter something more than just intimacy. Identification is replaced by introjections-the subject is projected inward into an "other". The subject (player) and the "other" (the onscreen avatar) do not stand at the opposite sides of the mirror anymore-they become one.[35]

How to square this rather contradictory argument? Here, as somewhat obliquely alluded to above, we find a common ground between 1.0 constative subjection theory and 2.0 reflexive performative theory. Both are equally symptomatic of an ideology of *'the arrival'*. In both wrapping up a *constative* completion of a subjection to the apparatus (1.0) or conversely a completion of *reflexive-performative* absolute self-presence (2.0) both positions end up equally saying the same thing: *"the space and the user are indivisible"*. For as *a program-space* we cannot be divided apart from it and as a *me-space* we equally cannot be divided apart from it (for it gives me everything *I* would want whatever this *I* turns out to be when floating around itself). To begin to close-up the 2.0 performative stage of our argument: by being able to *choose* our avatar and then *change* their position we would seem to float-free upon cyberspatial air, destabilising any previously dominant Cartesian or Euclidean coordination.

So here *on* the internet and *within* cyberspace we are within the presence of very concrete and open wormholes and thus the *true* death of the boundary would seem to be imminently or immanently upon us. The private, carved-off space of the previously dominant *'cogito-text'* now gives way to a sort of infinite bleeding-out, as all the connections which previously were furtively sought out (by merely reading) become open and available as destinations (of reflexive *self*-becoming). Within six hyperlinks then we experience a giddy separation from our original *"location"*. The olde texts of 1.0 then give-way to a mere *resource* and thus throw us back upon our own giddy and now free-roaming self-present identities. This self-present first-person performative self-movement will need much deconstructive unpacking.

4.   First-Person Multiple: Iterable Performatives

> Could a performative utterance succeed if its formulation did not repeat a "coded" or iterable utterance, or in other words, if the formula I pronounce in order to open a meeting, launch a ship or a marriage were not identifiable as conforming with an iterable model, if it were not then identifiable in some way as a "citation"?...In such a typology, the character of intention will not disappear; it will have its place, but from that place it will no longer be able to govern the entire scene or system of the utterance. [36]

The Performative, here reinterpreted by Derrida (and also quoted by Butler[37] to underline her own Derridean use of the performative) as quasi-citation, always-already *penetrates* into the Constative (which we, and by extension 2.0 labelled as 1.0). Austin's performative[38] would be the *self-*

presenting first-person singular-pronominal active present-participle of the "*I*-do" (furnishing the, for example, the famous speech act of the *I-do* of the wedding rites[39]). This singular presence however is predicated and reliant upon (iterative) the 'past-perfect' of the "*you-did*" that would seem *in comparison* to this first-person singularity to be an externally cold and stale recording, citation or writing technology[40]. Thus the *citational* writing-*within*-speech (we could recoin it arché-citation) that is Derrida's own reworked 'performative'[41] points to a *différantial-undecideability* (between – but not *beyond*- 'performative' and 'constative' as opposites) that can also be seen to be at the heart of the videogame which neither a *constative 1.0 theory* nor the *performative 2.0 theory* could circumscribe. For in the game, as we will see, there is an *excess* or *dissemination* that overruns or *invaginates* the boundary of any third or first-person position.

Beyond these (1.0 vs. 2.0) views then, it is preferable that the game should *not* be conceived of as a program*(me)* at all. For within this compounded neologism both a closed '*program*' (1.0) and a closed '*(me)*' (2.0) presumes a *violatory* concept of an *outer* hacking or breaching of erected 'meta' fences that would attempt to fend off such incursions or breechings by some notionally errant *alterity*. For in the old 'sovereign-spaces' of the linear media text or program(me) there are the countless protections against fore-seen audience dissention, dialogically contained *within*, as constitutive of their very boundary or notionally 'cleaved' singular-existence[42]). As a concomitant of this *non-limit* in the game, and at this point still in a measure of agreement with 2.0, we must also be wary of utilising unproblematised concepts from film or literary-linear studies such as '*diegetic space*'. For here a *distinct* or internal 'diegetic space' (to be divided off from the notionally 'extra-diegetic space' of the 'audient' *encountering* that "theatrical" en-closure) would create a too neat divide, frame or *parergon* which does no justice to the *openly* invaginated nature of the space that is the *game-staging*[43]: the outlying districts of the game are not so circumavigable. This lack of a diegetic framing or of a carved-off narrative space becomes all the more conspicuous when we see that there is no '*One*' in the sense of a clear narrative *agency*. Here we come upon the importance of the first/third person problem for the videoogame.

In the game there is a clear (and essential) *undecidability* between the first and the third person subject positions (performative and constative respectively) whose vibrating-interlace will deny the ability of the space-of-play to wrap up its incorporated 'protagonist'. Before coming to land squarely on this however we must briefly look at a very important transition between the game and its linear subject-position forebears, one also that makes it very different to the *externality* of subject positions within the internet experience (could one here even think in the region of first or third person?). Within literature, and in its transportation to film, the *difference* of the first and the third-person never hands over an active 'signifier' arranging role to the person who is doing the reading or the spectating (hence now the neat new celebratory baptismal-neologism of the morphed *reader+writer=wreader*). The handing over of the optical first-person position in a few select linear-films *never* hands over the reigns to the viewer however. This is a very different to first and third undecidables within the game[44]. One need only look at one of film's famous (and few) incursions into the "first-person" territory to see the difficulties of taking up the optic alignment and concomitantly then assuming to make of the spectator the *key player*.

Montgomery's Film-Noir '*Lady in the Lake*'[45] was an experiment in film which took cinematic suture and the dominant *point*-of-view and transformed these into a constant *optical*-point-of-view. Here then we rarely saw the star of the show (Montgomery himself) for all the 'other' eyes in the film looked directly into 'our' protagonistic ones. This experiment was famously a failure for the voyeuristic *distance* so beloved of cinema (Mulvey[46] et al) would paradoxically prevent the 'immersion' of stepping into the shoes of the screen-party rather than witnessing the scene from an associational distance. Another problem is the *control of a space of comparison* where we would be needed to be ever-present and thus outside of the constant locked character-optic. For if every component within the narrative-space is *restricted* to our optical-presence then *unrestricted aspects* unperceived by us 'the character' could not be compared or controlled by the omniscient narration (the obvious point about suspense as Hitchcock pointed out to Truffaut[47] is showing more than the character knows and thus *increasing* our sense of empathy at their plight; for example a bomb ticking away under their seat). Thirdly, and most obviously for our purposes, the optical aspect does not hand over the reins, for nothing in the space is ever re-arranged by any extra-diegetic empirical viewing. On these three grounds at least[48] then the game is prevented from coinciding with such narrational first or third personage; for the interactivity of the game makes a mockery of the taking-up of these inside/outside positions: *the game invaginates this divide*.

Games then in being a haunted[49] différance-engine operate on the very boundary distinction of first and third person, text/and non-text, of performative and constative and of presence and absence. Designers are still mistakenly fighting (*pragmatologically*) to create a first-person performative with the additional security of the cinematic third-person constative: hence the promised 'Cinematic' experience which game's covers and cutscenes often wish to foreground[50]). This battle however is headed in entirely the wrong direction and cannot complete its mission, as the game is situated *from bottom* on openings. Let us look at a game which more openly welcomes or embraces its gamic nature.

Like many games 'Black and White'[51] starts with a cutscene which helps to situate the player in relation to the gamespace they are about to embark on. Here they are given their 'character' and welcomed into the world of the game's 'parameters'. Once this universal-constative cutscene is over and the particular-performative game-element embarked upon, the player finds they are actually occupying at least *two* positions, to a large extent fracturing any perspectivisation in that traditionally *unified* sense. Firstly there is the God-mimicking 'above' position (literally 'a hand') where all areas of the game can be mobilised and manipulated, as in any decent top-down civilisation game. This leaves however a certain sense of de-focalised third-personage, placed as we are within the "third-person" position of distance or identificatory absence: 'outside' the *occupied* space of the ground level. Godlike. A second position is offered in answer to this hovering absent-outside whereby a second 'stand-in' character, now *within* the space, can be influenced, coaxed as of a proxy (a 'Beast' character chosen from a line-up of cow, lion or monkey; each with their own *initial* attributes). Here is where this game gets its impetus or identity, in this fractured sewing-*between third and first*. We are a God who chooses to intervene but we also intervene *on* a character which also *intervenes* on further characters (the population of a village it will interact with). A *double*-intervening. A *double* placement and interest: expanding as the game unfolds.

One interaction is constant, ready-to-hand and *ours;* obeying our controls, one-to-one, as in some *I-extension*. This extended-*I* is omnipotent, immanent and always seemingly ours. The second stand-in however is relatively autonomous and *capable* of change, without any exacting guarantee. Through a sort of Pavlovian conditioning, the *as yet* ill-formed Beast's activities in this island-world are circumscribed, to an extent, given its relative autonomy, by reward and punishment (a stroke or a punch for example as it eats up villager *or* saves one from drowning). Thus the God-hand (for that is the tool with which we reward, punish and coax) *upon* the beast forms a sort of clumsy steering wheel that in *attempting* to drive the beast becomes a sort of *conscious* extension of it, in a Heideggerian sense. Our boundary with the beast is thus more fluid and removed than our *ready-to-hand* (of God) character which would seem *also* to be the first-person avatar of ourselves *in-play* (replacing the gun of the first-person shooter with the hand of our God-self). The beast-character acted upon by our *extending-I* hand then forms a secondary tool more *present-to-hand*, a *tool-towards-a-narrative-branching* that we are constantly and consistently aware of. This character itself is however *never* consistent or determined. A problem already. For these two *différant* loci of operation (the hand *and* the beast; operator *and* operand) within *themselves* and within their *difference* provide also a variable and bleeding boundary dynamic *between* positions of first and the third person (God: for we are the position of the narratological third as in a linear text, *experienced* also as first in this game-text) and third-person-*ed* (beast) with attributes of a first which then provides the game's *irresolvable* identity-play (*and thus showing the game to be beyond constative and performative as distinctives*). Three narratological dynamical parties then are at play in their presence in this game. The complex, even *psychotic*, status of first and third person is rarely addressed or problematised within the critical literature and tends to be reduced to easy *positional* differentiations (as we have seen) of first *or* third and a *clear diegetic arena* within which their activities are thus then circumscribed.

Let us concentrate briefly a little more here then, for economic simplicity, on one of the boundary-between parties only: the beast. This beast, this *other-self*, has fluidly open-closed (invaginated) boundaries which prevent us from landing it as some diegetically encircled third person constative position. Also however as acted-upon it cannot be wrapped in any performative first-person immediacy.

The opening few transactions of the game are centred on demonstrating to us its *openness*, its *choices*. Two character-guides or preliminary-chaperones, one angelic and one demonic (*momentary* helpers or traditional omniscient narrators as far as the game allows for such stabilised *guiding hands*) unravel the function of many of the game's core components. They foreground for example the concept of the building up of the behaviours of the beast that we have *taken on*. In this rather camp parody[52] of the cartoon's (Good vs. Evil) disembodied 'inner voices' we are told how we can affect various outcomes. Here then after this restrictive nursery-slope (once we are on our own) the game becomes far from black and white. This is why a textual analysis cannot really take us any further down these multiply-forking paths. How can one textually analyse such a shaded uncertain and undecidable object? How then can one talk of a diegetically locked temporo-spatiality, where by definition either a first or third person position could be defined?

The beast, as neither constative third-person character nor performative first-person *occupied* tool, never sleepwalks along a path of calendar pre-destination. By coaxing the character, and by having it continually on the edge of a slipping-away-from-grasp, we find a haunting *sense* of its future attributes in its de-centred present movements within the story-world 'we-*it*' occupies; making of 'it-*we*' a flickering undecidable performative-constative (or as we saw earlier a Derridean *re-coined* performative). The beast is then is a *de*-central character of a morphous identity within this différance engine that is the *slippery diegesis* of the game's fluid *futurity*. The important *fluidity* of this future and the haunting of the *other-path* cannot help but make us aware of the question of *other* always-already hanging over present-absences.

That the 'present-diegesis' (the spacetime that the beast is "presently" inhabiting) is haunted by an-other diegesis makes any narrational *absolute* positioning of *third-person constative* eminently undecidable. That we are not free to operatively or performatively *roam* makes any metaphorical first-person 'experiential' equally undecidable. Such undecidabilities that we are opening up here cannot be closed down by the wishful thinking of the *protective absolute oppositions* of third or first person. Thus we must put in place a more knowing, open and avowedly undecidable recoined performative which *contains and admits* of its constative-iterative.

This more knowing and thus *less certain* re-coined iterative-performative must recognise that neither a 1.0 locked constative (third-person) beloved of apparatus theory, nor an open and free-roaming performative (first-person) beloved of reflexive models is *correct* for these new media spaces such as the game. Identity here is never *knitted* nor *unknitted* but also never simply a happy combination or resolution of the two (hence no 3.0 synthetically appreciating or sublating these differences). This irresolvable un-becoming *flickering* of the first and the third persons provides a telling problem in this différance-engine that is the videogame. That we cannot *resolve* this différance in the spacetime of the game may be something to celebrate...

...For the game itself does not end in either definition *by the game* or by *walking away free* within it. The game goes *far beyond* the game and we will not be walking away from it. For we are not *really* playing it.

We are facing our incompletion...

Notes

[1] This of course purposefully and rather self-confidently utilises a computer program nomenclature to display a theoretical goodness of fit to the momentum of this modern world.

[2] Again we must underline the somewhat ironic sense of this progressive 1.0 versus 2.0 mounting of hostilities. A younger generation of media theorists (typified in the parties of Merin, Gauntlet et al) parcel-up as "1.0" a seeming homogenous unity which does not recognise *ludic play*. More particularly they seem to say that media studies 1.0 does not seem to recognise that the world has moved on into the more client-sided pursuits of games, the internet and social networking sites. Thus the *technologies-of-the-teaching* need an overhaul as they are in grave danger of being left behind and outstripped by

their pedagogic student/objects (now turned teacher). Of course media theory was not previously sewn-up (or even sutured) by non-playful explanations. For example, one need only think of Fiske's classical re-deployment of de Certeau and Bakhtin (almost a repeat of Merin's re-deployment of Caillois) to see the role that play as *tactics* have had in the face of a seemingly faceless and *strategic* ideological power. It is of course this latter 'strategic' aspect (as representative of 'the server' serving media to a linear down-stream consumer) that has here come into question. Still does this create a neat 2.0 departure?

[3] See Fiske, J., *Television Culture*. Routledge, London, 1987 for a clear example of this position of carnivaleque consumption which refuses to unwrap its parcel in the symmetrical way that the *giving* institution would prefer.

[4] See de Certeau, M., *The Practice of Everyday Life*, University of California Press, Berkeley and Los Angeles, 1988 for a classic examination of the organising strategies of institutions versus the resistant counter-tactics of their users, consumers, etc.

[5] In 1987 with its System 6 operating system Macintosh Hypercards were much hyped and lead famously to popular games such as Myst as well as the popularising of interactive multimedia along with the Commodore Amiga's 'Amigavision' authoring system.

[6] See Aarseth, A,. *Cybertext: Perspectives on Ergodic Literature*. The Johns Hopkins University Press, Baltimore and London, 1997. Though Aarseth rightly points out the difficult notion of a reader writing through choosing pathways, he points out that such choice does not in any way compete with a notion of writing.

[7] Here we could name Jay .G. Blumer, Wolfgang Iser, John Fiske, Stuart Hall, David Morley, Ien Ang, Standley Fish, Henry Jenkins, Martin Barker and others

[8] See MacCabe's 'Realism: Notes on Some Brechtian Theses' for a clear explanation of the workings of meta-narration within classic narrative texts.

[9] *http://www.jiscmail.ac.uk/cgi-bin/webadmin?A2=ind0801&L=MECCSA&P=R386&I=-3* for a brief entry on Merrin's thinking on keeping up with strudent's ludic experiences also the intereseted reader could search the archive for "media studies 2.0" for other entries in this debate. This debate also responded to an outline by Gauntlet of his thinking on media theory 2.0 to be found here: *http://www.theory.org.uk/mediastudies2.htm*.

[10] See Caillois R., *Man, Play and Games*, University of Illinois Press, Urbana and Chicago, 2001, for an influential analysis of the social functions of play

from a number of angles including the ludic angle influential with Media 2.0 scholars.

[11] Rehak, B. 'Playing at Being' in *The Video Game Theory* Reader ed. M.J.P. Wolf & B. Perrron (Routledge, 2003) New York and London. p103-127.

[12] Of course the use of the phrase '*hey you!*' comes from Althusser in relation to the multitude of ideological state apparatuses but here interpellation makes us think of the use of subject positioning by writers of the cinematic apparatus such as Baudry, Comoli, Mulvey and Heath as well as others centering around the journals *Screen* and *Cinetracts* in the 1970's and 80s. For the interested reader, the every edition of *Cinetracts* is available in pdf format at the following website: *http://dl.lib.brown.edu/cinetracts/*

[13] MacCabe, C., 'Realism and the Cinema: Notes on Some Brechtian Theses' in *Popular Television and Film*, Tony Bennett (ed), BFI Press, London, 1981.

[14] Rehak op cit p.119.

[15] Indeed we could open up a whole can of worms here in the use of *diegesis* in any sense or conjoining of terms, difficult as it would be to throw it away; thus reducing the open-closed of the game to the openness and thus entire lack of diegesis of the internet, for example. We use 'extra-diegetic' here *heuristically* to denote the distance of the game from the diegesis of the film (and in the absence of a better concept) but *extra-diegetic* has been utilized rightly to refer to things like titles or peacocks in Eisenstein's 'October' which exist outside their respective story-spaces. This can may be worth opening however to expose the insurmountable narrative problems of the game. We can only mount an insubstantial challenge here ourselves.

[16] See Dayan D., 'The Tutor Code of Classical Cinema' in *Movies and Methods*, Bill Nichols (ed), University of California Press, Berkeley and Los Angeles, 1976, pp.438-450, as well as the chapter 'On Suture' in Heath, S., *Questions of Cinema*, Palgrave Macmillan, London, 1981, pp76-112.

[17] For the suturing of the spectator "completed" within the film's shot-reverse-shot takes the third-person 'juxtapositions' of the film's dominant specularity and enacts for the audience a *misrecognition* of first-person identity. For more on misrecognition see Rosen, P., *Narrative, Apparatus, Ideology*, Columbia University Press, New York, 1986. Also see the two entries immediately below.

[18] Doane M.A.,'Misrecognition and Identity'in *Explorations in Film Theory: Selected Essays from Cinetracts,* Ron Burnett (ed), Indiana University Press, Bloomington and Indianapolis, 1991, p15-25.

[19] See Metz, C., *The Imaginary Signifier: Psychoanalysis and the Cinema*, Indiana University Press, Bloomington and Indianapolis, 1986.

[20] Doane op. cit. p.19

[21] Rehak, op. cit. p121.

[22] Heidegger's phrase (translated from '*das-man*') for an inauthentic 'Being' which follows the machinic flock showing for example an inauthentic being-towards-death (a disavowal of its real-coming) and thus a lack of authenticity in one's present comportments.

[23] Rehak, op. cit. p122.

[24] Here we see a paradox of 'the break' which there is no real time to go into here but which would take the 'break' of the shot-reverse-shot (something screen theory takes to *actually* suture) and by taking them away would suture ever the more. Here lies an illogical paradox in Rehak's argument that would be worth unpicking further (beyond its confines in Rehak's usage to further issues within notions of remediations of the cinematic).

[25] Here again there is the paradox of 'programming' which some remediating Screen theorists take as an enslaving power of the game: programming as if to program audient outcomes. We will be looking into this a little further in.

[26] Bolter a little like Rehak sees video games as carrying on or 'remediating' the work achieved by earlier media.

[27] Gauntlett, D. *Media, Gender and Identity: An Introduction*, Routledge, 2002 p97.

[28] Ibid p. 142

[29] Osborne, P. & Segal, L., '*Gender as Performance: An Interview with Judith Butler*', Radical Philosophy 67 (Summer 1994), pp32-39.

[30] Here performative is closed down from any prior materiality to a radical free-choice without standing-order. This combination of self-presence and reflexivity provides a tautological self-security which repeats the notion of the free-flowing individual, so beloved of the tradition. In dressing this tradition up in the garb of an escape-from-tradition the 2.0 theorist gains a very flexible tool.

[31] To match with portfolio *identities* we have portfolio *work* which contours identity within the ambit or ecology of the infrastructural move from a previous industrial lifelong *workplacedness* to a post-industrial 'portfolio working' where work focuses down to a highly mobile individual (the *smallest company*, as some have coined 'him'). Countless employment studies (for example: Gold. M. 'Managing Self-management: Successful Transitions to Portfolio Careers' *in Work, Employment and Society Vol. 16, No 4.)* point out this change in the dominant life-time. For a more worked out sociological view see Harvey, D.,   *The Condition of Postmodernity*, Blackwell, Oxford, 1989 as well as Smart, B., *Modern Conditions, Postmodern Controversies*, Routledge, London and New York, 1992. Such a transition (and self-reflexive freedom) is however figurally 'triangulated' in the (rather patronisingly self-confident) film '*Billy Elliot'*, where a boy in a British northern industrial town 'comes out' to his locale as a ballet dancer

(and to his somewhat pre-portfolio or 'industrially' situated dad). The key moment in the film comes when the dad *recognises* his own attitudes are those of a passing age and that he must give way to these new and more mobile identities: his son should be able to choose the mode and identity he likes. Here we have a marked move in the figure of the problematic position of the 'offspring' from '*Saturday Night and Sunday Morning*' where Arthur Seaton is punished for his coming-out-of-the-collective through his use of music, drink and adulterous affairs. The traditional pre-reflexive ecology of the time was not yet ripe for choice.

[32] Turkle, S., *Life on the Screen: Identity in the Age of the Internet*, Simon & Sschuster, New York, 1997.

[33] Filiciak, M., 'Hyperidentities' in *The Video Game Theory* Reader ed. M.J.P. Wolf & B. Perrron (Routledge, 2003) New York and London. pp87-102

[34] Ibid p95-97.

[35] ibid. p91

[36] Derrida, J. '*Signature, Event, Context*' in 'Margins of Philosophy' (Press, London) p.149

[37] Bulter ibid. p.13

[38] As father of Speech-Act theory Austin spoke of acts which could not be judged on any constative truth value but which inaugurate or perform an *activity* in the very act of saying. This *causal-inaugurating* of such acts of speech are what Derrida (like his ongoing deconstruction of the speech and writing opposition) problematises back into a citational anteriority, making of the performative a sort of *arché-citation* much like the famous arché-writing he makes of speech which he then goes on to mobilize as a borrowed and retargeted (against the very conceptual framework borrowed from) tool to work on the tradition.

[39] This is one of Austin's famous *performatives* with which Derrida takes issue: self-presence as non-iterable (within '*Signature, Event, Context*') and in sympathy with which Butler anchors the reading to engage with questions or notions of sex/body (as probmematisers or contourings of 'gender'). Gauntlett ignores this important influence, as some fast and loose freedom with the concept might then have been threatened by such noted conceptual filiations.

[40] One need only think here of the '*verb*' and its connection with the '*verbal*'. A 'doing' word can only seem here to 'be done' when it is an originary 'doing'; as assumed in a performative speech act.

[41] We have to reinforce that the performative that Derrida uses is stretched from the contradictions noted within Austin's theory. Austin's 'performative'

haunted by 'constative' (by iteration for example) is Derrida's knowing *mis*use.

[42] Hence the notion of a 'copyright' that marks off an internal limit from its citational outside (wherein the latter possibility is repressed).

[43] Games as such then are not to be seen as strategic campaigns inviting resistant and escalating tactical *counter* campaigns on the part of the player (a la the counter-tactics cherished by de Certeau and his followers such as Fiske and his playful polysemically-equipped 'semi-active' consumers). Such notions of a *firewallable* identity are not a part of the game no matter how many boundaries are tried and tested. Here again is a contradiction which both defines the game and reveals why its future, *to come,* does not lie in any form of recalculated or reconditioned filmic *presence*. The game involves and always-already accounts for the free-play of the player. The computer can do nothing else than *accept* such user input. It is not then a war and thus not a real *hacking*.

[44] Could one talk about a Deleuzean *becoming-first* or *becoming-third* or of a *fold* between? Such a rhizomatic *becoming* from-the-divide however does not recognise the radicallity of the flickering undecideability between these '*position*s' as we hope to elaborate.

[45] Montgomery, R., *Lady in the Lake*, MGM, 1947.

[46] Mulvey, L., '*Visual Pleasure and Narrative Cinema'* in Popular Film and Television Tony Bennett (ed), BFI Press, London, pp.206-215.

[47] Scott, H.G. & F. Truffault, *Hitchcock*. Simon & Schuster, New York, 1985

[48] This small list of three could be expanded and an interesting study undertaken to further problematise the difference between so-called first-person videogames and traditional narrative or *diegetic genres* that employ the first-person but within the larger narratological web that is the text. This difference needs to be unlocked much more than it is within the literature and the *gamic* (which should not be reduced either to the *ludological*, after Caillois and Frasca) quality of the videogame exorcised from these differences.

[49] For an examination of the haunted or hauntological nature of the spacetime in videogames see Lockwood, D. & Richards, T., '*Presence-Play: The Hauntology of the Computer Game* in 'Games Without Frontiers, War Without Tears: Computer Games as a Sociocultural Phenomenon'. Jahn-Sudmann A., and Stockmann, R., (eds),Palgrave Macmillan, 2008, pp175-185.

[50] This perhaps is where the conceptual mistake can occur that games are *necessarily like* film, because so many games still want *to be* film (to *remediate* film). They have perhaps not *attuned* yet to their gamic potentiality. We would strongly argue then that the game is *always already*

the game no matter how conservatively the nostalgia for film is evidenced, enforced, inscribed or seemingly concretised. There can then, as a product of this view, only be *degrees* of gamic rather than locatable or ontological differences of *'kind'* within the game. A film-game is from bottom a contradiction.

[51] Lionhead Studios., *'Black & White'*

Bibliography

Aarseth, A,. *Cybertext: Perspectives on Ergodic Literature*. The Johns Hopkins University Press, Baltimore and London, 1997.

Althusser, L., 'Ideology and Ideological State Apparatuses', in *Lenin and Philosophy*. New Left Books, London 1972.

Austin, J.L., *How to do Things With Words*. Harvard University Press, Cambridge, Massachusetts, 1975.

Butler, J., *Bodies That Matter*. Routledge, New York, 1993.

Butler, J., *Gender Trouble*. Routledge, New York, 1990.

Caillois, R., *Man, Play and Games*. University of Illinois Press, Urbana and Chicago, 2001.

Dayan, D., 'The Tutor-Code of Classical Cinema' in *Movies and Methods Volume One*, Bill Nichols (ed), University of California Press, Berkeley and Los Angeles, 1976, pp.438-450.

de Certeau, M., *The Practice of Everyday Life*, University of California Press, Berkeley and Los Angeles, 1988.

Derrida, J., *Margins of Philosophy*. The University of Chicago Press, Chicago, 1982.

Derrida, J., *Limited Inc* Northwestern University Press, Evanston, 1988.

Doane, M.A., 'Misrecognition and Identity' in *Explorations in Film Theory*, ed. Ron Burnett. Indiana University Press, 1991.

Fiske, J.,*Television Culture*. Routledge, London, 1987.

Gauntlett, D., *Media Gender and Identity: An Introduction*. Routledge, London, 2002.

Giddens, A. '*Modernity and Self-Identity: Self and Society in the Late Modern Age*' Stanford University Press, Stanford, 1991.

Gold, M., 'Managing Self-management: Successful Transitions to Portfolio Careers' in *Work, Employment and Society Vol. 16, (No 4.)*.

Harvey, D., *The Condition of Postmodernity*, Blackwell, Oxford, 1989.

Heath, S., *Questions of Cinema*, Macmillan, London, 1981.

Heidegger, M., *Being and Time*. Blackwell, London 1998.

Lash, S., & Giddens, A., & Beck, U., *Reflexive Modernisation: Politics, Tradition and Aesthetics in the Modern Social Order*, Polity Press, Cambridge and Oxford, 1994.

Lockwood, D. and Richards, T., 'Presence-Play: The Hauntology of the Computer Game' in *Computer Games as a Sociocultural Phenomenon: Games Without Frontiers, War Without Tears*. Jahn-Sudmann A., and Stockmann, R., (eds), Palgrave Macmillan 2008, pp175-185.

MacCabe, C. 'Realism and the Cinema: Notes on Some Brechtian Theses' in *Popular Television and Film*, Tony Bennett (ed), BFI Press, London, pp.216-235.

Metz, C., *The Imaginary Signifier: Psychoanalysis and the Cinema*, Indiana University Press, Bloomington and Indianapolis, 1986.

Mulvey, L., 'Visual Pleasure and Narrative Cinema' in *Popular Television and Film*, Tony Bennett (ed), BFI Press, London, pp.206-215.

Osborne, P. & Segal, L., '*Gender as Performance: An Interview with Judith Butler*', Radical Philosophy 67 (Summer 1994), pp32-39.

Rehak, S., 'Playing at Being' in *The Video Game Theory Reader* ed. M.J.P. Wolf & B. Perrron, Routledge, New York and London, 2003. pp. 103-127

Rosen, P., *Narrative, Apparatus, Ideology*, Columbia University Press, New York, 1986.

Scott, H.G. & F. Truffault, *Hitchcock*. Simon & Schuster, New York, 1985

Smart, B. *Modern Conditions, Postmodern Controversies*. Routledge, London and New York, 1992.

Turkle, S., *Life on the Screen: Identity in the Age of the Internet*, Simon & Schuster, New York, 1997.

Technology on Screen: Projections, Paranoia and Discursive Practice

Alev Adil and Steve Kennedy

Abstract

This paper explores the manner in which visual representations might be positioned in relation to more traditional political discourses around contemporary media technologies. Visual representation is discourse – not viewed as preceding as Baudrillard might have us believe, but as a link in a discourse chain connecting intermediate events or intensities. The way technology is seen and discussed, is integral to its essence (and therefore to digital/technological/cyber cultures) from a Heideggerian perspective. The discursive practices that shape technology will be explored using cinema as an example. Conceptual boundaries between seeing and feeling, perception and reality, past and present (memory and perception), the individual and collective are problematised and breached in contemporary cinematic representations of technology. Using Freud's conceptualisation of paranoia, arising from his analysis of Schreber's memoirs, this paper will address several questions about the paranoid film text and its relationship to new technologies. Discursive practices both shape technology, and are technologies in themselves. This essay will challenge hierarchies and position cinema as a key element within a network of discourses, exploring the extent of linkage and asking how situated practises shape these discourses.

Key Words: Technology, Cinema, Paranoia, Situated practice, Discourse, Visual Representation, Psychoanalysis, Freud, Schreber, Heidegger, Deleuze and Guattari

*****

Film and its visualisation of other technologies can and should be seen as *operational* within discourse, existing not solely in the symbolic realm but bound up in the world materially. But what is a discourse? What is it that film is a part of? For Michel Foucault a discourse is an amalgamation of statements that exist within a specifically prescriptive modality that allows them to have a material impact.[1] The films examined here are statements within a discourse that form a relationship with the 'real'. It is not an empty reality composed of representations in the manner put forward by Slavoj Žižek or Jean Baudrillard.[2] Films do more than simply reflect or set up a model for imposing vacuity wherein the real world is reduced to a screenplay

– rather they make varying and specific contributions to the nature of that reality.

This essay explores the extent to which film can be viewed as a discursive practice and as such the extent to which it can be seen as an element central to the essence of 'technology' when the concept is more carefully defined using the work of Martin Heidegger. Our analysis of recurring visual and narrative motifs and metaphors around the representation of technology in specific films will consider how these representations are part of wider discursive practices concerned with conceptualising technology. Film is a form of language that makes visible things that *are* (in this case technology), and in doing so contributes to the bringing forth of that which is *not yet*. In doing so it contributes to what technology *is*. Film is therefore immanent to technology and is implicated in its development, adoption and ultimate utilisation – its Heideggerian essence. The way in which it does this is complex.

Because of media convergence film is no longer a single medium, yet the cinematic apparatus still presumes and asserts modes of distribution and consumption whose commercial dominance is challenged by new media platforms. This paper will demonstrate the extent to which mainstream Hollywood, as situated aesthetic and industrial practice, produces representations of technology and viewing experiences which are marked by anxiety around the crisis facing the cinematic apparatus in the new media landscape.

In The *Question Concerning Technology* Heidegger sets out a framework for thinking about technology in a contemporary setting that urges the quest for *essence*. It is a framework that is still of use to us and is employed here to assess the importance of certain specific films' contribution to the contemporary technological landscape. In the essay Heidegger dismisses instrumental and anthropological assessments of technology as by themselves being insufficient in revealing this essence. He pushes us beyond simple means/ends ways of thinking and invites us to consider a more complex model where cause is itself a complex contrivance of factors. The essence of technology, it is suggested, might be better arrived at through an examination of the 'four causes' as traditionally employed in western philosophy[3] For Heidegger the most significant of these, *causa finalis* – ironically the one that in contemporary terms is the most overlooked - involves circumscription and setting bounds. It is claimed here that film contributes significantly to this process of circumscription in so far as it contributes to a discourse on technology, which in turn has a significant impact on our relationship to it. Heidegger tackles this relationship specifically when he moves his analysis on to consider the way in which we engage as humans with instrumental means within the context of the 'four causes'. In doing so he introduces the concepts of *poiesis* and *enframing*. The former relates to an essential aspect of technology which draws on human creativity to give form and function to material artefacts. This union of human creativity and material production had, according to Heidegger, become stretched as technology increasingly brought the world under control as *standing reserve*, or as a resource waiting to be utilized. The result of this has been a distancing between mankind, the natural world and technology. The essence of technology instead of being present within *poiesis* then, becomes characterised by what Heidegger called *enframing*: a mindset that privileges instrumental logic and separates the creative arts from technical production and material reality.

Thus technology, when exposed to an enquiry pertaining to its essence, is not present in anything technological but must be viewed within the context of its own discourse. The discursive practices which surround, contextualise and bring technology forth are important and maybe even primary. Within this context film can be seen as an instrument or a cause. But it can also be seen as an end or effect in itself, as specific finished product. When these two elements combine in films *about* technology or about film's relationship to other media/technologies, our analysis reveals something of the essence *of* technology.

The relationship between discursive practice and the material or 'real' world was further developed by Michel Foucault. In *The Order of Things* Foucault demonstrated how language and things became detached. He said:

> The Profound kinship of language with the world was thus dissolved. The primacy of the written word went into abeyance. And that uniform layer, in which the seen and the read, the visible and the expressible, were endlessly interwoven, vanished too. Things and words were to be separated from one another. The eye was henceforth destined to see and only to see, the ear to hear and only to hear. Discourse was still to have the task of speaking that which is, but it was no longer to be anything more than what it said. [4]

This dissolving does not mean however that there is no longer any meaningful relationship between 'reality' and representation as argued by Baudrillard and Žižek, but stresses the change in that relationship; a change in the order. The position here is that rather than existing as pure simulacra or representation, film as discourse has a serious role in informing the 'real' and the material – stressing the correlative not the causal. In support of this a better interpretation of Foucault's position comes from Deleuze, who points out:

"talking isn't seeing... a difference that means that by
saying what one can't see, one's taking language to its
ultimate limit, raising it to the power of the unspeakable."[5]

This according to Deleuze is not what Foucault is doing. There
comes to reside in language the power to significantly affect without
fundamentally determining. In accordance with this position and in a manner
that seems to support the inclusion of film within an expanded category of
discourse, Deleuze has described Foucault's archaeological method as audio
visual:

Archaeology is to do with archives, and an archive has two
aspects, it's audio-visual. A language lesson and an object
lesson. It's not a matter of words and things. We have to
take things and find visibilities in them. And what is visible
in a given period corresponds to its system of lighting and
scintillations, shimmerings, flashes produced by the contact
of light and things.[6]

It is these 'shimmerings' in cinematic form that are the object of
analysis here. Such an approach seems to echo/draw on Heidegger's position
regarding the centrality of discursive practice to essence as set out above. If
what is said and how it is said is recognised as important in locating the
essence of technology, then technological determinism and instrumental
reasoning can be challenged. Film, when seen as more than a technological
means to an end, can help us do this. Both economic and political, existing as
both cultural text and within a wider social context, it is a
medium/technology that is situated in relation to other media/technologies
both old and new. This situated relationship is sometimes explicit, as in the
films being analysed here. At times paranoia may be identified when film is
seen as being aware of itself as a technology, with a direct relationship to
other technologies, but it is unaware of itself as central to the essence of
technology in the form of *causa finalis*. As such it does more than simply
reflect the so-called real world.

Let's examine how mainstream Hollywood as a 'system of lighting
and scintillations' 'speaks' from an industrially located ideology and what it
has to 'say' about technology. The big screen (cinematic apparatus) tries to
articulate its supremacy – as the 'premiere' or licit platform of film in a
media landscape where films become computer games, can be 'ripped' –
downloaded, sampled and collaged, shared through peer-to-peer file sharing
viewed in their entirety or as clips or stills on the small screen of television
and PCs as well as on the tiny screens of mobile phones and ipods. At the
same time cinema must engage and contain the fantasies engendered by new

technology and adapt to the demands of new viewing subjects. Hollywood is rarely flattering about competing modes of film dissemination. Films about television like *The Truman Show*, *Pleasantville* and *Quiz Show* for instance, all represent television as an autocratic anti-intellectual medium/technology that produces undemocratic and dumbed-down viewing subjects. The small screen is represented as small-minded, conformist and simplistic, explicitly fascistic in both *The Truman Show* and *Pleasantville*. Cinema iterates itself as, by implied contrast, the space of Technicolor, high art and individualism, offering opportunity and free will. As in *The Matrix*, *eXistenZ* and *Minority Report* most cinematic representations of new technology commonly make free will a crucial anxiety/ problem in the new media environment. Beyond its characterisation of new technologies as totalitarian, cinema also posits (as both threat and perhaps tantalising promise) technology as penetrative and prosthetic, as threatening the autonomous Enlightenment subject. In *Videodrome* and *eXistenZ* David Cronenberg represents both video and gaming as penetrative technologies that produce subjugated users tied to an organic/ prosthetic medium, as do the Wachowski brothers in *The Matrix*.

What's at stake here is not simply representational: the positive or negative properties attributed to new media platforms in mainstream Hollywood cinema but relational: the kind of viewing subject being interpellated/ constructed. Film viewing, as much as film making, is a situated practice. The viewing subject is to some extent technologically determined, their relationship to the text shaped by their mode of reception. The cinematic apparatus is predicated on a mode of viewing which renders the viewer as an essentially scopophilic and passive subject: alone in the dark watching the film according to dictates set by the cinema's timetable and the director's sequencing. Yet, ironically, new media viewing environments that offer more choice in modes, qualities and intensities of reception are presented as more threatening to individual autonomy, as deterministic and breaching the boundaries of the self. Laura Mulvey contends that mainstream Hollywood organises meaning around the active (penetrative and sadistic) male gaze both through narrative and visual construction. Her argument is relevant here, not only because it attempts to configure the psychological relation between the viewing subject and the technological mode of reception but also because it invites us to see the film consumption in the classic mode as creating a subject for whom film is a prosthetic through the phantasy of the penetrating gaze.

Technology as a signifier in cinema takes on a variety of signifieds but ultimately acts as a fetish, that asserts that technology is 'thing', outside sentience, that there is an essentially human sense of self as clearly distinguishable from the machine. This acts as a fetish in both an economic, anthropological and psychoanalytic sense. In its very articulation the assertion undermines itself : whereas the Freudian fetish both acknowledges and represses the difference of the Other, and thus the threat of castration ; the technological fetish recognises the impossibility of distinguishing between the sentience that interacts with a medium and the sentience the medium interpellates through both form and content. Cinematic representations of technology speak (with much anxiety) of a realm of representation and subjecthood which threaten the boundaries of spectacle and voyeur, image and viewer, mechanical and organic. Rather than the comfort of the gaze penetrating (and controlling) the phantasy space, new media environments show us a world where it is impossible to distinguish between the 'real' and technologically mediated. "Are we still in the game?" Ted asks Allegra at then end of *eXistenZ*. The audience's anxiety about the ontological status of the narrative is as comprised as the protagonists'.

Films such as *The Matrix* and *eXistenZ* infer a new model of specularity. The representation of new media environments, of virtual realities conjures up a new viewing paradigm, a shift from a visual voyeuristic model to a diffused paranoid model. Here the acoustic (hearing voices) is as important as the visual, the panopticon is as prevalent as the voyeur because seeing and being watched are contemporaneous, the vision itself is organic, opaque and tactile. The game players plug into the game in *eXistenZ*, the Matrix plugs into and feeds off humans, the precogs in *Minority Report* are attached to the machines that screen their visions. The screen is either nonexistent or an interactive social space as in *Minority Report*. The conceptual boundaries between seeing and feeling, perception and reality, past and present (memory and perception), the individual and the collective are all problematised and breached. These films concern themselves with phantasies of persecution and penetration. They present us with the return of the (cinematic) repressed: our desire for a more immersive interactive medium returns in the paranoid delusion of it as a threat . The inability to distinguish between reality and illusion is a crucial component of paranoid psychopathology. The impossibility of distinguishing between reality and simulation is the central narrative anxiety of *The Matrix* and *eXistenZ* and speaks to the central epistemological anxiety/desire of postmodernism. This returns us to the central dilemma of the Cartesian meditations. The supposition is that "there is an evil spirit, who is supremely powerful and intelligent, and does his utmost to deceive me. I will suppose that sky, air, earth, colours, shapes, sounds and all external objects are mere delusive dreams, by means of which he lays snares for my credulity."[7] The rational 'I' who thinks, whom Descartes proposes, is breached in paranoia; and according to these films in new media environments. Paranoia operates not merely as an individual pathology, a breakdown of reason, but as an epistemological method of enquiry, an attempt to make sense of a compromised subjectivity, in this context the new subjectivities engendered by new technologies. Thus the paranoid gaze on/of technology in these films not only articulates anxieties about the threat to the boundaries between self and Other, animate and inanimate and most crucially reality and illusion, but also marks an attempt to imagine a new kind of subjectivity.

There are marked and extensive similarities between Neo in *The Matrix* and Schreber, whose memoirs form the basis of Freud's conceptualisation of paranoia. Both are penetrated by something which feeds off them, both hear voices, both are convinced that they are 'the One'. Undoubtedly the dominant reading offered is that this new subjectivity is a space of crisis, a pathologised, abject space. However we can also draw useful parallels between Deleuze and Guattari's definition of the Body-without-Organs and Neo's description of the Matrix. Deleuze and Guattari tell us that "The field of immanence is not internal to the self, but neither does it come from an external self or a nonself. Rather, it is like the absolute Outside that knows no Selves because interior and exterior are equally a part of the immanence in which they have fused."[8] At the end of *The Matrix* as the screen shows a computer screen with binary code and the words 'System Failure' Neo tells us "I'm going to show these people a world with you, a world without rules and controls, without borders or boundaries; where anything is possible. Where we go from there is a choice I leave to you".

It's worth noting that while the narrative externalizes and configures the Matrix as hostile, as an empty BwO the ending of the film is ambivalent. Neo speaks from within the Matrix, the sequels promise us more, not less of the virtual. Technology is visualized as a threat, the space of abject maternity, a womb-space that feeds off rather than nourishing its collectivized subjects. Yet it is also the topoi of spectacle, where we can eat steak and look streamlined and sleek in black leather in contrast to 'real' where, denied fantasy, we must subsist on gruel looking grubby and grizzled in homespun hemp." Extending Deleuze and Guattari's categorization of psychoanalysis, we can characterise the cinematic apparatus as a 'priest' of vision. Thus it is no surprise that mainstream Hollywood tends to translate/repress the desire for this new specularity and its attendant collective subjectivity as a projection of persecution rather than as internal desire for collective illusory sentience (although that reading is still present). This is because cinema's traditional medium of existence is threatened by the prevalence of this new model of specularity.

The point here is not simply that cinema tends towards dystopian representations of new technologies because as an 'old' technologically situated practice it is under threat. Beyond this economically (and culturally) determined discourse we can see older discourses woven though differing media which shape the representation of technology on film. Rutsky identifies two contrasting 'impulses' of technology which predate cinema: the Frankenstein complex and the mummy complex.[9] In the former technology comes to life whilst the mummy complex elides technology and the distinction between copy and original. Bazin traces a genealogy from cinema, painting and sculpture to the religion of ancient Egypt and the 'mummy complex' – the desire to preserve life against death.[10] Film and photography, before cg imaging presents us with an archive, which "must be described in relation to death. ... a contract with what has ceased to exist, a contract with death."[11]

Spielberg's *Artificial Intelligence: A.I.* inhabits both these discourses. We see an elision from the dystopian creation myth of the machine: *Frankenstein* (and the birth of modernism), to a utopian vision of the machine as the benevolent receptacle of memory (and thus of the dead). The robots read David's memory just as we look at old photos, for the punctum, the 'really' essentially human transitive, ephemeral qualities preserved there. The loved one is lost, but is revived or recreated through technology: Sean as a ghostly hologram in *Minority Report*, David as an uncanny automaton. David and the pre-cogs are variants of the automaton, the zombie and the double: figures that Freud identifies in his essay on the uncanny[12] as occupying a liminal space that breaches the division between alive and dead, human and non-human. The uncanny effect (in literature and film), as the etymology of the German word *unheimlich* makes clear, renders the familiar strange and reveals that which makes us uneasy about it. The domestic bliss David longs for is a disconcerting experience for Monica and for the film's audience, for instance when David laughs unnaturally at the dinner table, or leaps out when Monica is in the bathroom. The unheimlich often takes on an auditory nature, as when David acts as a telephone or in *Minority Report* when the innocent pre-cogs speak in the voices of the guilty.

The recurrence of the double and of multiples in both films also raises questions around originality and reproduction. Whereas David is a copy (of the original David Hobby), the many Davids and Darlenes David discovers in Professor Hobby's headquarters remind us of the questions Benjamin raises around aura and authenticity in his essay *The Work of Art in Age of Mechanical Reproduction*. David is distraught to find he is a simulacrum of the 'real' (lost) David Hobby. He rejects his multiplicity and insists on his singularity – an individuality borne chiefly out of the singularity of his love for Monica. As a simulacra David lacks the 'aura' of the real child, just as Benjamin proposes art loses its aura in the age of mechanical reproduction However the mechanical, through memory, is imbued with aura. "The cult of remembrance of loved ones, absent or dead, offers a last refuge for the cult value of the picture. For the last time the aura emanates from the early photographs in the fleeting expression of a human face. This is what constitutes their melancholy, incomparable beauty."[13] The blue fairy is a cheap simulacrum but through ritual worship (a 2,000 year prayer) she becomes 'real' or at least realised as the conduit though which the future machines communicate with David.

In *High Techne* R.L Rutsky identifies how utopian representations of technology are "'spiritualized', infused with an eternal fully present spirit of life" whereas "in dystopian representations, the coming to life of technology is presented as the product of an occult or supernatural knowledge, of black magic.... The 'dead' technological object never becomes fully living; it remains merely a simulation, undead, a technological monster or zombie."[14] Whilst anxieties around master/slave dialectic are commonly expressed in cinema, and Spielberg seems to be making explicit visual and verbal references to the Holocaust in depiction of the Flesh Fairs in *Artificial Intelligence: A.I.*, the crucial issue isn't simply about whether humanity is served or subjugated but whether the machine, cyborg or alien attains individual sentience and morality –becomes auratic. From Rachel in *Blade Runner,* the Terminator in *Terminator 2: Judgment Day* to David, we love the machine that manages to become imbued with the aura of individual identity.

In *Artificial Intelligence: A.I*, David's genealogy stretches from the classical Hellenic myth of Pygmalion through Collodi's *Pinocchio* to Shelley's *Frankenstein*. The film is inspired by a Brian Aldiss short story *Super Toys Last All Summer Long*. The weave of discourses contained in the imprinting spell or formula that makes David love Monica eternally reflects this mixture of discourses – the natural (hurricane), aesthetic (tulip, dolphin), philosophical (Socrates) and scientific (particle). A binaristic opposition between machine utility and aesthetics is refused. Like cinema itself, David needs both "flat fact" and "fairy tale" in his quest to become real. Cinema is a medium whose aim is primarily psychological, and certainly in its popular and commercial incarnation, film speaks to a collective imaginary or unconscious rather than straightforwardly representing any individual authorial intention or psyche. Symbols, whatever the medium they are communicated in, operate in a discursive mode, which is distinct from logical analysis or any rational epistemology, although they engage with the same ontological dilemmas. Where technology becomes penetrative and aggressive in the (paranoid) Frankenstein complex, it is prosthetic (memorial) in mourning. The two approaches to conceptualizing technology are not mutually exclusive. These films move between paranoia and mourning: between the fear that the collective intelligence of technology will enslave individual sentience and the hope that technology can stop time and return our lost loved ones to us. In doing so they contribute to the Heideggerian quest for essence.

As a technology film belongs in the modern world characterised by *enframing*. As such it can be seen as an element central to dominant discourse and normalising practice. However, it can equally operate at the level of *poiesis* within a postmodern setting as Rutsky points out, to the extent that the aestheticization of life to which film has contributed, has now moved us beyond enframing.

"Thus, for Heidegger , the mode of representation involved in the Greek techne is a mode of unsecuring that is non-instrumental , and thus more closely related to artistic production (poeisis) than to the production of modern technology, which regulates and secures the world in instrumental terms. The world is thus set in place (gestellt), which is why Heidegger figures the essence of modern technology, its mode of representation as a kind of Enframing [Ge-stell]. Thus, while Enframing stresses setting in place, regulating, and securing, the emphasis in techne is on setting free, on unsecuring, on allowing the world to be brought forth in non instrumental terms... In a high-tech world, then, the proliferation of technological reproducibility begins to outstrip the ability to resecure it."[15]

Rutsky's argument suggests that the distance between *poiesis* and *techne* as set out by Heidegger has been breached within a postmodern setting that is characterized by the re-adoption of technology into the artistic process. Technology is viewed as having slipped its leash - its constant renewal and reinvention making it impossible to secure within a bureaucratic discourse of the kind which characterised modernism.

The film texts considered here acknowledge the possibility of film as a discursive practice that is characterised neither by enframing *nor* poiesis, but a movement between the two. This fluidity operates in a manner that exposes relations of cause and effect to perpetual critique wherein the real and symbolic are seen as confluent and not divergent.

Notes

[1] Michel Foucault, 2004b: 120
[2] Slavoj Žižek, *Welcome to the Desert of the Real* (2001) and Baudrillard, J *The Precession of the Simulucra* in *Simulations* (1983)
[3] The four causes are (1) *causa materialis* (2) *causa formalis* (3) *causa finalis* (4) *causa efficiens* Heidegger, (1977): 6
[4] Michel Foucault, 2004a: 48.
[5] Gilles Deleuze, G (1995): 97.
[6] Gilles Deleuze, G (1995): 96.

[7] Rene Descartes, *Discourse on Method and the Meditations* Trans. and ed. Anscombe, Elizabeth and Geach, Peter Thomas. (London: Nelson's University Paperbacks, 1979), 65.

[8] Deleuze, Giles and Guattari, Felix. *A Thousand Plateaus* trans. Brian Massumi (London: The Athalone Press. 1988), 156.

[9] Randolph L. Rutsky, *High Techne: Art and Technology from the Machine Aesthetic to the Posthuman* (Minneapolis: University of Minnesota Press. 1999)

[10] Bazin, Andre. *What is Cinema? Volume 1.* Trans Hugh Gray. (Berkeley and London: University of California Press, 1967)

[11] Roland Barthes, *The Grain of the Voice* trans. Linda Coverdale (New York: Hill and Wang, 1985): 356.

[12] Sigmund Freud. *The Uncanny" 1919* in *Penguin Freud Library, Vol.14, Art and Literature,* ed. Albert Dickson. (London: Penguin, 1990.)

[13] Walter Benjamin. *Illuminations* Trans Harry Zohn (London: Fontana, 1999), 219

[14] R.L Rutsky (1999): 24.

[15] R.L Rutsky (1999):7-8.

Bibliography

Baudrillard, J. *Simulations* New York: Semiotext. 1983.

Bazin, Andre. *What is Cinema? Volume 1.* Trans Hugh Gray; Berkeley and London: University of California Press, 1967.

Benjamin, Walter. *Illuminations* Trans Harry Zohn: London: Fontana, 1999.

Cronenberg, David. *eXistenZ* London: Momentum Pictures Home Entertainment. 2002. DVD.

Deleuze, Giles. *Negotiations* New York: Columbia University Press, 1995

Deleuze, Giles. *Cinema 1: The Movement-Image.* Trans. Hugh Tomlinson and Barbara Habberjam. 1983. London: The Athlone Press, 1986.

Deleuze, Giles. *Cinema 2: The Time-Image.* Trans. Hugh Tomlinson and Robert Galeta. London: The Athlone Press, 1989.

Deleuze, Giles and Guattari, Felix. *A Thousand Plateaus* (trans. Brian Massumi) The Athalone Press, London, 1988.

Descartes, Rene. *Discourse on Method and the Meditations* Trans. and ed. Anscombe, Elizabeth and Geach, Peter Thomas, London: Nelson's University Paperbacks, 1979.

Foucault, Michel. The Order of Things. London: Routledge, 2004a.

Foucault, Michel. The Archaeology of Knowledge. London: Routledge, 2004b.

Freud, Sigmund. 'Schreber, notes on a case of Paranoia' in *Case Histories II* Vol. 9 London: Penguin, 1991.

Freud, Sigmund. "The Uncanny" 1919 in *Penguin Freud Library*, Vol.14, *Art and Literature*, ed. Albert Dickson. London: Penguin, 1990.

Heidegger, Martin. *The Question Concerning Technology and Other Essays* New York: Harper & Row, 1977.

Mulvey, Laura. 'Visual Pleasure in Narrative Cinema' in *Visual and Other Pleasures*. London: Macmillan, 1989

Rutsky, Randolph L. *High Techne: Art and Technology from the Machine Aesthetic to the Posthuman* Minneapolis: University of Minnesota Press, 1999.

Spielberg, Steven. *Artificial Intelligence: A.I.* Los Angeles, Calif.: Warner Home Video, 2000. DVD.

Spielberg, Steven. *Minority Report* London: 20th Century Fox Home Entertainment, 2003. DVD.

Wachowski, Andy and Larry Wachowski. *The Matrix*. Los Angeles, Calif.: Warner Home Video, 1999. DVD.

Žižek, S. Welcome to the Desert of the Real *re: constructions: reflections on humanity and media after tragedy* (2001)

Desistant Media

Seppo Kuivakari

Abstract
Through analyses of works from contemporary media artists I argue for a certain mode of information I call desistant. Desistance can be understood in terms of mise-en-abyme, considered here as an abyss following the logic of the paradox, or the logic of the hyperbologic, as French philosopher Philippe Lacoue-Labarthe calls it. For him, mise-en-abyme must always reflect in order to ensure (re)presentation, namely, reflection itself as (re)presentation. Thus, hyperbology is the logic of mimesis: the hyperbological is unceasing, endless and thus without resolution. As opposite to a mirror, which holds the truth as adequation, mise-en-abyme is a tool for folding the truth by producing hyperbological folders of uncertainty into the operations of the truth itself. Hyperbologic is indifferentiable as such, imperceptible and always superlative: the greater the attempt at any identification with the other, the more this intention fails. This, finally, is "desistance". To "desist", in Jacques Derrida's vocabulary, is to correspond to a kind of madness, obsession, siege and caesura, a double bind and the impossibility of reappropriation: not just formal oscillation but hyperbology.

Key Words: mimesis, media art, desistance

*****

1.   Introduction

Within Western traditions of aesthetic thought, the concepts of imitation and mimesis have been central to attempts to theorize the essence of artistic expression, the characteristics that distinguish works of art from other phenomena, and the myriad of ways in which we experience and respond to works of art. In most cases, mimesis is defined as having two primary meanings – that of imitation (more specifically, the imitation of nature as object, phenomena, or process) and that of artistic representation. Mimesis is an extremely broad and theoretically elusive term that encompasses a range of possibilities for how the self-sufficient and symbolically generated world created by people can relate to any given "real", fundamental, exemplary, or significant world, Mimesis is thus understood as integral to the relationship between art and nature.[1]

Different media have treated this relationship differently. For example, Jay Bolter and Richard Grusin make an argument in their theory of remediation that the desire for immediacy would appear to be fulfilled by the transparent technologies of straight photography, live television, and three-dimensional, immersive computer graphics. Such transparent technologies, however, cannot satisfy that desire because they do not succeed in fully denying mediation. Each resolves to define itself with reference to other technologies, so that the viewer never sustains that elusive state in which the objects of representation are felt to be present; therefore the oscillation between media modes that, according to Bolter and Grusin, finally construct the viewer's identity. Whenever we engage ourselves with media, we become aware not only of the objects of representation but also of the media themselves. Instead of trying to be in the presence of the objects of representation, we, due to oscillation, define immediacy as being in the presence of media. This can be questioned through the hyperbologic of media: this fascination, as Bolter and Grusin say, with media works as the sublimation of the initial desire for immediacy is something as central to the Western tradition, the desire to be immediately present to oneself – something that has an onto-typological philosophy as a guarantee. Still, oscillation means that this idea of investing to oneself is too narrow explanation. We can admit that the double logic of remediation recapitulates the Lacanian psychic economy – but it does not yet open the field of "frustration" to be recognized: the very problematics of identification.[2]

Western thought, believes Jacques Derrida, has always been structured in terms of dichotomies or polarities like truth versus error and identity versus difference. These polar opposites do not, however, stand as independent and equal entities. The second term in each pair is considered the negative, corrupt, undesirable version of the first, a fall away from it. Hence, the absence is the lack of presence error is the distortion of the truth, etc. In other words, the two terms are not simply opposed in their meanings, but are arranged in a hierarchical order, which gives the first term *priority*, in both the temporal and the qualitative sense of the word. In general, what these hierarchical oppositions do is to privilege unity, identity, immediacy, and temporal and spatial *presentness* over distance, difference, dissimulation, and deferment. In its search for the answer to the question of Being, Western philosophy has indeed always determined Being as *presence*. Derrida's critique of Western metaphysics focuses on its privileging of the spoken word over the written word. The spoken word is given a higher value because the speaker and listener are both present to the utterance simultaneously. There is no temporal or spatial distance between speaker, speech, and listener, since the speaker hears himself speak at the same moment the listener does. This immediacy seems guarantee the notion that in the spoken word we know what we mean, mean what we say, say what we mean, and know what we have said. Derrida has termed this belief in the self-presentation of meaning "logocentrism" from the Greek word *Logos* (meaning speech, logic, reason, the Word of God). Writing, on the other hand, is considered by the logocentric system to be only a representation of speech, a secondary substitute designed for use only when speaking is impossible. Writing is thus a second-rate activity that tries to overcome distance by making use of it: the writer puts his thought on paper, distancing it from himself, transforming it into something that can be read by someone far away.[3]

Responding to the constraint of an originary programmation – *in fine*, the Platonic determination of being as *eidos/idea*, and therefore of being as the fundamental *tupos*, or repeating formula, of a transcendental production – the epoch of onto-theology is nothing other than the epoch of the bestowal of (the) meaning (of being, of existing) through figures. And this means, most decisively, through the figure of man, the figure of a human *tupos* determined as the *subjectum* or as the Subject of meaning. It is in this sense that, following Derrida's analyses in "The Ends of Man", also Philippe Lacoue-Labarthe and Jean-Luc Nancy will speak of what completes itself is the discourse of the actualisation of the genre of the human. It is this actualisation, and hence exhaustion, of the human as the absolute figure of meaning that Lacoue-Labarthe and Nancy identify as the figural completion of metaphysics. Distinguishing themselves from Martin Heidegger, they insist upon the figure not as the metaphysical echo of a more originary experience of being, but being itself as an original *mimeme*; as the mark of an originary fiction at the heart of metaphysics.[4]

Derrida challenges the metaphysical assumption of an original unity of meaning and being in discourse and suggests means of introducing the effects of passion, irony, and ambiguity into the semiotic study of representation. He thus enables us to locate the limitations of (Saussurian) sign theory. Deconstruction is Derrida's term for the critical manoeuvre that reveals the moment of negation inscribed in any notion of presence, including the presence of the subject to consciousness as the condition of possibility of meaning, the presence of signifier to signified, and the presence of reality to perception. Deconstruction calls into question metaphysical hierarchies that allow self-presence, meaning, and reality supposedly to transcend the moment of their inscription in representations. Derrida argues that because metaphysical philosophy defines being with reference to its other (nonbeing), the meaning of discourse with reference to its negation in graphic notation, and reality in terms of its capacity to be copied in representations, then nonbeing, writing, and representation can no longer be considered supplements to an original reality or perversions of an original closure of the

subject in spoken discourse, but as moments in the very constitution of the
subject and signified of discourse.[5]

For Lacoue-Labarthe onto-typology is ontology, which lies hidden
in every – traditional or contemporary – definition of mimesis: truth means
placing the world itself in its own truth, the revelation of truth, regardless of
the subject positing this phenomenon. Onto-typology is a transcendental
production of the world in itself in a away the world opens up and will be
stabilized by the being – whether it is the question of ideas which mark the
things by Plato, or Heidegger's technic, which essence, *Ge-stell* (meaning
"framework") is nothing technical but the marking of the being, installation –
typing its seal on it. Onto-typology is a philosophical effort to set together the
demand for truth and the idea of the world as pre-constructed. World is a
"work", but it is not depended on any subjective discretion (in other words,
from the threat of mimesis), but it constructs itself from within. Lacoue-
Labarthe's thought on onto-typology is primarily as follows: onto-typological
philosophies are, because of their emphasis on infinity, too near the
Christian-platonic thinking to be free to think about the transcendentality
itself. In onto-typological philosophies the world appears as types, characters
or forms (idea, schema, Ge-stell): even if transcendental type cannot be seen
or be represented as such, directly, a thought about type is attached with an
idea of its own permanence, a certain a priori shape of the world. This is why
onto-typological philosophies are culminated – even though this cannot be
seen in Hegelianism – in a thought about a system, perfect categorization of a
whole, which could, at least in principle, be seen as a complete illumination.
Lacoue-Labarthe's thought about the essence of the world demands to its pair
a notion of an image that a finite subject will from this pretension construct.[6]

By onto-typology Lacoue-Labarthe means finally a term he – in his
own words – forged on the model of the Heideggerian philosopheme of
"onto-theology" to designate the ontology that underlies at once the most
ancient thought of mimesis and the modern thought about figures (*Gestalt*)
that proceeds from it.[7] Onto-typology is by nature a belonging of the
"Western metaphysics"; it overthrows the thematic values proposed by an
"original mimesis".

A convincing form of onto-typology, forming a type or schema, is
hidden in the ecological media theorization that relies also on the Aristotelian
apparatus of identification by emotional involvement, namely, empathy, pity,
sorrow, and finally, catharsis as a powerful "emotion machine" described by
Ed Tan, psychologist Joseph Anderson and other media ecologists,[8] but
elaborated also by Bolter, who holds that television in particular seeks to
foster the illusion that it is pure perception, a perfect recreation of the world –
persuading the viewer that he or she is looking through the screen at the "real
world beyond"[9]. Bolter and Grusin say that one in all its various forms the
logic of hypermediacy expresses the tension between regarding a visual space

as mediated and as a "real" space that lies beyond mediation. The logic of hypermediacy, in its full form, means logic of (formal) oscillation.

Richard Lanham calls this a tension between looking *at* and looking *through*. He sees it as a feature of 20th century art in general and digital representation in particular.[10] A viewer confronting a collage, for example, oscillates between looking at the patches of the paper and paint on the surface of the work and looking through to the depicted objects as if they occupied a real space beyond the surface. What for Lanham characterizes modern art is an insistence that the viewer keep coming back to the surface of, in extreme cases, an attempt to hold the viewer at the surface indefinitely.[11] He regards *collage* as the "central technique of the 20th century mainstream, which has often created heterogeneous spaces and made viewers conscious of the act of representation".[12]

To fulfil this thought, Lev Manovich pinpoints the oscillation protocol in a same manner as does Peggy Phelan. Manovich says the production machinery can be revealed next to the creation of an illusion, and the cyclical shifts between illusion and its deconstruction neither distract nor support in giving a reality effect.[13] Phelan, from a feminist perspective, citing extensively Lacan, says that the real is read through representation, and representation is read through the real. Each representation relies on and reproduces a specific logic of the real; this logical real promotes its own representation. The real partakes of and generates different imagistic and discursive paradigms. Phelan gives an example: a legal right in which concepts such as "the image" and "the claimant" are defended and decided through recourse to pre-established legal concepts such as copyright, trademark, property, the contract, and individual rights. Within the physical universe, the real of the quantum is established through a negotiation with the limitations of the representational possibilities of measuring time and space. She continues, within Lacanian psychoanalysis the real is full being itself. Within the diverse genre of autobiography, the real is considered the motivation for self-representation. The discourse of Western autobiography and psychoanalysis are alike in believing their own terms to be most comprehensive, the most basic, the most fundamental route to establish or unsettling the stability of the real.[14] What Phelan thinks here is that autobiography is an artistic method for shattering the stable real as a resistant mode to something we can consider as "onto-typology", a haunt for the truth of illus

Donna Haraway postulates that in Renaissance visual technology, form and narrative implode, and both seem merely to reveal what was already there, waiting for unveiling or discovery. This epistemology underlies in Haraway's eyes the European-indebted sense of what counts as reality in the culture, believed by many of its practitioners, to transcend all culture, called modern science. Reality, as Westerners have known it in story and image for several hundred years, is an effect but cannot be recognized as such without great moral and epistemological angst. The conjoined Western modern sense of the "real" and the "natural" was achieved by a set of fundamental innovations in visual technology beginning in the Renaissance.[15]

Now comes the question presented by Derrida: why is the space of the one not the space of the other? Deconstruction questions the fundamentality of onto-typology: if space were "objective" – or universal, as we have spoken here –, geometric, ideal, no difference in economy would be possible between the two systems of incision. According to Derrida, the space of geometric objectivity is an object or an ideal signified produced at a moment of writing. Before it, there is no homogenous space, submitted to one and the same type of technique and economy. Before it, space orders itself wholly for the habitation and inscription in itself of the body "proper". There still are factors of heterogeneity inside a space to which one and the same "proper" body relates, and therefore there are different, indeed incompatible, economic imperatives, among which one must choose and among which sacrifices and an organization of hierarchies become necessary. An original economy is prescribed each time.[16] This opinion challenges the universality of different programming of media and is the key factor in differencing the media modes from each other practically.

We can continue this elaboration with Lacan. In contrast to the tactile, "visuality" is the space of light that Lacan calls "dazzling, pulsatile": there's an atmospheric aura that illuminates the viewer from both back and front, so that from the start there is no question of mastery. And in the context of this space of the luminous, the viewer is not the surveyor, but, caught within the onrush of light, he is what interrupts its flow. Into this interruption the viewer enters a picture created by this light as a "stain" or blind spot, as the shadow cast by the light, its trace, and its deictic mark. The viewer's position is one of dependence on an illumination that both marks him (the deictic) and escapes his grasp (the distich). This illumination Lacan calls the "gaze".[17] Gaze in fact exists in relation with illusion, pointing still to a certain attempt to master the seen, not leaving it without comprehension but with failure, whereas the cognitive look upon this defines it rather as a universal way of media homogenizing the human experience.[18]

With Lacan's psychoanalytic understanding of thought, deconstructive philosophy problematizes this latter tradition of thinking at a technological momentum that differs with each effort to determine it. Kaja Silverman, for instance, interprets Lacan to affirm that through the gaze a subject relies for his or her visual identity on an external representation,[19] but at the core of Lacan's work is the idea that the unconscious is structured like language. The passion of the signifier is Lacan's name for something Silverman calls the language of desire. Signification comes into play with displacement – which the mirror experience produces – both in the sense that it is *there* that meaning is produced, and that each new term functions as a representative of what came before. Each new memory is ultimately a signifier "of" passion. We can also become passionate about the signifier itself – about what makes it distinct from what it represents, claims Silverman.[20] This abyss will remain in focus as we proceed further, to the extent that there is no proper image, no pure image, no whole picture for us to comprehend or, as Derrida says, an entire theory of the structural necessity of the abyss will be gradually constituted: the indefinite process of supplementarity has always already infiltrated presence, always already inscribed there the space of repetition and the splitting of the self. Representation in the *abyss* of presence is not an accident of presence, the desire of presence is, on the contrary, born from the abyss (the indefinite multiplication) of representation.[21] Thus, no patterns of presence in media can be surely erected. Already the notion of the unconscious by Lacan has challenged the metaphysics of presence and of the self-conscious subject.[22]

The relationship between art and imitation has always been a primary concern in examinations of the creative process, and already in Aristotle's *Poeisis* the "natural" human inclination to imitate is described as "inherent in man from his earliest days; he differs from other animals in that he is the most imitative of all creatures, and he learns his earliest lessons by imitation." The very *pedagogy* of this thought is shared by Plato, but in contradiction to him, whose skeptical and hostile perception of mimesis and representation operate as mediations that we must get beyond in order to experience or attain the "real", Aristotle views mimesis and mediation as fundamental expressions of our human experience within the world – as means of learning about nature that, through the perceptual experience, allow us to get closer to the real. In this thinking, works of art are encoded in such a way that humans are not duped into believing in them as "reality", but rather to recognize features from their own experience of the world within the work of art that cause the representation to seem valid and acceptable. Mimesis for Aristotle functions not only to re-create existing objects or elements of nature, but also to beautify, improve upon, and universalize them. Mimesis creates a fictional, *supplementary* world of representation in which there is no capacity for a non-mediated relationship to reality. Here Aristotle locates two types of mimesis: general, and the one that is restricted, productive. He looks upon mimesis as something that both nature and humans have in common, something not only embedded in the creative process but also in the constitution of the human species.[23] This thought, which ultimately accounts for no meaningful space to the "otherness" of our reality, is quite ecological in its constitutional manner.

Onto-typology assumes the world to be pretended, or to be fictioned. As far as we think that metaphysical thinking is onto-typological, its essence is *fictionnement* – a word that Lacoue-Labarthe creates from the French word fiction (figure, creation) as translation for German word *(Ein)bildung* (*einbildung* = imagining; *Bildung* = shaping, formation, pedagogy etc.) This "fictionnement", which is translated here as figuration, is evident in Plato's ideas, categorizations of Aristotle, Kant's schematization or in *Ge-stell* from Heidegger. They are based exactly on what Kant called the forming force (*bildende kraft*) of transcendental imaginative power (*Einbildungskraft*), in other words, in transcendence or metaphysics itself. It is a kind of "schematism" that defines the essence of reason as the "positing of the same". Schematization, the constitution of the same, fashioning and fictioning, is categorization in the Aristotelian sense or idea in the Platonic sense. Idea, category, and schema consequently connect to the same fictioning force of reason that Kant called the "forming force" of reason or transcendental imagination.[24] And despite its always being a question of a formation of a world of man, of how the world always produces or *pretends* itself, this transcendental *bildungskraft* has nothing to do with the presentation of the subject. The world, being, and the truth remain as a stela, they are characterized by slowness or even permanence – and this is the very articulation of the being itself.[25] Stelae of man, of representation and thereby a finalizing system of belief: a myth that calls us to be a part of the world giving within this closure a gift of defining "us".[26]

Since Freud (and Nietzsche), the installation of the system – modification of the Aristotelian schema of "recognition" by accounting for processes of identification such as they do – implies an exclusion which in turn is no longer merely that of physical suffering and illness, but that of mental illness as well, of neurosis that is realized, constituted and "foreign" and thus resistant to recognition. Lacoue-Labarthe tells us that this exclusion, which pertains to insanity or madness, is not treated adequately in theories implicating identification through recognition.[27] This "theory" is hidden even in the realms of interactivity – at the precise point where any thought about "protagonism" arises. Still, Malcolm Le Grice avers that if the early traditions of (pictorial) representation can be characterized by the representation of the object to us – confirming our power over objects – and if the more recent state of our representational (cinematic) technologies have placed us as spectators within the representation of unfolding events, then interactivity for Le Grice seems to offer a representation of our intervention in those events. He argues that where the cinematic implicates us as viewers through the processes of identification supported on a layer of photographic, sensory simulation, and an illusion of instantaneous presence, interactivity promises us implication as protagonists, which means a continuity of psycho-cultural enterprise from pictorial representation using perspective to the dynamic "narrative" of represented events.[28]

But Lacoue-Labarthe and Nancy hold that, in the history of the notion of identification, the experience of hysteria joins identification when one traces its examination, on this side of imitation and contagion, right back to an appropriation of the other, who can only result from a community, from an *already* given being-with-the-Other. Through the double path of narcissistic and hysterical identifications, a path never absolutely reduced, one does not end up with a concept, but with the formation, which endlessly redoubles and undoes itself, of a constitution of identity through a being-with-the-Other which only takes place in the negation of the Other. This negation is also an appropriation, but the one who appropriates has no "proper", he is not a subject. Consequently, if there must be a question of origin, the latter takes place (or arrives) neither through a subject nor through an other, nor through the Same nor through the Other (*l'Autre*) but through asociality, or through an altered sociality.[29] This is not only a modernist rupture in the transparency of the visual regime – Bolter and Grusin say hypermediacy, the "hold" of technology, becomes the sum of all the unconventional unusual, and in some sense deviant ways of looking: it is multiple and deviant in its suggestion of multiplicity, a multiplicity of viewing positions and a multiplicity of relationships to the object in view[30] – but a centuries old technique of the artist. Philosophically, we can understand this not as inter-, but alteration.

Within this, the identification process as such will not be finalized. Or fragmented, as the myth of "modern" in the evaluation of modernism suggests. Instead, it will continue, infinitely.

Now, with extensive use of desistant motifs in art, there might be a certain deconstructive process happening that *dis-erects* the human from the image – simulation from the emotion machine, as ecological media theory supposes – of ourselves: an unstructuring of being and its relation to the world. Hypothetically, we can understand that desistant media are misappropriated tools and thereby produce, as we will see, the uncanniness within (and of) mimesis.

To "desist" is, in Derrida's words,[31] to correspond to a kind of madness, obsession and schiz, siege and caesura, double bind and impossibility of reappropriation, hyperbology, ineluctable dis-identification. What interests us here is neither the subject nor the author. Nor is it the "other", whatever one places under the term, of the subject of the author. It would be rather what is *also* at play in the subject; what, in the subject, "deserts" the subject *itself*, and which, prior to any "self-possession" (and following another mode than that of dispossession), is the dissolution, the defeat of the subject in the subject or *as* the subject. The (de)constitution of the subject, or the loss of the subject is to conceive of the loss of what one has never had, a kind of "originary" in a sense of "constitute" loss (of self). Lacoue-Labarthe's way of parenthesizing the "de" in "(de)constitution" signifies for Derrida that one must not hear it (any more than in the case of desistance) as a negativity affecting an originary and positive constitution.

The italicizing of the *as* signifies that the "subject", as such, (de)constitutes itself in this movement of desistance and *is nothing other than* the formation of this movement. For this reason it also signifies that the subject cannot be simply omitted or dissolved, or passed over in silence in the name of a deconstruction of subjectivity.[32]

To "desist" is thereby more than "to oscillate"; it goes *beyond* any formal structuring. Understanding desistance as a strategy for analysing media, desistant media are by definition disappropriate and obsessive; also, they produce a kind of realm that makes Friedrich Kittler, among few, to wonder if certain basic assumptions remain unquestioned also in the psychoanalytic verification of the fantastic – because it transfers poetry into science.[33] But the incoherence, the excess, the lack of control, a mad machine, as Lacoue-Labarthe calls a desistant mode, escapes mastery. Or else, one must oppose it – arrest thought, or remove it, by a step back, from this danger: draw back. And so, measure, maintain, economize: A determinative mode means an economical mode. Save and safeguard: truth against everything that could shake it. Nothing is accidental if its safeguards some sense of truth, the very truth of aletheia in the sense of Heidegger – the master word.[34]

Keywords in the quest for defining desistant mode of media, to name a few explicitly, are *mirror, mise-en-abyme*, and *mimesis*. Lacoue-Labarthe, with his colleague Nancy, teases out all the philosophical force of the terms generated from within the tragic of the Greek word *opsis*: mimesis, poeisis, techné – a whole theatrics of thinking, in other words, which falls within the essential lexicon of the figure. Figure is a central theme in Lacoue-Labarthe´s thinking, a suspicion concerning what he has called "onto-typology", concerning a figural and fictional assignation of the presentation of the being and/or the truth.[35]

Within but few pages in a book about Heidegger and art, Lacoue-Labarthe elaborates his ideas concerning mimesis and appropriation:

> Since Plato, education or training, political Bildung, has been thought taking the mimetic process as starting point: Plato challenges this, dreaming precisely of a (philosophical) self-grounding of the political, i.e. cutting through the mimetological double bind – admittedly with an idea of the Idea that is itself paradigmatic (and belonging, in consequence, to the mimetological) [...] the programme emerges of what Schiller calls an 'aesthetic education' of humanity [...] The crucial point is that Bildung is always thought on the basis of archaic mythic paideia [...] It is not by chance that the 'myth' of the cave – a myth that has no 'mythic' source, a myth that is self-

formed and self-grounded – lays the foundations of Plato's
political project. Identification or appropriation – the self-
becoming of the Self – will always have been thought as
the appropriation of a model, i.e. as the appropriation of a
means of appropriation, if the model (the example) is the
ever-paradoxical imperative of propriation: imitate me in
order to be what you are.[36]

After this important question concerning paideia Lacoue-Labarthe asks how,
and why, identity derives from mimetic appropriation:

Yet the question remains of how, and above all why,
identity (properness/property (la propiété) or being-in-
oneself/being-proper (être-propre)) derives from mimetic
appropriation. The speculative dialectic is eschatology of
the identical; and so long as this logic, more or less
explicitly, underpins the interpretation of mimesis, one can
only ever move endlessly from the same to the other –
under the authority of the same. Conceived more
rigorously, however, mimetologic (la mimétolologique)
complicates and de-stabilizes this schema: in the
dialecticization of mimesis, a subject is presupposed, albeit
a virtual one. However, by definition, mimetism forbids
such a presupposition, and Diderot has very convincingly
established this: no subject, potentially identical to himself
or related to himself, can pre-exist the mimetic process,
except to render it impossible.[37]

For Lacoue Labarthe, philosophy's true essence lies in its own
figuration. The sign represents the present in its absence. It takes the place of
the present. When we cannot grasp or show the thing, state the present, the
being-present, when the present cannot be presented, we signify, we go
through the detour of the sign. We take or give signs. We signal. The sign, in
this sense, is deferred presence. Whether we are concerned with the verbal or
the written sign, with the monetary sign, or with electoral delegation and
political representation, the circulation of signs defers the moment in which
we can encounter the thing itself make it ours, consume or expend it, touch it,
see it, intuit its presence. And this structure presupposes that the sign, which
defers presence, is conceivable only on the *basis* of the presence that it defers
and *moving toward* the deferred presence that it aims to reappropriate. Within
this classical semiology, the substitution of the sign for the thing itself is both
secondary and *provisional*: secondary due to an original and lost presence
from which the sign thus derives; provisional as concerns this final and

missing presence toward which the sign in this sense is a movement of mediation. Still there is no justice to be found within these processes, but violence, and not just any violence; it is arche-violence.[38]

According to Lacoue-Labarthe, the classical conception of figure or fiction, that is, to a fictioning such as philosophy, from Plato to Christian allegorism, from Dante to Descartes and Leibniz, has always opposed, under whatever name, to the *e-vidence* of truth. This does not mean that it was ever a question of excluding fictioning (even less of "repressing" it). It has always functioned, on the contrary, either as a propaedeutic to the revelation of truth, or, as in Cartesian thought, as an auxiliary to the presentation of truth, that is, as a supplement to evidence. This is why fiction is never absolutely in the class of error or lie (even in Plato), even if it is in the space of shadow, of phenomenal Darkness, of indistinctness, of confusion, of veiling, and of the veiled. There are – Lacoue-Labarthe now citing Leibniz – two kinds of eloquence, there are two kinds of fiction, the "good" one, and the "bad" one; the one that leads to truth, effaces itself before truth or even heightens it – and then the other one, the one that resists, that does not efface itself, does not lift the aberrant one. A double veil, two kinds of veil: transparency and the obstacle. Fiction, for Lacoue-Labarthe is always divided.[39]

In an essay written by Lacoue-Labarthe and Nancy, "The Nazi Myth" (originally "Le mythe nazi", 1981), this thought culminates in a notion that Nazism understands itself through the terms of aesthetic politics – not by giving attention to aesthetic phenomenon but by being an aesthetic ideology. Like Nancy, Lacoue-Labarthe elaborates the figurative essence of politics from the standpoint of identification, myth or mimesis. Their emphasis on the figurative essence of politics and the political is fundamental to each moment of treating the political (and beyond). This essence takes many names: identification, poetry, mimesis, poeisis, mimetology, oeuvre, immanentism, fiction, myth, a sacrifice, scène. One might say that this series is the very lexicon of the political itself. It is not by chance that this can also be seen as the lexicon of onto-theology itself, now rethought as onto-typo-logy or, what amounts to the same thing, onto-politi-ology.[40]

Processes of identification Lacoue-Labarthe examines by creating two specific categories of imitation. First one is

> 1) Mimetism, which paragon is heroism. The question in mimetism is about identification and commitment, appropriation of pre-given models, but also about a myth as a way of identification.

Besides this traditional perspective on identification Lacoue-Labarthe has created a mechanism he considers as

2) hyperbologic, where every exaggerated construction of a model leads at the same time to its own underway. Because the relationship stays unsolved, it constantly erects itself again. Instead of appropriating any model, the idea of hyperbology is in an unstable repetition due to oscillation between two figures without any final destination to this logic.

In Lacoue-Labarthe's deconstructive reading of mimesis, it is not a matter of simple imitation but in fact turns on a logic of endless reflections following each other in an infinite chain. This is one disposition of *mise-en-abyme*, reflective abyss. Abyss is a basic and speculative motif in his thinking, from which he draws his own view concerning the subject of philosophy and its mimetic agony, which derives from the incompetence of mimetical movement to achieve the truth – and by so doing, remains within the territory of speculation. For Lacoue-Labarthe, the same theoretical speculation is typical of modern art, in fact, modernist art has provided Lacoue-Labarthe with a method for elaborating the (fictive) constitution of subject. Within this project it is not the passions that are "erected" by memory, but an obsessive hunt for the closure that will itself never come (to an end).

Insofar as hyperbology refers to structural oscillation, Lacoue-Labarthe's mimesis also reminds us of Derrida's *Writing* – or *Gram*. But where Derrida searches the motifs of Writing out from the margins of philosophy, Lacoue-Labarthe scans for the very core of metaphysics, where its influence is essential because its context is illimitable.[41]

Inasmuch as we think mimesis has always been led by processes of truth, there still remain persistent types of *Unheimlich* of *fictionnement* that could even be fragmentary. Lacoue-Labarthe and Nancy hold that fragments are definitions of the fragment and this is what forms the totality of the fragment as a plurality and its completion as the incompletion of its infinity. The truth, then, of the fragment is not only in infinite progressivism, but also in the actual infinity, by means of the fragmentary apparatus, of the very process of truth. Purely theoretical completion is impossible because the theoretical infinite remains asymptotic. Thus, work in progress becomes the infinite truth of the work.[42]

By the virtue of difference, truth is delayed. This conclusion differs from the theoretical assumption of truth that is shattered and fragmented; what is noteworthy here is that Lacoue-Labarthe and Nancy locate the fragmentary – the very fragment – earlier than Friedrich Kittler, for whom Romanticism was a period of monograph, and modernism; simply put, a time of polygraph. Lacoue-Labarthe and Nancy assume a mimetical account for modernist art and its aesthetic values somewhat earlier, through a specific study of early Romanticism in literature. Still, Lacoue-Labarthe is *not* drawing substantial differences between fragmentative and desistant modes of art; modernist art seems for him a monolith of resistant information modes, modes of counter-reading and counter-picturing.

Figure, for Lacoue-Labarthe, cannot present the true story of man, instead, the word "figure" always contains fiction.[43] If we follow the thought of desistance carefully enough, we might point out that camera, as a modelling tool, lies us, in an act of dispossession, into the picture – even when it is monitoring us. This means participation as dispossessive desistaction: a poetic paradox instead of proprioceptivity, which derives etymologically from *proprius*, personal and characteristic, and *capere*, to grasp, to catch.[44] This, in short, alludes to personal grasping and, ultimately, possession akin to *safeguard*.

Mimesis is a concept of fascination. Historically, the word *mimesis* has denoted representation and imitation, but, when chained to imitation, it has also meant repetition. Greek word "mimesis" belongs to the word family, whose root is *mimos,* an imitator or mime. Other members of the family are *mimesthai* (imitate, represent), *mimetes* (person who represents or imitates), *mimesis* (practise of imitation), *mimetikos* (something capable of imitating; also the object of) and *mimema* (representation).[45] Mimesis could also mime something that is missing – and, interestingly, also the truth. For Derrida repetition means giving meaning to multiplicity of reality and experience. Repetition, a structuring of reality and experience within a certain historical context, works as a supplement for nature: by giving certain structure to natural phenomena, not unproblematically.[46]

Lacoue-Labarthe postulates that repetition creates the manners of construction, of *Ge-stell,* so to speak. Repetition helps us to draw the line between mimetic and non-mimetic, but also between the real and the fantastic, familiar and non-familiar, life and fiction. In his celebrated essay on typography, Lacoue-Labarthe holds that the absence of rhythm is equivalent to the infinite paradoxical appearances of the mimetic itself. The lack of the imitated reveals what is in fact unpresentable – the imitated, repeated. This signifying faculty is a mimetic faculty: music (harmony and instrumentation on the other, rhythm on the other hand) imitates.[47] The weird and the fantastic, madness, these all assemble to create a world of stories, and vice versa: stories are weird, or they are mad: they are *fantastic.* This means also the stories produced by media art exhibit a certain faculty of possession, which makes the mental guarantees of aprioric world tremble, the supposed *a priori* order of things.

Mise-en-abyme is a term used for multiple purposes from heraldry to art history and literature. The principle of *mise-en-abyme* is that of a miniaturised form within the work, which either reflects the work as a whole or at least a major theme. The term was coined by Andre Gide, who borrowed it from the heraldic custom of crest design – *l'abyme*, literally meaning abyss, refers to the interior space of the blazon or crest. *Mise-en-abyme* might therefore be described as the Russian doll or Chinese box principle in art. *Mise-en-abyme* participates in artistic reflexivity in the sense that it draws attention to the constructedness of art, and in the sense that the fragment en abyme acts as a kind of mirror image of the larger work. In modernist art *mise-en-abyme* also constitutes a questioning of the concept of origin as it opens up the possibility of infinite regress.[48] This technique of reflection can reinforce the meaning and structure of a work and may even function as a self-conscious intrusion of the author, who deliberately draws attention to the fictionality – to the poetry – of art. Current literary theories place emphasis on aspects of the term that remind the reader of the artificer who has crafted the narrative, and therefore focus on the coming into being of the work itself, in short, the mirror in the text concentrates on the process of production of the text containing the mirror – possibly even as a metanarrative level of the poetic self-consciousness.

Lacoue-Labarthe does not define the term *mise-en-abyme* in any theoretically detailed manner but uses it strategically to present the idea of an abyss in modernist art. In short, he means by the term more an infinite imitation of the imitated. *Mise-en-abyme*, for him, means that a work reflects what it is doing, its presence of "the already presented": that is, re-presentation as desistance.

For Lacoue-Labarthe, desistance has to be dealt within the limits of imitation. For him, there exist at least two conditions under which this *imitatio* is possible:

> 1) The subject of the imitation (subjective genitive) or, in other words, the imitant, has to be nothing in and of itself or must, in Diderot's words have "nothing characteristics of itself". It therefore must not already be a subject. This supposes an inherent impropriety, an "aptitude for all roles" – on condition that this im-propriety or this aptitude should not in turn be considered as subject or support. This could comprise the "negative" variant – negative as in negative theology – of onto-typology, of mimetology for which the figural is the very presupposition of the identical.

> 2) The "subject of the imitation" therefore must be a "being" in the sense of being something (which is, an essent) originally *open to* or originally "outside itself", ek-static. This is precisely what Heideggerian *Da-sein* is. But this ecstatic (de)constitution has itself to be thought as lack

or as insufficiency – according to a strict thinking of finitude. The subject is originally the infirmity of the subject and this infirmity is its very intimacy, in a state of dehiscence. Or, in other words, differance is inherent in the subject, forever preventing it from being subject (or, in other words, from being a stable essent) and essentially determining it as mortal.

Derrida has suggested that this inherent infirmity – without which no relation (either to oneself or to others) could be established and in whose absence there would be neither consciousness nor sociality – should be, ultimately, termed desistance.[49] Desistance brings to the light of day the insanity or unreason, the *anoia* against which Platonic onto-ideology, or even Heidegger's interpretation of it is established, installed, stabilized. But just as it is not reducible to a negative mode of the stance, it is not to be confused with madness – though in doubling or disinstalling everything that secures reason, it can resemble insanity. Madness against madness. The double bind oscillates between two madnesses, for there can also be a madness of reason, of the defensive stiffening in assistance, imitation and identification.[50]

When we look into the depths of a mirror we must remember that false positioning of the figure of man can be, as Derrida argues elsewhere, forged signature as a sign of our presence. In all, it is not a mastering program. According to him, play is the disruption of presence. The presence of an element is always a signifying and substitutive reference inscribed in a system of differences and the movement of a chain. Play is always play of absence and presence. This movement of play is the movement of supplementary. One cannot determine the centre and exhaust totalization because the sign, which replaces the centre, which supplements it, taking the centre's place in its absence – this sign is added, occurs as a surplus, as a floating supplement.[51]

Within *mise-en-abyme* we are at the threshold of distortion and complexity, instead of the threshold of the visible, as Kaja Silverman proposes in her book under the same title. Mimesis is not an interpretation of the seen but as mentioned, a relation that itself is problematised.

Analyses of art work such as Lynn Hershman Leeson's 1995 *Paranoid Mirror* and Joachim Sauter's and Dirk Lüsebrink's 1992 *Zerseher* (transl. *De-Viewer*) show that interactivity, or, rather, the participatory threatens the Lacanian idea of an eye as camera – camera understood here as one of our primary identification tools.[52] To construct the strange our eye must function like fertile vulva: *Paranoid Mirror* and *Zerseher* both come into being in the act of perception, and in the first of these, pictures of ourselves emerge only through our sight apparatus. *Paranoid Mirror* changes through a sensor under a rug on the floor and in *Zerseher* the picture changes at the precise spot where the spectator fixes his/her gaze. This is a strange world, producing strange perceptions.

In this sense I speak about the desistant figure of man in the mirrors of *Paranoid Mirror* or *Zerseher*: although we see ourselves represented in the mirror it is not "us" in a sense of autobiography but of allobiography. Florian Rötzer holds that in Hershman Leeson's works we see how the avant-garde's "escape from the image" leads consistently toward the appropriation and use of new media. He continues that it is possible to remove boundaries in one place without erecting them somewhere else. Rötzer seeks an oscillation between image and its viewer: there are interfaces everywhere connecting us to the world, even as they simultaneously separate us from it.[53]

What the poststructuralists call mimetology involves subordinating mimesis to a deadening logic based on visual reproduction, which they see as typical of the western ontotheological project in general. Mimesis understood as rhythmic repetition without closure, an infinite oscillation between original and copy, is posited as a never fully successful hyperbological antidote to mimetology, as the uncanny caesura in a speculative system that seeks to stifle its playful uncertainties. The hyperbologic, as I take it, targets Lacan's privileging of vision in the mirror stage and in the imaginary, which depend on a conceptualisation of the subject in narcissistic terms. As Silverman has condensed the problem under discussion here, the category through which Lacan concretises the gaze is not God or the master, but the camera. The camera, like God and master, represents one of the persistent screens through which we have traditionally apprehended the gaze. Lacan metaphorizes the gaze as a camera so as to characterize it as an apparatus whose only function is to put us in the picture – it does not determinate what that picture will be, nor what it will mean for us to be "there". Finally, Lacan's metaphorization of the gaze as a camera represents that gesture through which he most energetically dissociates it not only from such psychoanalytically specific signifiers of the subjectivity as "lack" and "desire", but also from such conventional designators of the human as "psyche", "spirit", or "soul".[54]

Lacoue-Labarthe (partly with Lacan, partly against him) constructs a nonidentical, uncanny version of the self. He calls it "allobiographical" – the "novel" of an other (be it a double) – rather than autobiographical. Such a self, he claims, is not based on specular reflection, on the imitation of the same, but rather on the *Unheimliche*, rhythmic repetition of an original that never existed in itself, a perpetual spacing without end and instead of being reality, echoing Aristotelian empowerment over nature, is replaced by self-defined and reinvented reality.[55]

The transgression goes further yet: before Grahame Weinbren's 1999 work *Frames*, viewers are able to transform a present day person into a moulded "there", recalling something of Lacan.[56] To participate is not to engage. It is, as is the case with *Zerseher*, to enter the obscure, the very abyssal of the strange. In Weibren's work, viewers are implicated in a sharing of the hysteria and tension that female inmates felt in an 1850's experience of imprisonment. In this strict sense *Unheimliche*, as strange or uncanny, is to be understood as that which throws us back outside of the *Heimliche*, that is to say, outside the innermost, outside the habitual, the familiar, the unthreatened security. It is in relation to the *Unheimliche* thus defined or redefined, in relation to this overpowering or this original violence that is nothing other than the incommensurability of being or the nothing, that man himself is determined as *das Unheimlicheres*, that which is more uncanny. In his book Poetry as Experience Lacoue-Labarthe claims that the Umheimliche, estrangement, affects existence, undoes its reality. The *Unheimliche* does not open up another domain as something to take us "outside the human", but ratrher opens up a domain "turned toward that which is human" – existence itself made strange. The *Unheimliche* is thus essentially a matter of language. Language is the locus of the *Umheimliche*. Language is that what "estranges" the human and is, at the same time, essential part of his humanity. Language is not the Umheimliche, though only language contains the possibility of the *Umheimliche*. But the *Unheimliche* appears, or rather, sets in (and is it always, already there) something turns in man and displaces the human, something in man even overturns, expulsing him from the human – along with a certain posture in language: the artistic posture, or the mimetic. That is, the most natural posture in language, as long as one thinks or pre-understands language as a mimeme. In the infinite cross-purposes of the "artistic" and the "natural", in linguistic misprision, the *Unheimliche* is, finally, forgetfulness. The motif of forgetfulness and turnaround (reversal) indicates here that the *Unheimliche*, because of language, is the catastrophe of the human.[57]

An allobiography of man can now be defined, in Lacoue-Labarthe´s vocabulary, as the one who does violence, which is to say, the one who transgresses the limits of the *Heimliche* and is heading towards the *Unheimliche*.[58] This is to place oneself in danger, not just to cross the tragic, but to stay in the abyssal of strange. Entrance into *Frames* traces a transformation from a visible, symbolic order to a more imaginary realm that desists (endlessly) meaningful interpretations and suppressive behaviour of media technology, the very *stele* of media ecology.

Lacoue-Labarthe stresses that the figure is never one and that the imaginary destroys at least as much as it helps construct. This explains, perhaps, why the subject in the mirror (of media) is first of all a subject in "desistance". There is no essence of the imaginary, and the subject desists because it must always confront at least two figures (or one figure that is at least double). Lacoue-Labarthe postulates that destabilizing division of the figural muddles the distinction between the imaginary and the symbolic, and broaches at the same time the negativity or absolute alterity of the "real", whereas Lacan – in seminar VII – says that the mirror image fulfils a role as limit: it is that which cannot be crossed.[59] This thought can be seen as limiting as the other philosophical postulations of the repressing regime of visuality.

A few words on the differences between onto-typology and the concept of mimesis by Derrida and Lacoue-Labarthe are probably necessary to distinguish existing theorization of "mimetology" from the very approach of deconstruction.

First, we can ask if media histories are often told as crossing points of experience or if they've been based on dualistic systems of perception in which a rapt, timeless presence of perception constructed by onto-typological philosophy is contrasted with lower, mundane or quotidian forms of seeing or listening that challenge this Western tradition of thought. We can even ask, as Rosalind Krauss has done, whether modernist vision with its "all-at-oneness" is founded on the cancellation of the empirical conditions of perception, including the very experience of successiveness. Despite the endless flow of questions we can say that attention and distraction have been not two essentially different states but been existing on a single continuum and thus, as Jonathan Crary emphasizes, attention has been a dynamic process, intensifying and diminishing, rising and falling, ebbing and flowing according to an indeterminate set of variables.[60] Inasmuch as Walter Benjamin suggests that distraction and concentration form polar opposites, Crary argues that attention and distraction cannot be thought outside of a continuum in which the two ceaselessly flow into one another, but as part of a social field in which the same imperatives and forces incite one and the other.[61]

Instead of a cancellation of successiveness, a certain field of the type might be the one of the hyperbologic. Cancellation, a serious myth of the modern, turns into an infinite grasp for identification as is the case with many deserting characters within media arts: there's simply no pedagogical ahistorical oscillation in one of the crossings at stake here.

2.   Unheimliche Art

During our efforts thus far to demonstrate what is valid processing of the very thing hyperbologic we have been forced to defer certain aspects of the problem. But now we historically distinguish two different definitions for an (id)entity represented in arts: (1) traditional, autobiographical, and (2) transgressive, allobiographical.

In the continuum of transgression – without any sustainable destination for our identification process – *Paranoid Mirror* produces a lack which, in turn, leaves us within the field of the threatened security: infelicity is embedded, as Derrida points out, in the act's very structure, the structure that can taken over by anyone at any time, the same structure which assumes

invagination. With Lacoue-Labarthe's words, mirror is there for the
mimetician. It is only a certain means, a trope, for (re)presenting the
mimetician. One must understand that the ´trick of the mirror´ is a turn or
trick of conjuring or illusionism (*thaumatopoiia*, from *thauma*, *thaw*,
teaomai). From the mirror we pass to painting, from there to poetry, and – in
the sense of *techne* – back to technology, but even before that the matter for
Lacoue-Labarthe is settled. For him specularization, the actual trick of the
mirror, has precisely this function: it assigns to mimesis its means. It makes
of mimesis a "theoretical" practice that organizes itself within the visible. It
delimits mimesis as (re)presentation/reproduction, as "imitation", as
installation with a character of veri-similitude (the true here being determined
in terms of idea and aletheia), speculation (the mise-en-abyme, the theoretical
reduction) does not happen all by itself. It remains fragile: mimesis is
precisely the absence of appropriative means whereas platonic philosophy
behind onto-typology presupposes the possession of a proper image (of
man).[62]

Within this framework, a work of art schematised here should not be
seen as a mirror for a subject, as it is framed by psychoanalysis and cinema,
but as a *mise-en-abyme*, an endlessly reflective abyss, an enunciation of our
identity. I suggest that we read *Paranoid Mirror* as we read Lacoue-Labarthe
by rejecting the privileging of vision in speculative mimetology and contrast
it with a presensual and rhythmic repetition of a nonexistent original.
Hershman Leeson says that *Paranoid Mirror*

> uses reflection as a means of portraiture and reflected self-
> portraiture. Though obscured and distanced, the artist's
> reflection watches from behind the central figures.
> *Paranoid Mirror* engages ideas of reflection, tracking,
> surveillance and voyeurism and uses the viewer as a direct
> interface [...] underscoring the often mistaken paranoid
> fear of being watched as well as the relationship of
> paranoia to voyeurism and surveillance. [63]

As viewers walk in the room where Leeson's mirror is installed,
they see images on the mirror, but the closer they walk to the mirror the
stranger it gets. For instance, they see themselves reflected but behind them
they also see themselves from behind – now, when we see ourselves merge
into the abysses of a paranoid mirror, we can say that mimesis is finally a
polysemic, even catachrestic concept, an infinite oscillation between original
and copy.[64]

This is a commentary on control and surveillance: how are we in the
picture? Abigail Solomon-Godeau, in a feminist interpretation of *Paranoid
Mirror*, says that the work contains sequences that stage the conflict between

the viewer's desire to look and the (imaged) woman's protest at that look. Mimesis strikes back at the viewer: *Paranoid Mirror* implicates the spectator in the visual spectacle, inasmuch as the viewer is herself photographed from behind by a wall-mounted video camera and projected into the image field of the mirror.[65] We see ourselves looking at the mirror. It is not a mirror any more; it is *mise-en-abyme*, of face(s) so familiar turning into strange and unfamiliar.[66] Here is an oscillation between absence and presence never achieving its goal in a sense of a meaningful ending. Within frames such as *Paranoid Mirror*, the subject desists. Desistance resists. With Lacoue-Labarthe's words, it remains paradoxically constructive, fictionable at its very origin.[67]

Because in the *Unheimliche* there's no solid ground for any type of reasoning, hyperbologic (as in *Paranoid Mirror*) stays indifferentiable as such, always imperceptible. The greater the reach for identification with the other, the more the attempts fails: the closer it is, the further it is, the more proper, the more improper, and vice versa.[68] Desistant experience machinery creates paranoid fiction through circumstances of surveillance. Fictionable media speculate, as is the case with *Paranoid Mirror*, the *Unheimliche* of our identity, the possibility of transformation. This is the potential for transgression that Rokeby considers in the opening of his highly influential article *Transforming Mirrors*, such that

> the medium not only reflects back, but also refracts what is given; what is returned is ourselves, transformed and processed. To the degree that the technology reflects ourselves back recognizably, it provides a self-image, a sense of self. To the degree that the technology transforms our image in the act of reflection, it provides us with a sense of relation between this self and the experienced world.[69]

The first possibility given by Rokeby is again a narcissistic loop; it is *autopoeisis*, mimetology of the autobiographical self, which has the power to predict the world, the symbolic order of things. Second possibility, processed image of our selves, is on the contrary a subject on arrival. Through the double path of narcissistic and, in paranoid mirror, at the same time hysterical identifications, one does not thus end up with a concept, but with the formation which endlessly redoubles and undoes itself, as Lacoue-Labarthe says, of a constitution of identity through a being-with-the-Other which only takes place in the negation of the Other. This negation is also an appropriation: but the one who appropriates has no "proper", he is *not* a subject. Consequently, if there must be a question of origin, the latter takes place (or arrives) neither through a subject nor through an other, nor through the Same nor through the Other but through an asociality, or through an altered sociality.[70] It is imaginary in a sense that there is no oneness to depend upon but understandably at the end not forming any such (id)entity. It stays, as inside Rokeby's cybernetic loop, in a state of arrival. We must remember that in passing, as Lacoue-Labarthe says, subject is destabilizing the Lacanian distinction between the imaginary and the symbolic. What Lacoue-Labarthe undergoes here is the experience of the ineluctable: I present myself, or rather write myself, sign my own desistance, the impossible itself, as an experience of the double bind, the poetic experience of the double bind, whereas, according to Silverman, the successful imaginary alignment with an image can be seen as something that evokes values like "wholeness" and "unity". Silverman accentuates that all this radiates "ideality".[71]

Hyperbology as such critiques the idea of mimesis as adequation. Any work like *Paranoid Mirror* or *Zerseher* is a story how the new born sight has yet no identity to hold onto, to identify with in terms of passion and catharsis: as in *Paranoid Mirror* or *Zerseher*, or as in Alba d´Urbano's 1995 work *Touch Me* or in Max Dean and Kristian Horton's *Be Me* (2002), our passion turns into obsession, to look, to see, finally, beyond man.[72] This is a modern thought, still, from James Joyce and T.S. Eliot to Franz Kafka and Claude Simon: art is escape from personality. What is left behind is not catharsis but, as Lacoue–Labarthe has named one of his key essays, the "echo of the subject". A deconstructive reading of Aristotelian heritage shows that it is a distortion in the continuum of evercoming. As desistance, Lacan's camera is out of order – at least for the symbolic order as a structure for imitating the world in the name of the "real".

For Lacoue-Labarthe, the paradox of mimesis lies in the fact that in order to do everything, to imitate everything, in order to (re)present or (re)produce everything, one must oneself be nothing and have nothing proper to oneself. Only the being without properties or specificity is able to present or produce in general.[73] The logic of paradox is always articulated around the division between appearance and reality, presence and absence, the same and the other, or identity and difference.[74] Through becoming something else, as both *Touch Me* and *Be Me* by nature propose, mimesis is always a matter of disappropriation,[75] or even dispossession. Deconstructive power of a constant identification of the other by semblance threatens the traditional schemata of truth as adequation in the work of art. What is set forth in *mise-en-abyme* is the law of impropriety. The hyperbological is unceasing, endless – thus, without resolution.[76] For Lacoue-Labarthe, the logic of mimesis is controversy. *Mise-en-abyme*, in the works of art, can be seen as a tool for "folding" the truth, producing folders of uncertainty into the operations of the truth itself. Here mirror image does not represent, it re-presents any information available.

For Lacoue-Labarthe, the more the tragic is identified with the speculative desire for the infinite and the divine, the more tragedy presents it as a casting into separation, differentiation, and finitude. Tragedy, then, is the catharsis of the speculative. This is why Lacoue-Labarthe presents disappropriation as that which secretly animates and constitutes it; tragedy presents (dis)appropriation: from the moment the mimetic structure no longer guarantees in principle the reconciliatory and reappropriating "return to the same", from the moment the tragic spectacle presupposes, behind it, the irremediable loss of every secure position and determination on enunciation, and sees itself condemned, as a consequence, to represent the process of (dis)appropriation, everything then forces the dynamic and productive successivity that structurally organized tragedy to give way to a mechanism of pure equilibrium. The structure of tragedy itself becomes immobilized and paralysed, although as I see it, there is still the desistant movement in the *mises-en-abyme* of media art. Also Lacoue-Labarthe believes this does not prevent this neutralization of the dialectical dynamic from being constantly active – comes down to "disorganizing" tragedy in the strongest sense of the term: desystematizing it and disjointing it.[77]

But why a question of pedagogy, there, in the history of philosophy, where the essence of man is elaborated? For Lacoue-Labarthe the essence of man, against the conventional tradition of philosophy, is not simply *animal rationale*, thinking, sensible animal, but mimesis. Mimesis is not submissive to reason: it makes thinking possible, not vice versa. It is a faculty to repeat, reflect, change and generally produce, it is the original *technai*, the basis for the essence of man. In a classical setting it might be explained as a faculty of a soul, not a spirit; it does not contain information on good or bad but it is a faculty for good and bad, true and delusion. Because mimesis does not resolve questions between good and bad, or truth and delusion, such criteria must be carried to soul from the outside – from reason, which in the theory of education exists as an ethical model for good. Mimetic soul implies infinite adaptability, and the purpose of education is to guide and direct this ability in a way that it would operate for good against bad.[78]

Lacoue-Labarthe identifies at least two conditions for imitation:

> 1. The subject of the imitation (subjective genitive). In other words, the imitant, must be nil of itself or must, in Diderot's words have 'nothing characteristic of itself'. It therefore must not already be a subject. This presupposes an inherent impropriety (impropriété), an 'aptitude for all roles' – on condition, however, that this im-propriety or this aptitude should not in turn be considered as subject or support. (This could be the 'negative' variant – negative as in negative theology – of onto-typology.)

> 2. The 'subject of the imitation' therefore must be a 'being'
> (in the sense of being something which is, an essent)
> originally open to (ouvert à) or originally 'outside itself',
> ek-static. This is precisely what Heideggerian Da-sein 'is'.
> But this ecstatic (de)constitution has itself to be thought as
> lack or insufficiency – according to a strict thinking of
> finitude. The subject is originally the infirmity of the
> subject and this infirmity is its very intimacy, in a state of
> dehiscence. Or, in other words, difference is inherent in the
> subject, forever preventing it from being subject [...] The
> 'subject' desists. This is why it is fictionable at its very
> origin and [...] In other words, it remains paradoxically
> constitutive.[79]

The paradox of the mirror is not only a contradicting or surprising opinion (out of the ordinary and shocking). It implies a passing to the extreme, a sort of "maximization", as is said in logic nowadays. It is in reality a hyperbolic movement by which the equivalence of contraries is established (probably without ever establishing itself) – the contraries themselves pushed to the extreme, in principle infinite, of contrariety. This is why the formula for the paradox is always that of the double superlative: the madder it is, the wiser it becomes; the maddest is the wisest. Paradox is defined by the infinite exchange, or the hyperbolic identity, of contraries. This paradoxical logic, finally, Lacoue-Labarthe calls hyperbological, properly abyssal. The hyperbological is unceasing, endless, which also means without resolution.[80] A conclusion can be drawn: hyperbological abysses form the desistant mode of media, when the actual crossing is *mise-en-abyme*.

The space in media is not to be proclaimed only by onto-typological relation to the image, although some have said cyberspace is "Platonism as a working product". Here, "with an electronic infrastructure, the dream of perfect forms becomes the dream of information: filtered through the computer matrix, all reality becomes patterns of information. Here the idea of the universe as imagined by Plato takes shape".[81] This forming is against something Benjamin described as his work's pedagogy: to see dimensionally, stereoscopically into the depths of historical shade.[82]

Lacoue-Labarthe claims that image or figure is never one, neither is the one of man. It is always and already dimensional: every angle shows only another, endlessly. This is *mise-en-abyme* in where Benjamin's pedagogy lays shattered: in mimesis without origin there is no myth, of man, of mankind, neither there is an awakening. Man is not asleep, as Benjamin figures; man's purpose is to measure his actions without such a mythical history. Depth (of times) is not as much as concealed as it is rising through desistance. Desistance cuts through history in a way that it violates the wait for perfect technological modes, violate against the passivity of waiting.

Participatory art as such, we might agree with Frank Popper, ended in deadlock in the 1970s, but continued life under "interaction" in the art of Jeffrey Shaw, Lynn Hershman Leeson and Myron W. Krueger. For Popper, interactive art, with its vast number of experiments and innovations in different media, presents the flow of data (pictures, texts, sounds) and a catalogue of cybernetic, intelligent structures, environments and networks in a way that the viewer could now project some effect on this flow, to alter the structures with interactive environment or navigate the networks and participate in this way in altering and changing the content and form or art – even in creation of art.[83] Popper understands interactivity differently as, for example, Söke Dinkla does: interactivity means here not the one and only path from the closures of participation art in the mid 1900s. Altering of the structures and thereby the decay of the mimetic through participation not necessarily means interaction.

Krueger has elaborated closely different responsive environments. According to him, interface design should concentrate on features and possibilities of man, instead of arguing for the technological development. Interaction should be unstraining and talkative to the body of man as a whole. Krueger launched the concept "artificial reality" in 1973 in order to represent the responsive, computer-controlled environment, which took an aesthetic approach to the human/computer interface. In 1972 he spoke of his experiments with artificial reality installation called *Videoplace* (1969-1973):

> Videoplace's main aesthetic statement is that response is the medium. The composition is the relationship between what you do and what you perceive as being the computer-generated consequences of your action. The quality of the computer's perception of your actions is even more important than the responses' visual or musical quality. Realistic graphic environments are irrelevant unless you can interact realistically with them.[84]

He declares that in the term "artificial reality", "reality" refers to the causal laws that operate between your body's movements and their effect on the graphic world.[85] "An artificial reality perceives a participant's action in terms of the body's relationship to a graphic world, he wrote, "and generates responses that maintain the illusion that his or her actions are taking place within that world". Krueger is playing with the suppositions presented by ecological media theories: *Videoplace* celebrates the unexpected possibilities provided by technology and simultaneously indicts the currently restricted means of interacting with computers.[86] For Krueger, an environment has no self-sufficient values. "Realistic" interaction, though, demands intelligence from the system. Resisting the immersing mode of virtual reality as a mode of linkage to technology, Krueger's ethical pre-mission is that man should maintain his/her freedom and mobility. When a participant performs an action in a Videoplace interaction, he/she does not necessarily know what the system's response will be. It may be based on what happened before, or it could offer an element of surprise. Krueger says we need surprises to keep people interested in responding. That is why we have always focused on fun types of interactions, and on instantaneous response.[87]

This already implies desistance. We move rapidly from Duchamp's dream and John Cage's notions of change to a direction of surprise and possible joy. But "participation" as such must be questioned when the user's actions are blurred by the intelligence of the machine.

Although Krueger uses terminology familiar to us mainly from ecological media studies, he says that artificial reality works could also cut and mutilate us – in an act of desistance, presumably. But with a reading from Krueger we can believe that Oliver Grau's stress on the idea that artistic visions reflect a continuing search for illusion through technologically advanced media is true only in part: we must question here Grau's thought that *without exception* the image fantasies of oneness, of symbiosis allied to media are utopian[88]. This is a task not proper to Krueger's oeuvre as an artist.

This argues also against the idea of "joy without harm" that Aristotle, in the *Politics* (VIII, 1341b), attributes to catharsis in its specifically medical, homeopathic, "pharmaceutical" function (catharsis used *pharmakeias charin*). This is also an argument against how Freud posits mimesis (that is, to use his own term, identification) as what makes the "cathartic machine" itself possible. Freud transfers Aristotelian *recognition (anagnorisis)* to the relation between stage and audience in such a way as to "interest" the spectator in it. Krueger's play with the participant tells us something about how Freud actually introduces something that does not belong to the Aristotelian "program" but explains the connection between catharsis and mimesis that had remained unthought throughout the entire tradition, namely, that tragic pleasure is essentially a masochistic pleasure, and thus maintains some relationship with narcissism itself: "reality" in the concept of "artificial reality" is connected to the causal laws that operate between one's bodily movements and their effect on the graphic world. Artificial reality is an enriched reality beyond computer by the actions of the user, a reality that speaks to people by responses like sounds, images and lights. It could greet, introduce itself or even say goodbye.[89]

Theatrical pleasure, stresses Lacoue-Labarthe, is thoroughly masochistic: the only pleasure that comes from suffering is prepared – formally – by this supplement of pleasure which itself, however, implies pain. The modern "break" occurs with the introduction into the tragic conflict of the unconscious, that is, of the difference between the repressed and the nonrepressed.[90] The greatest joy of *Videodesk* (or *Glowflow*, 1969, *Psychic Space*, 1971 and *Metaplay*, 1972 as prototypes to *Videodesk*) is to interrupt the recognition project the user is practising. Erection of narcissistic projection manifolds into the abysses of a *mise-en-abyme* that do not reflect back the image but withdraws. A certain development can be seen from change to surprise and finally to desistance. Engineer Krueger is searching for the functional, ecological use of technology; the artist Krueger, then, creates effects of withdrawal from these functions. A technological structure can hold in itself different modes of use. On the introduction to "Artificial Reality" he says "the computer should adapt to the human rather than the human adapting to the computer".[91]

Perhaps Krueger is right in believing that "the response is the medium": the structure is not *media* in itself, in the sense predicted by Marshall McLuhan and Kittler. Technology does not adjust artistic imagination; this imagination enters the determinations of technology. Krueger says that the user is not in *real* interaction with the system – also this relationship is fictioned. Homeopathic scenography is translated in the hands of an artist into a hyperbological abyss, into something that Freud was not able to comprehend in his system: the disruptive functions of modern art. Within this apparatus of derealization art takes more than a simply "secondary" function, that it has the power to confront us (only) with the real itself.[92]

As with Krueger, other artists play with the user; one might think of a 1995 work by Paul Sermon, *The Tables Turned* as much as *Touch Me* by d'Urbano, both in a sense *tintamarresques*. *Tintamarre*, as posing through a hole in the picture means a step away from the familiar paradoxically in the tradition of the popular culture. *Tintamarresque* means not tragedy in a traditional sense, but merely a carnival. In both example works the "actor" partly disappears into the theatrical space through (technically produced) masks. We can say that in *tintamarresque* this question concerns the appropriation of the unthought, as Lacoue-Labarthe calls us for "exorcising madness" as an abyss for a subject always to enter, instead of a narcissistic relation to what is seen.[93] To describe this he uses the word "obliteration". The figure of the identification about to happen disappears in the manifold of figures. *Obliteration* is the strategy of the thought, but the meaning of obliterate is ambiguous: it means at once to efface and to surcharge (superimpose). In each case, it is obviously a question of making an inscription to disappear. A *tintamarresque* defers man: a masochistic pleasure in losing yourself in an art of recognition. The movement that leads from "madness" to the unthought is the same as that which leads from writing to the unexpressed.

Writing and madness must be sublated together, claims Lacoue-Labarthe. This is why the hermeneutics of the unthought finds in obliteration – in a certain erasure of the letter – its surest defence against madness. It is obliteration that all of Heidegger's operations ultimately take place. Obliteration is the other of the "stratagem of *é-loignement*" and the primitive operation or manoeuvre on which the whole strategy of thought is built: *é-loigment* means both to bring nearer and carrying away. If danger lies in madness, the enemy for Heidegger is the letter.[94] Lacoue-Labarthe thinks this "stratagem" could be reversible; this madness is not to be fought back but to make it the logic of identification, which finally *is* the erasure of the letter of man.

Closed circuit video was among the first inventions of context awareness in media art, if we understand context awareness now as awareness of the other as allobiography: the spectator enters the stage that could be imagined but never as familiar but strange. For Dan Graham, the mirror takes on a much wider meaning. He uses it as a device for creating awareness of identifications and identities that are essentially social. All Graham's works are directly or indirectly concerned with bringing about such identifications. He refers to his performances and mirror spaces as being "a feedback device governing behaviours – a superego" or "subconscious" to the *conalienation*, specifically to the longing for a sense of identity and home. The mirror as it is used by Graham – in my mind, as *mise-en-abyme* – therefore has a direct connection with architecture, and not only with architecture as such but also with power. The necessity of deconstructing the image and the position of the subject has produced a paradigm shift in the art. The inappropriateness of previous forms of art is neither the cause of that paradigm shift nor a mere fed, but a necessity and logical consequence of the shift but for me, the motif of mise-en-abyme is not a consequence of the shift but a theme underlying in arts' essence.[95] An illuminating example of *mise-en-abyme* in closed-circuit video art of the era is Graham's other installation *Opposing Mirrors and Video Monitors on Time Delay* (1974) with multiple echoes of dispossession. Visitors to this space find a variety of available scenarios: a view of what had happened five seconds earlier, as reflected with delay in the mirror on the other side of the room; a view, in the mirror nearest them, of themselves and the nearby video monitor; or a faraway view in the opposite mirror.[96] This uncanniness of reflection – Graham arguing that there is no autonomous subject and that he uses mirrors to create alluring spaces that at the same time impose subtle forms of authority and self-censorship[97] – reminds us of the reflecting trap of Velasquez' painting *Las Meninas* (1656), which comes near the conjunction that Lacoue-Labarthe set between the binary oppositions such as presence and absence of the observer and the observed, the artist and the model, a play that is never ceased.[98]

Graham's "cinema" is also arranged to enable an encounter with this danger, in which a contrary effect, that is, a different "remembering", is produced. This corresponds to Benjamin's concept of history: "To articulate that which has passed historically is not to recognize how it then really was. It is to empower a memory as it flashes up in a moment of danger." The prerequisite for this is a consciousness of the "nowtime" (*Jetztzeit*) which makes time "stand still" so that the "true image of the past" can come alive in a unique way — it "rushes silently past" and allows in this movement the recognition of that which has relevance for the present.[99]

Still, we can argue that acts of the viewers are not reflections of unmediated mind but the past and the present are always divided by the abyss. Even the past is produced in Graham's mirrors as something other. Graham breaks down the now-time signifiers with uncentered *mise-en-abyme*, and dreamwork becomes abysmal. The subject remains in a state of (de)constitution in the economy of the mirror, which is uncomfortable, as Dixon says, but not self-conscious state.[100]

A search for an adequate memorabilia folds naturally into the very elaboration of truth in arts: Marie-Claire Ropars-Wuilleumier claims – already in another, deconstructive context – that a property of the outside is precisely that it breaks down the opposition between inside and outside, and the operation always tends toward an exteriority that comes to ruin the identity of the proper term, even that of an exterior space. The truth in painting thus leads painting into the orbit of a truth that is outside of painting, because it is incumbent upon truth to decenter what it describes. In order to unfold, the truth in painting supposes a dissimulation of painting: the demand for an unveiling (of truth) can be realized only by the logic of a diversion (of painting), by means of which, and in order to respond to the truth in brings to light, painting would be led to give reflecting its own visibility. Captured in the mirror of painting, the truth will see the abyss of its discourse open up; but painting, in subscribing to the obligation of truth, will have to give in to the rule of exteriority that makes the truth of painting pass through the breaking open of its propriety. The reflection of painting in truth is both reciprocal and asymmetrical, and if painting resists anyone who claims to speak the truth about it, it is nonetheless caught in the originary attraction of a truth that occludes it. The obliteration of the traits of painting – the face – even Velasquez's absent model or Graham's vanishing visitors in time – of which is erased from the picture – belongs in this sense to the truth of painting.[101] The dilemma thus changes into a deconstructive paradox, which, in turn, is willing to cross the boundaries laid up by onto-typologies from the Western tradition of philosophy.

The more context aware a work of art is, the more it operates on particular levels of recognition than identification (with the other), which, for Lacoue-Labarthe, means appropriation.[102] Disappropriation borne of the massive collapse of recognition – forming something like a (mis)recognition, as Lacan would suggest – or, as Dixon believes, the body appearing as "lines of fragilization".[103]

Inasmuch the active mimesis of the viewer is not radically changed, historical change in our trajectory lies in repetition of a passive mimesis that former thaumatic machines could not yet produce. Still we can argue that *mise-en-abyme* has been a commonly repeated (de)constructive visual motif in media art not just since the daylight of video but already from the mirror culture of Baroque. Thus the history of the use of the motif goes far deeper in the history than those remarks concerning the relations between contemporary media art and historical avant-garde, as an example of art's own historical understanding.

Lacoue-Labarthe stresses that we cannot miss the repetition from which the division might be made between the mimetic and the non-mimetic: a division between the recognizable and the non-recognizable, the familiar and the strange, the real and the fantastic, the sensible and the mad – life and fiction.[104] Lacoue-Labarthe says that mimesis is by definition active, virile, and formative; according to the very logic of paradox, it presupposes no preliminary subject. This is played against passive mimesis, which is an involuntary possessive role as nothing other than mimetic passivity itself: pity or sympathy, compassion, the catharsis of passion,[105] reflecting the general Aristotelian idea of catharsis. Toni Dove argues that in a traditional film the position of viewer (voyeur) is physically passive – the process of spectatorship is physically still.[106] The film becomes the eyes and point of view of the viewer and the body is left behind or even forgotten – in this though much alike Lacan's point concerning the eye as a camera – we enter the screen. Even in "action movies", as Dove calls this genre, which use the eyes as a visual trigger into the internet of the sensorium to produce physical thrills, the body is largely left behind: inactive. In a responsive interface, the body is active and the experience becomes embodied. A viewer is simultaneously aware of their body – "in" their body and "in" the screen. The space between the two activated. This charged space is a key characteristic of telepresence. It is the space through which the body extends itself into the movie or virtual space. It is the invisible experience of the body's agency beyond its apparent physical edge.[107]

Within this *mise-en-abyme* installed by interface, any sympathetic identification with mirror image would simply be a narcissistic operation.[108] This the desistant mode of media denies by arguing that with writing also comes madness, the uncanny sense of the Other.

3.   Definitions

In terms of desistance, it feels wrong to speak about a conclusion for a text. In no way can one article cover a field that is (historically) expanding, never ceasing and teleologically fulfilling its journey as a media history. Instead, an afterword sounds more appropriate way to take a final look on to this what we have defined as a breakdown of binary opposition between classical, traditional and modern media modes. Nevertheless we ought to be careful; Spivak says in the preface for Derrida's "Of Grammatology" that the desire of deconstruction has also the opposite allure. Deconstruction seems to offer a way out of the closure of knowledge. By inaugurating the open-ended indefinites of textuality – by thus "placing the abyss" (*mettre en abîme*), as the French expression would literally have it – it shows us the lure of the abyss as freedom. The fall into the abyss of deconstruction inspires us with a much pleasure as fear. We are intoxicated with the prospect of never hitting bottom.[109]

Deconstruction's impact on the research of media art has been minimal. One reason for this might be, as Spivak reminds us, that deconstruction can never be a positive science. Dixon is ready to argue that Derrida's linguistic plague darkens, divides, and undermines notions of meaning and truth.[110] But we are also about to notice that by creating new categories of information modes we never can say it is the final categorization of the media modes but a humble start in a search for more. Here Lacoue-Labarthe's mimesis can be interpreted as a positive concept: not as conceptative and sheltering, not as radical and resisting, but as a logic that always works "in-between" these polarities to overcome, for instance, the discontinuities of modernist art and the very negation proposed by the modern.

Discussions informed by the grounding of the myth of the modern hint at the presence of oscillation in art, constrained by the specific media of the period. The idea stretches back at least far as the Renaissance but surprisingly little attention has been paid to it. Certain features of new media have been found here, features such as the geometry of space being a space of several traces left by different media art modes such as participative and recording modes and that promulgate not binary oppositions but rather an ungeometrical space of being.

We have seen how in specific *mises-en-abyme* of media art, or of the machinery of media art, the tension between binary oppositions like truth-false and absence-presence have collapsed into an abyss of infinite reflections of identity work what we can describe as hyperbologic.

We have read assumptions towards hyperbological mode of media art (for Krauss it favours solublution between the poles) and technology (Bolter and Grusin) but these openings haven't been sufficiently satisfactory. As mentioned, not even deconstruction, as a method of investigation, can present us with sufficient interpretation of media art works; rather, deconstruction can erect questions concerning the mode of media and its ethical impacts in terms of mimesis, in terms of questioning *how* media can

Desistant Media

provide the world to us and *how* media see us within this world. In this query of information modes, we have to keep in mind the words of Lacoue-Labarthe: nothing differs from mimesis more than possession.

We have also seen how mimesis for Lacoue-Labarthe means a paradox, a logic that is intertwined in the relation between presence and absence, same and different or identity and the other. This logic is not dialectical but endless, infinite and unclear: it is also a faculty of producing real and delusion. It is a faculty without a principle, which in the end could answer whether a production is truthful or not. Mimesis is thus an endless, infinite paradox; it is not a concept, or an object, at most it can be seen as logic. At the same time it is impurity; a relation to something else, a try to make adequate with something else without assurance to this desire for identity to be certain.[111]

The subject of philosophy appears to Lacoue-Labarthe as a (de)constitution of the subject and therefore it is unclean, wrenched from itself. It is a subject identifying itself endlessly. The self is a subject of its own infinite, unfinished and fragmented utterance, which mimetics make unclean and contaminated. Its identity is always uncertain, vanishing, present but still beyond any reach. Lacoue-Labarthe:

> Mirror is there for the mimetician. It is only a certain means, a trope, for (re)presenting (darstellen) the mimetician [...] one must understand that the "trick of the mirror" is a turn or trick of conjuring or illusionism (thaumatopoiia, from thauma, thaw, cf. theaomai) [...] From the mirror we pass to painting, from there to poetry, and the matter is settled [...] Specularization ("the trick of the mirror") has precisely this function: it assigns to mimesis its means. It makes of mimesis a "theoretical" practice that organizes itself within the visible. It delimits mimesis as (re)presentation/reproduction, as "imitation", as installation with a character of veri-similitude (the true here being determined in terms of idea and aletheia), speculation (the mise-en-abyme, the theoretical reduction) does not happen all by itself. It remains fragile [...] mimesis is precisely the absence of appropriative means"[112]

In place of the identical, mimesis names the similar. Rokeby, through *The Giver of Names* (1997), refers to this difference in a fascinating way: the giver of names creates thought from the objects put in front of the work. The installation includes an empty pedestal, a video camera and a computer system. The camera observes the top of the pedestal. A visitor may place any of the items filling the installation space on the pedestal. When the system senses something new on it, it records an image of the object. It then performs many levels of image processing, which are visible on a computer screen or video projection. The results of these analytical processes are used to stimulate a metaphorically linked associative knowledge-base of about 150,000 known objects, ideas, sensations, words, etc. The sentence that the computer produces from what is recorded is not random, yet it often does not make sense – these sentences could be described, in terms of mimesis, as Dadaistic poems rather than an adequate relation to what is seen. Rokeby says that works like *The Giver of Names* present the (mimetic) challenge of replicating parts of the human mental system in computer code. Many of the functions of the human (or even animal) system that we take for granted are actually remarkably complex. This does not mean that the function cannot be replicated by computer code; the question remains open[113], but speaking in terms of mimesis, the complexity of the visual world we inhabit generates equally complex interpretations of the seen, and mimesis, as *aletheia*, seems to be an impossible dream to achieve the truth.

But what does the mimetic challenge of *The Giver of Names* look like? Lacoue-Labarthe postulates that the idea of a pretending world with perfect categorization of the whole demands an image that a finite subject from this pretending produces. An image can no longer be an apparition of the whole, it is only a space opened to existence by this subject, like a lightened scene where the subject could measure the relations between different elements. There is no truth, no *aletheia* in its purity of revelation the existing world without a certain adequation. But this adequation, says Lindberg, made possible by a representation, does not mean the pure adequation between idea and thing, as was the case for Plato, but in the desire to produce adequation as mimesis: resemblance, representation. Rokeby says – with special emphasis on mimesis – that *The Giver of Names* knows a fair bit about language, but all it knows of the world is kind of bookish knowledge. It may have read a novel or two and glanced through an encyclopaedia, but it has never cuts its finger, fallen in love, been hungry or lonely. The sentence is the expression of a naïve, highly idiosyncratic, *subjective* point of view. The adequation produced by this being cannot be interpreted as the sameness of an idea, even though there has to be possibility to interpret and understand reality for limited minds – like the one of *The Giver of Names* – as well. Its only function is to name a thing, and thus, to understand. Rokeby says that the computer offers us the opportunity and a device through which to ask in a new way what it means to be human[114]: allobiography as "presented" image of the human.

For Margaret Morse *The Giver of Names* explores the symbolic field and the correspondence between signs and objects created through the enunciate power of words. The results are not necessarily predictable, for

they activate alternative or poetic possibilities for correspondences or links
between language and the object world that are different than the tacit
associative network of links and the automatisms in everyday language. In
fact, it is this difference that for Morse makes the well-worn traces of the
mystic writing pad first visible and that also reveals the *Giver of Names* as a
machine for poeisis or fresh or creative meaning-making from the substance
of the material world.[115] Enigmatism, the poetic strange consumes the
rational: mind means not automatics, and in the case of *The Giver of Names*,
no "new" structures of truth are necessarily revealed. I see that a trace is an
abyss in the sense defined by Lacoue-Labarthe: our task is not to surpass it
but to understand it from its own conditions.

By our critical excavation we can assume a slow withdrawal from
the metaphors such as the light of the sun (of truth) to the metaphor of the
black sun (of mimesis) provided by the *mekhane* of media art. The good of
sun, as Plato thought, turns into a metaphor of, not bad but disappropriation:
concrete references are gone with the light. What is left is the black sun of
madness as Georges Bataille has predicted. Thus the historical shift in the
reasoning of art takes place between pedagogy and madness. This is not to
suggest that madness has been historically produced for us as an alternative,
but as the way it has always been a part of us, our essence as human beings,
the familiar of us.

History of desistance in media art has been a history, rather than
denying madness, to predict it, to *form* it in various ways. To comprehend the
world also implies the acknowledgment of the *Unheimlich* within this world,
within us: we negotiate, with all our capability, how to organize the known
and the unknown, *Heimlich* and *Unheimlich*, in our lives. This, For Lacoue-
Labarthe, means mimesis.

We have to be fully aware of that there is no goal for this
negotiation in a strict, teleological sense. From the pedagogical perspective,
we must understand this project as an endless, infinite process of producing
the other in the self. In this tradition, augmentation is a guarantee for
allobiography. Desistant media mode is dispossessive in its allobiography;
there, it doesn't divide the teleological aporias of any given dialectics,
including interpretations of the binary oppositions presented by Derrida. In its
withdrawal desistance, however, shares something in common with Derrida's
concept of dissemination, processes of truth and non-truth set upon each
other endlessly and without destination.

This means that we cannot see the presence itself in the mirrors of
media art, since presence does not present itself; instead, in the erasure of the
letter there is the multiplication of screens as emblems.

The argument Derrida makes about the polysemy is that this kind of
project belongs to the attending discourse. Its style is that of the
representative surface. It forgets that its horizon is framed. The difference

between polysemy and textual dissemination is precisely difference itself, "an implacable difference". This difference is of course indispensable to the production of meaning (and that is why between polysemy and dissemination the difference is very slight). But to the extent that meaning presents itself, gathers itself together, says itself, and is able to stand there, it erases difference and casts it aside. Structure (the differential) is a necessary condition for the semantic, but the semantic is not itself, in itself, structural. The seminal, on the contrary, disseminates itself without ever having been itself and without coming back to itself. Its very engagement, its division, its involvement in its own multiplication, which is always carried out at a loss and unto death, is what constitutes it as such in its living proliferation.[116] Likewise, desistance veils the processes of truth, as Lacoue-Labarthe has pronounced; it is there, and it is not, it has it freedom in its own multiplication.

Works from Lynn Hershman Leeson, of which *A Room of One's Own* (1991-1993) and *Deep Contact* (1990) produce ironic interpretations of possession, evoking the Lacanian problem proposed by Lacoue-Labarthe. In *A Room of One's Own,* Hershman Leeson lets the spectator be immersed, gazing into the peep show of the work – into the bedroom of the woman under surveillance. The viewer observes a total of four video scenes or tableaux featuring a seductive, blonde woman. These tableaux can be experienced in a total of seventeen ways, depending on how the sequence is sparked by the viewer's mobilization of the interactive mechanism. In one of the four video sequences, the woman carries out what resembles a commercial phone sex conversation with the caller; the agreed-upon fantasy is that of a prison cell in which the two have sex. In another, and for our inquiry more important sequence, the woman addresses the viewer directly as she strips to her underwear, protesting her visual objectification and surveillance ("Don't look at me", "Go away"). The monologue here is an extremely cold coquetry, mirroring with no shame back the viewer to him/herself.

Each of these sequences is visually activated according to where the viewer focuses the movable viewer within a miniature roomlike environment in the "real" space in front of the virtual space of the video screen. Containing a bed, a video monitor in which the viewer's eyes are both projected and mirrored, a telephone, a chair, and a heap of clothing, each of these objects, when focused on by the viewer, activates one of the audio/video sequences. Focusing on the bed, for example, produces an audio track of jouncing bedsprings, the sounds of lovemaking, a tinny radio song, and a ghostly composite image of a woman imprisoned behind the bedposts. With its erotised atmosphere, seductive protagonist, and privatised viewing conditions, the work deliberately mimics the scopic economy of the peep show. Invited to peep and provided the desired spectacle of femininity staged for the looking, the viewer is, in effect, both captivated and made acutely aware of the equivocal nature of this voyeuristic scenario. The work becomes a self-reflective space of ethical reflection, the critical intervention into the mechanics of spectacle that is one of the consistent features of Hershman's work. [117]

Lacoue-Labarthe says that myth is considered as the originary poem (*Urgedicht*) of a people. Which means that a people originates, exists as such or identifies itself, appropriates itself – and that is to say, properly is itself – only on the basis of myth. According to the mimetic logic or mimetologic just evoked, myth is the means of identification, and the appeal to myth is the demand for the appropriation of the means of identification, judged, in short, more decisive than those of the means of production.[118] But already for Derrida the principle of mimesis is differ*a*nce, a productive freedom, but not any elimination of ambiguity; mimesis contributes to the profusion of images, words, thoughts, theories and action, without itself becoming tangible. Mimesis thus resists theory and constructs a world of illusion, appearance, aesthetics, and images in which existing worlds are appropriated, but changed and re-interpreted in the processes of invagination: images are non-disposable doubles that always stand in relation to what has preceded them and thus are never the origin, the inner, never outer but always by *gestaltung* doubled.[119]

Derrida argues that Lévi-Strauss, like Rousseau, associates writing with simple binary-opposition violence and falls preys to structuralism. He points out that writing is violent insofar as it classifies and pigeonholes, going against the *différance*-structured economy of writing. Accordingly, Derrida believes that Lévi-Strauss's anthropology fails to recognize the original violence in writing. He then distinguishes three levels (tertiary structure) of violence of writing: first, 1) the " arche-violence": "the originary violence of language which consists in inscribing within a difference, in classifying, in suspending the vocative absolute"; second, 2) the totalizing violence: the force which organizes and assimilates the first violence into effects of propriety; and, third, 3) the resistant violence: the returning force of what is excluded and repressed in the disciplinary system of language.[120]

For Derrida the structure of violence is complex and its possibility – writing – no less so. Arche-violence, loss of the proper, of absolute proximity, of self-presence, in truth the loss of what has never taken place, of a self-presence which has never been given but only dreamed of and always already split, repeated, incapable of appearing to itself except in its own disappearance (oscillation of the hyperbologic). Out of this arche-violence, forbidden and therefore confirmed by a second violence that is reparatory, protective, instituting the "moral", prescribing the concealment of writing and the effacement and obliteration of the so-called proper name which was already dividing the proper, a third violence can possibly emerge or not (an empirical possibility) within what is commonly called evil, war, indiscretion, rape; which consists of revealing by effraction the so-called proper name, the originary violence which has severed the proper from its property and its self-sameness (*proprété*). Derrida names the third violence as violence of reflection, which denutes the native non-identity, classification as denaturation of the proper, and identity as the abstract moment of the concept. We can all accept Derrida's idea that it is on this tertiary level, that of the empirical consciousness, that of the common concept of violence (and the system of the moral law and of transgression) whose possibility remain yet unthought, should no doubt be situated. The last violence is all the more complex in its structure because it refers at the same time to the two inferior levels of arche-violence and of law (modern art has many times been confronted by law). In effect, it reveals the first nomination which was already an expropriation, but it denudes also that which since then functioned as the proper, the so-called proper, substitute of the deferred proper, perceived by the *social* and *moral consciousness* as the proper, the reassuring seal of self-identity, the secret.[121]

We can see from this differentiation how desistant modes of art differ from resistant art in the deferral of the proper instead of resisting this substituted proper presented through totalising violence of media machinery through ages.

As effects of *arche-writing*, these three levels of violence together constitute the endless cycle of the violence *against* violence phenomenon or what Derrida calls an "economy of violence". For Derrida, discourse can only do itself violence and negate itself in order to *affirm* itself. Philosophy, as the discourse of the Self, can only open itself to the question of violence *within* and *by* it. It is an economy: "violence against violence, light against light". "One never escapes the economy of war". In other words, if metaphysics is a violence of assimilation, one must fight against this violence with a certain other violence. It is this endless cycling, or the tertiary structure, of violence, which makes the economy of violence *irreducible*.[122] But what are the ethical impacts of allobiography? The writing of media art from our standpoint stays not in a state of aporia of discontinuity, but in a latent state of a infinite mise-en-abyme. Writing chews writing. Thus, the ethics are: arche-violence waves from within us. In mirrors of art analysed here we are more than just an autobiography, which always censors the image of ourselves – mastery over submission in search for identity over difference. This *logos* which today defines differently the circumstances of the culture of mirrors than those pedagogical perspectives of, let's say, Kircher's *mises-en-abyme*. Still the desistant mode is the same than the Baroque mirror culture already produced: allobiography instead of autobiography that Phelan thinks is a resistant representational mode of information towards the stability of media – or transparency.

We are witnessing a "strange perspective", but not without a price to pay. Paz refers to Duchamp's *Given* as a work that will be fulfilled only through voyeurism additionally defines an act in which somebody sees him/herself seeing something. As well, the target sees us, and my gaze will complete the work only on condition that I voluntarily become part of the work. This means that mimesis is construction made only a priori by the subject, not as pro priori relation set by the world beyond us. This is a self deconstruction of the truth in the artwork, the impossibility of exposure – even the lesson from early anamorphoses was that it, according to Sabine Melchior-Bonnet, forces us to admit that reality must be interpreted, and, everything that seems enduring is in fact transitory[123].

Derrida has been criticized for lacking positive and concrete socio-political aims and purposes. Despite his selective focus — linguistic and philosophical thought over political and social thought — the spirit of deconstruction remains the same for him. Deconstructive interrogation for Derrida destabilizes and complicates the opposition between *droit* (as law, convention, institution, positive law) on the one hand and Nature and natural law on the other. It mimics the oscillation of difference or the displacement of oppositionalism and puts into question the authority of the questioning-form itself in order "to show the constitutive undecidability, radical incompletion or untotalizability of textual, institutional, cultural, social and economic structures".[124]

For Lai deconstruction is a double-movement between an empirical interrogation of *law-as-droit* and an interrogation of the subjection of this interrogation; an apolitical movement that formulates logico-formal paradoxes together with the events that are evidently political. In relation to justice and *law-as-droit*, Derrida writes that "deconstruction takes place in the interval that separates the undeconstructibility of justice from the deconstructibility of *droit* (authority, legitimacy and so on)". Accordingly, justice is an experience of *aporia*: experience is a passage, a traversal towards a destination. Aporia, as the *impasse of meaning*, does not permit (direct) passage. The experience of this impossibility is the *aporia* of justice. Or, in this sense, media is traumatized with two or more madnesses: in the heart of the media modes, whether psychological or desistant, lies trauma towards the represented. *Mimesis* will never cease to be the same as it is, as an aporia of imitation. There's a long history of communicative trauma following each other besides the latent desistant media mode, as Kittler has already shown.[125] But should consider the *mises-en-abyme* produced by media technology: within desistance, as a passage, there is no absolute destination, no end for the search of the figure of man. Our picture of ourselves stays unclear within this undecidable process – and this is our part, instead of any ethical or aesthetical aporia, within humanity. Different modes of violence do not necessarily mean technological determination (Kittler, Williams) as a possessive media program, even if we now can, after Derrida, claim that the idea of "Cartesian oppression" is in fact correct.

Even though the cultural content of voyeurism and the mode of the gaze are inseparable from each other, the images will still break down and we will remain in the middle of things, of pictures, of words, in the blindness where Tiresias lives and tells infinitely the stories of him never actually interpreting them. Lacoue-Labarthe argues that blindness is the empty space between words, it is the gaze beyond the gaze. Also this is why poetry occurs as the brutal revelation of the abyss that contains art and nevertheless constitutes it, as such, in its strangeness.[126]

Instead of the interpretations made by psychoanalytical media theory, the reflections in media art are often the deconstruction of the very concept of "the self". This renders all categories violently impure and results in a destabilisation of all distinctions by what Derrida calls "differantielle contamination". Purity without violence is an impossibility due to the fact that "iterability requires the origin to repeat itself originarily, to alter itself so as to have the value of origin, that is, to conserve itself".[127] Lacoue-Labarthe and Nancy claim that it would be fruitless to identify the philosophical and the political: the political marks the place where the distinction between philosophy and non-philosophy, between philosophy and its unthought, becomes blurred. This place, the place of the political, would always have the character of a limit. But this limit is not simply restrictive: it marks both an inside and an outside. In marking out the limit of philosophy it therefore traces an identity. The political is both at the limit of philosophy and forms its limit.[128] We can see now how this political form of thinking is tending towards an aporia of totalising, repressing violence, whereas within desistance there's still a trifle of contamination.

Totalizing madness can also be elaborated through concept of "scopic regime" with which Martin Jay referred to as Cartesian perspectivalism and Chris Jenks to modern power. Jenks says this modern power has the deft touch of a "look" in interaction. It no longer requires the hard-edge and the explicit realization of the *ancien régime*, through a "look" it can absorb all and do so without being noticed, or say all without ever revealing its true intentions. Modern power to Jenks means pervasive power, though not omnipotent, because it cautiously acts on and in relation to the scopic regime. Also for Jenks the "gaze" and the conscious manipulation of images are the dual instruments in the exercise and function of modern systems of power and social control. This cultural network, grid, is, finally, our scopic regime.[129] But there are also uneconomical procedures, disorder, of course, but, as Derrida says, differance that produces what it forbids makes possible the very thing that it makes impossible.[130] What, then, happens with this oscillation to madness, or, rather, to the myth of madness?

Mimesis, as opposed to possession as an optical discipline, and as opposed to ideology of mythical censorship technologies, which in all their mimetology deny the possible mad(n)essence of man, shows that desistant media, producing obscure sights of madness, are not a modern, psychoanalytical master-machine. Instead, these thaumatic machines are – in all of their violent deferrals – differance engines. For Lacoue-Labarthe the incoherence, the excess, the lack of control, this whole movement of a racing motor, a mad machine indeed escapes mastery. The appearance of separation in particular *mise-en-abyme* is the mechanism of desistance. We have seen how the question of the "artist" for artists like Della Porta, Kircher, Duchamp and Hershman Leeson forms an ambiguous project: whereas the engineer is the controller of the knowledge to technology, the artist uses this knowledge to question the nature of the technology at hand. Hence, arche-violence. It is not resistant towards technology, but looks upon the nature of technology's power to enunciate: arche-writing, or original mimesis. We can say that the oeuvre of the artists here is set against possession, against totalising violence of economical media mode.

Mirror is one mode of media that encompassed the production of no one, but two madnesses. Madness of media does not start with the typewriter as Kittler claims; we have seen desistant features from the mirror cabinets of Della Porta and Kircher, features where gestures are not autobiographical but allobiographical and thus the other of us deferring from ourselves as ethical trait clinging between freedom and responsibility laid by history of an endless mimesis of man.

This challenges onto-typology in a violent manner: since Plato, education or training, political *Bildung* has been understood as taking the mimetic process as starting point. Plato challenges this, dreaming precisely of a (philosophical) self-grounding of the political (i.e. cutting through the mimetological double bind), admittedly with an idea of the Idea that is itself paradigmatic (and belonging, in consequence, to the mimetological). The crucial point is that *Bildung* is always thought on the basis of archaic mythic *paideia*. It is not by chance that in the "myth" of the Cave – a myth that has no mythic source, a myth that is self-formed and self-grounded[131] – lays the foundations of Plato's political project.

Identification or appropriation – the self-becoming of the self – will always have been thought of as the appropriation of a model, as the appropriation of a means of appropriation, if the model (the example) is the ever paradoxical imperative of propriation: imitate me in order to be what you are. Difference does not resist appropriation, it does not impose an exterior limit upon it.[132]

Yet the question remains of how, and above all why, identity (properness/propriety, or being-in-oneself/being proper) – in what art works like *Touch Me* and *Be Me* ask – derives from mimetic appropriation. It is by no means obvious that self-identity presupposes that there will be an other, because the other also presupposes the identical. The speculative dialectic is an eschatology of the identical; and so long as this logic, more or less explicitly, underpins the interpretation of mimesis, one can only ever move endlessly from the same to the other – still under the authority of the same. Conceived more rigorously, however, mimetologic complicates and de-stabilizes this schema: in the dialecticization of mimetism, a subject is presupposed, albeit a virtual one. But, by Lacoue-Labarthe's definition, mimetism forbids such a presupposition (something already convincingly established by Diderot): no subject, potentially identical to himself or related to himself, can exist prior to the mimetic process, except to render it impossible. If something pre-exists, it is not even, as Plato believed, a substance, in the form of a pure malleability or plasticity which the model would come to stamp as its own "type" or on which it would imprint its image. Such a substance is, in reality, already a subject, and it is not on the basis of an eidetics that one can hope to think the mimetic process, if the eidos – or, more generally, the figural – is the very presupposition of the identical. We remember that such an eidetics – from Plato to Nietzsche and Wagner and even to Heidegger – underpins mimetology in the form that Lacoue-Labarthe calls onto-typology, where an entire tradition has thought that the political is the sphere of the *fictioning* of beings and communities.[133]

We have seen that, instead of the dialectics this tradition of thought, the deconstructive displacement of the subject does not merely reverse an oppositional dissymmetry while leaving the opposition and its terms intact. Rather, it seeks to articulate a relation other than that of opposition itself, a relation of differential intrication in which the involvement of terms with each other constitutes their only identity or quidity. This excess over closure, this failure of closure, meaning or sense is always *à venir*, yet to come, indefinitely deferred – which is to say that this is essentially a question, an indecision, an ambiguity[134] instead of possession produced both by economical and uneconomical (resistant) modes of media.

Gregory Ulmer believes that Benjamin's comparison of psychoanalysis and film shows the optimistic side of the education, holding out the hope for film as a cognitive medium. For Benjamin, one of the revolutionary functions of film would be "to demonstrate the identity of the artistic and scientist uses of photography which heretofore usually were separated – and from the pedagogical point of view: the illiterate of the future would be one who did not know how to take a photograph. Dream-work, as Lacan and structuralist psychoanalysis have tried to show, amounts to a generic codification of the organizing principles of a wide range of non-analytical texts, including dreams, jokes, myths, all the forms of everyday life, as well as of the arts. Freud was among the first ones to point out the essence of dream work as condensation and displacement. With this he may have alluded to dream's affinity to all artistic activity, for his entire psychoanalytical method may, in some respect, be considered the working out of the science of tropes: metaphors and their variations. Freud proved that consciousness can operate without logic – and now we have come to the main point of hyperbologic – but not without any guiding dream-image, which also controls the realm that gives birth to logic. Similarities and oppositions appear as images in the dream unifying, not dividing, the various elements. Freud's project reflects the invention of an alternative mode of thought, whose form, style, and function are still in the process development. Taking dream-work as the logic of primal thinking Ulmer argues that the film or video media provide the technology for primal writing. Such writing functions as the representation of invention. The point here is that dream-work is "logic", and within that, every logic is the logic of relationships. The relations specific to dream-work are those of figuration.[135]

Dream-work paths the way to the deconstruction *mises-en-abyme* erected with various media *mekhane*. Works we have analysed are constructed generally by (visual) jokes and puns, of myths and dreams. This is also a way of approaching how double images, for instance, have remained invisible in our culture since the days of Della Porta and Kircher: not as a main mode of media production, but as the pedagogy of a betrayal (just as a joke or pun is a betrayal of the meaning of the content), of speech, of logos, of the memory of technology. If Ulmer's post-pedagogy finds the answer to the pedagogical problem of Avant-Garde – the discontinuity – in grammatology growing from the recognition of this break in the tradition, in the separation, we must keep in mind the oscillation *between* things (instead of the dialectical): the memory of an open artwork is open also to allobiographical notes. The memory of the specific artworks is something Plato feared: the memory in the works of Della Porta, Kircher, Duchamp, Cage, Rokeby, and others is open to changes in an infinite manner. Moreover, the trick of the mirror is to stay in some *in-between*, which is, and has been, a "magical" stage. This magic of augmentation has been interpreted differently in several historical stages, from religious to political and finally historio-structural phases, but up to this point art has always flirted with the history of the popular, of the mirror cabinets, of anamorphoses, of tintamarres: popular history has been a history of the fun of the pun, *pun-fun*, so to speak.

What is, then, at stake with desistant media? It is a matter of discharging the tragedy – or to be more precise, to replace the appropriative mode of tragedy with a disappropriative mode, which will then loosen itself from the matrix of truth: desistant mirror withdraws itself from the truth, any socially determined truth to consider its own representations. Desistance is a play of semblance, not essence: where semblance can be a cheating mode altogether, control of the essence means total control with no safe haven left.

This is finally a state of metatechnology. If we recall the GPS, the iris code, infrared or biochips under our skin there is no question of mimesis, likeness but pure essence.

Bolter and Grusin imagine that ubiquitous computing – a pervasive mode of computer technology – is an extreme form of hypermediacy that carries in itself the possibility of total surveillance,[136] but we must also remember that the *Unheimliche* – the other in us – is delivered into us in the form of a chip. Lacoue-Labarthe says that possession presupposes a matrix in which the imprint – or, in this case, the chip – is stamped or installed.[137] The oscillation here is opened up also by Haraway. Through her "Cyborg Manifesto" she argues that in similar circumstances the certainty of what counts as nature is undermined, probably fatal. The transcendent authorization of interpretation is lost, and with it the ontology grounding "Western" epistemology.[138] Technological determination is only one ideological space, opened up by the reconceptions of machine and organism as coded text, through which we engage in the play of writing and reading the world.[139] From one perspective, a cyborg world is about the final imposition of a grid of control, but from another perspective, a cyborg world might be about lived social and bodily realities, being *un*afraid of permanently partial identities and contradictory standpoints.[140]

As already mentioned, for Lacoue-Labarthe nothing differs more from mimesis than possession. Mimesis is active, possession, on the contrary, presupposes the supposition itself or the supportive medium. Possession, in other words, presupposes a subject. It is the monstrous, dangerous form of passive mimesis.[141] Any transparent, functional media use, which clings to Aristotelian emotive-cognitive theory of imitation, can be seen as much possessive as ecological in its own totalising violence, but in terms with mimesis, fertility of an eye cannot be considered as such. Instead, it must stay violent towards any human closure in order to give birth to the type, to the imprint, in order to *tupein* – Greek for typing, here, the original man. In my interpretation, here is arche-violence instead of the totalising violence the ecological media mode erects through, for example, Gibson's "universality" of ecology. *Be Me* particularly shows that there is recognition, but only the recognition of one's own actions; therefore there can be no identification with the seen – or this identification would be narcissistic. Furthermore, it is a question of violence, of madness, of *Unheimliche*: it is allobiographical if we think this kind of contemporary media art is producing any source of *muthos* for the visitor to live with – to live with the strange of our own lives.

This implies strongly that allobiography is the betrayal, which, in turn, *is* arche-violence. Writing – or mimesis – writes always the other instead of the same, *friendship* of the same. Violence inside the friendship; arche-violence, where totalising violence is not betrayal, is also justice and injustice, but in a mode of surveillance, keeping the visual regime untouched.

It is not the Lacanian unconscious of a machine but metatechnology: as augmentation, the outside inhabits the inside – a *hymen*. There's no limit grounded by the mirror, as Lacan would suggest.

What we have seen here is that the desistant mode of media has been with us for centuries – from the distorted mirror image of an ancient man to the context aware media technology of today. Any history to deny this past is an invalid history of media technology. Through desistance, the pedagogical approach of media exposes itself as "archeration" of justice-injustice with a certain betrayal of meaning. It is probably not the post-pedagogy Ulmer predicts, but a pre-pedagogy in a sense of arche-violence. Desistance is the pedagogy of the other as a productive tension of *"o(the)riginal"* obsession.

The same obsession can be found in Peter Greenaway's 1996 film *The Pillow Book*, in which the protagonist's body is written over and over again, at the peak of obsession with six languages at the same time. Behind the film lies the ancient Japanese story of the creation of man – man made of clay turns into human being with the writing (from god). Even *logos* here – as in the writing of visitors in many desistant media art works – is allobiography in the flesh: god gone mad, as Kittler mentions in a different historical context.

An absolute desistant mode of media is not the only mode media establishes – I am not positing a theory for only one mode of media – there has always been a paradigm of desistance within media, or a tendency towards a desistant mode as well as theoretical tendencies toward an economical media mode, the media in us and us, with media. The argument Derrida makes, that writing is not an independent order of signification, can be used here as a key for analyses of this work: it is weakened speech, something not completely dead; a living dead, a reprieved corpse, a deferred life, a semblance of breath.[142] It is a waste of energy, uneconomy of energy: aporia is *not* the denial but the betrayal – a deception of technology.

Within this mode of media, there is no sign of fusion (rather, vice versa), no trace of unity, even no feeling of synthesis, there is only the trust of *distance* that the concept of hymen does not tolerate. The injustice of desistance is the rupture of the illusion of the world for which persistent media economy is constantly striving. Instead of understanding the world as a fulfilment of laws, we are actively 'forgetting' it into its constituent parts and this, as a representation, means decay (of fiction).

Still, we can argue, desistance is a different mode than the one that Margaret Morse describes in the 1996 article "Nature Morte". Some, she argues, speculate that a subject immersed in virtual reality, with its mobile perspective and multiple narrative paths, would lose its identity, splinter, and fall apart. Perhaps, says Morse, the opposite is true – by constructing binary oppositions between persistent and resistant media modes she argues that the multiple aspects of personhood and agency may offer more possibilities for subjective integration and control.[143]

The art works briefly studied don't claim that man is autobiographical in the modern implications of a socio-cultural state of man, but more or less subconsciously, the vision they're proposing is allobiographical as such – always re-figuring itself in a manner state of hyperbology. Like psychophysics (for which it is a technological precondition as well), the typewriter or contemporary media tools alter the status of discourse and repositions literature, science, and theory. The end of "man" postulated by Foucault is not an aporia but brought on by a mechanism that writes writing – or, now, is it allobiography in a sense the *Umheimliche* was covered on a man's body with the torture machines in Kafka's short story?

This is the realm of the black sun of madness: we must understand that black sun is not a condition of the "absence of light", as the binary oppositions in a European tradition lead us to think, but merely the "desistance of light" in the sense of persistence of "black speculation", speculation in terms of "mirror gazing" via the literal meaning of the word "speculation"[144].

An ending here means, of course, not an ending but merely an opening: supplementing a void instead of complementing it. After this discussion my proposal to media studies is not to consider media only in terms of immersion (into the image) or distraction (of the image), but also in terms of desistance (from the image), in all their implications of dissemination. Theoretically, when desistance stays persistent in *mises-en-abyme* of media art, remaining constant in its efforts to lock the hyperbological relation, then in terms of mimesis it must stay open, unended. Then desistance can be seen as violent towards figuration's own limits: it is the interruption in the myth of man, as Nancy has proposed. Madness of desistance means not, as the polygraph for Kittler, the psychopathology of modern culture, but a deferral from corporeal punishment of violence, from an idol erected in various identification protocols by persistent media ecologies.

Can we say that deconstruction of media theorization has provided us a means for seeing the tradition of media art as apart from another, larger perspective? For me the answer is yes. We have seen that the desistant mode, as Derrida has defined it as correspondence to obsession and hyperbology, something that is at play in the subject, is neither a post-modern mode (Poster), nor a network of 1900 by Kittler as a network of cultural psychopathology; rather, we can think of it as a mode of madness of supplementary logic.

We can see that none of these historical steps, paradigms of possession and control, deal with a withdrawal or desistance with certain hyperbological accordance to a substantial subtext of dispossession. I suggest that besides the historical phases we must also look for the ahistorical threads – the very continuums through the phases of different media technologies. Dispossessive media modes of both Baroque and Romanticism show that modern and modernist media art are not plain historical paradigm shifts but also certain continuums of dispossession produced by media differencing from the possessive mode, theorized historically by the onto-typology within Western thinking. This onto-typological safeguard of mimesis now has its twin, not oppositional to the first mentioned but as an *Unheimlich* pair, or strange couple.

Desistance, finally, is an oscillation protocol of media art that cannot be historicized as a historical paradigm but as a manifestation of an artist free from the constraints of technology. As a Kunstkammer, art is a trace of ahistorical motifs and themes, pedagogically concerned with a myth of man.[145] Even though the resistant mode of information can be seen as domesticated, still many indicators let us speculate that the "Kunstkammer" – the media lab – is still a place for magic to occur.

Notes

[1] Cf. Puetz 2002.

[2] Cf. Bolter & Grusin 2000, 236.

[3] Johnson in Derrida 2004, viii-ix.

[4] Sparks 1997, xxii-xxiii. Compare "mimeme" to "meme" in Fuller 2005, 109-116.

[5] Oswalds 1994, 254.

[6] Cf. Lacoue-Labarthe 1995, 46 and Lacoue-Labarthe 1994, 152 and especially Lindberg 1998, 33-36. About Nazi onto-typology, see Lacoue-Labarthe 1990, 93-99.

[7] Lacoue-Labarthe 1994, 152.

[8] This discussion is described in Tikka 2005, see e.g. 106 and 120. The very problematic substance of this thinking is cited in a direct quotation from Jean Mitry: "a film is a mirror in which we recognize only what we present to it through what it reflects back to us: all it ever reflects is our image". This is a loop (of consciousness). See also Zapp 2002, 78.

[9] Bolter 1991, 226. See also Bacon 1994, 80: audiovisual experience in general functions as a substitute for the lack of participation in the world; there's a movement away from tactile towards visual experience as a movement toward greater abstraction and formalism divorced from actual experience that, according to Bacon, increases the sense of consciousness as something separate and alienated from the world. What is behind this thought

is that film (audiovisuality) functions as a form of "epistemological repression" by suggesting that reality is essentially material and visible – capable of being captured by the camera.

[10] Lanham 1993, 3-28 & 31-52.

[11] Bolter & Grusin 2000, 41.

[12] Lanham 1993, 40-41 and Bolter & Grusin 2000, 39.

[13] Manovich 2001, 208.

[14] Phelan 2003, 106-107.

[15] Haraway 1997, 182.

[16] Derrida 1976, 288.

[17] Krauss 1994, 87.

[18] Cf. e.g. Bolter 1991, 226.

[19] Silverman 1996, 18.

[20] Silverman 1999, 81-82.

[21] Derrida 1976, 163.

[22] Ulmer 1985, 189.

[23] Cf. Puetz 2002; Lacoue-Labarthe 1989, 255. Interpretations, emphasized with italics, are mine.

[24] Lacoue-Labarthe 1989, 70. Cf. the "pretend theory" of media and film ecology.

[25] Lindberg 1998, 33-34. Fictioning differs from the mode speculated by pretend and simulation media theories.

[26] Lacoue-Labarthe 1994, 18. Lacoue-Labarthe recalls the mythic stages upon the idea: he says that myth, defined as the primitive and anonymous poem of the people is thought of in the modern age as the only means of identification that authorizes even the fitting recognition of a nation.

[27] Lacoue-Labarthe 1993, 107-109.

[28] Le Grice 2002, 234.

[29] Lacoue-Labarthe & Nancy 1997, 17.

[30] Bolter & Grusin 2000, 84.

[31] In Lacoue-Labarthe 1989, 15.

[32] Ibid. 16-17.

[33] Kittler 1997, 87.

[34] Lacoue-Labarthe 1993, 97-98.

[35] Lacoue-Labarthe 1994, 152.

[36] Lacoue-Labarthe 1990, 80-81.

[37] Ibid., 81.

[38] For arche-violence see Derrida 1976 and 1978.

[39] Lacoue-Labarthe 1993, 150.

[40] Simon Sparks in the introduction to Lacoue-Labarthe & Nancy 1997, xxiii-xxiv.

[41] Cf. Ulmer 1989, 14145-147.

[42] Cf. Lacoue-Labarthe and Nancy 1988, 44-48.

[43] Lacoue-Labarthe 1994, xvii.

[44] Silverman 1996, 16.

[45] Ikonen 2000, 9-10.

[46] Hintsa 1998, e.g. 32 and Kaarto 2003, 31.

[47] Lacoue-Labarthe 1989, 194, 195 and 201.

[48] See www.ssla.soc.usyd.edu.au/conference/Walker.html

[49] Lacoue-Labarthe 1990, 82-83.

[50] In Lacoue-Labarthe 1989, 24.

[51] Derrida 1978, 289 & 292.

[52] To view a certain trail from *Zerseher* to more contemporary media installations, see Le Meur 2002, 71-74, where she has also elaborated the fertility of seeing by wondering "if I can destroy by looking, can't I then create by looking as well?".

[53] Rötzer 1995, 37; Cf. Hardison, passim.

[54] Silverman 1996, 168.

[55] Zapp 2002, 80. According to her, majority of dramatic forms follow the Aristotelian idea of mimetic narration: the presentation of a dramatic action is understood as a copy or imitation (mimesis) of reality, in which the author talks through the figures that are the actors. The fictional action is represented by these personae, being either a character as an individual being or a type as a representative of a certain social group. They are put into a constellation, in which their specific and characteristic attributes are arranged in opposition to each other to show the different dimensions of the conflict and story. Protagonists, antagonists, main and sub-characters lead to a personification of story content and also of representative social behaviours. Most importantly they are all the author's creatures. The viewer is taking on the role of a voyeur, witness or emotional judge. He or she is immersed in the story by emotional means of identification, as the plot aims to provoke sympathy or antipathy with the characters or draws possible parallels to the viewer's subjective reality. Ibid. 78.

[56] Cf. Jay 1997, 42- 46. Poststructuralism, I argue – after many premonitions of modern and modernity in the discourse – ought to be understood here as a timeline and not so much as a philosophical paradigm.

[57] Lacoue-Labarthe 1999, 48-49.

[58] Lacoue-Labarthe & Nancy 1997, 73-74. Allobiography should not be read as a material notation system as is Kittler's polygraph as a solid proof of the madness of the media systems. Allobiography is a system occupied with the unfamiliar of ourselves, whereas autobiography produces unity, the very *Heimlich* of man.

---

[59] Lacoue-Labarthe 1989, 5 and Silverman 1996, 11.

[60] Crary 2000, 46-47.

[61] Crary 2000, 50-51.

[62] Lacoue-Labarthe 1989, 92-95.

[63] Hershman Leeson 1995, 19-20.

[64] Cf. Jay 1997, 46.

[65] Solomon-Godeau 1995, 29. She says *Paranoid Mirror* addresses at least some of the implications of what can be (inelegantly) called the "spectacularization" of women. The mirror has many associations: the vanitas of the Renaissance – the woman with the mirror, but also the mirror of truth and of surveillance. More details of *Paranoid Mirror* see Ibid., 30-31.

[66] Pictorial *mises-en-abyme*, in the thread of my study, are living portraits from the transforming faces of Della Porta to the unfamiliar face in the picture of *Be Me*.

[67] Lacoue-Labarthe 1990, 83.

[68] Lacoue-Labarthe and Nancy 1997, 76.

[69] Rokeby 1995, 133. This artistic approach is building a long bridge from the present to the baroque mirror culture and its playful taming of human passions with illusions and projective magic under the well known title "natural magic". Desistant features of media were embraced in the Baroque mirror cabinet of e.g. Athanasius Kircher and a century before him, Giovanni Battista Della Porta with passionworks of the mirror. A certain processing of the signal (non-organic fluctuation of the symbolic order) from these mirrors through Futurism and e.g. Fluxus even to the present day media I have called after Derrida rhythmotypical. Derrida says that rhythm belongs neither to the visible nor to the audible, neither to "spectacular" figuration nor to the verbal representation of music, even if it structures them insensibly, I see this as a symptom of rhythmic typing of any audiovisual material. E.g. for John Cage a rhythmic structure was as hospitable to non-musical sounds, noises, as it was to those of conventional scales and instruments – and the very hospitability of technology to process the signal as sounds. "Typorhythmics" can also be desistant, as are certain withdrawals of the signal in sound art. This "echoing" is slightly different mode than that of modernist fragmentation of sound. See Lacoue-Labarthe 1989, 32-33, cf. Nyman 1999, 32. See also Zapp 2004, 78-80.

[70] Lacoue-Labarthe & Nancy 1997, 17.

[71] Lacoue-Labarthe 1989, 34 and Silverman 1996, 20.

[72] Cf. Kuivakari 2005, 251.

[73] Lacoue-Labarthe 1989: 258–259.

[74] Ibid.

[75] Lacoue-Labarthe 1994: 110.

[76] Lacoue-Labarthe 1989: 253–260.

[77] Ibid., 233-234.

[78] Lindberg 1996, 39-40.

[79] Lacoue-Labarthe 1990, 82-83.

[80] Lacoue-Labarthe 1989, 252-253.

[81] Todd 1996, 180.

[82] Cf. Buck-Morss 1991, 292.

[83] Popper 1993, 172 About Hershman Leeson's participative art see Dietz 2005, especially about *Time and Time Again*, see Ibid., 196. In fact the features like the change of information from participant to participant, participant as a performer, the changes in signals passing through input and output devices, from the categorization made by Bell are vigorously present in contemporary art which has included in itself a variety of forms and functionalities also from games and plays. The last item in the list also contain a deliberation upon the faculty of the audience to comprehend the work of art. Directing the contents of art could happen through familiar schemas.

[84] Krueger 1992, 254.

[85] Ibid.

[86] Ibid., 245.

[87] Ibid., 254.

[88] Grau 2003, 350.

[89] See Lacoue-Labarthe 1993, 106 and Krueger 1992, 254.

[90] Lacoue-Labarthe 1993, 108.

[91] Krueger 1991, xiv.

[92] Lacoue-Labarthe 1993, 103.

[93] Lacoue-Labarthe 1993, 82.

[94] Lacoue-Labarthe 1993, 93-95.

[95] Cf. Foreword, p. 14.

[96] For more details see O'Dell 1990, 139.

[97] Graham 2001, 15.

[98] We must keep in mind that reflection as re-presentation, with any lack of *mythos*, already belongs to the era of the modern and modernity. It is a rupture in the story (of man) before modern art started to speculate on it – Cubism, Dadaism, etc.

[99] Stemmrich 2004.

[100] Dixon 2007, 245.

[101] Ropas-Wuilleumier 1994, 66. In his study, Dällenbach concentrates on couple of pages to the examples of *mise-en-abyme* in at history: among them *Arnolfini Marriage* by Van Eyck, and *Las Meninas* by Velasquez. Short, and

structural analyses of these examples tell for Dällenbach that the duplication that these paintings from history give rise to, far from being faithful, is distorted by the convexity of the mirror. We are witnessing the outside within inside, or external within the internal; Dällenbach says, for the optical illusion sought in all these pictures, which is their main attraction, lies in bringing into the painting items that (fictively) are outside it: the reflections provided in the mirrors complete the picture and function primarily as a medium for interchange. Dällenbach 1989, 11-12. Still, the attraction remains the distorted same in the contemporary mirrors of media art; what is changed is that the outside is not that "fictive", in Dällenbach's meaning, any more, but as real as the camera or other means of context awareness would provide.

[102] Lacoue-Labarthe 1997, 153.

[103] Dixon 2007, 245.

[104] Ibid., 194.

[105] Lacoue-Labarthe 1989, 264–265 and 1994, 21.

[106] Ecological media theory share the same view as Dove does.

[107] Dove 2002, 210.

[108] Cf. Ulmer 1989, 127: The drama is intrasubjective, corresponding to the theory of narcissism, supported by the myth of the androgyne (the desire to merge with the other), which, according to Lacan, represents the effort of the split psyche to regain (impossible–Imaginary) unity.

[109] Spivak in Derrida 1976, lxxvii.

[110] Dixon 2007, 146.

[111] Lindberg 1998, 28-29, 32-33 & 47

[112] Lacoue-Labarthe 1989, 92-95:

[113] Rokeby 2000, 101-102.

[114] Rokeby 100-102, Lindberg 1998, 36

[115] Morse 2000, 37.

[116] Derrida 2004, 385.

[117] Solomon-Godeau 1995, 25-27.

[118] Lacoue-Labarthe & Nancy 1997, 153. This can be questioned through the practise of media artists like Christa Sommerer and Laurent Mignonneau, who together creates a-life as a sign of technology, which produces the "interruption of a man". Note: this break only according to Nancy. On the other hand, history has shown us many times how technologies have been installed only for the limitation of the "original man" in favour of an idealized, clean and pure picture of mankind, which is the very *ge-stell* of eugenics, and more recently, genetics. Questions towards the madness of reason arise, not only ethical: in a world cleansed from madness, can we ever really understand the calmness of Antigone, or the reasons behind the madness of Hamlet and Macbeth, or, even, the symbolics behind the

transformation of Gregor Samsa? These classics are very much the preconditions also for the discussion about madness as metaphor and motive in contemporary media art, not only represented and formatted in *Paranoid Mirror*, or, *Frames,* but also in artworks like Eija-Liisa Ahtila's *The House* (2002) which explores the mind of a young woman undergoing severe episodes of psychosis. Dinkla says that in *The House* inside and outside, subject and object merge. As classic narrative means, Ahtila employs the stream-of-consciousness technique, by which we can leave the world of linearity, logic and clarity. According to Dinkla, Ahtila's works, like those of Lynn Hershman, take for granted the dissolution of the subject's boundaries. They demonstrate that the compulsive, the absurd and the fantastic are all parts of our reality. For this, see Dinkla 2004, 263.

[119] Cf. Puetz 2002.

[120] Derrida 1976, 112.

[121] Derrida 1976, 112. I'm willing to stress that arche-violence, in its double logic, could be interpreted also (in terms of satire and irony) as paradoxical humour.

[122] Lai 2003.

[123] Paz 1991, 110-111 & 129; Melchior-Bonnet 2004, 249.

[124] Critchley 1999: 163.

[125] Lai 2003, 23-46.

[126] Lacoue-Labarthe 1999, 37 & 54.

[127] Lai 2003.

[128] Sparks 1997, xvii.

[129] Jenks 1995, 14-15.

[130] Derrida 1976, 143.

[131] For Lacoue-Labarthe's relation to Plato's concept of mimesis, see especially Lacoue-Labarthe 1989, passim.

[132] Derrida 1976, 143.

[133] Lacoue-Labarthe 1990, 80-83.

[134] Lacoue-Labarthe 1993, xv.

[135] Ulmer 1989, 59-60.

[136] Bolter & Grusin 2000, 218. For art and "post-visual surveillance" see also Arns 2004, 235-236.

[137] Lacoue-Labarthe 1989, 264.

[138] Haraway 2003, 478.

[139] Ibid., 477.

[140] Ibid, 479.

[141] Lacoue-Labarthe 1989, 264. "Passive mimesis" is not an invention of Lacoue-Labarthe, but he has given it the very attention this thought regards.

[142] Derrida 2004, 144.

[143] Morse 1996, 199.

[144] Viola 1990, 483-484. Bill Viola is not an "interactive artist", as Rokeby has termed the work of many contemporary artists. In his latter works, with references to e.g. angels and other religious matter, there's a hint that his oeuvre can be defined with the Latin term "lustro" – spiritual cleansing with fire and water.

[145] Cf. Grau 2007, especially 146: this "Kunstkammer" turned into "Wunderkammer" as Grau says, cabinet of wonder, later at the 19th century including optical and aural attractions such as peep shows, distorting mirrors and tableaux of miniature landscapes. Also here art deals with the popular through "magic".

Bibliography

Aarseth, Espen (1997): *Cybertext. Perspectives on Ergodic Literature*. Baltimore & London, The Johns Hopkins University Press.

Abel, Manuela (ed.) (1997): *Jeffrey Shaw – a User' Manual. From Expanded Cinema to Virtual Reality*. Ostfildern, Edition ZKM/Cantz.

Allen, Richard and Murray Smith, (eds.) (1997): *Film Theory and Philosophy*. Oxford, Clarendon Press.

Anderson, Joseph D. (1996): *The Reality of Illusion: An Ecological Approach to Cognitive Film Theory*. Carbondale and Edwardsville, Southern Illinois University Press.

Aristotle (1992): *Politics*. Harmondsworth, Penguin Classics.

Aristotle (1996): *Poetics*. Harmondsworth, Penguin Classics.

Arns, Inke (2004): "Social Technologies. Deconstruction, Subversion and the Utopia of Democratic Communication" in Frieling, Rudolf & Dieter Daniels (Hg./eds. 2004): *Media Art Net 1 Survey of Media Art*. Wien/New York, Springer.

Bacon, Henry (1994): *Continuity and Transformation – The Influence of Literature and Drama on Cinema as a Process of Cultural Continuity and Renewal*. Helsinki, Suomalainen tiedeakatemia.

Blunck, Annika (2002):"Towards Meaningful Spaces", in Rieser, Martin & Andrea Zapp (eds.): *New Screen Media. Cinema. Art. Narrative.* Throwbridge, British Film Institute.

Boiarsky, Greg (1997): "The Psychology of New Media Technologies", in Convergence 3/1997.

Bolter, Jay David (1991): *Writing Space. The Computer, Hypertext, and the History of Writing.* Hillsdale, N.J & Howe and London, Lawrence Erlbaum Associates.

Bolter, Jay David & Richard Grusin (2000): *Remediation. Understanding New Media.* The MIT Press, Cambridge, Mass. London, England.

Bolter, Jay David & Diane Gromala (2003): *Windows and Mirrors. Interaction Design, Digital Art, and the Myth of Transparency.* The MIT Press, Cambridge, Mass & London, England.

Bolter, Jay David, Blair McIntyre, Maribeth Gandy & Petra Schweitzer (2006): "New Media and the Permanent Crisis of Aura", in Convergence vol. 12, Number 1, Spring 2006.

Bordwell, David and Noel Carroll eds. (1996): *Post-Theory: Reconstructing Film Studies.* Madison, University of Wisconsin Press.

Bowie, Malcolm (1979) "Jacques Lacan", in John Sturrock (ed.): *Structuralism and Since: From Lévi-Strauss to Derrida.* Oxford, Oxford University Press.

Bürger, Peter (1994): *Theory of the Avant-Garde.* University of Minnesota Press, Minneapolis.

Camenietski, Carlos Ziller (2004): "Baroque Science Between the Old and the New World", in Findlen, Paula (ed.): *Athanasius Kircher. The Last Man Who Knew Everything.* New York/London, Routledge.

Carey, James W. (1988): *Communication as Culture: Essays on Media and Society.* Boston, Unwin Hyman.

Churchland, Paul (1996): "The Neural Representation of the Social World", in Larry May, Marilyn Friedman, and Andy Clark, (eds.): *Mind and Morals: Essays on Ethics and Cognitive Science*. Cambridge, MA, The MIT Press.

Codognet, Philippe (2003): "Artificial Nature and Natural Artifice", in Shaw & Weibel (eds.) 2003.

Crary, Jonathan (1992): Techniques of the Observer. On Vision and Modernity in the Nineteenth Century. Cambridge & London, The MIT Press 1992.

Crary, Jonathan (2000): *Suspensions of Perception. Attention, Spectacle and Modern Culture*. Cambridge, Mass. & London England, The MIT Press.

D'Agostino, Peter (1990): "Interventions of the Present: Three Interactive Videodiscs 1981-90", in Hall, Doug & Sally Jo Fifer (eds.): Illuminating Video. An Essential Guide to Video Art. New York, Aperture/BAVC 1990.

D'Alleva, Anne (2005): *Methods & Theories of Art History*. London, Laurence King Publishing.
Daniels, Dieter (2004): "Media->Art/Art->Media. Forerunners of media art in the first half of the twentieth century", in Frieling, Rudolf & Dieter Daniels (Hg./eds.): *Media Art Net 1 Survey of Media Art*. Wien/New York, Springer.

Daniels, Dieter (2004): "Sound & Vision in Avant-garde & Mainstream". On-line at http://www.medienkunstnetz.de/themes/image-sound_relations/sound_vision/

Daniels, Dieter (2007): "Duchamp: Interface: Turing: A Hypothetical Encounter Between the Bachelor Machine and the Universal Machine", in Grau, Oliver (ed.): *MediaArtHistories.*, Cambridge, Mass. & London, England, The MIT Press.

Derrida; Jacques (1976): *Of Grammatology*. Baltimore & London, The Johns Hopkins University Press.

Derrida, Jacques (1978): *Writing and Difference*. Routledge, London.

Derrida, Jacques (1982): *Margins of Philosophy*. Chicago, Chicago University Press.

Derrida, Jacques (2004): *Dissemination*. Continuum, London & New York.

Dietz, Steve (2005): "Animating the Network", In Tromble (ed.) 2005.

Dinkla, Söke (1994): "The History of the Interface in Interactive Art", in Tarkka, Minna (ed.): *ISEA'94 Catalogue*. Helsinki: UIAH B 40.

Dinkla, Söke (1995): "From Participation to Interaction. Towards the Origins of Interactive Art", in Hershman Leeson, Lynn (ed.): *Clicking In. Hot Links to a Digital Culture*. Seattle, Bay Press.

Dinkla, Söke (2002): "The Art of Narrative – Towards the Floating Work of Art", in Rieser, Martin & Andrea Zapp (eds.): *New Screen Media. Cinema/Art/Narrative*. London, British Film Institute.

Dinkla, Söke (2004): "Virtual Narrations. From the crisis of storytelling to new narration as a mental potentiality", in Frieling, Rudolf & Dieter Daniels (Hg./eds.): *Media Art Net 1 Survey of Media Art*. Wien/New York, Springer.

Dove, Toni (2002): "The Space Between: Telepresence, Re-animation and the Re-casting of the Invisible", in Rieser, Martin & Andrea Zapp (eds.): *New Screen Media. Cinema/Art/Narrative*. London, British Film Institute.

Dreyfus, Hubert L.: "Intelligence Without Representation." On-line at <http://www.hfac.uh.edu/cogsci/dreyfus.html>.

Duve, Thierry de (2001): "Dan Graham and the Critique of Artistic Autonomy", in Brouwer, Marianne (ed.): *Dan Graham. Works 1965-2000*. Düsseldorf, Richter Verlag.

Dällenbach, Lucien (1989): *The Mirror in the Text*. Chicago & Cambridge, The University of Chicago Press & Polity Press.

Elsaesser, Thomas (1998): "Digital Cinema: Delivery, Event, Time", in Elsaesser, Thomas & Kay Hoffmann (eds.): *Cinema Futures: Cain, Abel or Cable?*. Amsterdam, Amsterdam University Press.

Elsaesser, Thomas (2006): "Early Film History and Multi-Media: An Archaeology of Possible Futures?" in Chun, Wendy Hui Kong & Thomas Keenan (eds.): *New Media Old Media. A History and Theory Reader*. New York & London, Routledge.

Findlen, Paula (2002): "Inventing Nature. Commerce, Art, and Science in the Early Modern Cabinet of Curiosities", in Smith, Pamela H. & Findlen (eds.): *Merchants & Marvels. Commerce, Science, and Art in Early Modern Europe*. New York & London, Routledge.

Freeland, Cynthia (1997): "Cognition Science and Film Theory", in Panel on Cognitive Science and the Arts, October 31, Santa Fe. On-line at http://www.hfac.uh.edu/Cogsci/CogSciFilTheory.html

Freud, Sigmund (1985): „The Uncanny", in *Pelican Freud Library Vol. 14*. Harmondsworth, Penguin.

Friedberg, Anne (1993): *Window Shopping. Cinema and Postmodern.*, Berkeley/Los Angeles/Oxford, University of California Press.

Frieling, Rudolf & Dieter Daniels (Hg./eds. 2004): *Media Art Net 1 Survey of Media Art*. Wien/New York, Springer.

Frohne, Ursula (1999): "Video Cultures", in Frohne ed.): *Video cult/ures. Multimedialle Installationen der 90er Jahre*. Köln: DuMont & ZKM.

Frohne, Ursula: "Agnes Hegedüs", in Shaw & Weibel (eds.) 2003.

Frohne, Ursula (2004): ""That's the only now I get": Immersion und Participation in Video-Installations by Dan Graham, Steve McQueen, Douglas Gordon, Doug Aitken, Eija-Liisa Ahtila, Sam Taylor-Wood". On-line at
http://www.medienkunstnetz.de/themes/art_and_cinematography/immersion_ participation/.

Fuller, Matthew (2005): *Media Ecologies. Materialist Energies in Art and Technoculture*. Cambridge, Mass. & London, England, The MIT Press.

Föllmer, Golo (2004): „Audio Art", in Frieling, Rudolf & Dieter Daniels (Hg./eds.): *Media Art Net 1 Survey of Media Art*. Wien/New York, Springer.

Föllmer, Golo & Julia Gerlach (2004): "Audiovisions. Music as an Intermediate Art Form". On-line at
http://www.medienkunstnetz.de/themes/image-sound_relations/audiovisions/

Garver, Greg & Carol Gigliotti & Brenda Laurel & Joan Starcley & Rob Tow (1994):"Pedagogy of the Oppressed: Women, Men and the Cartesian Coordinate System", in Tarkka, Minna (ed.): *ISEA'94 Catalogue*. Helsinki: UIAH B 40.

Giannetti, Claudia (2004a): "Aesthetic Paradigms of Media Art". On-line at http://www.medienkunstnetz.de/themes/aesthetics_of_the_digital/aesthetic_p aradigms/

Giannetti, Claudia (2004b): "Aesthetics and communicative Context". On-line at http://www.medienkunstnetz.de/themes/aesthetics_of_the_digital/aesthetics_ and_communicative%20Context/

Gibson, J.J. *The Ecological Approach to Visual Perception*. Boston: Houghton Mifflin, 1979.

Goodwin, Jocelyn (1979)*: Athanasius Kircher. A Renaissance Man and the Quest for Lost knowledge*. London, Thames and Hudson.
Gorman, Michael John (2001): "Between the Demonic and the Miraculous: Athanasius Kircher and the Baroque Culture of Machines", in Stolzenberg (ed.): *The Great Art of Knowing. The Baroque Encyclopaedia of Athanasius Kircher*. Stanford, Stanford University Libraries.

Graham, Dan (1990): "Video in relation to Architecture", in Hall, Doug & Sally Jo Fifer (eds.): *Illuminating Video. An Essential Guide to Video Art*. New York, Aperture/Bay Are Video Coalition.

Grau, Oliver (2003): *Virtual Art. From Illusion to Immersion*. Cambridge, Mass. & London, England, The MIT Press.

Grau, Oliver (2004): "Immersion and Interaction. From circular frescoes to interactive image spaces", in Frieling, Rudolf & Dieter Daniels (Hg./eds.): *Media Art Net 1 Survey of Media Art*. Wien/New York, Springer.

Haraway, Donna (1997): Modest_Witness@Second_Millennium. FemaleMan©_Meets_OncoMouseTM. New York & London, Routledge..

Haraway, Donna (2003): "A Cyborg Manifesto: Science, Technology, and Socialist-Feminism in the Late Twentieth Century", in Jones, Amelia (ed.):

The Feminism and Visual Culture Reader. New York & London, Routledge
(originally 1985).

Haustein, Lydia (1999): Media Art or A Second Look at Reality", in Frohne
ed.): *Video cult/ures. Multimedialle Installationen der 90er Jahre*. Köln,
DuMont & ZKM.

Hayles, Katherine N. (1996): "Embodied Virtuality: Or How to Put Bodies
Back into the Picture", in Moser, Mary Anne (ed.): *Immersed in Technology.
Art and Virtual Environments*. Cambridge, The MIT Press.

Hayles, Katherine N. (2003): "Virtual Bodies and Flickering Signifiers" in
Jones (ed.) 2003 (originally 1993).

Hershman Leeson, Lynn (1990): "The Fantasy Beyond Control", in Hall,
Doug & Sally Jo Fifer (eds.*): Illuminating Video. An Essential Guide to
Video Art*. New York, Aperture/Bay Are Video Coalition.

Hershman Leeson, Lynn (1995): "Reflections and Preliminary Notes", in
Hershman, Lynn: *Paranoid Mirror*. Seattle, Seattle Art Museum.
Hershman Leeson, Lynn (2003): "Teknolust", in Shaw & Weibel (eds.) 2003.

Hintsa, Merja (1998): *Mahdottoman rajoilla. Derrida ja psykoanalyysi*.
Helsinki, Tutkijaliitto.

Huhtamo, Erkki (1996): "Time Travelling in the Gallery: An Archaeological
Approach in Media Art", in Moser, Mary Anne (ed.): *Immersed in
Technology. Art and Virtual Environments*. Cambridge, The MIT Press.

Huhtamo, Erkki (2003): "Media Art in the Third Dimension: Stereoscopic
Imaging and Contemporary Art", in Shaw & Weibel (eds.) 2003.

Huhtamo, Erkki (2007): "Twin-Touch-Test-Redux: Media Archaeological
Approach to Art, Interactivity and Tactility", in Grau (eds.) 2007.

Ikonen, Teemu (2000): Imitaation rajoilla. Täydentävä kirjoitus
Denis Diderot'n tuotannossa. Helsinki, Helsingin yliopisto.

James, David E. (2005): "Lynn Hershman: The Subject of Autobiography",
in Tromble, Meredith (ed.): *The Art and Films of Lynn Hershman Leeson*.
Berkeley & Los Angeles & London, University of California Press.

Jay, Martin (1997): "Mimesis and Mimetology: Adorno and Lacoue-Labarthe" in Huhn, Tom and Lambert Zuiderwaart (eds.): *The Semblance of Subjectivity. Essays in Adorno´s Aesthetic Theory*. Cambridge, Mass. & London, England, The MIT Press.

Jenks, Chris (1995): "The Centrality of the Eye in Western Culture: an Introduction", in Jencks, Chris (ed.): *Visual Culture*. London & New York, Routledge.

Johnson, Barbara (2004): "Translator's Introduction", in Derrida 2004.

Kaarto, Tomi (2003), "Derridan toiston käsitteen genealogiaa", in Synteesi 4/2003.

Kahn, Douglas (2007):"Between a Bach and a Bard Place: Productive Constraint in Early Computer Arts", in Grau (ed.) 2007.

Kittler, Friedrich (1990): *Discourse Networks 1800/1900*. Stanford, Stanford University Press.
Kittler, Friedrich (1997): *Literature, Media, Information Systems*. G+B Arts International, Amsterdam.

Kluszczynski, Ryszard W. (2005): "Arts, Media, Cultures: Histories of Hybridisation", in Convergence 4/2005.

Krauss, Rosalind (1986a): *The Originality of the Avant-Garde and the Other Modernist Myths*. Cambridge, Mass. & London, England, The MIT Press.

Krauss, Rosalind (1986b): "Video: The Aesthetics of Narcissism", in Hanhardt, John (ed.): *Video Culture. A Critical Investigation*. New York, Visual Studies Workshop Press.

Krauss, Rosalind (1994): *The Optical Unconscious*. Cambridge & London, The MIT Press.

Korkea-aho, Mari (2000): *Context-Aware Applications Survey*. Helsinki, Helsinki University of Technology, Dept. of Computer Science.

Krueger, Myron: *Artificial Reality*. Addison-Wesley 1991.

Kuivakari, Seppo (2005): "Mimesis and Media Art: Mise-en-abyme in Media Arts from Touch Me to Be Me", in Ylä-Kotola, Mauri, Sam Inkinen & Hannakaisa Isomäki (eds.): *The Integrated Media Machine 3-4: Aspects of Future Interfaces and Cross-Media Culture*. Rovaniemi, University of Lapland & European Society for a Sustainable Information Society.

Kuspit, Donald (2000): *Psychostrategies of Avant-Garde Art*. Cambridge, UK ,Cambridge University Press,.

Lacoue-Labarthe, Philippe (1989): *Typography. Mimesis, Philosophy, Politics*. Stanford University Press, Stanford.

Lacoue-Labarthe, Philippe (1990): *Heidegger, Art and Politics*. Basil Blackwell, Padstow, Cornwall.

Lacoue-Labarthe, Philippe (1993): *The Subject of Philosophy*, Minneapolis & London, . University of Minneapolis Press.

Lacoue-Labarthe, Philippe (1994): *Musica Ficta (Figures of Wagner)*. Stanford, Stanford University Press.
Lacoue-Labarthe, Philippe (1999): *Poetry as Experience*. Stanford, Stanford University Press.

Lacoue-Labarthe, Philippe & Jean-Luc Nancy (1988): *The Literary Absolute. The Theory of Literature in German Romanticism*. Albany, State University of New York Press.

Lacoue-Labarthe, Philippe & Jean-Luc Nancy (1997): *Retreating the Political*. London and New York, Routledge.

Lacoue-Labarthe, Philippe & Jean-Luc Nancy (2002): *Natsimyytti*. Helsinki, Tutkijaliitto.

Lai, Chung-Hsiung (2003): "On Violence, Justice and Deconstruction" in *Concentric: Studies in English Literature and Linguistics* January 2003: 23-46.

Landow, George P. (1997): *Hypertext 2.0*. Baltimore & London, Johns Hopkins University Press.

Lanham, Richard A. (2006): *The Economics of Attention. Style and Substance in the Age of Information*. Chicago & London, The University of Chicago Press.

Lauria, Rita (2001): "In Love with our Technology: Virtual Reality. A Brief Intellectual History of the Idea of Virtuality and the Emergence of a Media Environment", in Convergence 4/2001.

Lebensztejn, Jean-Claude (1994): "Starting out from the Frame (Vignettes)", in Brunette, Peter and David Wills (eds.): *Deconstruction and the Visual Arts. Art, Media, Architecture*. Cambridge: Cambridge University Press.

Le Grice, Malcolm (2002): "Virtual Reality – Tautological Oxymoron", in Rieser, Martin & Andrea Zapp (eds.): *New Screen Media. Cinema/Art/Narrative*. London, British Film Institute.

Le Meur, Anne Sarah (2002): "Into the Hollow of Darkness: A Virtual Environment Project on Interactive Peripheral Perception", in Kohmura, Masao & Kiyofumi Motoyama & Yoshiomi Yamaguchi (eds.): *Proceedings Isea 2002*. Nagoya, Isea 2002 Nagoya Steering Committee.

Lindberg, Susanna (1998): *Filosofien ystävyys*. Helsinki, Tutkijaliitto.

Lovejoy, Margot (1992): *Postmodern Currents. Art and Artists in the Age of Electronic Media*. New Jersey, Prentice Hall.

Manovich, Lev (2001): *The Language of New Media*. Cambridge, Mass. & London, England, The MIT Press.

Manovich, Lev (2002): "Spatial Computerisation and Film Language", in Rieser & Zapp (eds.) 2002.

Manovich, Lev (2003): "New Media from Borges to HTML", in Wardrip-Fruin, Noah & Nick Montford (eds.): *The New Media Reader*. Cambridge, Mass. & London, England, . The MIT Press.

Marvin, Carolyn(1988): *When Old Technologies Were New. Thinking About Electric Communication in the Late Nineteenth Century*. New York/Oxford, Oxford University Press.

Melchior-Bonnet, Sabine (2004): *Kuvastin. Peilin historiaa.* Jyväskylä, Atena.

Metz, Christian (1983): *Psychoanalysis and Cinema. The Imaginary Signifier.* London, Macmillan 1983.

Mitchell, W.J.T. (2005): *What Do PicturesWant? The Lives and Loves of Images.* Chicago & London, The University of Chicago Press.

Monaco, James (1981): *How to Read a Film. The Art, Technology, Language, History, and Theory of Film and Media. Revised Edition.* New York & Oxford, Oxford University Press.

Morse; Margaret (1990): "Video Installation Art: The Body, The Image and the Space-in-Between", in Hall &Fifer (eds,) 1990.

Morse, Margaret (1994): "Enthralling Spaces. The Aesthetics of Virtual Environment", in Tarkka (ed.) 1994.

Morse, Margaret (1996): "Nature Morte", in Moser (ed.) 1996.

Morse, Margaret (2000): "Gort! Klaatu Barada Nikto On Alien Intelligence", in Huhtamo, Erkki (ed.):2000: *Alien Intelligence.* Helsinki, Museum of Contemporary Art Publication 63/2000.

Nicholls, Bill (2003): "The Work of Culture in the Age of Cybernetic Systems", in Wardrip-Fruin & Montfort (eds.) 2003.

O'Dell, Kathy (1990). Performance, Video and Trouble in the Home. In: Hall, Doug & Fifer, Sally Jo (eds.), *Illuminating Video. An Essential Guide to Video Art.* New York, Aperture/Bay Area Video Coalition.

Oswalds, Laura R (1994): "Cinema-Graphia: Eisenstein, Derrida, and the Sign of Cinema" in Brunette, Peter and David Wills (eds.): *Deconstruction and the Visual Arts. Art, Media, Architecture.* Cambridge, Cambridge University Press.

Paul, Christiane (2003): *Digital Art.* London & New York, Thames and Hudson.

Paul, Christiane (2007): "The Myth of Immateriality: Presenting and Preserving New Media", in Grau (ed.) 2007.

Paz, Octavio (1981): *Marcel Duchamp. Appearance Stripped Bare*. New York, Seaver Books.

Phelan, Peggy (2003): "Broken Symmetries: Memory, Sight, Love", in Jones (ed.) 2003 (originally 1993).

Popper, Frank (1993): *Art of the Electronic Age*. New York, Abrams, Inc. Publishers.

Poster, Mark (1990): *The Mode of Information. Poststructuralism and Social Context*. Cambridge, UK, Polity Press.

Poster, Mark (1995): *The Second Media Age*. Cambridge, UK, Polity Press.

Poster, Mark (1997): *Cultural History and Postmodernity. Disciplinary Readings and Challenges*. Columbia University Press, New York.

Pramaggiore, Maria (2001): "Seeing Double(s)", in Nicholls (ed.) 2001.

Puetz, Michelle (2002): "Mimesis". On-line at http://chicagoschoolmediatheory.net/glossary2004/mimesis.htm

Rajagopal Arvind (2006): "Imperceptible Perceptions in Our Technological Modernity", in Chun & Keenan (eds.) 2006.

Rokeby, David (1995): "Transforming Mirrors", in Penny, Simon (ed.): *Critical Issues in New Media*. Albany, State University of New York Press.

Rokeby, David (2000): "The Giver of Names", in Huhtamo (ed.) 2000.

Ropars-Wuilleumier, Marie-Claire (1994): "The Dissimulation of Painting", in Brunette, Peter and David Wills (eds.): *Deconstruction and the Visual Arts. Art, Media, Architecture*. Cambridge, Cambridge University Press.

Rosler, Martha (1990): "Video: Shedding the Utopian Moment", in Hall & JoFifer (eds.) 1990.

Ross, Christine (2003): "To Touch the Other: A Story of Corpo-Electronic Surfaces" in Jones (ed.) 2003 (originally 1996).

Ross, Christine (2005): "New Media Arts Hybridity: The Vases (Dis)communicants Between Art, Affective Science and AR Technology", in Convergence 4/2005.

Rush, Michael (2001): *New Media in Late 20th-Century Art*. London & New York, Thames and Hudson.

Rötzer, Florian (1995): "The Viewer is a Voyeur", in Hershman 1995.

Schwarz, Hans-Peter (1997). *Media-Art-History: Media Museum*. München, Prestel-Verlag & Karlsruhe, ZKM Center for Art and Media.

Sederholm, Helena (1996): *Vallankumouksia norsunluutornissa. Modernismin synnystä avantgarden kuolemaan*. Jyväskylä, Jyväskylän yliopiston ylioppilaskunta, Jyy julkaisuja 37,

Sederholm, Helena (2000): *Tämäkö taidetta?* Porvoo, WSOY.

Shaw, Jeffrey & Peter Weibel (eds.) (2003): *Future Cinema. The Cinematic Imaginary after Film*. Cambridge, MA, The MIT Press & Karlsruhe, ZKM Center for Art and Media.

Sihvonen, Jukka (1991): *Exceeding the Limits. On the Poetics and Politics of Audiovisuality*. Turku, SETS.

Silverman, Kaja (1996): *The Threshold of the Visible World*. London and New York, Routledge.

Silverman, Kaja (1999): "Prolegomena to "World Spectators"", in Frohne (ed.): *Video cult/ures. Multimedialle Installationen der 90er Jahre*. Köln, DuMont & ZKM.

Slater, Don (1995): "Photography and Modern Vision. The Spectacle of 'Natural Magic'", in Jencks, Chris (ed.): *Visual Culture*. London & New York, Routledge.

Sparks, Simon (1997): "Introduction: Politica ficta", in Lacoue-Labarthe & Nancy 1997.

Spielmann, Yvonne (1999): "Vision and Visuality in Electronic Art", in Frohne, Ursula (ed.): *Video cult/ures. Multimedialle Installationen der 90er Jahre*. Köln, DuMont & ZKM.

Spielmann, Yvonne (2000): "Visual Forms of representation and Simulation: A Study of Chris Marker's level 5", in Convergence 2/2000.

Solomon-Godeau, Abigail (1995): "Conscientious Objectification: Lynn Hershman's Paranoid Mirror", in Hershman 1995.

Stemmrich, Gregor (2004): "Dan Graham's 'Cinema' and film theory". On-line   at http://www.medienkunstnetz.de/themes/art_and_cinematography/graham/

Stiegler, Bernard (1998): *Technics and Time 1. The Fault of Epimetheus*. Stanford, Stanford University Press.

Stolzenberg, Daniel (2001): The Connoisseur of Magic", in Stolzenberg (ed.): *The Great Art of Knowing. The Baroque Encyclopaedia of Athanasius Kircher*. Stanford, Stanford University Libraries.

Tan, Ed S. (1996): *Emotion and the Structure of Narrative Film: Film as an Emotion Machine*. Mahwah, New Jersey, Lawrence Erlbaum Associates.

Tikka, Pia (2005): "Dynamic Emotion Ecologies of Cinema", in Ylä-Kotola, Inkinen & Isomäki (eds.) 2005.

Todd, Loretta (1996): Aboriginal Narratives in Cyberspace", in Moser, Mary Anne (ed.): *Immersed in Technology. Art and Virtual Environments*. Cambridge, The MIT Press.

Trezise, Thomas (1993): "Foreword" to Lacoue-Labarthe 1993.

Turim, Maureen (1990): "The Cultural Logic of Video", in Hall, Doug & Sally Jo Fifer (eds.): *Illuminating Video. An Essential Guide to Video Art*. New York, Aperture/Bay Are Video Coalition.

Ulmer, Gregory (1985): *Applied Grammatology. Post (e)-Pedagogy from Jacques Derrida to Joseph Beuys*. Baltimore & London, The Johns Hopkins University Press.

Ulmer, Gregory (1989): *Teletheory.Grammatology in the Age of Video*. New York & London, Routledge.

Viola, Bill (1990): "Video Black – The Mortality of the Image", in Hall, Doug & Sally Jo Fifer (eds.): *Illuminating Video. An Essential Guide to Video Art*. New York, Aperture/Bay Are Video Coalition.

Viola, Bill: "On Transcending the Water Glass", in Jacobsen (ed.) 1992.

Wands, Bruce (2006): *Art of the Digital Age*. London, Thames and Hudson.

Wellbury, David E. (1990): "Foreword", in Kittler 1990.

Wilden, Anthony (1981): "Lacan and the Discourse of the Other" in Lacan, Jacques: *The Language of the Self: the Function of Language in Psychoanalysis*. London and Baltimore, Johns Hopkins University Press.

Wilson, Jason (2004): "'Participation TV': Early Games, Video Art, Abstraction and the Problem of Attention", in Convergence 3/2004.

Wooster, Ann-Sargent (1990): "Reach Out and Touch Someone: The Romance of Interactivity", in Hall & Fifer (eds.) 1990.

Zapp, Andrea (2002): "net.drama://myth/mimesis/mind_mapping/", in Rieser & Zapp (eds.) 2002.

Zerseher. On-line at http://www.artcom.de/

Zielinski, Siegfried (1996): "Media Archaeology". Originally published on-line at www.ctheory.net.

Zielinski, Siegfried (2003): "Backwards to the future. Outline for an Investigation of the Cinema as a Time Machine", in Shaw & Weibel (eds.) 2003.

Zielinski, Siegfried (2006): *Deep Time of the Media. Toward an Archaeology of Hearing and Seeing by Technical Means*. Cambridge, Mass. & London, England, The MIT Press.

List of Contributors

Francisco J. Ricardo, Ph.D. is Research Associate in the University Professors Program and codirector of the Digital Video Research Archive at Boston University, and teaches critical theory at the Rhode Island School of Design. His work investigates historical and conceptual intersections between new media and contemporary art.

Sheizaf Rafaeli, Ph.D. (http://sheizaf.rafaeli.net) is director of INFOSOC - Center for the Study of the Information Society and Professor - Graduate School of Management (Business Administration) University of Haifa, Israel.

Tsahi Hayat (http://com.haifa.ac.il) is a graduate student at the Department of Communication, University of Haifa, Israel.

Yaron Ariel (http://yaronariel.com) is a doctoral student at the Graduate School of Management, University of Haifa, Israel.

Mahmoud Eid, Ph.D. is an Assistant Professor at the Department of Communication, University of Ottawa (Ontario, Canada) and the editor of *Global Media Journal – Canadian Edition*. His professional expertise, teaching experience, research interests, and publications concentrate on international communication, media studies, communication research methods, terrorism, crisis management and conflict resolution, modernity, and the political economy of communication.

Rita Zaltsman, Ph.D. is currently working at the GFL (German as a Foreign Language) Project at the Catholic Education Center in Reutlingen, Germany. She is also publishing articles and taking part in German and international conferences. Her main research interests include psycholinguistics, web-based discourse analysis, cross-cultural e-learning, and intercultural conflicts in e-learning communities.

Nicole Ridgway is an interdisciplinary scholar whose most recent publications, 'Of the Between - Thinking the (Im)Mediate,' and 'In Excess of the Already Constituted: Interaction as Performance,' explore the intersection of philosophy and art. She currently works in the MSc Programme in Multimedia at Trinity College Dublin.

Nathaniel Stern (http://nathanielstern.com) is a writer, teacher and interdisciplinary artist. He continues to research, write and publish on digital art, continuity and embodiment, which inform his own practice as an artist. His media span experimental and interactive installation, video, net.art and printmaking.

Leman Giresunlu, Ph.D. is Assistant Professor at American Culture and Literature in Western Languages and Literature Department at Dokuz Eylül University, Turkey. Her research and writing covers American Studies theory and methods, American literature and history of technology, gender studies, critical theory, travel literature and popular culture.

Maria Bäcke is currently a Ph.D. Candidate in Digital Games at Blekinge Institute of Technology (Karlskrona, Sweden). As a university lecturer of English at Karlstad University, Sweden, her main focus was how information and communication technologies were framed and problematised in fiction novels. Her current research project focuses on frameworks, hierarchies and power relations in online 3D games.

Tony Richards is a Senior Lecturer in Media Theory and Production in the Faculty of Media, Humanities and Technology at the University of Lincoln (Lincoln, UK). His main research interests revolve around the relationship of deconstruction to video games as well as the interface of media theory to practice.

Alev Adil is Head of the Department of Creative, Critical and Communication Studies, University of Greenwich, United Kingdom

Steve Kennedy is a Lecturer in Media and Programme Leader for BA Hons Media Culture and Communication, University of Greenwich, United kingdom.

Seppo Kuivakari is lecturer at the University of Lapland, Finland. His recent research work examines media art and history.

Index

Printed in the United States
by Baker & Taylor Publisher Services